If it's APRIL 2007
and you are still using this Directory,
it's time to order the NEW Edition.

Please visit our website

www.cabells.com

or contact us at

Box 5428, Beaumont, Texas 77726-5428
(409) 898-0575
Fax (409) 866-9554
Email: publish@cabells.com

Cabell's Directory of Publishing Opportunities in Marketing

VOLUME II   J of I THROUGH W, INDEX
TENTH EDITION 2006-2007

David W. E. Cabell, Editor-in-Chief
McNeese State University
Lake Charles, Louisiana

Deborah L. English, Executive Editor
Twyla J. George, Associate Editor
Lacey E. Earle, Associate Editor

To order additional copies
or electronic versions
visit our web site
www.cabells.com

or contact us at:

Box 5428, Beaumont, Texas 77726-5428
(409) 898-0575; Fax: (409) 866-9554

$119.95 U.S. for addresses in United States
Price includes shipping and handling for U.S.
Add $60 for surface mail to countries outside U.S.
Add $150 for air mail to countries outside U.S.

ISBN # 0-911753-34-6

Printed by Technical Communication Services, 110 West 12th Avenue, North Kansas City, MO 64116

Cover Design by Wayne Hale/Alphabet Soup, Inc.

Journal of Interactive Marketing

ADDRESS FOR SUBMISSION:

Barbara W. Hruska, Managing Editor
Journal of Interactive Marketing
Direct Marketing Educational Foundaiton
14th Floor
1120 Avenue of the Americas
New York, NY 10036-6700
USA
Phone: 212-768-7277
E-Mail: bhruska@the-dma.org
Web: www.interscience.wiley.com

CIRCULATION DATA:

Reader: Academics
Frequency of Issue: Quarterly
Sponsor/Publisher: DMEF / John Wiley &
  Sons

PUBLICATION GUIDELINES:

Manuscript Length: 21-25
Copies Required: Electronic
Computer Submission: Yes Email
Format: MS Word preferred or PDF
Fees to Review: 0.00 US$

Manuscript Style:
  American Psychological Association

REVIEW INFORMATION:

Type of Review: Blind Review
No. of External Reviewers: 2
No. of In House Reviewers: 0
Acceptance Rate: 11-20%
Time to Review: 2 - 3 Months
Reviewers Comments: Yes
Invited Articles: 0-5%
Fees to Publish: 0.00 US$

MANUSCRIPT TOPICS:

Communication; Customer Relationships & Lifetime Value; Direct Marketing; E-Commerce; Interactive Marketing; Internet Marketing; Marketing Theory & Applications; Multichannel Marketing; Technology/Innovation

MANUSCRIPT GUIDELINES/COMMENTS:

The *Journal of Interactive Marketing* is an important and timely undertaking in the evolution of the marketing discipline. The *Journal's* goal is help shape the issues and ideas associated with the emerging interactive/electronic commercial environment and to elevate the level of research in direct and interactive marketing. The *Journal* seeks original research in interactive marketing, broadly defined. Suggested research areas include, but are not limited to:

- The strategic use of information and information technology as corporate assets
- The analysis of interactive databases
- Network-based communications
- Customer and managerial behavior in interactive environments
- The evolution of interactive institutions
- The design and testing of interactive marketing decisions

The *Journal of Interactive Marketing* is sponsored by the Direct Marketing Educational Foundation (a unit of the Direct Marketing Association).

Call for Papers
The *Journal of Interactive Marketing* invites papers for upcoming issues. The policy of *Journal of Interactive Marketing* is to publish significant manuscripts–papers that may change the way direct and interactive marketing are viewed, studied, and practiced. If this invitation speaks to the potential *Journal of Interactive Marketing* author in you, take us up on it: RSVP.

Manuscript Guidelines
The *Journal* strongly encourages the electronic submission of manuscripts. Please send manuscripts as e-mail attachments in Microsoft Word 97 or Microsoft Word 2000 format, or as a *.pdf file, to the managing editor, Barbara Hruska (**bhruska@the-dma.org**).

Manuscripts should be double-spaced, with pages numbered consecutively. Allow margins of at least one inch on all four sides. Tables and references should be typed on separate pages. Indicate their placement in the text.

Length. Up to 25 double-spaced pages, including charts, tables, exhibits, and references. Shorter manuscripts are appreciated. Manuscripts should be accompanied by an abstract of 100 to 125 words on a separate page.

Footnotes. The use of footnotes should be **avoided**. If the author feels that a footnote would clarify, extend a point, or improve the readability of the text, a *few* footnotes may be included but never for reference sources. They should appear double-spaced on a separate page and be numbered consecutively throughout the text.

References. References are to be arranged in numbered alphabetical order at the end of the body of the paper, beginning on a separate page.

Style. On all matters of style, including treatment of references, the *Journal* requests authors to follow the stylebook of the American Psychological Association.

Disk Submission Instructions for Papers Accepted after Review
Only when your paper has been fully accepted, please return your final, revised manuscript on disk as well as hard copy. The hard copy must match the disk.

The *Journal* strongly encourages authors to deliver the final, revised version of their accepted manuscripts (text, tables, and, if possible, illustrations) on disk. Given the near-universal use of computer word-processing for manuscript preparation, we anticipate that providing a disk will be convenient for you, and it carries the added advantages of maintaining the integrity of your keystrokes and expediting typesetting. Please return the disk submission slip below with your manuscript and labeled disk(s).

GUIDELINES FOR ELECTRONIC SUBMISSION
Text
Storage Medium. 3½" high-density disk in IBM MS-DOS, Windows or Macintosh format.

Software and Format. Microsoft Word 6.0 is preferred, although manuscripts prepared with any other microcomputer word processor are acceptable. Refrain from complex formatting; the Publisher will style your manuscript according to the *Journal* design specifications. Do not use desktop publishing software such as Aldus PageMaker or Quark XPress. If you prepared your manuscript with one of these programs, export the text to a word processing format. Please make sure your word processing program's "fast save" feature is turned off. Please do not deliver files that contain hidden text: for example, do not use your word processor's automated features to create footnotes or reference lists.

File Names. Submit the text and tables of each manuscript as a single file. Name each file with your last name (up to eight letters). Text files should be given the three-letter extension that identifies the file format. Macintosh users should maintain the MS-DOS "eight dot three" file-naming convention.

Labels. Label all disks with your name, the file name, and the word processing program and version used.

Illustrations

All print reproduction requires files for full color images to be in a CMYK color space. If possible, ICC or ColorSync profiles of your output device should accompany all digital image submissions.

Storage Medium. Submit as separate files from text files, on separate disks or cartridges. If feasible, full color files should be submitted on separate disks from other image files. 3-1/2" high-density disks, CD, Iomega Zip, and 5 1/4" 44- or 88-MB SyQuest cartridges can be submitted. At authors' request, cartridges and disks will be returned after publication.

Software and Format. All illustration files should be in TIFF or EPS (with preview) formats. Do not submit native application formats.

Resolution. Journal quality reproduction will require greyscale and color files at resolutions yielding approximately 300ppi. Bitmapped line art should be submitted at resolutions yielding 600-1200ppi. These resolutions refer to the output size of the file; if you anticipate that your images will be enlarged or reduced, resolutions should be adjusted accordingly.

File Names. Illustration files should be given the 2- or 3-letter extension that identifies the file format used (i.e., .tif, .eps).

Labels. Label all disks and cartridges with your name, the file names, formats, and compression schemes (if any) used. Hard copy output must accompany all files. [Print Diskette Label form at www.interscience.wiley.com/jpages/1094-9968/authors.html]

Journal of International Business and Economics

ADDRESS FOR SUBMISSION:

Tahi J. Gnepa & Z. Radovilsky, Man. Eds.
Journal of International Business and
  Economics
Academy of International Business
  and Economics
PO Box 2536
Ceres, CA 95307
USA
Phone: 209-667-3074
E-Mail: akhade@aibe.org
  Review@aibe.org
Web: www.aibe.org

PUBLICATION GUIDELINES:

Manuscript Length:
Copies Required: Two
Computer Submission: Yes Disk, Email
Format: MS Word
Fees to Review: 0.00 US$

Manuscript Style:
  Chicago Manual of Style

CIRCULATION DATA:

Reader: Academics, Business Persons
Frequency of Issue:
Sponsor/Publisher: Academy of
  International Business and Economics
  (AIBE)

REVIEW INFORMATION:

Type of Review: Blind Review
No. of External Reviewers: 2
No. of In House Reviewers: 1
Acceptance Rate: 21-30%
Time to Review: 1 - 2 Months
Reviewers Comments: Yes
Invited Articles: 21-30%
Fees to Publish: 0.00 US$

MANUSCRIPT TOPICS:

Advertising & Promotion Management; Business Education; Business Information Systems (MIS); Business Law, Public Responsibility & Ethics; Communication; Direct Marketing; Economics; Global Business; Health Care Administration; Labor Relations & Human Resource Mgt.; Marketing Research; Marketing Theory & Applications; Non-Profit Organizations; Office Administration/Management; Operations Research/Statistics; Organizational Behavior & Theory; Organizational Development; Production/Operations; Public Administration; Purchasing/Materials Management; Sales/Selling; Services; Small Business Entrepreneurship; Strategic Management Policy; Technology/Innovation; Transportation/Physical Distribution

MANUSCRIPT GUIDELINES/COMMENTS:

Please use following manuscript Guidelines for submission of your papers for the review. Papers are reviewed on a continual basis throughout the year. Early Submissions are welcome! Please email your manuscript to Dr. Alan S. Khade at **Review@aibe.org**.

552

Copyright. Articles, papers, or cases submitted for publication should be original contributions and should not be under consideration for any other publication at the same time. Authors submitting articles/papers/cases for publication warrant that the work is not an infringement of any existing copyright, infringement of proprietary right, invasion of privacy, or libel and will indemnify, defend, and hold AIBE or sponsor(s) harmless from any damages, expenses, and costs against any breach of such warranty. For ease of dissemination and to ensure proper policing of use papers/articles/cases and contributions become the legal copyright of the AIBE/IABE unless otherwise agreed in writing.

General Information. These are submission instructions for review purpose only. Once your submission is accepted you will receive submission guidelines with your paper acceptance letter. The author(s) will be emailed result of the review process in about 6-8 weeks from submission date. Papers are reviewed and accepted on a continual basis. Submit your papers early for full considerations!

Typing. Paper must be laser printed/printable on 8.5" x 11" white sheets in Arial 10-point font single-spaced lines justify style in MS Word. All four margins must be 1" each.

First Page. Paper title not exceeding two lines must be CAPITALIZED AND CENTERED IN BOLD LETTERS. Author name and university/organizational affiliation of each author must be printed on one line each. Do NOT include titles such as Dr., Professor, Ph.D., department address email address etc. Please print the word "ABSTRACT" in capitalized bold letters left justified and double-spaced from last author's name/affiliation. Abstract should be in italic. Please see the sample manuscript.

All other Headings. All other section headings starting with INTRODUCTION must be numbered in capitalized bold letters left justified and double-spaced from last line above them. See the subsection headings in the sample manuscript.

Tables Figures and Charts. All tables figures or charts must be inserted in the body of the manuscripts within the margins with headings/titles in centered CAPITALIZED BOLD letters.

References and Bibliography. All references listed in this section must be cited in the article and vice-versa. The reference citations in the text must be inserted in parentheses within sentences with author name followed by a comma and year of publication. Please follow the following formats:

Journal Articles
Khade Alan S. and Metlen Scott K. "An Application of Benchmarking in Dairy Industry" *International Journal of Benchmarking* Vol. III (4) 1996 17

Books
Harrison Norma and Samson D. Technology Management: Text and Cases McGraw-Hill Publishing New York 2002

Internet
Hesterbrink C. E-Business and ERP: Bringing two Paradigms together October 1999; PricewaterhouseCoopers *www.pwc.com*.

Author Profile(s). At the end of paper include author profile(s) not exceeding five lines each author including name highest degree/university/year current position/university and major achievements. For example:

Author Profile:
Dr. Tahi J. Gnepa earned his Ph.D. at the University of Wisconsin Madison in 1989. Currently he is a professor of international business at California State University Stanislaus and Managing Editor of Journal of International Business Strategy (JIBStrategy).

Manuscript. Absolutely no footnotes! Do not insert page numbers for the manuscript. Please do not forget to run spelling and grammar check for the completed paper. Save the manuscript on your diskette/CD or hard drive.

Electronic Submission. Send your submission as an MS Word file attachment to your Email to Dr. Alan S. Khade at **Review@aibe.org**.

Journal of International Business Research

ADDRESS FOR SUBMISSION:

Current Editor / Check Website
Journal of International Business Research
Digital Submission Through Website
Address other questions to:
 Jim or JoAnn Carland at # below
USA
Phone: 828-293-9151
E-Mail: info@alliedacademies.org
Web: www.alliedacademies.org

CIRCULATION DATA:

Reader: Academics
Frequency of Issue: Yearly
Sponsor/Publisher: Allied Academies, Inc.

PUBLICATION GUIDELINES:

Manuscript Length: 16-20
Copies Required: Submit Through Web
Computer Submission: Yes
Format: MS Word, WordPerfect
Fees to Review: 0.00 US$

Manuscript Style:
 American Psychological Association

REVIEW INFORMATION:

Type of Review: Blind Review
No. of External Reviewers: 3
No. of In House Reviewers: 2
Acceptance Rate: 21-30%
Time to Review: 3-4 Months
Reviewers Comments: Yes
Invited Articles: 0-5%
Fees to Publish: 75.00 US$ Membership

MANUSCRIPT TOPICS:
Global Business; International Economics; International Finance; International Trade

MANUSCRIPT GUIDELINES/COMMENTS:

The journal publishes theoretical or empirical research concerning any of the Manuscript Topics.

Comments. All authors of published manuscripts must be members of the appropriate academy affiliate of Allied Academies. The current membership fee is $75.00 U.S.

Editorial Policy Guidelines
The primary criterion upon which manuscripts are judged is whether the research advances the discipline. Key points include currency, interest and relevancy.

In order for a theoretical manuscript to advance the discipline, it must address the literature to support conclusions or models which extend knowledge and understanding. Consequently, referees pay particular attention to completeness of literature review and appropriateness of conclusions drawn from that review.

In order for an empirical manuscript to advance the discipline, it must employ appropriate and effective sampling and statistical analysis techniques, and must be grounded by a thorough literature review. Consequently, referees pay particular attention to the research methodology and to the conclusions drawn from statistical analyses and their consistency with the literature.

Journal of International Business Strategy

ADDRESS FOR SUBMISSION:

Tahi J. Gnepa & W. Cordeiro, Man. Eds.
Journal of International Business Strategy
Academy of International Business
and Economics
PO Box 2536
Ceres, CA 95307
USA
Phone: 209-667-3448
E-Mail: Review@aibe.org
Web: www.aibe.org

CIRCULATION DATA:

Reader: Business Persons, Academics
Frequency of Issue: 2 Times/Year
Sponsor/Publisher: Academy of
International Business and Economics
(AIBE)

PUBLICATION GUIDELINES:

Manuscript Length: 11-15
Copies Required: One
Computer Submission: Yes Disk, Email
Format: MS Word
Fees to Review: 0.00 US$

Manuscript Style:
Chicago Manual of Style

REVIEW INFORMATION:

Type of Review: Blind Review
No. of External Reviewers: 2
No. of In House Reviewers: 1
Acceptance Rate: 11-20%
Time to Review: 1 - 2 Months
Reviewers Comments: Yes
Invited Articles: 0-5%
Fees to Publish: 0.00 US$

MANUSCRIPT TOPICS:
Advertising & Promotion Management; Direct Marketing; Global Business; Marketing Research; Marketing Strategy; Marketing Theory & Applications; Non-Profit Organizations; Operations Research/Statistics; Production/Operations; Purchasing/Materials Management; Sales/Selling; Services; Small Business Entrepreneurship; Strategic Management Policy; Technology/Innovation; Transportation/Physical Distribution

MANUSCRIPT GUIDELINES/COMMENTS:

Please use following manuscript Guidelines for submission of your papers for the review. Papers are reviewed on a continual basis throughout the year. Early Submissions are welcome! Please email your manuscript to Dr. Alan S. Khade at **Review@aibe.org**.

Copyright. Articles, papers, or cases submitted for publication should be original contributions and should not be under consideration for any other publication at the same time. Authors submitting articles/papers/cases for publication warrant that the work is not an infringement of any existing copyright, infringement of proprietary right, invasion of privacy, or libel and will indemnify, defend, and hold AIBE or sponsor(s) harmless from any damages, expenses, and costs against any breach of such warranty. For ease of dissemination and to ensure proper policing of use papers/articles/cases and contributions become the legal copyright of the AIBE/IABE unless otherwise agreed in writing.

General Information. These are submission instructions for review purpose only. Once your submission is accepted you will receive submission guidelines with your paper acceptance letter. The author(s) will be emailed result of the review process in about 6-8 weeks from submission date. Papers are reviewed and accepted on a continual basis. Submit your papers early for full considerations!

Typing. Paper must be laser printed/printable on 8.5" x 11" white sheets in Arial 10-point font single-spaced lines justify style in MS Word. All four margins must be 1" each.

First Page. Paper title not exceeding two lines must be CAPITALIZED AND CENTERED IN BOLD LETTERS. Author name and university/organizational affiliation of each author must be printed on one line each. Do NOT include titles such as Dr., Professor, Ph.D., department address email address etc. Please print the word "ABSTRACT" in capitalized bold letters left justified and double-spaced from last author's name/affiliation. Abstract should be in italic. Please see the sample manuscript.

All other Headings. All other section headings starting with INTRODUCTION must be numbered in capitalized bold letters left justified and double-spaced from last line above them. See the subsection headings in the sample manuscript.

Tables Figures and Charts. All tables figures or charts must be inserted in the body of the manuscripts within the margins with headings/titles in centered CAPITALIZED BOLD letters.

References and Bibliography. All references listed in this section must be cited in the article and vice-versa. The reference citations in the text must be inserted in parentheses within sentences with author name followed by a comma and year of publication. Please follow the following formats:

Journal Articles
Khade Alan S. and Metlen Scott K. "An Application of Benchmarking in Dairy Industry" *International Journal of Benchmarking* Vol. III (4) 1996 17

Books
Harrison Norma and Samson D. Technology Management: Text and Cases McGraw-Hill Publishing New York 2002

Internet
Hesterbrink C. E-Business and ERP: Bringing two Paradigms together October 1999; PricewaterhouseCoopers *www.pwc.com.*

Author Profile(s). At the end of paper include author profile(s) not exceeding five lines each author including name highest degree/university/year current position/university and major achievements. For example:

Author Profile:
Dr. Tahi J. Gnepa earned his Ph.D. at the University of Wisconsin Madison in 1989. Currently he is a professor of international business at California State University Stanislaus and Managing Editor of Journal of International Business Strategy (JIBStrategy).

Manuscript. Absolutely no footnotes! Do not insert page numbers for the manuscript. Please do not forget to run spelling and grammar check for the completed paper. Save the manuscript on your diskette/CD or hard drive.

Electronic Submission. Send your submission as an MS Word file attachment to your Email to Dr. Alan S. Khade at **Review@aibe.org**.

Journal of International Consumer Marketing

ADDRESS FOR SUBMISSION:

Erdener Kaynak, Executive Editor
Journal of International Consumer
    Marketing
International Business Press (IBP)
PO Box 399
Middletown, PA 17057
USA
Phone: 717-566-3054
E-Mail: k9x@psu.edu
Web: www.haworthpress.com

PUBLICATION GUIDELINES:

Manuscript Length: 21-25
Copies Required: Three
Computer Submission: No
Format: MS Word
Fees to Review: 0.00 US$

Manuscript Style:
    American Psychological Association

CIRCULATION DATA:

Reader: Academics
Frequency of Issue: Quarterly
Sponsor/Publisher: International Business
    Press / Haworth Press, Inc.

REVIEW INFORMATION:

Type of Review: Blind Review
No. of External Reviewers: 2
No. of In House Reviewers: 1
Acceptance Rate: 11-20%
Time to Review: 1 - 2 Months
Reviewers Comments: Yes
Invited Articles: 0-5%
Fees to Publish: 0.00 US$

MANUSCRIPT TOPICS:

Advertising & Promotion Management; All From International Perspective; Business Information Systems (MIS); Global Business; Marketing Research; Sales/Selling; Services

MANUSCRIPT GUIDELINES/COMMENTS:

About the Journal. Articles of highest quality, written by practitioners and public policymakers as well as academicians from a variety of countries, offer managerial insights to other practitioners and policymakers to enable them to formulate need-oriented action programs and policies. The journal caters to all professionals who are dealing with overseas customers and/or catering to the needs of international consumers. The journal also benefits teachers of marketing and international business, consultants, and business researchers with "insiders' information" on cross-cultural/national consumer marketing issues.

In particular, persons working within the following fields would find the journal very useful: international marketing departments, trading companies, banks and other financial institutions, government departments and international organizations of dealing with trade, commerce and industry, academics teaching or with research interests in international consumer behavior, research institutions, professional and commercial organizations, firms, and publicly owned international corporations.

Instructions for Authors
1. Original Articles Only. Submission of a manuscript to this journal represents a certification on the part of the author(s) that it is an original work, and that neither this manuscript nor a version of it has been published elsewhere nor is being considered for publication elsewhere.

2. Manuscript Length. Your manuscript may be approximately **15-25 typed pages** double-spaced (including references and abstract). Lengthier manuscripts may be considered, but only at the discretion of the Editor. Sometimes, lengthier manuscripts may be considered if they can be divided up into sections for publication in successive *Journal* issues.

3. Manuscript Style. References, citations, and general style of manuscripts for this *Journal* should follow the APA style (as outlined in the latest edition of the *Publication Manual of the American Psychological Association*). References should be double-spaced and placed in alphabetical order.

If an author wishes to submit a paper that has been already prepared in another style, he or she may do so. However, if the paper is accepted (with or without reviewer's alterations), the author is fully responsible for retyping the manuscript in the correct style as indicated above. Neither the Editor nor the Publisher is responsible for re-preparing manuscript copy to adhere to the *Journal's* style.

4. Manuscript Preparation
Margins. Leave at least a one-inch margin on all four sides.
Paper. Use clean white, 8½" x 11" bond paper.
Number of Copies. Four (the original plus three photocopies)
Cover Page. *Important*—Staple a cover page to the manuscript, indicating only the article title (this is used for anonymous refereeing).
Second "Title Page." Enclose a regular title page but do not staple it to the manuscript. Include the title again, plus:
- full authorship
- an ABSTRACT of about 100 words. (Below the abstract provide 3-10 key words for index purposes)
- an introductory footnote with authors' academic degrees, professional titles, affiliations, mailing addresses, and any desired acknowledgment of research support or other credit.

5. Return Envelopes. When you submit your four manuscript copies, also include:
- a 9" x 12" envelope, self-addressed and stamped (with sufficient postage to ensure return of your manuscript);
- a regular envelope, stamped and self-addressed. This is for the Editor to send you an "acknowledgement of receipt" letter.

6. Spelling, Grammar, and Punctuation. You are responsible for preparing manuscript copy which is clearly written in acceptable scholarly English, and which contains no errors of spelling, grammar, or punctuation. Neither the Editor nor the Publisher is responsible for correcting errors of spelling and grammar: the manuscript, after acceptance by the Editor, must be immediately ready for typesetting as it is finally submitted by the author(s). Check your paper for the following common errors:

- dangling modifiers
- misplaced modifiers
- unclear antecedents
- incorrect or inconsistent abbreviations

Also, check the accuracy of all arithmetic calculations, statistics, numerical data, text citations, and references.

7. **Inconsistencies Must Be Avoided.** Be sure you are consistent in your use of abbreviations, terminology, and in citing references, from one part of your paper to another.

8. **Preparation of Tables, Figures, and Illustrations.** All tables and figures, illustrations, etc. must be "camera-ready". That is, they must be cleanly typed or artistically prepared so that they can be used either exactly as they are or else used after a photographic reduction in size. Figures, tables, and illustrations must be prepared on separate sheets of paper. Always use black ink and professional drawing instruments. On the back of these items, write your article title and the journal title lightly in pencil, so they do not get misplaced. In test, skip extra lines and indicate where these figures and tables are to be placed (please do not write on the face of art). Photographs are considered part of the acceptable manuscript and remain with the publisher for use in additional printings.

9. **Alterations Required By Referees and Reviewers.** Many times a paper is accepted by the Editor contingent upon changes that are mandated by anonymous specialist referees and members of the Editorial Board. If the Editor returns your manuscript for revisions, you are responsible for retyping any sections of the paper to incorporate these revisions (if applicable, revisions should also be put on disk).

10. **Typesetting.** You will not be receiving galley proofs o your article. Editorial revisions, if any, must therefore be made while your article is still in manuscript. the final version of the manuscript will be the version you see published. Typesetter's errors will be corrected by the production staff of The Haworth Press. Authors are expected to submit manuscripts, disks, and art that are free from error.

11. **Electronic Media.** Haworth's in-house typesetting unit is able to utilize your final manuscript material as prepared on most personal computers and word processors. This will minimize typographical errors and decrease overall production time lag. Please send the first draft and final draft copies of you manuscript to the *Journal* Editor in print format for his/her final review and approval.

After approval of your final manuscript, please submit the final approved version both on printed format ("hard copy") and floppy diskette. On the outside of the diskette package write:
1. the brand name of your computer or word processor
2. the word-processing program that you used
3. the title of your article, and
4. file name

Note. Disk and hard copy must agree. In case of discrepancies, it is The Haworth Press' policy to follow hard copy. Authors are advised that no revisions of the manuscript can be made after acceptance by the Editor for publication. The benefits of this procedure are many with speed and accuracy being the most obvious. We look forward to working with you on this, knowing we will be able to serve you more efficiently in the future.

12. **Reprints.** The senior author will receive two copies of the journal issue and 10 complimentary reprints of his or her article. The junior author will receive two copies of the journal issue and 10 complimentary reprints of his or her article. The junior author will receive two copies of the journal issue. These are sent several weeks after the journal issue is published and in circulation. An order form for the purchase of additional reprints will also be sent to all authors at this time. (Approximately 4-6 weeks is necessary for the preparation of reprints.) Please do not query the Journal's Editor about reprints. All such questions should be sent directly to The Haworth Press, Inc. Production Department, 37 West Broad Street, West Hazleton, PA 18202 USA. To order additional reprints (minimum: 50 copies), please contact The Haworth Document Delivery Center, 10 Alice Street, Binghamton, NY 13904-1580 USA; 1-800-342-9678, (607) 722-5857 or Fax (607) 722-6362.

13. **Copyright.** Copyright ownership of your manuscript must be transferred officially to The Haworth Press, Inc. before we can begin the peer-review process. The Editor's letter acknowledging receipt of the manuscript will be accompanied by a form fully explaining this. All authors must sign the form and return the original to the Editor as soon as possible. Failure to return the copyright form in a timely fashion will result in delay in review and subsequent publication.

14. **Examples to Format**
Reference to Periodicals
Journal Article. One Author
> Levitt, T. (1983). The Globalization of Markets, *Harvard Business Review.* (May-June), 61 (3), 92-102.

Journal Article. Multiple Authors
> Kaynak, E. and Mitchell A.L. (1981). Analysis of Marketing Strategies Used in Diverse Cultures, *Journal of Advertising Research* (June), 21 (3), 25-32.

Magazine Article
> Tinnin, D.B. (1981, November 16) The Heady Success of Holland's Heineken, *Fortune*, pp. 158-164.

Newspaper Article
> The opportunity of world brands, (1984, June 3), *The New York Times*, p. 6F.

Monograph
> Franko, L.G. (1979). *A Survey of the Impact of Manufactured Exports From Industrializing Countries in Asia and Latin America*, Changing International Realities [Monograph] No. 6.

References to Books
Reference to an Entire Book
Kaynak, E. (1986) *Marketing and Economic Development*, New York: Praeger Publishers Inc.
Book with a Corporate Author
Committee For Economic Development (1981) *Transnational Corporation for Developing Countries*, New York: Author.
Edited Book
Kaynak, E. (ed.) (1985) *Global Perspectives in Marketing*, New York: Praeger Publishers Inc.
Book with No Author or Editor
Marketing Opportunities in Japan (1978). London: Dentsu Incorporated.
Article or Chapter in an Edited Book
Bucklin, L.P. (1986). Improving Food Retailing in Less Developed Asian Countries. In E. Daynak (Ed.) *World Food Marketing Systems* (pp. 73-81) London: Butterworth Scientific Publishers.

Proceedings of Meetings and Symposia
Published Proceedings, Published Contributions to a Symposium
Lee, K.H. (1981). From Production Orientation to Marketing Orientation—Hong Kong in the International Trade Setting. In D.B. Yeaman (Ed.) *Developing Global Corporate Strategies* (pp. 753-766). Conference held at the University of Navarra, Barcelona, Spain, 2 (December 17-19).
Unpublished Paper Presented at a Meeting
Yucelt, U. (1987). *Tourism Marketing Planning in Developing Economies.* Paper presented at the annual meeting of the Academy of Marketing Science, Bal Harbour, Florida.

Doctoral Dissertations
Unpublished Doctoral Dissertation
Czintoka, M.F. (1980). An Analysis of Export Development Strategies in Selected U.S. Industries. *Dissertations Abstract International* (University Microfilms No. 80-15, 865).

For reference to unpublished manuscripts, publications of limited circulation, reviews and interviews and nonprint media please refer to the latest edition of *Publication Manual of American Psychological Association*.

Journal of International Food & Agribusiness Marketing

ADDRESS FOR SUBMISSION:

Erdener Kaynak, Executive Editor
Journal of International Food &
  Agribusiness Marketing
International Business Press
PO Box 399
Middletown, PA 17057
USA
Phone: 717-566-3054
E-Mail: k9x@psu.edu
Web: www.haworthpress.com

CIRCULATION DATA:

Reader: Academics
Frequency of Issue: Quarterly
Sponsor/Publisher: Haworth Press, Inc.

PUBLICATION GUIDELINES:

Manuscript Length: 21-25
Copies Required: Three
Computer Submission: No
Format: MS Word
Fees to Review: 0.00 US$

Manuscript Style:
  American Psychological Association

REVIEW INFORMATION:

Type of Review: Blind Review
No. of External Reviewers: 2
No. of In House Reviewers: 1
Acceptance Rate: 21-30%
Time to Review: 2 - 3 Months
Reviewers Comments: Yes
Invited Articles: 6-10%
Fees to Publish: 0.00 US$

MANUSCRIPT TOPICS:

Advertising & Promotion Management; All From an International Perspective; Business Information Systems (MIS); Food & Agribusiness; Global Business; Marketing Research; Marketing Theory & Applications; Purchasing/Materials Management; Sales/Selling

MANUSCRIPT GUIDELINES/COMMENTS:

The *Journal of International Food & Agribusiness Marketing* is a timely journal that serves as a round-table for the exchange and dissemination of food and agribusiness marketing knowledge and experiences on an international scale. Designed to study the characteristics and workings of food and agribusiness marketing systems around the world, the *Journal of International Food & Agribusiness Marketing* critically examines marketing issues in the total food business chain prevailing in different parts of the globe by using a systems and cross-cultural/national approach to explain the many facets of food marketing in a range of socioeconomic and political systems.

Practical and informative, the *Journal of International Food & Agribusiness Marketing* enables food marketing specialists from both developed and developing countries to make informed decisions by providing them with nuts and bolts information of doing business in a variety of targeted foreign markets. It is an indispensable source of reference for all those involved in the planning and implementation of food and agribusiness marketing policy and practice, such as food business firms, government food departments, and agencies and institutions related to food marketing internationally. The journal will also be valuable to professionals in many other roles—executives from international food companies; policymakers and officials in government; researchers, scholars, and consultants of food and agricultural marketing, economics, business administration, food science, nutrition, and home economics.

This journal looks at such marketing issues as:

- export/import of food and agribusiness products
- cross cultural, cross-national food purchasing and consumption habits and behaviors
- comparative food and agribusiness distribution systems
- Third World food and agribusiness marketing
- international food quality control and standardization
- marketing practices of agribusiness industries in C.I.S. countries
- strategic planning in international food and agribusiness marketing process and analysis
- basic economic and social developments affecting food and agribusiness marketing in world markets
- supply chain management issues for food and agribusiness industry

A managerially oriented publication, the *Journal of International Food & Agribusiness Marketing* examines contemporary food and agribusiness marketing issues at cross-national/cultural levels from the perspectives of the two types of active participants—micro and macro. The micro (firm level) approach examines the behavior of participants in the international food production and distribution systems whereas the macro (country level) approach studies the consequences of a particular food marketing system that occur over time and affect the well-being of various participants in the system such as consumers, retailers, wholesalers, processors, assemblers, and farmers.

Instructions for Authors

1. **Original Articles Only.** Submission of a manuscript to this *Journal* represents a certification on the part of the author(s) that it is an original work, and that neither this manuscript nor a version of it has been published elsewhere nor is being considered for publication elsewhere.

2. **Manuscript Length.** Your manuscript may be approximately 15–25 typed pages double-spaced (including references and abstract). Lengthier manuscripts may be considered, but only at the discretion of the Editor. Sometimes, lengthier manuscripts may be considered if they can be divided up into sections for publication in successive *Journal* issues.

3. **Manuscript Style.** References, citations, and general style of manuscripts for this *Journal* should follow the Chicago style (as outlined in the latest edition of the *Manual of Style of the University of Chicago Press*). References should be double-spaced and placed in alphabetical order. For reference to unpublished manuscripts, publications of limited circulation, reviews and interviews and nonprint media please refer to the latest edition of *Publication Manual of American Psychological Association*.

If an author wishes to submit a paper that has been already prepared in another style, he or she may do so. However, if the paper is accepted (with or without reviewer's alterations), the author is fully responsible for retyping the manuscript in the correct style as indicated above. Neither the Editor nor the Publisher is responsible for re-preparing manuscript copy to adhere to the *Journal's* style.

4. Manuscript Preparation
Margins. Leave at least a one-inch margin on all four sides.
Paper. Use clean white, 8 ½" x 11" bond paper.
Number of copies. 4 (the original plus three photocopies).
Cover page. Important—staple a cover page to the manuscript, indicating only the article title (this is used for anonymous refereeing).
Second "title page". Enclose a regular title page but do not staple it to the manuscript. Include the title again, plus:
- full authorship
- an ABSTRACT of about 100 words. (Below the abstract provide 3–10 key words for index purposes).
- an introductory footnote with authors' academic degrees, professional titles, affiliations, mailing addresses, and any desired acknowledgment of research
- support or other credit.

5. Return Envelopes. When you submit your four manuscript copies, also include:
- a 9 x 12 envelope, self-addressed and stamped (with sufficient postage to ensure return of your manuscript);
- a regular envelope, stamped and self-addressed. This is for the Editor to send you an "acknowledgment of receipt" letter.

6. Spelling, Grammar, and Punctuation. You are responsible for preparing manuscript copy which is clearly written in acceptable scholarly English, and which contains no errors of spelling, grammar, or punctuation. Neither the Editor nor the Publisher is responsible for correcting errors of spelling and grammar: the manuscript, after acceptance by the Editor, must be immediately ready for typesetting as it is finally submitted by the author(s). Check your paper for the following common errors:
- dangling modifiers
- misplaced modifiers
- unclear antecedents
- incorrect or inconsistent abbreviations

Also, check the accuracy of all arithmetic calculations, statistics, numerical data, text citations, and references.

7. Inconsistencies Must Be Avoided. Be sure you are consistent in your use of abbreviations, terminology, and in citing references, from one part of your paper to another.

8. Preparation of Tables, Figures, and Illustrations. All tables, figures, illustrations, etc. must be "camera-ready." That is, they must be cleanly typed or artistically prepared so that they can be used either exactly as they are or else used after a photographic reduction in size. Figures, tables, and illustrations must be prepared on separate sheets of paper. Always use black ink and professional drawing instruments. On the back of these items, write your article title and the journal title lightly in pencil, so they do not get misplaced. In text, skip extra lines and indicate where these figures and tables are to be placed (please do not write on face of art). Photographs are considered part of the acceptable manuscript and remain with Publisher for use in additional printings. If submitted art cannot be used, the Publisher reserves the right to redo the art and to charge the author a fee of $35.00 per hour for this service

9. Alterations Required by Referees and Reviewers. Many times a paper is accepted by the Editor contingent upon changes that are mandated by anonymous specialist referees and members of the Editorial Board. If the Editor returns your manuscript for revisions, you are responsible for retyping any sections of the paper to incorporate these revisions (if applicable, revisions should also be put on disk).

10. **Typesetting**. You will not be receiving galley proofs of your article. Editorial revisions, if any, must therefore be made while your article is still in manuscript. The final version of the manuscript will be the version you see published. Typesetter's errors will be corrected by the production staff of The Haworth Press. Authors are expected to submit manuscripts, disks, and art that are free from error.

11. **Electronic Media**. Haworth's in-house typesetting unit is able to utilize your final manuscript material as prepared on most personal computers and word processors. This will minimize typographical errors and decrease overall production timelag.
a. Please continue to send your first draft and final draft copies of your manuscript to the journal Editor in print format for his/her final review and approval;
b. Only after the journal editor has approved your final manuscript, you may submit the final approved version both on:
   - printed format ("hard copy")
   - floppy diskette
c. Please make sure that the disk version and the hard copy (printed copy) are exactly the same.
d. Wrap your floppy diskettes in a strong diskette wrapper or holder, and write on the outside of the package:
   - the brand name of your computer or word processor
   - the word-processing program that you used to create your article, book chapter, or book
   - file name

The benefits of this procedure are many with speed and accuracy being the most obvious. We look forward to working with you on this, knowing we will be able to serve you more efficiently in the future.

12. **Reprints.** The senior author will receive two copies of the journal issue as well as complimentary reprints of his or her article. The junior author will receive two copies of the journal issue. These are sent several weeks after the journal issue is published and in circulation. An order form for the purchase of additional reprints will also be sent to all authors at this time. (Approximately 6–8 weeks is necessary for the preparation of reprints.) Please do not query the journal's editor about reprints. All such questions should be sent directly to The Haworth Press, Inc., Production Department, 37 West Broad Street, West Hazleton, PA 18202. To order additional reprints (minimum: 50 copies), please contact The Haworth Document Delivery Center, 10 Alice Street, Binghamton, NY 13904–1580; 1–800–342–9678 or Fax (607) 722–6362.

13. **Copyright.** Copyright ownership of your manuscript must be transferred officially to The Haworth Press, Inc. before we can begin the peer-review process. The Editor's letter acknowledging receipt of the manuscript will be accompanied by a form fully explaining this. All authors must sign the form and return the original to the Editor as soon as possible. Failure to return the copyright form in a timely fashion will result in delay in review and subsequent publication.

14. **Examples to Format**
Examples of Reference to Periodicals
1. Journal Article: One Author.
Levitt, T. (1983). The Globalization of Markets, *Harvard Business Review*, (May-June), 61 (3), 92-102.

2. Journal Article: Multiple Authors.
Kaynak, E. and Mitchell A.L. (1981). Analysis of Marketing Strategies Used in Diverse Cultures, *Journal of Advertising Research* (June), 21 (3), 25-32.

3. Magazine Article.
Tinnin, D.B. (1981, November 16) The Heady Success of Holland's Heineken, *Fortune*, pp. 158-164.

4. Newspaper Article.
The opportunity of world brands, (1984, June 3). *The New York Times*, p. 6F.

5. Monograph.
Franko, L.G. (1979). *A Survey of the Impact of Manufactured Exports From Industrializing Countries in Asia and Latin America*, Changing International Realities [Monograph] No. 6.

Examples of References to Books
1. Reference to an Entire Book.
Kaynak, E. (1986) *Marketing and Economic Development*, New York: Praeger Publishers Inc.

2. Book with a Corporate Author.
Committee For Economic Development (1981) *Transnational Corporation for Developing Countries*, New York: Author.

3. Edited Book.
Kaynak, E. (ed.) (1985) *Global Perspectives in Marketing*, New York: Praeger Publishers Inc.

4. Book with No Author or Editor.
Marketing Opportunities in Japan (1978). London: Dentsu Incorporated

5. Article or Chapter in an Edited Book.
Bucklin, L.P. (1986). Improving Food Retailing in Less Developed Asian Countries. In E. Kaynak (Ed.) *World Food Marketing Systems* (pp. 73-81) London: Butterworth Scientific Publishers.

Proceedings of Meetings and Symposia
1. Published Proceedings, Published Contributions to a Symposium.
Lee, K.H. (1981). From Production Orientation to Marketing Orientation-Hong Kong in the International Trade Setting. In D.B. Yeaman (Ed.) *Developing Global Corporate Strategies* (pp. 753-766). Conference held at the University of Navarra, Barcelona, Spain, 2 (December 17-19).

2. Unpublished Paper Presented at a Meeting.
Yucelt, U. (1987). *Tourism Marketing Planning in Developing Economies*. Paper presented at the annual meeting of the Academy of Marketing Science, Bal Harbour, Florida.

Doctoral Dissertations
1. Unpublished Doctoral Dissertation.
Czintoka, M.F. (1980). An Analysis of Export Development Strategies in Selected U.S. Industries. *Dissertations Abstract International* (University Microfilms No. 80-15, 865).

Journal of International Marketing

ADDRESS FOR SUBMISSION:

Daniel C. Bello, Editor
Journal of International Marketing
Georgia State University
Department of Marketing
35 Broad Street, Suite 1300
Atlanta, GA 30303-3083
USA
Phone: 404-651-2740
E-Mail: jim@gsu.edu
Web: www.marketingpower.com/jim

PUBLICATION GUIDELINES:

Manuscript Length: 35 Maximum
Copies Required: Four
Computer Submission: No
Format: N/A
Fees to Review: 0.00 US$

Manuscript Style:
　　See Manuscript Guidelines,
　　References/Chicago Manual, 15th ed.

CIRCULATION DATA:

Reader: Academics, Practitioners
Frequency of Issue: Quarterly
Sponsor/Publisher: American Marketing
　　Association

REVIEW INFORMATION:

Type of Review: Blind Review
No. of External Reviewers: 2
No. of In House Reviewers: 1
Acceptance Rate: 20%
Time to Review: 1 - 2 Months
Reviewers Comments: Yes
Invited Articles: No Reply
Fees to Publish: 0.00 US$

MANUSCRIPT TOPICS:

Advertising & Promotion Management; Communication; Direct Marketing; E-Commerce; Global Business; Public Administration; Purchasing/Materials Management; Sales/Selling; Services; Strategic Management Policy

MANUSCRIPT GUIDELINES/COMMENTS:

Introduction

As the globalization of markets continues at a rapid pace, business practitioners and educators alike face the challenge of staying current with the developments. Marketing managers require a source of new information and insights on international business events. International marketing educators require a forum for disseminating their thoughts and research findings.

Journal of International Marketing (JIM) is designed to serve both the practitioner and educator audiences. Its primary mission is to contribute to the advancement of international marketing practice and theory. *JIM* brings to the readership a selection of original articles, executive insights, and book reviews. The journal is published quarterly with issues appearing spring, summer, fall and winter.

Editorial Guidelines

Journal of International Marketing is an international, peer-reviewed journal dedicated to advancing international marketing practice, research, and theory. Contributions addressing any aspect of international marketing management are welcome. The journal presents scholarly and managerially relevant articles on international marketing. Aimed at both international marketing/business scholars and practitioners at senior and middle level international marketing positions, the prime objective is to bridge the gap between theory and practice in international marketing.

The editors encourage scholars and practitioners from around the world to submit articles with a diverse approach to international marketing. They welcome traditional empirical articles on important international marketing management issues, thoughtful essays on international marketing trends and practices, in-depth case studies of individual companies or industries, and integrative research reviews. These articles can be traditional narrative reviews or meta-analyses that result in theories, models, or further research agenda. Articles should be written in a clear, concise, and logical manner.

All submissions are subject to a double-blind refereeing process. *Journal of International Marketing* strives to publish work of the highest quality. Synthesis, replication with advancement, systematic extension, and work that disconfirms assumptions about international marketing are appropriate for submission. Managerial relevance is a key criterion in the final decision process.

The *JIM* Editorial Board is committed to providing authors with timely and constructive reviews. Turnaround time for most manuscripts is seven weeks. Manuscript acceptance rate for the past year is 21 percent.

Editorial Philosophy

The following provides a more specific articulation of the editorial position of *JIM*:

The domain is international marketing management. The principal topical area is marketing aspects of global business operations. The journal strives to give special emphasis to mainstream issues in international marketing management and strategy such as market entry, segmentation, positioning, pricing, channel development, product/service innovation, customer service, company organization, and globalization.

JIM's **Audience** includes educators and students of international marketing, thoughtful practitioners of business enterprises engaged in international business activities, and those involved in formulating public policy for international marketing activity.

Coverage is managerial. The ultimate criterion for publication in *JIM* is relevance for international marketing practice. Does the work offer rich managerial insights? Will it have some impact on practice? Please note that purely comparative studies are not appropriate for *JIM*. Comparisons of marketing institutions, concepts, etc., are not automatically suitable for *JIM* unless they explore an issue of importance for the international marketing manager and develop some broader conceptual insights.

The focus is on firm strategy and practice, not consumer behavior. *JIM* prefers to publish articles about business enterprises engaged in international marketing, such as manufacturers, service firms, intermediaries, trading companies, franchisors, licensors, and facilitators in international business (e.g., freight forwarders). Equal attention is given to small and large company players (e.g., multinationals) as well as to all modes of international business entry (e.g., exporting, contractual arrangements, and direct investment). Discussion of newer forms of cross-border business activity such as strategic alliances and global sourcing is also encouraged.

Although the typical consumer behavior studies may not meet the editorial objectives of *JIM*, this does not imply indifference to consumer needs and wants. On the contrary, such issues as the implications of customer orientation in multinational business, cross-cultural market segmentation, and market research are of concern to international marketing management and, therefore, to *JIM*.

The approach is interdisciplinary. In practice, marketing functions are intertwined with other business activities such as corporate strategy, procurement, logistics, human resource management, research and development, manufacturing, etc. Therefore, *JIM* especially encourages articles that provide holistic views of international marketing phenomena and those that explore interrelationships between marketing and other business functions.

Article formats are diverse. *JIM* publishes works in a variety of formats. First, traditional empirical articles on important international marketing management issues are welcome. Second, thoughtful essays on international marketing trends and practices are desirable. Third, in-depth case studies of individual companies or industries are welcome. Fourth, integrative research reviews are also of interest. These articles can be traditional narrative reviews or meta-analyses that result in theories, models, or further research agenda. Fifth, *JIM* encourages "Executive Insights"—pieces that report and express opinions on important and timely issues in international marketing practice—and "Educator Insights"—articles that are useful teaching tools.

The writing style is non-technical. Although the articles published must meet rigorous methodological criteria, the *JIM* editorial board strives to publish works that are written in an interesting, highly readable style. Articles should be written in a clear, concise, and logical manner. The text should appeal to a wide audience by avoiding the use of methodological/ technical jargon wherever possible. It may be more appropriate to include technical details in an appendix rather than in the body of the article.

MANUSCRIPT GUIDELINES
Manuscript and Electronic Preparation
Submit four (4) paper copies of your manuscript to the Editor. (Do not submit electronic copies until directed to do so by the editor.) Keep an extra, exact copy for future reference.

Manuscripts should not exceed thirty-five (35) pages, inclusive of all text, tables, figures, appendices, etc. Manuscripts should be typed double-paced throughout (including references) on 8½ x 11-inch white, non-erasable paper.

Allow margins of at least one inch on all four sides and do not justify your right-hand margin. Type on one side of the paper only.

What Goes Where

- **First page**. Name of author(s) and title; authors(s) footnote, including present position, complete address, telephone number, fax number, and e-mail address (if available). Also include any acknowledgment of financial or technical assistance.
- **Second page**. Title of paper (without author's name) and a brief abstract of no more than 50 words substantively summarizing the article. It should be informative, giving the reader a "taste" of the article.
- **Next**. The text with major headings centered on the page and subheadings flush with the left margin.
- **Then**. Technical appendices if applicable.
- **Followed by**. Endnotes numbered consecutively on a separate page. *JIM* does not use footnotes.
- **Then**. Tables, numbered consecutively, each on a separate page. If tables appear in an appendix, they should be numbered separately and consecutively, as in Table A-1, A-2, and so on.
- **Last**. References, typed double-spaced in alphabetical order by author's last name.

Mathematical Notation

JIM discourages the use of mathematical notations in the body of the article. If essential, these can be included in an endnote or appendix.

Tables

- Tables should consist of at least four columns and four rows; otherwise they should be left as in-text tabulations or their results should be integrated in the text.
- The table number and title should be typed on separate lines, centered.
- Use only horizontal rules.
- Designate units (e.g., %, $) in column headings.
- Align all decimals.
- Refer to tables in text by number. Avoid using "above," "below," and "preceding."
- If possible, combine closely related tables.
- Indicate placement in text.
- Make sure the necessary measures of statistical significance are reported with the table.

Figures and Camera-Ready Artwork

Figures should be prepared professionally electronically and as camera-ready copy. PhotoShop, Illustrator, and PowerPoint formats are preferred.

Label both vertical and horizontal axes. The ordinate label should be centered above the ordinate axis; the abscissa label should be placed beneath the abscissa.

Place all calibration tics inside the axis lines, with the values outside the axis lines. The figure number and title should be typed on separate lines, centered.

Once a manuscript has been accepted, complex tables and all figures must be submitted on CD or electronically and as camera-ready. Table and figure headings should be typed on a separate page and attached to the appropriate camera-ready art. These titles will be set in our own typeface.

Lettering should be large enough to be read easily with 50% reduction.

Do not submit camera-ready art until your manuscript has been accepted. When the artwork is completed, submit photocopies.

Reference Citations within the Text

Citations in the text should be by the author's last name and year of publication enclosed in parentheses without punctuation: "(Thorelli 1960)." If practical, the citation should stand by a punctuation mark. Otherwise, insert it in a logical sentence break. If you use the author's name within the sentence, there is no need to repeat the name in the citation; just use the year of publication in parentheses, as in "...The Howard Harris Program (1966)."

If a particular page, section, or equation is cited, it should be placed within the parentheses: "(Thorelli 1960, p. 112)." For multiple authors, use the full citation for up to three authors; for four or more, use the first author's name followed by "et al." (no italics). A series of citations should be listed in alphabetical order and separated by semicolons: (Terpstra 1961; Thorelli 1960; Welch 1981).

Reference List Style

References are to be listed alphabetically, last name first, followed by publication date in parentheses. Use full first name, not just initials. The reference list should be typed double-spaced on a separate page. Do not use indents or tabs. Put two hard returns between each reference. Limit the references to only those that are essential.

Authors are responsible for the accuracy of their references. Check them carefully.

Single- and multiple-author reference for books
Terpstra, Vern and Ravi Sarathy (1991), International Marketing. Chicago: The Dryden Press.

Single- and multiple-author reference for periodicals (include author's name, publication date, article title, complete name of periodical, volume number, month of publication, and page numbers)
Green, Robert T. and A.W. Allaway (1981), "Identification of Export Opportunities: A Shift-share Approach," Journal of Marketing, 49 (Winter), 83-88.

Single- and multiple-author reference for an article in a book edited by another author(s)
Cavusgil, S. Tamer (1982), "Country of Origin Effects on Product Evaluations: A Sequel to Bilkey and Ness," in Export Management-An International Context, Michael R. Czinkota and George Tesar, eds. New York: Praeger Publishers, 276-86.

If an author appears more than once, substitute four hyphens (this will appear as a 1-inch line when typeset) for each author's name (do not use underlines)

Bartlett, Christopher A. and Sumantra Ghoshal (1986), "Tap Your Subsidiary for Global Reach," Harvard Business Review, (November-December), 87-97.

____ and ____ (1987a), "Managing Across Borders: New Strategic Requirements," Sloan Management Review, (Summer), 7-17.

If two or more works by the same author have the same publication date, they should be differentiated by letters after the date. The letter should appear with the citation in the text:

____ and ____ (1987b), "Managing Across Borders: New Organizational Requirements," Sloan Management Review, (Fall), 43-53.

References to unpublished works, such as doctoral dissertations and working papers, should be included in the reference list as follows:

Katcher, Max (1975), "An Analysis of the Effectiveness of the Overseas Trade Fair Program of the U.S. Department of Commerce as an Exporter Promotion," doctoral dissertation, The George Washington University.

Papers printed in published proceedings of meetings
Cavusgil, S. Tamer and John R. Nevin (1981), "State-of-the Art in International Marketing: An Assessment," in Review of Marketing 1981, Ben M. Enis and Kenneth J. Roering, eds. Chicago: American Marketing Association, 195-216.

Technical Appendix
To improve the readability of the manuscript, any mathematical proof or development that is not critical to the exposition of the main part of the text may be placed in a technical appendix.

Readability
JIM manuscripts are judged not only on the depth and scope of the ideas presented and their contributions to the field, but also on their clarity and whether they can be read and understood. *JIM* readers have varied backgrounds and include many practitioners. Hence, the following guidelines should be followed:
- Write in an interesting, readable manner with varied sentence structure.
- Reduce the discussion of methodology to a minimum. *JIM* readers are most interested in implication for managerial action.
- Avoid using technical terms that few readers are likely to understand. If you use these terms, include definitions. Remember: The journal is designed to be read, not deciphered.
- Keep sentences short so the reader does not get lost before the end of a sentence.

Review Procedure
The procedures guiding the selection of articles for publication in *JIM* require that no manuscript be accepted until after is has been reviewed by the editor and at least two members of the editorial review board. The decision of the editor to publish the manuscript is influenced considerably by the judgments of these advisors, who are experts in their respective fields. The author's name and credentials are removed prior to forwarding a manuscript to reviewers to maximize objectivity and ensure that a manuscript is judged solely on the basis of its content and contribution to the field.

Acceptance Criteria

All manuscripts are judged on their contributions to the advancement of the science and/or practice of marketing. All articles are expected to follow the rules for scholarly work, namely:

- Use references to previous work when developing your arguments. Do not assume other work on the subject does not exist, giving yourself credit for all the ideas in your manuscript.
- When data collection is discussed, consider the relevance of the sample to the subject matter. Carefully chosen sample groups are preferable to haphazardly chosen subjects who have little knowledge of or relevance to the subject being studied.
- Give as much information as possible about the characteristics of the sample and its representation of the population being studied.
- Do not ignore the non-respondents. They might have different characteristics than the respondents.
- Give consideration to the limitations of your study, model, and/or concepts and discuss them explicitly in your manuscript. Be objective.
- Use appropriate statistical procedures.
- Address the reliability and validity of any empirical findings.

Preparing the Final Version

After a manuscript is accepted for publication, the final version must be submitted either electronically or on CD. It should contain the entire manuscript, including tables, figures, endnotes, and references. Although authors can prepare the manuscript using any work processing software that is Macintosh or IBM compatible, submission of the manuscript using Microsoft Word 6.0 for Windows is required. Save Word 7.0 files as Word 6.0. Please adhere to the following guidelines when preparing the final version:

1. Type everything in upper and lower case letters.
2. Footnotes are not accepted. If necessary to improve the readability of the text, a few endnotes may be included. They should appear double spaced on a separate page and be numbered consecutively throughout the text. Do not use footnote feature in your word processing program.
3. Begin each new paragraph with a single hard return, not a tab. Also, use only a single space after each period, not a double space. Use the italic attribute rather than the underline attribute.
4. Write the name of the software program used on the CD submitted.

Other Information

All published material is copyrighted by the American Marketing Association with future-use rights reserved. This does not limit the author's right to use his or her own material in future works.

For details on manuscript preparation not covered here, see *Chicago Manual of Style: The Essential Guide for Authors, Editors, and Publishers*, 14th edition, Chicago: University of Chicago Press, 1993. For specific questions on content or editorial policy, contact the editor.

AMA Journals Editorial Policy

1. Replication and/or Extension of Results

The American Marketing Association supports the meaningful exchange of information to help create an environment for constructive criticism and free exchange of ideas. Such an environment requires the authors of AMA manuscripts to share their research findings and insights. Authors of manuscripts that report data dependent results will make available, upon request, exact information regarding their procedures, materials (excluding data), and stimuli during the editorial review process. The same information will also be made available, upon request, for at least five years after the date of publication for the benefit of researchers interested in replicating or extending their results.

Authors of articles published in AMA journals are required to footnote the availability of their research instruments and other stimuli as appropriate and provide information on how the materials may be obtained. Authors of manuscripts based on proprietary data sets or other restricted material must so notify the editor at the time a manuscript is submitted. The editor will then decide whether to accept the manuscript for review. Published articles in this genre will contain a footnote stating that the data or other elements of the research process as identified are proprietary.

2. Concurrent Reviews

AMA policy prohibits an article under review at an AMA journal from being concurrently reviewed at another journal without prior discussion with and written permission from the involved AMA journal editor.

3. Multiple Submissions

Multiple reports based on essentially the same data and results should not be submitted for publication in AMA journals. The publication of a manuscript in a non-AMA journal or other publication outlet precludes publication in an AMA journal if the manuscript is based on essentially the same data set and analysis as the AMA publication. Upon request, the AMA journal editor will make a binding decision about whether a manuscript submitted to an AMA journal is too similar to a previous publication elsewhere based on the same data set to warrant review for possible publication. Each article published must also contain references to the previously published papers.

4. Conflicts of Interest

Conflicts of interest may arise in a variety of situations. A conflict of interest may exist when a manuscript under review puts forth a position contrary to the reviewer's published work or when a manuscript reviewer has a substantial direct or indirect financial interest in the subject matter of a published manuscript. Since it is AMA policy to engage in a double-blind review process, a conflict of interest may also exist when a reviewer knows the author of a manuscript. The reviewer should consult the journal editor in such situations to decide whether to review the manuscript. A conflict of interest does not exist when an author disagrees with a reviewer's assessment that a problem is unimportant or disagrees with an editorial outcome.

Journal of Internet Commerce

ADDRESS FOR SUBMISSION:

John M. Pearson, Editor
Journal of Internet Commerce
Southern Illinois University
    at Carbondale
Department of Management
Mailcode 4627
Carbondale, IL 62901-4627
USA
Phone: 618-453-7802
E-Mail: jpearson@cba.siu.edu
Web: www.cba.siu.edu/faculty/pearson/

PUBLICATION GUIDELINES:

Manuscript Length: 16-20
Copies Required: Electronic
Computer Submission: Yes Required
Format: MS Word, WordPerfect
Fees to Review: 0.00 US$

Manuscript Style:
    Chicago Manual of Style

CIRCULATION DATA:

Reader: Academics
Frequency of Issue: Quarterly
Sponsor/Publisher: Haworth Press, Inc.

REVIEW INFORMATION:

Type of Review: Blind Review
No. of External Reviewers: 2
No. of In House Reviewers: 1
Acceptance Rate: 20-30%
Time to Review: 3-4 Months
Reviewers Comments: Yes
Invited Articles: Limited
Fees to Publish: 0.00 US$

MANUSCRIPT TOPICS:
Business Information Systems (MIS); E-Commerce; Global Business; Internet Commerce;
Technology/Innovation

MANUSCRIPT GUIDELINES/COMMENTS:

About the Journal
The business world has undergone many changes because of information technology, and the
impact of the Internet may cause one of the biggest yet. While many people use the Internet
for educational and entertainment purposes, organizations and companies are looking for ways
to tie their internal networks to this global network to conduct electronic commerce. While
companies have been conducting business electronically with suppliers and customers for
many years, conducting online commerce via the Internet offers even greater opportunities for
multinational, national, and even small businesses to cut costs, improve efficiency, and reach a
global market.

According to some, the Internet will "drive the economy into the next century." Numerous companies already conduct business on the Internet while others scramble to create a presence and catch up. The ability to conduct business anywhere at anytime with anybody who has access to the Internet is definitely moving society a little closer to the "global village" concept that has been touted as a future way of life. More importantly, it is changing the face of business and commerce.

Because of the significance of the impact of the Internet on business and organizations, the *Journal of Internet Commerce* is devoted to publishing articles that discuss issues vital to conducting electronic commerce on the Internet. Additionally, the journal will also solicit and publish manuscripts dealing with educational issues related to Internet commerce.

Thus, the purpose of the *Journal of Internet Commerce* is to provide a forum for researchers and practitioners for publishing high-quality materials and discussing issues related to conducting business on the Internet. Because of the global nature of the Internet, the journal is international in nature and will publish articles on international issues as well as country-specific research. Important issues include, but are not limited to, the impact of the Internet on all aspects of commerce, organizations, and the decision-making framework within an organization. Additional issues include adoption and implementation of Internet technology, assessment, security, and strategic considerations related to Internet commerce.

Researchers studying these and other related issues are encouraged to submit manuscripts directly to the editor. Manuscripts will undergo a blind, peer-review process consisting of at least two reviewers.

With peer-reviewed research studies, cases, and practitioner experiences, the *Journal of Internet Commerce* hopes to provide an outlet for sharing knowledge and experiences related to conducting business on the Internet. The intention of the journal is to provide a source of information that will bring practitioners and academicians together as the dynamic technology of the Internet continues to change the many aspects of commerce.

Manuscript Guidelines

1. **Original Articles Only**. Submission of a manuscript to this *Journal* represents a certification on the part of the author(s) that it is an original work, and that neither this manuscript nor a version of it has been published elsewhere nor is being considered for publication elsewhere. Plagiarism detecting software will be run on all submitted manuscripts

2. **Manuscript Length**. Your manuscript may be approximately 15-30 typed pages double-spaced (including references and abstract.) Lengthier manuscripts may be considered, but only at the discretion of the Editor. Sometimes, lengthier manuscripts may be considered if they can be divided up into sections for publication in successive journal issues.

3. **Manuscript Style**. References, citations, and general style of manuscripts for this *Journal* should follow the Chicago style (as outlined in the latest edition of the *Manual of Style of the University of Chicago Press.*) References should be double-spaced and placed in alphabetical order.

If an author wishes to submit a paper that has been already prepared in another style, he or she may do so. However, if the paper is accepted (with or without reviewer's alterations), the author is fully responsible for retyping the manuscript in the correct style as indicated above. Neither the Editor nor the Publisher is responsible for re-preparing manuscript copy to adhere to the *Journal's* style.

4. Manuscript Preparation.

Margins. Leave at least a one-inch margin on all four sides.

Cover Page. Important - Attach a cover page to the manuscript in a separate file, indicating only the article title (this is used for anonymous refereeing).

Second "Title Page." Enclose a regular title page. Include the title again, plus:

- Full authorship
- An ABSTRACT of about 100 words. (Below the abstract provide 3-5 key words for index purposes)
- An introductory footnote with authors' academic degrees, professional titles, affiliations, mailing addresses, and any desired acknowledgment of research support or other credit.

5. Spelling, Grammar, and Punctuation.

You are responsible for preparing manuscript copy which is clearly written in acceptable scholarly English, and which contains no errors of spelling, grammar, or punctuation. Neither the Editor nor the Publisher is responsible for correcting errors of spelling and grammar: the manuscript, after acceptance by the Editor, must be immediately ready for typesetting as it is finally submitted by the author(s). Check your paper for the following common errors:

- Dangling modifiers
- Misplaced modifiers
- Unclear antecedents
- Incorrect or inconsistent abbreviations

Also, check the accuracy of all arithmetic calculations, statistics, numerical data, text citations, and references.

6. Inconsistencies Must Be Avoided.

Be sure you are consistent in your use of abbreviations, terminology, and in citing references, from one part of your paper to another.

7. Preparation of Tables, Figures, and Illustrations.

All tables, figures, illustrations, etc. must be "camera-ready". That is, they must be cleanly typed or artistically prepared so that they can be used either exactly as they are or else used after a photographic reduction in size. Figures, tables, and illustrations must be prepared on separate sheets of paper. Always use black ink and professional drawing instruments. In text, skip extra lines and indicate where these figures and tables are to be placed. Photographs are considered part of the acceptable manuscript and remain with the publisher for use in additional printings. If submitted art cannot be used, the publisher reserves the right to redo the art and to charge the author a fee of $35.00 per hour for this service.

8. Revisions Required By Referees and Reviewers. Many times a paper is accepted by the Editor contingent upon changes that are mandated by anonymous referees and members of the Editorial Board. If the Editor returns your manuscript for revisions, you are responsible for retyping any sections of the paper to incorporate these revisions.

10. Typesetting. You will not be receiving galley proofs of your article. Editorial revisions, if any, must therefore be made while your article is still in manuscript. The final version of the manuscript will be the version you see published. Typesetter's errors will be corrected by the production staff of The Haworth Press. Authors are expected to submit manuscripts and art that are free from error.

11. Electronic Media. Haworth's in-house typesetting unit is able to utilize your final manuscript material as prepared on most personal computers and word processors. This will minimize typographical errors and decrease overall production time lag. Please send the first draft and final draft copies of you manuscript to the *Journal* Editor in print format for his/her final review and approval.

Note. Authors are advised that no revisions of the manuscript can be made after acceptance by the Editor for publication. The benefits of this procedure are many with speed and accuracy being the most obvious. We look forward to working with you on this, knowing we will be able to serve you more efficiently in the future.

12. Reprints. The senior author will receive two copies of the *Journal* issue and 25 complimentary reprints of his or her article. The junior author will receive two copies of the *Journal* issue. These are sent several weeks after the *Journal* issue is published and in circulation. An order form for the purchase of additional reprints will also be sent to all authors at this time. (Approximately 4-6 weeks is necessary for the preparation of reprints.) Please do not query the *Journal's* Editor about reprints. All such questions should be sent directly to The Haworth Press, Inc. Production Department, 37 West Broad Street, West Hazleton, PA 18202 USA. To order additional reprints (minimum 50 copies), please contact The Haworth Document Delivery Center, 10 Alice Street, Binghamton, NY 13904-1580 USA; 1-800-342-9678, (607) 722-5857 or Fax (607) 722-6362.

13. Copyright. Copyright ownership of your manuscript must be transferred officially to The Haworth Press, Inc. before we can begin the peer-review process. The Editor's letter acknowledging receipt of the manuscript will be accompanied by a form fully explaining this. All authors must sign the form and return the original to the Editor as soon as possible. Failure to return the copyright form in a timely fashion will result in delay in review and subsequent publication.

Journal of Macromarketing

ADDRESS FOR SUBMISSION:

Clifford J. Shultz, II, Editor
Journal of Macromarketing
Arizona State University
Morrison School of Agribusiness
7001 E. Williams Field Rd.
Mesa, AZ 85212
USA
Phone: 480-727-1242
E-Mail: jmm.agb@asu.edu
  atcjs@asu.edu
Web: http://agb.east.asu.edu/jmm

PUBLICATION GUIDELINES:

Manuscript Length: 16-30
Copies Required: Five
Computer Submission: Yes Preferred
Format: See Guidelines and/or Website
Fees to Review: 0.00 US$

Manuscript Style:
  Chicago Manual of Style

CIRCULATION DATA:

Reader: Academics
Frequency of Issue: 2 Times/Year
Sponsor/Publisher: Sage Publications

REVIEW INFORMATION:

Type of Review: Blind Review
No. of External Reviewers: 3
No. of In House Reviewers: 1
Acceptance Rate: 11-20%
Time to Review: 2 - 3 Months
Reviewers Comments: Yes
Invited Articles: 0-5%
Fees to Publish: 0.00 US$

MANUSCRIPT TOPICS:
Business Law, Public Responsibility & Ethics; Marketing Theory & Applications

MANUSCRIPT GUIDELINES/COMMENTS:

Topics Include. Distributive Justice; Macromarketing; Marketing & Economic Development; Marketing Behavior; Marketing History; Marketing & Society; Public Policy Regarding Marketing; Quality of Life Studies

The *Journal of Macromarketing* focuses on important societal issues as they are affected by marketing and on how society affects the conduct of marketing. The journal covers macromarketing areas such as marketing and public policy, marketing and development, marketing and the quality of life, and the history of marketing. Articles may involve explanatory theory, empirical studies, or methodological treatment of tests.

Four kinds of material are published in the *Journal of Macromarketing*. Feature articles explain relationships, analyze data, or examine methodological concepts, tests, or approaches to a problem. Reader response letters confirm or challenge viewpoints expressed in feature articles. Reviews and communications summarize and evaluate books and published research studies. Seminar abstracts summarize papers presented at the annual Macromarketing Conference.

The procedures guiding the selection of articles for publication in the journal require that no manuscript be accepted until it has been reviewed by the editor, the section editor (if applicable), and at least three outside reviewers who are experts in their respective fields (often members of the Editorial Review Board). Manuscripts are reviewed simultaneously by geographically separated reviewers. It is journal policy to remove the author's name and credentials prior to forwarding a manuscript to a reviewer to maximize objectivity and ensure that manuscripts are judged solely on the basis of content, clarity, and contribution to the field. All manuscripts are judged on their contribution to the advancement of science, the practice of macromarketing, or both. Articles should be written in an interesting, readable manner, and technical terms should be defined. In some highly exceptional circumstances, the journal will publish an invited manuscript from a noted scholar on a topic deemed of particular interest to the development of the field of macromarketing.

Manuscripts submitted to the journal can be processed most expeditiously if they are prepared according to these instructions.

Manuscript Preparation
Manuscripts should be typed double-spaced, including references, formatted for letter (8.5" x 11") paper size. Do not use single spacing anywhere except on tables and figures. Page numbers are to be placed in the upper right-hand corner of every page. A tab indent should begin each paragraph. Please allow the text to wrap, rather than placing a hard return after every line. Manuscripts ordinarily should be between 4,000 and 6,000 words (ca. 15 typewritten pages of text) using Times New Roman 12-point type or larger. Articles of shorter length are also acceptable and encouraged. Please refrain from using first person singular in the text of the manuscript unless it is an invited article or book review.

Electronic submissions are preferred; manuscripts should be submitted via e-mail, as an attachment in Word format, to **jmm.agb@asu.edu**. Alternatively, authors may submit five (5) copies of each manuscript along with a diskette containing the manuscript in Word format. The author's name should not appear anywhere except on the cover page. The author should keep an extra, exact copy for future reference.

In the manuscript, please be sure that acronyms, abbreviations, and jargon are defined, unless they are well-known (such as FBI) or in the dictionary or Chicago manual (e.g., Table 13.1 and sec. 14.50). Quotes of 10 or more words include page number(s) from the original source. Every Citation has a reference, and every reference is cited.

For details of manuscript preparation not covered in the following sections, see *The Chicago Manual of Style*, 14th edition, Chicago and London: University of Chicago Press, 1993, and review recent issues of the journal.

1. What Goes Where

The sections of the manuscript should be placed in the following order: cover page, title page, body, appendixes, endnotes, reference list, tables, figures. Each section should begin on a new page.

Cover Page. Article title, with full name of author(s), present position, organizational affiliation, full address including postal code and country, telephone/fax numbers, and e-mail address. Author(s) must be listed in the order in which they are to appear in the published article. Please clearly indicate which author will serve as the primary contact for the journal and be especially sure to provide a fax number and e-mail address for this person. A 40-word (maximum) narrative on each author's specialty or interests should also appear on this page, as should any acknowledgment of financial or technical assistance. (This page will be removed prior to sending the manuscript to reviewers.)

Title Page. Title of paper, without author(s) name(s), and a brief abstract of no more than 150 words substantively summarizing the article. Four or five keywords to facilitate electronic access to this manuscript should also be listed on this page.

Body. The text, with major headings centered on the page and subheadings flush with the left margin. Major headings should use all uppercase letters; side subheadings should be typed in upper- and lowercase letters. Do not use footnotes in the body of the manuscript. If used, please place endnotes in a numbered list after the body of the text and before the reference list; however, avoid endnotes wherever possible because they interrupt the flow of the manuscript. Acronyms, abbreviations, and jargon are defined unless they are well-known (such as FBI) or they can be found in the dictionary. Quotes of 10 or more words include page number(s) from the original source. Every citation has a reference and every reference is cited.

Tables and Figures. Each table or figure should be prepared on a separate page and grouped together at the end of the manuscript. The data in tables should be arranged so that columns of like materials read down, not across. Non-significant decimal places in tabular data should be omitted. The tables and figures should be numbered in Arabic numerals, followed by brief descriptive titles. Additional details should be footnoted under the table, not in the title. In the text, all illustrations and charts should be referred to as figures. Figures must be clean, crisp, black-and-white, camera-ready copies. Please avoid the use of gray-scale shading; use hatchmarks, dots, or lines instead. Please be sure captions are included. Indicate in text where tables and figures should appear. Be sure to send final camera-ready, black-and-white versions of figures and, if possible, electronic files.

References. References should be typed double-spaced in alphabetical order by author's last name (see 3).

2. Reference Citations within Text

Citations in the text should include the author's last name and year of publication enclosed in parentheses without punctuation, for example, (Kinsey 1960). If practical, the citation should be placed immediately before a punctuation mark. Otherwise, insert it in a logical sentence break.

If a particular page, section, or equation is cited, it should be placed within the parentheses, for example, (Kinsey 1960, 112). For multiple authors, use the full, formal citation for up to three authors, but for four or more use the first author's name with "et al." For example, use (White and Smith 1977) and (Brown, Green, and Stone 1984). For more than three authors, use (Hunt et al. 1975), unless another work published in that year would also be identified as (Hunt et al. 1975); in that case, list all authors, for example, (Hunt, Bent,. Marks, and West 1975).

3. Reference List Style

List references alphabetically, principal author's surname first, followed by publication date. The reference list should be typed double-spaced, with a hanging indent, on a separate page. Do not number references. Please see the reference examples below as well as reference lists in recent issues. Be sure that all titles cited in the text appear in the reference list and vice versa. Please provide: translations for non-English titles in references; page ranges for articles and for book chapters; and provide all authors'/editors names (note "et al.," unless it appears that way in the publication).

Journal Article
Smith, J.R. 2001. Reference style guidelines. *Journal of Guidelines* 4 (2): 2-7 [or 4:2-7].

----------- 2001. Reference style guidelines. *Journal of Baltic Studies* 4 (2): 2-7.

Book
Smith, J.R. 2001. *Reference style guidelines.* Thousand Oaks, CA: Sage.

Chapter in a Book
Smith, J.R. 2001. Be sure your disk matches the hard copy. In *Reference style guidelines,* edited by R. Brown, 155-62. Thousand Oaks, CA: Sage.

Editor of a Book
Smith, J.R., ed. 2001. *Reference style guidelines.* Thousand Oaks, CA: Sage.

Dissertation (Unpublished)
Smith, J.R. 2001. Reference style guidelines. Ph.D. diss., University of California, Los Angeles.

Paper Presented at a Symposium or Annual Meeting
Smith, J.R. 2001. A citation for every reference, and a reference for every citation. Paper presented at the annual meeting of the Reference Guidelines Association, St. Louis, MO, January.

Online
Smith, J.R. 2001. Reference style guidelines. In MESH vocabulary file [database online]. Bethesda, MD: National Library of Medicine. [cited 3 October 2001]. Available from www.sagepub.com

4. Mathematical Notation

Mathematical notation must be clear within the text. Equations should be centered on the page. If equations are numbered, type the number in parentheses flush with the right margin. For equations that may be too wide to fit in a single column, indicate appropriate breaks. Unusual symbols and Greek letters should be identified by a marginal note.

5. Permission Guidelines

Authors are solely responsible for obtaining all necessary permissions and for paying any associated fees. Permission must be granted in writing by the copyright holder and must accompany the submitted manuscript. Authors are responsible for the accuracy of facts, opinions, and interpretations expressed in the article.

Permission is required to reprint, paraphrase, or adapt the following in a work of scholarship or research:

- Any piece of writing or other work that is used in its entirety (e.g., poems, tables, figures, charts, graphs, photographs, drawings, illustrations, book chapters, journal articles, newspaper or magazine articles, radio/television broadcasts);
- Portions of articles or chapters of books or of any of the items in the preceding paragraph, if the portion used is a sizable amount in relation to the item as a whole, regardless of size, or it captures the "essence" or the "heart" of the work;
- Any portion of a fictional, creative, or other nonfactual work (e.g., opinion, editorial, essay, lyrics, commentary, plays, novels, short stories); and
- Any portion of an unpublished work.

Manuscript Submission

Please send all manuscripts to the Editor.

All published material is copyrighted by Sage Publications, Inc. Every author and co-author must sign a contract before an article can be published.

Submission of Final Manuscripts

Authors of final manuscripts accepted for publication should send a final copy as Word attachment to this e-mail address: **jmm.agb@asu.edu**; alternatively, authors may provide two hard copies of the final version of their article and a matching version on a 3.5-inch computer disk. Please group all sections of the article in one file on the disk; do not use separate files for tables, references, and so forth. Please do not include figures on disk. Figures are acceptable as camera-ready copy only.

Journal of Marketing

ADDRESS FOR SUBMISSION:

Roland T. Rust, Editor
Journal of Marketing
ONLINE SUBMISSION ONLY
Phone:
E-Mail: rrust@rhsmith.umd.edu
Web: www.marketingjournals.org/jm/

PUBLICATION GUIDELINES:

Manuscript Length: 50 maximum
Copies Required: Electronic
Computer Submission: Yes Required
Format: PDF
Fees to Review: 0.00 US$

Manuscript Style:
See Manuscript Guidelines

CIRCULATION DATA:

Reader: Academics, Marketing
    Practitioners
Frequency of Issue: Quarterly
Sponsor/Publisher: American Marketing
    Association

REVIEW INFORMATION:

Type of Review: Blind Review
No. of External Reviewers: 3
No. of In House Reviewers: 1
Acceptance Rate: 11%
Time to Review: 2 Months
Reviewers Comments: Yes
Invited Articles: 0-5%
Fees to Publish: 0.00 US$

MANUSCRIPT TOPICS:
Advertising & Promotion Management; Business Education; Business Information Systems (MIS); Business Law, Public Responsibility & Ethics; Communication; Direct Marketing; E-Commerce; Global Business; Health Care Administration; Labor Relations & Human Resource Mgt.; Marketing Research; Marketing Theory & Applications; Non-Profit Organizations; Office Administration/Management; Operations Research/Statistics; Organizational Behavior & Theory; Organizational Development; Production/Operations; Public Administration; Purchasing/Materials Management; Retailing; Sales/Selling; Services; Small Business Entrepreneurship; Strategic Management Policy; Technology/Innovation; Tourism, Hospitality & Leisure; Transportation/Physical Distribution

MANUSCRIPT GUIDELINES/COMMENTS:

Editorial Policy
The following policies are applicable to the *Journal of Marketing*, *Journal of Marketing Research*, *Journal of International Marketing*, and *Journal of Public Policy & Marketing*.

1. Replication and/or Extension of Results
The American Marketing Association supports the meaningful exchange of information to help create an environment for constructive criticism and free exchange of ideas. Such an environment requires the authors of AMA manuscripts to share their research findings and insights. Authors of manuscripts that report data dependent results will make available, upon

request, exact information regarding their procedures, materials (excluding data), and stimuli during the editorial review process. The same information will also be made available, upon request, for at least five years after the date of publication for the benefit of researchers interested in replicating or extending their results.

Authors of articles published in AMA journals are required to footnote the availability of their research instruments and other stimuli as appropriate and provide information on how the materials may be obtained. Authors of manuscripts based on proprietary data sets or other restricted material must so notify the editor at the time a manuscript is submitted. The editor will then decide whether to accept the manuscript for review. Published articles in this genre will contain a footnote stating that the data or other elements of the research process as identified are proprietary.

2. Concurrent Reviews

AMA policy prohibits an article under review at an AMA journal from being concurrently reviewed at another journal without prior discussion with and written permission from the involved AMA journal editor.

3. Multiple Submissions

Multiple reports based on essentially the same data and results should not be submitted for publication in AMA journals. The publication of a manuscript in a non-AMA journal or other publication outlet precludes publication in an AMA journal if the manuscript is based on essentially the same data set and analysis as the AMA publication. Upon request, the AMA journal editor will make a binding decision about whether a manuscript submitted to an AMA journal is too similar to a previous publication elsewhere based on the same data set to warrant review for possible publication. Each article published must also contain references to the previously published papers.

4. Conflicts of Interest

Conflicts of interest may arise in a variety of situations. A conflict of interest may exist when a manuscript under review puts forth a position contrary to the reviewer's published work or when a manuscript reviewer has a substantial direct or indirect financial interest in the subject matter of a published manuscript. Since it is AMA policy to engage in a double-blind review process, a conflict of interest may also exist when a reviewer knows the author of a manuscript. The reviewer should consult the journal editor in such situations to decide whether to review the manuscript. A conflict of interest does not exist when an author disagrees with a reviewer's assessment that a problem is unimportant or disagrees with an editorial outcome.

5. Protecting Intellectual Property

Protecting intellectual property is a primary responsibility of the reviewer and the editor. Reviewers, therefore, will not use ideas from or show another person the manuscript they have been asked to review without the explicit permission of the manuscript's author, obtained through the journal editor. Advice regarding specific, limited aspects of the manuscript may be sought from colleagues with specific expertise, provided the author's identity and intellectual property remain secure.

6. Sharing of Reviewing Responsibilities

Sharing of reviewing responsibilities is inappropriate. The review is the sole responsibility of the person to whom it was assigned by the journal editor. Students and colleagues should not be asked to prepare reviews unless the journal editor has given explicit prior approval. Each person contributing to a review should receive formal recognition.

7. Review Process

All reviews will use a double-blind review process. Reviewers and journal editors are expected to provide comments and critiques in a confidential, constructive, prompt, and unbiased manner appropriate for their position of responsibility. Collegiality, respect for the author's dignity, and the search for ways to improve the quality of the manuscript should characterize the review process. The editor has the final authority for the acceptance or rejection of any article.

Editorial Guidelines

Editorial Statement. The *Journal of Marketing* (*JM*), a quarterly publication of the American Marketing Association (AMA), is one of the premier refereed scholarly journals of the marketing discipline. Since its founding in 1936, *JM* has played a significant role in the dissemination of marketing knowledge grounded in scholarly research, as well as in shaping the content and boundaries of the discipline.

Two AMA objectives have a direct bearing on the publication policies of *JM*: (1) to lead in the development, dissemination, and implementation of marketing concepts, practice, and information and (2) to probe and promote the use of marketing concepts by business, not-for-profit, and other institutions for the betterment of society.

Editorial Goals. The editorial goals of *JM* are:

- The advancement of the science and practice of marketing (to make a difference by adding to what we know about marketing phenomena and changing how we study and practice marketing).
- To serve as a bridge between the scholarly and the practical, each of which has a vital stake in what's happening on the other side.

Primary Reader Targets. Thoughtful marketing practitioners and educators concerned with marketing theory and practice.

Positioning. Every discipline needs a broad-based journal that can serve as a vehicle for the publication of papers that have the potential to make a significant contribution to knowledge in any area of marketing. *JM* is positioned as the premier, broad-based, scholarly journal of the marketing discipline focusing on substantive issues in marketing and marketing management.

The target audience for *JM* articles are the thoughtful marketing academicians and practitioners. The word "thoughtful" in the statement of target audience has important implications. It implies that the reader, whether academician or practitioner, is knowledgeable about the state-of-the-art of the topic areas covered in *JM*.

Implications of Goals and Positioning for Editorial Content. By design, *JM* will publish articles on a variety of topics contributing to the advancement of the science and/or practice of marketing. Given *JM's* positioning as a broad-based journal of the discipline, and a readership comprised of heterogeneous groups of academics and practitioners with diverse substantive areas of interest and philosophical orientations, *JM* cannot devote a disproportionate amount of space to any one area.

Appropriate Editorial Content. As a literature-based scholarly journal, *JM* is committed to publishing a broad spectrum of conceptual and empirical articles that make a new theoretical and/or substantive contribution to the field. The following is a partial list of the nature of articles appropriate for submission to the journal for review and publication consideration:

- Articles focusing on any substantive area that falls within the field of marketing, addressing problems or issues deemed significant by one or more of *JM's* constituencies.
- Articles providing critical syntheses and reviews of relevant areas within marketing
- Articles reporting generalizable empirical findings
- Articles focusing on neglected areas of marketing
- Articles that critically reexamine existing concepts and theories in marketing
- Articles focusing on important forces, events, and trends affecting the present and future of marketing
- Articles that provide insights into emerging and evolving concepts and theories in marketing
- Articles that lead the discipline—push marketing into new frontiers
- Articles that have the potential to stimulate further research and, by doing so, alter the nature and scope of marketing's foundation
- Articles focusing on substantive areas characterized by a dearth of research, emerging and evolving areas that might potentially impact on the boundaries and frontier of the discipline, and areas that currently lack a theory base but constitute substantive issues that merit serious inquiry by marketing scholars
- Articles integrating concepts from allied disciplines such as economics, strategic management, finance, accounting, organizational behavior, sociology, psychology and anthropology into marketing

Manuscript Guidelines
See Websites:
 www.marketingjournals.org/jm/ms_prep.php
 www.marketingjournals.org/jm/ms_stylespecs.php

Journal of Marketing Channels

ADDRESS FOR SUBMISSION:

Lou E. Pelton, Editor
Journal of Marketing Channels
University of North Texas
College of Business Administration
PO Box 31196
Denton, TX 76203-1396
USA
Phone: 940-565-3124
E-Mail: pelton@unt.edu
Web: www.haworthpress.com

PUBLICATION GUIDELINES:

Manuscript Length: 21-25
Copies Required: Electronic
Computer Submission: Yes Email
Format:
Fees to Review: 0.00 US$

Manuscript Style:
American Psychological Association

CIRCULATION DATA:

Reader: Academics
Frequency of Issue: Quarterly
Sponsor/Publisher: Best Business Books /
Haworth Press, Inc.

REVIEW INFORMATION:

Type of Review: Blind Review
No. of External Reviewers: 2
No. of In House Reviewers: 0
Acceptance Rate: 12-16%
Time to Review: 2 - 3 Months
Reviewers Comments: Yes
Invited Articles: 0-5%
Fees to Publish: 0.00 US$

MANUSCRIPT TOPICS:

E-Commerce; Franchising; Global Business; Marketing Channels; Marketing Research; Operations Research/Statistics; Production/Operations; Purchasing/Materials Management; Retailing; Technology/Innovation; Transportation/Physical Distribution

MANUSCRIPT GUIDELINES/COMMENTS:

About the Journal. The purpose of the *Journal of Marketing Channels* is to provide the knowledge and tools needed to develop superior distribution systems, strategies, and management. Leading authorities from around the world will present the most up-to-date and in-depth thought, analysis, and research on these topics in this refereed international quarterly.

Each article will provide solid information, insights, or tools of analysis for dealing with such crucial marketing channel issues as:

- How will changing economic, competitive, and technological developments affect marketing channels?
- How can marketing channels be designed to provide superior customer service while enhancing profitability?
- How can effective channel partnerships be created through the selection of channel members?

- How can distributors, dealers, and other channel members be motivated to do a more effective selling job?
- How can the performance of marketing channels be evaluated more accurately?
- How can cooperation in marketing channels be fostered and conflict reduced?
- How can marketing channel strategy be used to gain a competitive advantage?
- How can marketing channels be used to gain access to international markets?

Instructions for Authors

1. **Original Articles Only.** Submission of a manuscript to this *Journal* represents a certification on the part of the author(s) that it is an original work, and that neither this manuscript nor a version of it has been published elsewhere nor is being considered for publication elsewhere.

2. **Manuscript Length.** 20-25 typed pages

3. **Manuscript Style.** *Chicago Manual of Style*

4. **Manuscript Preparation**
Margins. Leave at least a 1" margin on all four sides.
Paper. Use clean white, 8½" x 11" bond paper.
Number of Copies. 4 (the original plus three photocopies)
Cover Page. Important—Staple a cover page to the manuscript, indicating only the article title (this is used for anonymous refereeing).
Second "Title Page." Enclose a regular title page but do not staple it to the manuscript. Include the title again, plus:

- Full authorship
- An **abstract** of about 100 words. (Below the abstract provide 3-1 0 key words for index purposes).
- An introductory footnote with authors' academic degrees, professional titles, affiliations, mailing addresses, and any desired acknowledgment of research support or other credit.

5. **Return Envelopes.** When you submit your four manuscript copies, also include:

- A regular envelope, stamped and self-addressed. This is for the Editor to send you an "acknowledgement of receipt" letter.
- Manuscripts will not be returned.

6. **Spelling, Grammar, and Punctuation.** You are responsible for preparing manuscript copy which is clearly written in acceptable scholarly English, and which contains no errors of spelling, grammar, or punctuation. Neither the Editor nor the Publisher is responsible for correcting errors of spelling and grammar: the manuscript, after acceptance by the Editor, must be immediately ready for typesetting as it is finally submitted by the author(s). Check your paper for the following common errors:

- Dangling modifiers
- Misplaced modifiers
- Unclear antecedents
- Incorrect or inconsistent abbreviations

Also, check the accuracy of all arithmetic calculations, statistics, numerical data, text citations, and references.

7. **Inconsistencies Must Be Avoided**. Be sure you are consistent in your use of abbreviations, terminology, and in citing references, from one part of your paper to another.

8. **Preparation of Tables, Figures, and Illustrations**. All tables, figures, illustrations, etc. must be "camera-ready." That is, they must be cleanly typed or artistically prepared so that they can be used either exactly as they are or else used after a photographic reduction in size. Figures, tables, and illustrations must be prepared on separate sheets of paper. Always use black ink and professional drawing instruments. On the back of these items, write your article title and the journal title lightly in pencil, so they do not get misplaced. In text, skip extra lines and indicate where these figures and tables are to be placed (please do not write on face of art). Photographs are considered part of the acceptable manuscript and remain with Publisher for use in additional printings. If submitted art cannot be used, the Publisher reserves the right to redo the art and to charge the author a fee of $35.00 per hour for this service.

9. **Alterations Required by Referees and Reviewers**. Many times a paper is accepted by the Editor contingent upon changes that are mandated by anonymous specialist referees and members of the Editorial Board. If the Editor returns your manuscript for revisions, you are responsible for retyping any sections of the paper to incorporate these revisions (if applicable, revisions should also be put on disk).

10. **Typesetting**. You will not be receiving galley proofs of your article. Editorial revisions, if any, must therefore be made while your article is still in manuscript. The final version of the manuscript will be the version you see published. Typesetter's errors will be corrected by the production staff of The Haworth Press. Authors are expected to submit manuscripts, disks, and art that are free from error.

11. **Electronic Media**. Haworth's in-house typesetting unit is able to utilize your final manuscript material as prepared on most personal computers and word processors. This will minimize typographical errors and decrease overall production time lag. Please send the first draft and final draft copies of your manuscript to the *Journal* Editor in print format for his/her final review and approval. After approval of your final manuscript, please submit the final approved version both on printed format ("hard copy") and floppy diskette. On the outside of the diskette package write:
a.   The brand name of your computer or word processor
b.   The word-processing program that you used
c.   The title of your article, and
d.   File name

Note. Disk and hard copy must agree. In case of discrepancies, it is The Haworth Press's policy to follow hard copy. Authors are advised that no revisions of the manuscript can be made after acceptance by the Editor for publication. The benefits of this procedure are many with speed and accuracy being the most obvious. We look forward to working with you on this, knowing we will be able to serve you more efficiently in the future.

594

12. **Reprints**. The senior author will receive two copies of the *Journal* issue and 25 complimentary reprints of his or her article. The junior author will receive two copies of the *Journal* issue. These are sent several weeks after the *Journal* issue is published and in circulation. An order form for the purchase of additional reprints will also be sent to all authors at this time. (Approximately 4-6 weeks is necessary for the preparation of reprints.) Please do not query the *Journal*'s Editor about reprints. All such questions should be sent directly to The Haworth Press, Inc., Production Department, 21 East Broad Street, West Hazleton, PA 18201.

To order additional reprints (minimum 50 copies), please contact the Haworth Document Delivery Center, 10 Alice Street, Binghamton, NY 13904-1580; 1-800-342-9678 or Fax (607) 722-6362.

13. **Copyright**. Copyright ownership of your manuscript must be transferred officially to The Haworth Press, Inc., before we can begin the peer-review process. The Editor's letter acknowledging receipt of the manuscript will be accompanied by a form fully explaining this. All authors must sign the form and return the original to the Editor as soon as possible. Failure to return the copyright form in a timely fashion will result in delay in review and subsequent publication.

Journal of Marketing Communications

ADDRESS FOR SUBMISSION:

Patrick de Pelsmacker, Deputy Editor
Journal of Marketing Communications
University of Antwerp
Department of Applied Economics
Middelheimlaan 1
Antwerp, B-2020
Belguim
Phone: +32-3-2180-715
E-Mail: patrick.depelmacker@ua.be
Web: www.tandf.co.uk

CIRCULATION DATA:

Reader: Academics, Practitioners
Frequency of Issue: Quarterly
Sponsor/Publisher: Routledge (Taylor &
   Francis Ltd.)

PUBLICATION GUIDELINES:

Manuscript Length: 21-25
Copies Required: Four
Computer Submission: No
Format: N/A
Fees to Review: 0.00 US$

Manuscript Style:
   See Manuscript Guidelines

REVIEW INFORMATION:

Type of Review: Blind Review
No. of External Reviewers: 2
No. of In House Reviewers: 0
Acceptance Rate: 40%
Time to Review: 1 - 2 Months
Reviewers Comments: Yes
Invited Articles: 0-5%
Fees to Publish: 0.00 US$

MANUSCRIPT TOPICS:

Advertising & Promotion Management; Communication; Corporate & Marketing Communications Case Studies; Corporate Communications; Direct Marketing; E-Commerce; Global Business; Internet & Database Marketing; Marketing Theory & Applications; Public Relations; Sales/Selling; Services

MANUSCRIPT GUIDELINES/COMMENTS:

Editor
Professor Philip J. Kitchen, Hull University Business School, Hull University, Hull, UK HU17 7RP. Phone: +44 (0) 1482 463532, Fax: +44 (0) 1482 463689 Email: **p.j.kitchen@ hull.ac.uk**, Web: **http://www.tandf.co.uk**

Associate Editors
USA/Canada. Professor Don E. Schultz, Integrated Marketing Communications, Medill School of Journalism, Northwestern University, 1908 Sheridan Road, Evanston, Illinois 60208-1290, USA. Tel: 001 847 491 5665, Fax: 001 847 491 5925. Email: **dschultz@lulu. acns.nwu.au**

596

European Community. Professor W. Fred van Raaij, Faculty of Social and Behavioural Sciences, University of Tilburg, Warandelaan 2, PO Box 90153, 5000 LE Tilberg, The Netherlands. Tel: 00 31 13 466 2434, Fax 00 31 13 466 2067. Email: **W.F.vanRaaij@uvt.nl**

Pacific Rim. Professor Charles H. Patti, Head – School of Communication, Queensland University of Technology, Level 10, Z Block, 2 George Street, Brisbane, Queensland 4001, Australia. Email: **c.patti@qut.edu.au**

Book Reviews Editor
Professor Lynne Eagle, Middlesex University Business School, Middlesex University, The Burroughs, London, UK NW4 4BT. Tel: 0044 20 8411 5864, Fax 0044 20 8411 5357. Email: **L.Eagle@mdx.ac.uk**

Aims and Scope
The *Journal of Marketing Communications* is devoted to publishing research papers and information concerning all aspects of marketing and corporate communication, branding—both corporate and product-related, and promotion management. It is a channel for discussing issues such as customer relationship management, integrated marketing communication, together with behavioural foundations of marketing communications and promotion management. The *Journal* will also consider paper sin internal marketing and in the corporate communications domain.

Issues that the *Journal* covers includes:
- Marketing communications—communications via any or all of the marketing mix elements
- The way(s) the marketing mix elements are interrelated and operationalized for communication purposes in marketing planning process
- The general area of corporate communication as it relates to the development of communication programmes designed to influence the support of, and relationships with, various stakeholder groups
- Promotional elements—this not only includes the disciplines of advertising, sales promotion, marketing public relations, and personal selling, but also includes direct marketing, sponsorship, and Internet communications.
- Promotional management in terms of strategy development, implementation, and evaluation
- The mechanism or process of developing effective communication strategies via specific case studies
- Behavioural foundations of marketing communications and promotion management including semiotics, consumer behaviour, attitudes and persuasion, source and message factors, diffusion of innovation, and adoption
- Effects of changing environmental circumstance on marketing communications and promotional strategy—budget allocations, messages, and media vehicles adopted
- Issues such as brand equity, brand investment, brand marketing and performance, marketing communications ROI, the role of research in marketing communications, integrated marketing communication, relationship marketing, and on- and off-line marketing activities

- Examples of sound or innovative company or teaching practice in relation to marketing communication activities or promotional management
- Corporate communication and its interface with marketing communication

Instructions for Authors

All papers are subject to a double-blind refereeing process. There is no submission fee and no page charge. If a paper is considered suitable, it will be passed to an Associate Editor and thus to the review process. The Editor will make the final decision as to acceptability after taking into account reports from Associate Editors and referees. Authors will be provided with copies of the referees' reports.

Submission. Authors should submit four copies of their manuscript together with original illustrations and a covering letter to the Editor or to one of the Associate Editors. It is assumed that the author will keep one copy. Articles should be between 4000 and 6000 words. Submission of manuscripts in electronic form is also encouraged. Word, WordPerfect or ASCII files are acceptable, however four hard copies must be supplied.

The Manuscript. Manuscripts must be typed double-spaced on one side of A4 paper only, with a 4cm left-hand margin. Permission to reproduce previously published material or to use illustrations that identify individuals must be obtained by the author prior to submission. Information on the transfer of copyright will be sent to authors on acceptance of their manuscript for publication. The transfer of copyright from author(s) to publisher must be stated in writing before any manuscript can be published.

Title Page. The title page must include the following information: the full title; the affiliation and full addresses of all authors; a running title (maximum 50 characters); indication of the author responsible for correspondence and correction of proofs; a brief biographical outline.

Abstract and Keywords. The abstract should be comprehensible without reference to the text and should not exceed 200 words. The main findings and new and important aspects of the study should be emphasized. Up to five keywords or phrases must be submitted for indexing purposes.

References. The Harvard system is used. When quoted in the text the style is: ...Jones (1991) or (Smith and Jones, 1991). For three or more authors: Jones et al., (1991) or (Jones et al., 1991). References to papers by the same author(s) in the same year are distinguished in text and reference list by the letters a, b etc: Smith (1989a). References are listed at the end of the paper in alphabetical order giving the title of the paper and journal titles in full, together with the first and last page numbers. References to books and reports must include the year of publication, title, edition, editor(s), place of publication and publisher in that order.

Tables. Each table should be typed on a separate sheet, numbered consecutively and provided with a brief title. Tables should be comprehensible without reference to the text, but repetitions of methods that have been described in the text are not necessary. Explanatory material should be placed as a footnote to the table. When results are expressed as percentages, the absolute value(s) that correspond to 100% should be stated.

Illustrations. Line drawings should be supplied at double the intended size. Illustrations should not be inserted in the pages of the manuscript, but supplied separately with the typescript. Typewritten or handwritten annotations are not acceptable. Illustrations must be presented either as: (1) high-resolution, well-contrasted glossy photographs or (2) high-quality laser printed computer output. Colour illustrations should be supplied as colour prints grouped into plates; costs of colour printing will be charged to the author.

Footnotes. These should not be used unless absolutely essential. If included they should be kept to a minimum, and numbered separately on separate sheets.

Proofs. Proofs will be sent to the corresponding author for correction. The proofs must be corrected within three days of receipt and returned to the publisher. Alteration to proofs other than the correction of printer's errors may be charged to the authors.

Offprints. Each corresponding author will receive 25 free offprints and a bound copy of the journal.

Copyright. Submission of a paper to the *Journal of Marketing Communications* will be taken to imply that it presents original unpublished work, not under consideration for publication elsewhere. By submitting a manuscript, the authors agree that the copyright for their article is transferred to Taylor Francis Ltd if and when the article is accepted for publication. The copyright covers the exclusive rights to reproduce and distribute the article, including electronic distribution, reprints, photographic reproductions, microfilm or any other reproductions of a similar or any nature, and translations. Permission to publish illustrations must be obtained by the author before submission and any acknowledgements should be included in the captions.

Journal of Marketing Education

ADDRESS FOR SUBMISSION:

Douglas J. Lincoln, Editor
Journal of Marketing Education
Boise State University
College of Business and Economics
Department of Marketing and Finance
1910 University Drive
Boise, ID 83725
USA
Phone: 208-426-3246
E-Mail: dlincoln@boisestate.edu
Web: http://jmd.sagepub.com/

CIRCULATION DATA:

Reader: Academics
Frequency of Issue: 3 Times/Year
Sponsor/Publisher: Marketing Educator's
  Association / Sage Publications

PUBLICATION GUIDELINES:

Manuscript Length: 16-20
Copies Required: Electronic
Computer Submission: Yes Email Required
Format: MS Word
Fees to Review: 0.00 US$

Manuscript Style:
  Chicago Manual of Style

REVIEW INFORMATION:

Type of Review: Blind Review
No. of External Reviewers: 3
No. of In House Reviewers: 0
Acceptance Rate: 11-20%
Time to Review: 2 - 3 Months
Reviewers Comments: Yes
Invited Articles: 0-5%
Fees to Publish: 0.00 US$

MANUSCRIPT TOPICS:

Advertising & Promotion Management; Business Law, Public Responsibility & Ethics; Communication; Direct Marketing; E-Commerce; Global Business; Marketing Research; Marketing Theory & Applications; Pedagogical Topics in Marketing; Sales/Selling; Services; Technology/Innovation; Transportation/Physical Distribution

MANUSCRIPT GUIDELINES/COMMENTS:

Editorial Policy

The *Journal of Marketing Education is* the leading international scholarly journal devoted to issues in marketing education. The objective of the *Journal is* to publish articles focusing on the latest techniques in marketing education, emphasizing new course content and teaching methods. Its purpose is to provide a forum for the exchange of ideas, information, and experiences related to the process of educating students of marketing and advertising.

Our audience is largely composed of marketing faculty members at institutions of higher education where teaching is an important component of he assignment. The readership of the *Journal of Marketing Education is* international in scope, with a significant representation in university libraries.

The *Journal of Marketing Education* strives to enhance excellence in instruction by providing our readership with innovative plans for effective methods of teaching. First priority for publication goes to articles that specifically address this objective. The *Journal* also publishes articles that address various professional issues of importance to marketing faculty members. Development of the curriculum, career development, and the state of the profession are examples of such areas of interest.

Submission of Initial Manuscripts
To expedite initial consideration of your manuscript, please prepare and submit it according to the following guidelines.

Prior Publication
Manuscripts are considered for publication only if they have not been published or accepted for publication elsewhere and are not concurrently being reviewed for publication elsewhere. Publication of a one-page abstract of the manuscript in conference proceedings will not preclude consideration for publication in the *Journal*.

Manuscript Length and Evaluation Criteria
Manuscripts ordinarily should be between 4,000 and 7,000 words (15-30 pages), plus appropriate references, tables, and other supporting materials. Authors should strive for conciseness, readability, and a high density of contribution per page.

Manuscripts are (double blind) judged using the following seven criteria: (1) overall contribution to the marketing education literature, (2) significance of the topic to marketing education, (3) adequacy of literature review, (4) conceptual rigor, (5) content organization, (6) writing quality and, (7) strength of implications. Empirical manuscripts are also judged on methodological appropriateness and rigor, data analysis quality, and presentation of results and outcomes.

Style Guidelines
The entire manuscript, including references, should be double-spaced. Use only standard 12-point type. Place the sections of the manuscript in the following order: Cover Page, Title Page with Abstract, Body, Appendices, Footnotes, Reference List, Tables, Exhibits, Maps, and Figures. Begin each section on a new page.

Use standard author-date citations within the text. Note with item number and title where tables, exhibits, etc., should appear in the body of the text (e.g., between two paragraphs: Table 1—Respondent Characteristics).

Consult recent issues of the *Journal* for appropriate style and formatting of references, tables, etc. When in doubt, consult the latest edition of *The Chicago Manual of Style*.

Neither the names(s) nor the university affiliation(s) of the author(s) should appear anywhere in the manuscript. A separate cover sheet should provide this information and indicate a contact author and her or his full mailing address, telephone number, facsimile number, and e-mail address.

Submit one electronic file containing the manuscript and all tables, exhibits, etc. plus the separate cover sheet and a formal submission letter file. All three files should be in Microsoft Word (doc.) format. If an electronic submission is not possible, please mail (5) laser-printed originals, or *very* clean copies of the manuscript as well as a separate cover page and submission letter.

Send Submission Materials to:
Douglas J. Lincoln, Editor
Journal of Marketing Education
College of Business & Economics
Boise State University
1910 University Drive
Boise ID 83725
Phone: 208-426-3246; Fax: 208-426-5384
Email: **dlincoln@boisestate.edu**

Manuscript Review Procedures
Manuscripts are normally desk reviewed by the Editor and acknowledged within two weeks of receipt. If the manuscript passes this desk review, they are forwarded to three reviewers for a formal evaluation. Those reviews are usually completed within 10 weeks. Authors of non-rejected manuscripts can expect an invitation to make and submit either a major or minor revision. Major revisions are returned to the original three reviewers while minor revisions may or may not be sent to them depending on the editor's judgment. All accepted manuscripts are currently being published within one year of acceptance. At the present time, the *Journal* publishes approximately one in five manuscripts received for review.

Publisher and Sponsors
The *Journal of Marketing Education* is published three times a year by Sage Publications. The Marketing Educators' Association with additional financial support provided by Sage Publications and the College of Business and Economics, Boise State University sponsors the Journal.

Copyrights
The *Journal of Marketing Education* copyrights all published material, and the publisher reserves future use rights. (This does not limit authors' rights to use their own material.) Authors must obtain any necessary permissions and agree to incur any related expense.

Journal of Marketing for Higher Education

ADDRESS FOR SUBMISSION:

Thomas Hayes, Editor
Journal of Marketing for Higher Education
Xavier University
Williams College of Business
Department of Marketing
3800 Victory Parkway
Cincinnati, OH 45207-3214
USA
Phone: 513-745-3059
E-Mail: hayes@xavier.edu
Web: www.haworthpress.com

PUBLICATION GUIDELINES:

Manuscript Length: 21-25
Copies Required: Five
Computer Submission: Yes
Format: MS Word, WordPerfect
Fees to Review: 0.00 US$

Manuscript Style:
American Psychological Association

CIRCULATION DATA:

Reader: Academics, University Marketing
Frequency of Issue: 2 Times/Year
Sponsor/Publisher: Haworth Press, Inc.

REVIEW INFORMATION:

Type of Review: Blind Review
No. of External Reviewers: 2
No. of In House Reviewers: 1
Acceptance Rate: 21-30%
Time to Review: 2 - 3 Months
Reviewers Comments: Yes
Invited Articles: 0-5%
Fees to Publish: 0.00 US$

MANUSCRIPT TOPICS:

Advertising & Promotion Management; Direct Marketing; E-Commerce; Marketing Research; Non-Profit Organizations; Services

MANUSCRIPT GUIDELINES/COMMENTS:

The *Journal of Marketing for Higher Education* is the only journal devoted to academic marketing and promotion. The journal is a vital quarterly publication that provides guidance for all professionals involved in marketing for higher education. It serves a wide spectrum of schools from the community college to the private four-year university. It contains applicable, action-oriented information useful to those individuals responsible for advancing the institution, including public relations, admissions, development, and planning professionals. It also provides a focus through which the many aspects of marketing for higher education can be integrated into a coherent discipline. Each issue is designed to be a source of ideas, innovation, and inspiration to those individuals challenged with the responsibility of ensuring that their university not only survives, but thrives. To this end, every quarter, the *Journal of Marketing for Higher Education* offers readers fresh perspectives-with new ideas, approaches, and advice about promising new techniques and trends.

This *Journal* addresses practical matters and provides immediately usable data that can save institutions and professionals the effort of "reinventing the wheel." This unique *Journal* meets the needs of college administrators, instructors, and students.

Subscribing to the *Journal of Marketing for Higher Education* will help you to:
- Bring new students to your campus
- Identify and reach new groups of potential students
- Better utilize existing programs
- Make the best use of your marketing resources
- Improve retention rates
- Coordinate institution-wide efforts
- Get to and stay on the cutting edge

Manuscript Guidelines

1. Original Articles Only. Submission of a manuscript to this *Journal* represents a certification on the part of the author(s) that it is an original work, and that neither this manuscript nor a version of it has been published elsewhere nor is being considered for publication elsewhere.

2. Manuscript Length. Your manuscript may be approximately 5-50 typed pages, double-spaced (including references and abstract). Lengthier manuscripts may be considered, but only at the discretion of the Editor. Sometimes, lengthier manuscripts may be considered if they can be divided up into sections for publication in successive *Journal* issues.

3. Manuscript Style. References, citations, and general style of manuscripts for this *Journal* should follow the Chicago style (as outlined in the latest edition of the *Manual of Style* of the University of Chicago Press). References should be double-spaced and placed in alphabetical order.

If an author wishes to submit a paper that has been already prepared in another style, he or she may do so. However, if the paper is accepted (with or without reviewer's alterations), the author is fully responsible for retyping the manuscript in the correct style as indicated above. Neither the Editor nor the Publisher is responsible for re-preparing manuscript copy to adhere to the *Journal*'s style.

4. Manuscript Preparation

Margins. Leave at least a 1" margin on all four sides.
Paper. Use clean, white 8½" x 11" bond paper.
Number of Copies. 4 (the original plus three photocopies)
Cover Page. *Important*—Staple a cover page to the manuscript, indicating only the article title (this is used for anonymous refereeing).
Second "Title Page." Enclose a regular title page but do not staple it to the manuscript. Include the title again, plus:
- Full authorship

- An ABSTRACT of about 100 words. (Below the abstract provide 3-10 key words for index purposes).
- A introductory footnote with authors' academic degrees, professional titles, affiliations, mailing addresses, and any desired acknowledgment of research support or other credit.

5. **Return Envelopes**. When you submit your four manuscript copies, also include:
- A 9" x 12" envelope, self-addressed and stamped (with sufficient postage to ensure return of your manuscript);
- A regular envelope, stamped and self-addressed. This is for the Editor to send you an "acknowledgement of receipt" letter.

6. **Spelling, Grammar, and Punctuation**. You are responsible for preparing manuscript copy which is clearly written in acceptable, scholarly English and which contains no errors of spelling, grammar, or punctuation. Neither the Editor nor the Publisher is responsible for correcting errors of spelling and grammar: the manuscript, after acceptance by the Editor, must be immediately ready for typesetting as it is finally submitted by the author(s). Check your paper for the following common errors:
- Dangling modifiers
- Misplaced modifiers
- Unclear antecedents
- Incorrect or inconsistent abbreviations

Also, check the accuracy of all arithmetic calculations, statistics, numerical data, text citations, and references.

7. **Inconsistencies Must Be Avoided**. Be sure you are *consistent* in your use of abbreviations, terminology, and in citing references, from one part of your paper to another.

8. **Preparation of Tables, Figures, and Illustrations**. All tables, figures, illustrations, etc., must be "camera-ready." That is, they must be cleanly typed or artistically prepared so that they can be used either exactly as they are or else used after a photographic reduction in size. Figures, tables, and illustrations must be prepared on separate sheets of paper. Always use black ink and professional drawing instruments. On the back of these items, write your article title and the journal title lightly in pencil, so they do not get misplaced. In text, skip extra lines and indicate where these figures and tables are to be placed (please **do not write** on face of art). Photographs are considered part of the acceptable manuscript and remain with Publisher for use in additional printings. If submitted art cannot be used, the Publisher reserves the right to redo the art and to charge the author a fee of $35.00 per hour for this service.

9. **Alterations Required by Referees and Reviewers**. Many times a paper is accepted by the Editor contingent upon changes that are mandated by anonymous specialist referees and members of the Editorial Board. If the Editor returns your manuscript for revisions, you are responsible for retyping any sections of the paper to incorporate these revisions (if applicable, revisions should also be put on disk).

10. **Typesetting**. You will not be receiving galley proofs of your article. Editorial revisions, if any, must therefore be made while your article is still in manuscript. The final version of the manuscript will be the version you see published. Typesetter's errors will be corrected by the production staff of The Haworth Press. Authors are expected to submit manuscripts, disks, and art that are free from error.

11. **Electronic Media**. Haworth's in-house typesetting unit is able to utilize your final manuscript material as prepared on most personal computers and word processors. This will minimize typo- graphical errors and decrease overall production time lag. Please send the first draft and final draft copies of your manuscript to the *Journal* Editor in print format for his/her final review and approval.

After approval of your final manuscript, please submit the final approved version both on printed format ("hard copy") and floppy diskette. On the outside of the diskette package write:
a. The brand name of your computer or word processor
b. The word-processing program that you used
c. The title of your article, and
d. File name

Note. Disk and hard copy must agree. In case of discrepancies, it is The Haworth Press's policy to follow hard copy. Authors are advised that no revisions of the manuscript can be made after acceptance by the Editor for publication. The benefits of this procedure are many with speed and accuracy being the most obvious. We look forward to working with you on this, knowing we will be able to serve you more efficiently in the future.

12. **Reprints**. The senior author will receive two copies of the *Journal* issue and 25 complimentary reprints of his or her article. The junior author will receive two copies of the *Journal* issue. These are sent several weeks after the *Journal* issue is published and in circulation. An order form for the purchase of additional reprints will also be sent to all authors at this time. (Approximately 4-6 weeks are necessary for the preparation of reprints.) Please do not query the *Journal*'s Editor about reprints. All such questions should be sent directly to The Haworth Press, Inc., Production Department, 21 East Broad Street, West Hazleton, PA 18201. To order additional reprints (minimum 50 copies), please contact The Haworth Document Delivery Center, 10 Alice Street, Binghamton, NY 13904-1580; 1-800-342-9678 or Fax (607) 722-6362.

13. **Copyright**. Copyright ownership of your manuscript must be transferred officially to The Haworth Press, Inc. before we can begin the peer-review process. The Editor's letter acknowledging receipt of the manuscript will be accompanied by a form fully explaining this. All authors must sign the form and return the original to the Editor as soon as possible. Failure to return the copyright form in a timely fashion will result in a delay in review and subsequent publication.

Journal of Marketing Management

ADDRESS FOR SUBMISSION:

Susan Hart, Editor
Journal of Marketing Management
University of Strathclyde
Department of Marketing
173 Cathedral Street
Glasgow, G4 0RQ
Scotland
Phone: +44 (0) 141-548-4927
E-Mail: susan.hart@strath.ac.uk
Web: www.westburn.co.uk/jmm

PUBLICATION GUIDELINES:

Manuscript Length: 21-30+
Copies Required: Three + Electronic
Computer Submission: Yes
Format: MS Word, PDF
Fees to Review: 0.00 US$

Manuscript Style:
    See Manuscript Guidelines

CIRCULATION DATA:

Reader: Academics, Business Persons
Frequency of Issue: 5 Times/Year
Sponsor/Publisher: Academy of Marketing /
    Westburn Publishers, Ltd.

REVIEW INFORMATION:

Type of Review: Blind Review
No. of External Reviewers: 2
No. of In House Reviewers: 1
Acceptance Rate: 11-20%
Time to Review: 2 - 3 Months
Reviewers Comments: Yes
Invited Articles: 0-5%
Fees to Publish: 0.00 US$

MANUSCRIPT TOPICS:

Advertising & Promotion Management; Communication; Direct Marketing; Global Business; Marketing Research; Marketing Theory & Applications; Purchasing/Materials Management; Sales/Selling; Services; Small Business Entrepreneurship; Strategic Management Policy; Technology/Innovation; Transportation/Physical Distribution

MANUSCRIPT GUIDELINES/COMMENTS:

Aims

The *Journal of Marketing Management* (*JMM*) is concerned with all aspects of the management of marketing and is intended to provide a forum for the exchange of the latest research ideas and best practice in the field of marketing as a whole. As such it is intended to fill the middle ground between the often esoteric and/or highly technical treatment of the purist academic journal and the lightweight and often-anecdotal commentary typical of the "trade press". Thus *JMM* seeks to meet the needs of a wide but sophisticated audience comprising senior marketing executives and their advisors, senior line managers, teachers and researchers in marketing and undergraduate and postgraduate students of the subject. *JMM's* policy is to encourage the widest possible exchange of knowledge and ideas related to the theory and practice of marketing, in a thought-provoking way, but without resorting to jargon or journalism.

The *JMM* is a double-blind reviewed periodical in its 21st year of publication in 2005 and the official journal of the UK based Academy of Marketing. *JMM* was the most frequently cited academic journal for the field of Business Studies in the recent Research Assessment Exercise (RAE) in which the staff of British Universities were required to declare their most important publications for the period 1996-2001. In addition to Marketing the Business Studies unit of assessment included Hotel and Catering Management, Human Resource Management, Management Science, Management Studies and Travel and Tourism. However, citations for *JMM* outranked those for the leading journals for these subjects by a significant margin.

In addition to its pre-eminent position in the UK, *JMM* enjoys a strong reputation in many other countries, especially Europe, South East Asia, Japan and Australasia. Currently *JMM* has subscribers in over 45 countries and is available through the libraries of the major Universities and Business Schools in these countries. The composition of the Editorial Board reflects this international reach and reputation. As well as including the leading UK marketing scholars more than one third of Editorial Board members are drawn from countries other than the UK including such distinguished researchers as: Stephen Greyser, Abbie Griffin, Christian Grönroos, Evert Gummesson, Shelby Hunt, Kristian Möller, Hans Mülbacher and Rajan Varadarajan. Contributions to *JMM* also reflect its international importance with over 40% of the 455 authors published in the last 5 years based outside the UK.

JMM is published in five double issues a year and contains approximately 50 articles comprising around 1,100 pages. As a result of this frequency of publication *JMM* is able to offer shorter lead times than many of its major competitors and places great emphasis on early dissemination of accepted material.

Each Volume comprises ten printed issues of approximately 110 pages each, delivered in five dispatches. In a typical year Issues 1-2 are combined under the guest editorship of a leading expert to address a particular theme. At least six issues a year contain competitive papers including one made up of the best papers from the Academy's Annual Conference—usually eight from over 400 which have been through the blind review process. The remaining two issues address specific themes under the Guest Editorship of a distinguished expert. Recent and forthcoming special issues include: Effective Marketing Management in Financial Services Contexts, Political Marketing, Consuming Families: Marketing, Consumption and the Role of Families in the 21st Century and Critical Issues in Brand Management.

Guidelines

In accordance with its policy, the *JMM* welcomes contributions from theoreticians and practitioners in the following areas:

- State of the art papers on particular topics—e.g. portfolio planning, sales management, pricing.
- Management of the marketing mix—the practical issues of managing product, price, place and promotion efficiently and effectively.
- Customer behaviour—how and why both corporate and ultimate customers behave in the way they do.
- Marketing intelligence—the establishment and maintenance of marketing information systems and everything associated with them.

- Case studies—how an organization has tackled an important marketing problem.
- Meta marketing—how marketing ideas and techniques are applied to the less- or non-traditional areas of services, public and non-profit organizations

In addition to these core areas the journal also attracts:
- Marketing education and training papers
- Conference reports and commentaries
- Books reviews and abstracts
- Letters

Submissions (3 copies) should be of 4,000-6,000 words (excluding display material and references) typed double-spaced on A4 paper. The first page should consist of the title, authors' names, addresses and an indication of author for correspondence with his/her telephone/fax number. The second page should comprise an abstract of the paper (c. 150 words) and a biography (c. 150 words) detailing the authors' background, affiliations and interests. Display material must be numbered, captioned and cited in the text. Authors should avoid identifying themselves in the main body of the text.

References
References are indicated in the text by the Harvard (name and date) system: Either "Recent work (Smith 1970)" or "Recently Smith (1970) has found ..". All such references should then be listed in alphabetical order at the end of the paper in accordance with the following conventions:

1. *Books*
Baker, Michael J. and Hart, Susan J. (1989), *Marketing and Competitive Success*, Hemel Hempstead, Philip Allen.

2. *Journal Articles*
Star, Steven H. (1989), "Marketing and its Discontents", *Harvard Business Review*, November/December 1989 No.6, pp. 148-154.

3. *Contributions in Books, Proceedings, etc.*
Doyle, Peter (1990), "Managing the Marketing Mix". In: *The Marketing Book* 2nd Edition. (Ed.) Baker, Michael J. (London), William Heinemann Ltd, pp. 227-267.

Copyright of Prints
Authors submitting a manuscript do so on the understanding that if it is accepted for publication, copyright in the paper exclusive shall be assigned to the Publisher. In consideration of the assignment of copyright a PDF of each paper, and a copy of the *Journal* will be supplied. Further reprints may be ordered at extra cost. The Publisher will not put any limitations on the personal freedom of the author to use material contained in the paper in other works. Papers are accepted for the Journal on the understanding that they have not been or will not be published elsewhere in the same form, in any language.

Please note that all articles should be submitted to the Editor for review.

Submission of Accepted Papers

When supplying the final version of your article, please email the paper to journals@ westburn.co.uk

The accompanying email should clearly state the contents of the attachment which must fulfill the following requirements. Please follow these guidelines carefully.

- Include one copy of the word-processed article in MS Word including figures and tables. (If using an alternative word processing package please save into Word when possible and also send in original format)
- If the article includes a figure which is a photograph, or a particularly complex illustration, this should be saved in a separate .png file. All diagrams and figures should be in black and white. All figures should be at 300dpi quality minimum. If prepared on an Apple, include the file in ASCII format.
- Ensure that the files are not saved as read-only. Virus check all files before sending them.
- The directives for preparing the paper in the style of the journal as set out in the Instructions to Authors must be followed; i.e. ensure the document is in the following order: Title; Authors; Addresses; Abstract; Running heads; Introduction; Materials and methods; Results; Discussion; Acknowledgements; References; Appendices; Figure legends; Tables; Footnotes; Abbreviations.
- It is the responsibility of the author to ensure that all these points are fulfilled, and that the material on the disk is correct. References MUST be presented in the manner given in the guidelines.

Additional Points to Note

- Use two carriage returns to end headings and paragraphs.
- Type text without end-of-line hyphenation, except for compound words.
- Be consistent with punctuation and only insert a single space between words and after punctuation.

Final Formatting

All authors will be sent a PDF of their paper in proof format for their approval. Papers will not be published without the return to the publishers of the signed copyright assignment form, which must be signed by all authors involved in the paper. It is the author's responsibility to obtain clearance if they wish to use copyright material within their paper.

All other enquiries and accepted papers and accompanying disks should be directed to Westburn Publishers Ltd, 23 Millig Street , Helensburgh, Argyll G84 9LD, Scotland. Tel: +44 1436 678 699; Fax: +44 1436 670 328; Email: **jmm@westburn.co.uk**

Calls for Papers

The *JMM* has an email list which announces new Calls for Papers. If you would like to be contacted when the next call for papers is announced, please email us-**jmm@westburn.co.uk**.

Journal of Marketing Research

ADDRESS FOR SUBMISSION:

Joel Huber, Editor
Journal of Marketing Research
Duke University
Fuqua School of Business
Box 90120
Durham, NC 27708
USA
Phone: 919-660-7785
E-Mail: joel.huber@duke.edu
Web: www.marketingjournals.org/jmr;
    www.marketingpower.com/jmr

PUBLICATION GUIDELINES:

Manuscript Length: 50
Copies Required: Five
Computer Submission: Yes Email
Format: See Guidelines
Fees to Review: 0.00 US$

Manuscript Style:
    Chicago Manual of Style

CIRCULATION DATA:

Reader: Academics, Practitioners
Frequency of Issue: Quarterly
Sponsor/Publisher: American Marketing
    Association

REVIEW INFORMATION:

Type of Review: Blind Review
No. of External Reviewers: 2
No. of In House Reviewers: 1
Acceptance Rate: 11-20%
Time to Review: 1 - 2 Months
Reviewers Comments: Yes
Invited Articles: 0-5%
Fees to Publish: 0.00 US$

MANUSCRIPT TOPICS:
Marketing Research; Marketing Theory & Applications

MANUSCRIPT GUIDELINES/COMMENTS:

The *Journal of Marketing Research* is written for those academics and practitioners of marketing research who need to be in the forefront of the profession and in possession of the industry's cutting-edge information. *JMR* publishes articles representing the entire spectrum of research in marketing.

JMR concentrates on the subject of marketing research, from its philosophy, concepts, and theories to its methods, techniques, and applications. This quarterly, peer-reviewed journal is published for technically oriented research analysts, educators, and statisticians.

The editorial content is peer-reviewed by an expert panel of leading academics. Articles address the concepts, methods, and applications of marketing research that:
- Present new techniques for solving marketing problems.
- Contribute to marketing knowledge based on the use of experimental, descriptive, or analytical techniques.

- Review and comment on the developments and concepts in related fields that have bearing on the research industry and its practices.

In each issue, there are articles that pertain to new marketing research-related methods and techniques, clarifications of marketing research methodology and practice, and the state of the art in marketing research.

Manuscript and Electronic Preparation

1. Submit your manuscript electronically to the Editor. Do not submit disk copies until directed to do so by the Editor. Please refer to the section of Web site, "Preparing the Final Version and Editing Style Rules," when preparing the final version for publication.

2. The manuscript should be saved in Adobe Portable Document Format (PDF) and submitted by e-mail to *JMR*. Send one PDF file that contains all text, references, tables, figures and exhibits. Manuscripts should not exceed fifty (50) pages, inclusive of all text, tables, figures, appendices, and so on. Do not lock the PDF file because the *JMR* office will need to remove identifying information such as author's name and affiliation. Authors should keep an exact, extra copy of the manuscript for future reference.

3. PDF files allow automatic file compression, file concatenation, and, more important, manuscripts to have an identical appearance when viewed on almost any computer. If you are unable to submit your manuscript by e-mail as a PDF, you may mail five (5) paper copies of your manuscript—but (regrettably) the processing of your manuscript will take significantly longer.

4. All manuscripts must be double-spaced (including references) in 12-point font, with pages numbered consecutively throughout the entire paper. (The title page is page one.)

5. Allow margins of at least one inch on all four sides. Papers should be left justified; do not justify the right-hand margin.

6. Type on one side of the paper only.

If we receive a file that does not conform to the above requirements, we will inform the author(s) and will not begin the review process until the corrected file is received.

What Goes Where

- **First page**. Name of author(s) and title; author(s) footnote, including present positions, complete address, telephone number, fax number, email address, and any acknowledgment of financial or technical assistance.
- **Second page**. Title of paper (without author's name) and a brief abstract of no more than 50 words substantively summarizing the article. It should be informative, giving the reader a "taste" of the article.
- **Next**. The text with major headings centered on the page and subheadings flush with the left margin.

- **Then**. Tables, numbered consecutively, each on a separate page. If tables appear in an appendix, they should be numbered separately and consecutively, as in Table A-1, A-2, and so on.
- **Next**. Figures, numbered consecutively, each placed on a separate page. If tables appear in an appendix, they should be numbered separately, as in Figure A-1, A-2, etc.
- **Last**. References, typed double-spaced in alphabetical order by author's last name.

Mathematical Notation

1. Mathematical notation must be clear within the text.
2. Equations should be centered on the page. If equations are numbered, type the number in parentheses flush with the left margin.
3. Unusual symbols and Greek letters should be identified by a marginal note. If equations are too wide to fit in a single column, indicate appropriate breaks.
4. Please avoid using Equation Editor for simple in-line mathematical copy, symbols, and equations. Type these in Word instead. For display equations, using the Equation Editor is appropriate. In addition, please avoid stacking in-line equations. If the equation is difficult, place it as a display rather than in line and number it accordingly.

Tables

1. Tables should consist of at least four columns and four rows; otherwise they should be left as in-text tabulations or their results should be integrated in the text.
2. The table number and title should be typed on separate lines, centered.
3. Use only horizontal rules.
4. Designate units (e.g., %, $) in column headings.
5. Align all decimals.
6. Refer to tables in text by number. Avoid using "above," "below," and "preceding."
7. If possible, combine closely related tables.
8. Indicate placement in text.
9. Make sure the necessary measures of statistical significance are reported with the table.

Figures and Camera-Ready Artwork

1. Figures should be prepared professionally on disk and as camera-ready copy.
2. Label both vertical and horizontal axes. The ordinate label should be centered above the ordinate axis; the abscissa label should be placed beneath the abscissa.
3. Place all calibration tics inside the axis lines, with the values outside the axis lines.
4. The figure number and title should be typed on separate lines, centered.
5. When a manuscript has been accepted, complex tables and all figures must be on disk and camera-ready. Table and figure headings should be typed on a separate page and attached to the appropriate camera-ready art. These titles will be set in our own typeface.
6. Lettering should be large enough to be read easily with 50% reduction. Any art not done on a computer graphics program should be professionally drafted in India ink.
7. Do not submit camera-ready art until your manuscript has been accepted. If the artwork is completed, submit photocopies.

Reference Citations Within the Text

1. Citation in the text should be by the author's last name and year of publication, enclosed in parentheses without punctuation: "(Kinsey 1960)." If practical, the citation should stand by a

punctuation mark. Otherwise, insert it in a logical sentence break. If you use the author's name within the sentence, there is no need to repeat the name in the citation; just use the year of publication in parentheses, as in "...The Howard Harris Program (1966)."

2. If a particular page, section, or equation is cited, it should be placed within the parentheses: "(Kinsey 1960, p. 112)." For multiple authors, use the full citation for up to three authors; for four or more, use the first author's name followed by "et al." (no italics). A series of citations should be listed in alphabetical order and separated by semicolons: (Donnelly 1961; Kinsey 1960; Wensley 1981).

Reference List Style

1. References are to be listed alphabetically, last name first, followed by publication date in parentheses. Use full first name, not just initials. The reference list should be typed double-spaced on a separate page. Do not use indents, tabs, or symbols to delineate your paragraphs. Instead, use two hard returns between each reference.

2. Authors are responsible for the accuracy of their references. Check them carefully.

3. Single- and multiple-author references for books
Donnelly, James H. and William R. George (1981), Marketing of Services. Chicago: American Marketing Association.

4. Single- and multiple-author reference for periodicals (include author's name, publication date, article title, complete name of periodical, volume number, month of publication, and page numbers)
Wensley, Robin (1981), "Strategic Marketing: Betas, Boxes, or Basics," Journal of Marketing, 45 (Summer), 173-82.

5. Single- and multiple-author reference for an article in a book edited by another author(s)
Nevin, John R. and Ruth A. Smith (1981), "The Predictive Accuracy of a Retail Gravitation Model: An Empirical Evaluation," in The Changing Marketing Environment, Kenneth Bernhardt et al., eds. Chicago: American Marketing Association.

6. If an author appears more than once, substitute four hyphens (this will appear as a 1-inch line when typeset) for each author's name (do not use underlines)
Fornell, Claes and David F. Larcher (1981a), "Evaluating Structural Equation Models with Unobservable Variables and Measurement Error," Journal of Marketing Research, (February), 39-50.
----and---- (1981b), "Structural Equation Models with Unobservable Variables and Measurement Error: Algebra and Statistics," Journal of Marketing Research, 18 (August).

7. If two or more works by the same author have the same publication date, they should be differentiated by letters after the date. The letter also should appear with the citation in the text:
Day, George (1981a), "Analytical Approaches to Strategic Market Planning," in Review of Marketing 1981, Ben Enis and Kenneth J. Roering, eds. Chicago: American Marketing Association.

----(1981b), "The Product Life Cycle: Analysis and Applications Issues," Journal of Marketing, 45 (Fall), 60-67.

8. References to unpublished works, such as doctoral dissertations and working papers, should be included in the references list as follows:
Coughlin, Maureen (1980), "Fear of Success: Reaction to Advertising Stimuli and Intention to Purchase," doctoral dissertation, City University of New York.

Technical Appendix
To improve the readability of the manuscript, any mathematical proof or development that is not critical to the exposition of the main part of the text may be placed in a technical appendix.

Readability
JMR manuscripts are judged not only on the depth and scope of the ideas presented and their contributions to the field, but also on their clarity and whether they can be read and understood. Readers have varied backgrounds. Hence, the following guidelines should be followed.
• Write in an interesting, readable manner with varied sentence structure. Use as little passive voice as possible.
• Avoid using technical terms that few readers are likely to understand. If you use these terms, include definitions. Remember: The *Journal* is designed to be read, not deciphered.
• Keep sentences short so the reader does not get lost before the end of a sentence.

Review Procedure
The procedures guiding the selection of articles for publication in *JMR* require that no manuscript be accepted until after it has been reviewed by the editor and at least two members of the editorial review board. The decision of the editor to publish the manuscript is influenced considerably by the judgments of these advisors, who are experts in their respective fields. The author's name and credentials are removed prior to forwarding a manuscript to reviewers to maximize objectivity and ensure that a manuscript is judged solely on the basis of it content and contribution to the field.

Acceptance Criteria
All manuscripts are judged on their contributions to the advancement of the science and/or practice of marketing. All articles are expected to follow the rules for scholarly work, namely:
• Use references to previous work when developing your model or theory. Do not assume other work on the subject does not exist, giving yourself credit for all the ideas in your manuscript.
• When data collection is discussed, consider the relevance of the sample to the subject matter. Carefully chosen sample groups are preferable to haphazardly chosen subjects who have little knowledge of or relevance to the subject being studied.
• Give as much information as possible about the characteristics of the sample and its representativeness of the population being studied.
• Do not ignore the nonrespondents. They might have different characteristics than the respondents.

- Give consideration to the limitations of your study, model, and/or concepts and discuss these in your manuscript. Be objective.
- Use appropriate statistical procedures.
- Address the reliability and validity of any empirical findings.

Preparing the Final Version and Editing Style Rules

After a manuscript is accepted for publication, the final version must be submitted electronically. The electronic copy should contain the entire manuscript, including tables, figures, footnotes, and references, as well as author bios and executive summaries. Although authors may prepare the electronic copy using almost any word processing software that is Macintosh or IBM compatible, submission of the material using Word (any version) for Windows is preferred. LaTeX, PCTeX, OzTeX, Scientific Word, or any other form of TeX is incompatible with AMA's publishing software and therefore is not accepted. Please note the following guidelines when preparing the final version:

- The AMA follows its own supplementary house style so that articles in the same issue will not have conspicuously different styles. However, the AMA uses its style in accordance with the *Chicago Manual of Style: The Essential Guide for Authors, Editors, and Publishers*, 15th ed., Chicago: University of Chicago Press, 2004. In addition, *Merriam Webster's Collegiate Dictionary*, 11th edition, is used.
- The abstract should be written in third person.
- Whenever possible, authors should use active voice, as the passive voice is wordier and often comparatively clumsy. When passive voice is used excessively, it can make expression seem vague and evasive. If an author prefers passive voice, then the article setup should be in active voice only, for example, "In the next section, we compare two theoretically based message design strategies." For a single author, however, passive voice is acceptable; use active voice sparingly except for article setup. For single authors, the royal "we" is not acceptable.
- Per *Webster's*, the AMA distinguishes between words such as enable vs. allow, whereas and although vs. while, due to vs. because of, based on vs. on the basis of, believe vs. feel, and so on. If you have specific questions about this style, please contact the *Journal's* technical editor.
- Italics should only be used for emphasis, for definition of a term or set of terms, and for certain statistical abbreviations (p). Foreign words that are familiar and/or can be found in the main part of Webster's, such as a priori, are not italicized.
- Always spell out acronyms on first use, unless universally known (e.g., IBM, AIDS, AT&T).
- At all times, an author's meaning should be upheld. During copy editing, if the author's meaning has been changed, it is the *Journal's* policy to respect the author's desire to change back to the original wording. To assist the copy editor in ensuring the accuracy of the article, please make note of any technical terms or field-specific jargon that should not be modified during the editing process. This can be done on the second page of the document, directly following the abstract.
- Footnotes should not be used for reference purposes and should be avoided if possible. If necessary to improve the readability of the text, a few footnotes may be included. They should appear double-spaced on a separate page and be numbered consecutively throughout the text.

Other Information

All published material is copyrighted by the American Marketing Association with future-use rights reserved. This does not limit the author's right to use his or her own material or place it in future works, provided full credit is given to the American Marketing Association.

For details on manuscript preparation not covered here, see *Chicago Manual of Style: The Essential Guide for Authors, Editors, and Publishers*, 15th edition, Chicago: University of Chicago Press, 2004. For specific questions on content or editorial policy, contact the Editor.

Journal of Marketing Theory and Practice

ADDRESS FOR SUBMISSION:

Greg W. Marshall, Editor
Journal of Marketing Theory and Practice
Rollins College
Crummer Graduate School of Business
1000 Holt Avenue - 2722
Winter Park, FL 32789-4499
USA
Phone: 407-691-1150
E-Mail: jmtp@rollins.edu
Web: www.rollins.edu/jmtp

PUBLICATION GUIDELINES:

Manuscript Length: 40 Pages Total
Copies Required: Electronic
Computer Submission: Yes ·
Format: MS Word
Fees to Review: 0.00 US$

Manuscript Style:
   See Manuscript Guidelines

CIRCULATION DATA:

Reader: Academics
Frequency of Issue: Quarterly
Sponsor/Publisher: Society for Marketing
   Advances / M. E. Sharpe, Inc.

REVIEW INFORMATION:

Type of Review: Blind Review
No. of External Reviewers: 3
No. of In House Reviewers: 0
Acceptance Rate: 15%
Time to Review: 2 - 3 Months
Reviewers Comments: Yes
Invited Articles: 0-5%
Fees to Publish: 0.00 US$

MANUSCRIPT TOPICS:

Business Law, Public Responsibility & Ethics; Direct Marketing; E-Commerce; Global Business; Marketing Research; Marketing Theory & Applications; Non-Profit Organizations; Sales/Selling; Services; Strategic Management Policy; Technology/Innovation; Technology/Innovation; Transportation/Physical Distribution

MANUSCRIPT GUIDELINES/COMMENTS:

Topics Include. Areas of interest to *JMTP* readers include, but are not limited to, the following (listed in alphabetical order): Branding/Products, Consumer Behavior, Customer Relationship Management (CRM), E-Commerce, Entrepreneurship, Ethics, Innovation, International, Leadership, Marketing Education, Marketing Management, Marketing Metrics, Pricing, Promotion/Advertising, Public Policy, Relationships, Retailing, Research Methods, Selling and Sales Management, Services, Strategy, Supply Chain, Technology, and Theory.

Vision/Positioning

The *Journal of Marketing Theory and Practice* (*JMTP*) is positioned as a high quality journal internationally that is devoted to the publication of peer-reviewed articles addressing substantive, managerial issues in marketing. In the context of developing, enhancing, and disseminating marketing knowledge, *JMTP* values both conceptual and empirical work by academicians so long as the work provides strong implications for the managerial practice of marketing.

Initial Submission

All manuscripts must be sent directly to the Editor. Do not send manuscripts to the Publisher. JMTP processes all manuscripts electronically. Please do not mail or fax manuscripts. Submit all manuscripts to **jmtp@rollins.edu**. Please attach both the manuscript and your cover letter as separate MSWord documents.

Order of Inclusion
A. Front Matter
First Page: Title of paper (upper/lower case), name and position of author(s), each author(s)' complete contact information (complete postal address, phone number, fax number, and email address). Manuscripts received without complete contact information for each author will be desk rejected.

Second Page: Title of the paper (upper/lower case) and a brief sketch for each author limited to only the following information: name, highest degree held and awarding school, current title or position, current organization or institution, city, state, and email address. Example: William L. Cron (Ph.D., Indiana University), Professor of Marketing, M.J. Neeley School of Business, Texas Christian University, Ft. Worth, TX, b.cron@tcu.edu.

Do not include information on prior publications, courses taught, organizations consulted, etc. (i.e., limit the information to only the above). The email address of each author must be included.

If you have any acknowledgements of assistance, please place these on the second page under the brief author sketches.

Third Page: Title of paper (upper/lower case) without names of the author(s) and a brief abstract of no more than 100 words summarizing the article. Be sure the abstract walks the reader through major aspects of the article. Begin page numbering on this page, placing the numbers at the bottom center. This page will be Page 1.

B. Body of Text
Note: Do not use ALL CAPS anywhere in the manuscript!

Text begins on the fourth page. The title of the paper should not appear again at the top of this page. First-level headings (major headings) are to be centered; second-level headings are to be flush left; third-level headings are to be indented, followed by a period and the related copy beginning immediately thereafter. Headings should be in boldface type, in upper/lower case. Font for the entire manuscript should be 12 point Times Roman or the equivalent (i.e., serif).

Do not begin with the heading "Introduction." Of course, the first several paragraphs will be your introduction, but do not label it as such.

Footnotes are to be avoided. In an extraordinary case in which a footnote is needed, number it in the body of the text and place the note text just before the references.

Manuscript length should normally not exceed 40 pages including all appendices, tables, figures, and references. Use standard 8½ X 11 white paper.

Throughout the manuscript, use only one space after punctuation -- not two. This includes after periods, colons, questions marks, and other types of punctuation.

C. Technical Appendices

Technical appendices may be used to include mathematical or highly technical material that supports the main text but is not critical to the reader's interpretation of the text. Label these appendices "Appendix 1," "Appendix 2," etc. They must be referred to in the text of the article, but are not to be designated for placement (unlike tables and figures -- see below).

D. Tables and Figures

Each table or figure should be placed on a separate page and numbered consecutively beginning with Table 1 and Figure 1. A table or figure should not be included unless it is referenced in the text of the article. In the paper, tables come first followed by figures. Placement in the text should be indicated as follows:

- -
Place Table 2 about here
- -

Table or figure number and title should be typed on two separate lines in boldface type using upper/lower case. Example:

Table 1
Job Involvement Items

Footnotes in tables and figures should be designated by superscript numbers that correspond to notes at the bottom of the table or figure (outside the box or line).

E. References

References within the text should include the author(s)' last name(s) and year of publication with no comma immediately preceding the date, enclosed in parentheses. Example: (Brown and Peterson 1993). If practical, place the citation just before a punctuation mark, preferably at the end of a sentence. If the author(s)' names are used within the text sentence, place the year of publication in parentheses. Example: "The results reported by Brown and Peterson (1993) provide evidence of...." If a particular page or section is cited, it should be placed within the parentheses. Example: (Brown and Peterson 1993, p. 73) or Brown and Peterson (p. 73) depending on the context. For multiple authorship articles use up to three names in the citation. With four or more authors, use the first author's name and et al. Example: (Cravens et al. 1993) or Cravens et al. (1993) depending on the context.

A listing of references in alphabetical order should appear at the end of the manuscript (starting on a separate page), listed by the first author (last name/first name/middle initial), all other authors (first name/middle initial/last name), and then year of publication. **Complete names** of each author are to be cited. Do not use initials-only unless that author typically writes under initials-only. Example: list Cravens, David W. **not** Cravens, D.W. Articles by the same author(s) with the same publication year should be distinguished by a lower-case letter after the date. Example: 1992a and 1992b. For authors cited more than once, substitute six hyphens (dashes) for each repeated name in the reference list. Generally, within a series of articles by the same first author you will list any single-author papers first (ascending date order) followed by any two-author papers (also in ascending date order), then papers by three-authors, four-authors, etc. Examples:

Churchill, Gilbert A., Jr. (1996), "Better Measurement Practices are Critical to Better Understanding of Sales Management Issues," *Journal of Personal Selling & Sales Management*, 12 (Spring), 73-80.

------, Neil M. Ford, Steven W. Hartley, and Orville C. Walker, Jr. (1985), "The Determinants of Salesperson Performance: A Meta-Analysis," *Journal of Marketing Research*, 22 (May), 103-18.

Rackham, Neil and John DeVincintis (1999), *Rethinking the Sales Force: Redefining Selling to Create and Capture Customer Value*, 1st ed., New York: McGraw-Hill.

Walker, Orville C., Jr (1979), "Where Do We Go From Here? Selected Conceptual and Empirical Issues Concerning the Motivation and Performance of the Industrial Salesforce," in *Critical Issues in Sales Management: State-of-the-Art and Future Research Needs*, Gerald Albaum and Gilbert A. Churchill, Jr, eds., Eugene, OR: College of Business Administration/ University of Oregon, 10-75.

The second in a pair of page numbers should be elided as follows: *DO* – 100-103, 125-37; 108-25; 150-59. *DON'T* – 100-3, 140-9.

Special Requirements: Methods
For empirical articles authors must systematically document information about the sample(s) utilized, as well as the relationships among variables. With regard to the sample(s), complete information should be provided (concisely in the text or a table) about the sampling procedure (type, selection method), method of contact, sponsorship (if applicable), incentives provided to participants, number in the sampling frame, response rate, industries from which the sample was drawn, company characteristics, geographic scope of the sampling frame, major activities/job responsibilities represented, as well as respondent characteristics including age, gender, length of service, experience level, and any other relevant characteristics. Authors with manuscripts based on research using student samples need to contact the Editor prior to submission to determine if their use of students is acceptable to *JMTP*. It is expected that means, standard deviations, inter-correlations, and reliability/validity indices will be provided for measures in the study. Generally, all scale items not drawn from previously published literature should appear in a table or in an appendix (depending on how extensive the list).

Review Procedure
Manuscripts are reviewed independently by members of the *JMTP* Editorial Review Board and by ad hoc reviewers chosen by the Editor. Typically, three reviewers assess each

manuscript. The evaluations and recommendations of the reviewers guide the Editor in his decision. The reviews are double blind -- neither authors nor reviewers know the identity of the others.

It is the policy of *JMTP* that manuscripts submitted for review must not have been published or be under consideration for publication elsewhere. Manuscripts that are substantially similar in content to articles already published or accepted for publication in *JMTP* or elsewhere are ineligible for publication in *JMTP*. It is the responsibility of the author(s) to abide by these provisions when submitting a manuscript to *JMTP* for review.

JMTP strives for a review process that is thorough and constructive, so that regardless of the ultimate decision about publication in *JMTP* the author(s) can benefit from the feedback obtained on their work.

It is possible for a manuscript submitted to *JMTP* to be desk rejected by the Editor. Although several reasons might precipitate this action, common reasons are: (1) the topic or type of submission does not fit the editorial positioning of *JMTP*, or (2) the manuscript is not submitted according to the guidelines provided in this document.

Submitting Revised Manuscripts and Accepted Manuscripts
It is the responsibility of the author(s) to complete invited manuscript revisions in a timely manner. The maximum time allowed for resubmission of an invited revision is six months from the date of the invitation to revise. Instructions for handling revised manuscripts and accepted manuscripts can be located on the *JMTP* web site: **www.rollins.edu/jmtp**.

Call for Ad Hoc Reviewers
Individuals interested in serving as an ad hoc reviewer for *JMTP* should contact the Editor at **jmtp@rollins.edu**.

Journal of Medical Marketing

ADDRESS FOR SUBMISSION:

Emma Jones, Senior Publishing Editor
Journal of Medical Marketing
Palgrave Macmillan
Houndmills
Basingstoke, RG21 6XS
UK
Phone:
E-Mail: submissions@palgrave.com
Web: http://www.palgrave-journals.com/
jmm/index.html

CIRCULATION DATA:

Reader: Business Persons
Frequency of Issue: Quarterly
Sponsor/Publisher: Palgrave Macmillan

PUBLICATION GUIDELINES:

Manuscript Length: 2,000-5,000 Words
Copies Required: Two
Computer Submission: Yes
Format: MS Word
Fees to Review: 0.00 US$

Manuscript Style:
    Uniform System of Citation (Harvard
    Blue Book)

REVIEW INFORMATION:

Type of Review: Blind Review
No. of External Reviewers: 2
No. of In House Reviewers: 1
Acceptance Rate: 21-30%
Time to Review: 1 - 2 Months
Reviewers Comments: Yes
Invited Articles: 31-50%
Fees to Publish: 0.00 US$

MANUSCRIPT TOPICS:
Communication; Direct Marketing; E-Commerce; Global Business; Health Care Administration; Management; Marketing Research; Marketing Theory & Applications; Sales/Selling; Strategic Management Policy

MANUSCRIPT GUIDELINES/COMMENTS:

Under the guidance of its respected Editor and expert Editorial Board, *Journal of Medical Marketing* is the leading international journal for executives performing a marketing or commercial role at every company producing pharmaceuticals, medical devices or diagnostic equipment for the medical industry.

Instructions for Authors
1. Contributions should be between 2,000 and 5,000 words in length. All submissions should be typewritten and double spaced.

2. The *Journal's* Editors and Editorial Board particularly welcome submissions which present case study material, new approaches, techniques, empirical research or conceptual papers.

3. All articles should be accompanied by a short abstract outlining the paper's aims and subject matter.

4. All articles should be accompanied by up to six keywords.

5. Articles should be accompanied by a short (about 80 words) description of the author(s) and, if appropriate, the organization of which he or she is a member.

6. Authors should not seek to use the *Journal* as a vehicle for marketing any specific product or service.

7. Authors should avoid the use of language or slang which is not in keeping with the professional and academic style of the *Journal*.

8. Titles of organizations etc. should be written out first in full and thereafter in initials.

9. Papers should be supported by references. References should be set out in accordance with the Harvard style - that is, they should be indicated in the text by the author's surname followed by the year of publication, both in brackets (e.g. Boyle, 1992) and then set out in full in a corresponding alphabetical list at the end of the text in the following form: [for journal articles] Author (year) 'Title of article', *Journal name*, Vol., No., pp,; [for books] Author (year) 'Title of chapter' in 'Editor' (ed), 'Book title', Publisher, place of publication.

10. Photographs and illustrations supporting articles should be submitted where appropriate. Photographs should be good quality positives, printed from the original negatives and preferably in black and white only. Figures and other line illustrations should be submitted in good quality originals and a copy of the data should also be included.

11. Authors must ensure that references to named people and/or organizations are accurate, not racist or sexist and without libellous implications.

12. All contributions sent to the Publisher, whether invited or not, will be submitted to the Journal's Editors and Editorial Board. Any such contribution must bear the author's full name and address, even if this is not for publication. Contributions, whether published pseudonymously or not, are accepted on the strict understanding that the author is responsible for the accuracy of all opinion, technical comment, factual report, data, figures, illustrations and photographs. Publication does not necessarily imply that these are the opinions of the Editorial Board, Editors or the Publisher, nor does the Board, Editors or Publisher accept any liability for the accuracy of such comment, report and other technical and factual information. The Publisher will, however, strive to ensure that all opinion, comments, reports, data, figures, illustrations and photographs are accurate, insofar as it is within its abilities to do so. The Publisher reserves the right to edit, abridge or omit material submitted for publication.

13. All articles submitted for publication will be subject to a double-blind refereeing procedure.

14. **Copyright**. Authors are responsible for obtaining permission from copyright holders for reproducing through any medium of communication those illustrations, tables, figures or lengthy quotations previously published elsewhere. Add your acknowledgements to the typescript, preferably in the form of an "Acknowledgements" section at the end of the paper. Credit the source and copyright of photographs or figures in the accompanying captions.

The journal's policy is to own copyright in all contributions. Before publication, authors assign copyright to the Publishers, but retain their rights to republish this material in other works written or edited by themselves, subject to full acknowledgement of the original source of publication.

The journal mandates the Copyright Clearance Center in the USA and the Copyright Licensing Agency in the UK to offer centralised licensing arrangements for photocopying in their respective territories.

15. No contribution will be accepted which has been published elsewhere, unless it is expressly invited or agreed by the Publisher.

16. All reasonable efforts are made to ensure accurate reproduction of text, photographs and illustrations. The Publisher does not accept responsibility for mistakes, be they editorial or typographical, nor for consequences resulting from them.

17. Submissions should be sent to the Publisher:
Emma Jones,
Senior Publishing Editor
Palgrave Macmillan
Houndmills
Basingstoke RG21 6XS, UK
E-mail: **submissions@palgrave.com**

Please clearly state for which journal you are contributing.

18. Authors will be given the opportunity to purchase offprints of their paper once typesetting has been finalised. The Publishers will send first-named authors up to three free copies of the issue containing their paper.

Journal of Nonprofit & Public Sector Marketing

ADDRESS FOR SUBMISSION:

Walter W. Wymer, Jr., Editor
Journal of Nonprofit & Public Sector
  Marketing
Christopher Newport University
School of Business
Newport News, VA 23606
USA
Phone: 757-594-7692
E-Mail: wwymer@cnu.edu
Web: www.haworthpress.com;
  users.cnu.edu/~jnspm

PUBLICATION GUIDELINES:

Manuscript Length: 15-35
Copies Required: One
Computer Submission: Yes
Format: See Website
Fees to Review: 0.00 US$

Manuscript Style:
  Chicago Manual of Style

CIRCULATION DATA:

Reader: Academics
Frequency of Issue: Quarterly
Sponsor/Publisher: Haworth Press, Inc.

REVIEW INFORMATION:

Type of Review: Blind Review
No. of External Reviewers: 3
No. of In House Reviewers: 1
Acceptance Rate: 20-25%
Time to Review: 6-8 Weeks
Reviewers Comments: Yes
Invited Articles: 0%
Fees to Publish: 0.00 US$

MANUSCRIPT TOPICS:

Advertising & Promotion Management; Direct Marketing; E-Commerce; Health Care Administration; Marketing Research; Marketing Theory & Applications; Non-Profit Organizations

MANUSCRIPT GUIDELINES/COMMENTS:

Topics Include. All topics related to the effective marketing of nonprofit, membership, charitable, advocacy, political, and nongovernmental organizations.

See Website for description of manuscript format. Electronic submissions allowed. Book reviews of 500-700 words encouraged.

About the Journal

The *Journal of Nonprofit & Public Sector Marketing* is devoted to the study of the adaptation of traditional marketing principles for use by nonprofit organizations. Marketers who have struggled to adapt inappropriate marketing strategies from the profit-motivated sector will benefit from this resource targeted specifically for their nonprofit or public sector organizations.

The *Journal of Nonprofit & Public Sector Marketing* provides a vehicle for the development of marketing thought and dissemination of marketing knowledge in the nonprofit and public sectors of the economy. The nonprofit and public sectors share many common denominators, which separate them from the for-profit sector, including budgeting considerations, the measurement of disparate goals among various publics, and a general lack of knowledge of marketing concepts. Traditional marketers often miss these important nuances in attempting to adapt marketing strategies and concepts to these new domains. The Journal of Nonprofit & Public Sector Marketing is devoted to the study of the adaptation of marketing for use by these organizations.

Manuscript Guidelines
1. **Original Articles Only.** Submission of a manuscript to this *Journal* represents a certification on the part of the author(s) that it is an original work, and that neither this manuscript nor a version of it has been published elsewhere nor is being considered for publication elsewhere.

2. **Manuscript Length.** Your manuscript may be approximately 20-35 typed pages, double-spaced (including references and abstract). Lengthier manuscripts may be considered, but only at the discretion of the Editor. Sometimes, lengthier manuscripts may be considered if they can be divided up into sections for publication in successive *Journal* issues.

3. **Manuscript Style.** References, citations, and general style of manuscripts for this *Journal* should follow the Chicago style (as outlined in the latest edition of the *Manual of Style of the University of Chicago Press*). References should be double-spaced and placed in alphabetical order.

If an author wishes to submit a paper that has been already prepared in another style, he or she may do so. However, if the paper is accepted (with or without reviewer's alterations), the author is fully responsible for retyping the manuscript in the correct style as indicated above. Neither the Editor nor the Publisher is responsible for re-preparing manuscript copy to adhere to the *Journal's* style.

4. **Manuscript Preparation**
Margins. Leave at least a 1" margin on all four sides. Paper. Use clean, white 8 ½" x 11" bond paper.
Number of Copies. Two (the original plus one electronic copy).
Cover Page. Important-Staple a cover page to the manuscript, indicating only the article title (this is used for anonymous refereeing).
Second "Title Page." Enclose a regular title page but do not staple it to the manuscript. Include the title again, plus:
• Full authorship
• An ABSTRACT of about 100 words. (Below the abstract provide 3-10 key words for index purposes).
• A introductory footnote with authors' academic degrees, professional titles, affiliations, mailing addresses, and any desired acknowledgment of research support or other credit.

5. **Spelling, Grammar, and Punctuation**. You are responsible for preparing manuscript copy which is clearly written in acceptable, scholarly English and which contains no errors of spelling, grammar, or punctuation. Neither the Editor nor the Publisher is responsible for correcting errors of spelling and grammar: the manuscript, after acceptance by the Editor, must be immediately ready for typesetting as it is finally submitted by the author(s). Check your paper for the following common errors:

- Dangling modifiers
- Misplaced modifiers
- Unclear antecedents
- Incorrect or inconsistent abbreviations

Also, check the accuracy of all arithmetic calculations, statistics, numerical data, text citations, and references.

6. **Inconsistencies Must Be Avoided**. Be sure you are consistent in your use of abbreviations, terminology, and in citing references, from one part of your paper to another.

7. **Preparation of Tables, Figures, and Illustrations**. All tables, figures, illustrations, etc., must be "camera-ready." That is, they must be cleanly typed or artistically prepared so that they can be used either exactly as they are or else used after a photographic reduction in size. Figures, tables, and illustrations must be prepared on separate sheets of paper. Always use black ink and professional drawing instruments. On the back of these items, write your article title and the journal title lightly in pencil, so they do not get misplaced. In text, skip extra lines and indicate where these figures and tables are to be placed (please do not write on face of art). Photographs are considered part of the acceptable manuscript and remain with Publisher for use in additional printings. If submitted art cannot be used, the Publisher reserves the right to redo the art and to charge the author a fee of $35.00 per hour for this service.

8. **Alterations Required by Referees and Reviewers**. Many times a paper is accepted by the Editor contingent upon changes that are mandated by anonymous specialist referees and members of the Editorial Board. If the Editor returns your manuscript for revisions, you are responsible for retyping any sections of the paper to incorporate these revisions (if applicable, revisions should also be put on disk).

9. **Typesetting**. You will not be receiving galley proofs of your article. Editorial revisions, if any, must therefore be made while your article is still in manuscript. The final version of the manuscript will be the version you see published. Typesetter's errors will be corrected by the production staff of The Haworth Press. Authors are expected to submit manuscripts, disks, and art that are free from error.

10. **Electronic Media**. Haworth's in-house typesetting unit is able to utilize your final manuscript material as prepared on most personal computers and word processors. This will minimize typo- graphical errors and decrease overall production time lag. Please send the first draft and final draft copies of your manuscript to the Journal Editor in print format for his/her final review and approval.

After approval of your final manuscript, please submit the final approved version both on printed format ("hard copy") and floppy diskette. On the outside of the diskette package write:

A. The brand name of your computer or word processor
B. The word-processing program that you used
C. The title of your article, and
D. File name

Note. Disk and hard copy must agree. In case of discrepancies, it is The Haworth Press's policy to follow hard copy. Authors are advised that no revisions of the manuscript can be made after acceptance by the Editor for publication. The benefits of this procedure are many with speed and accuracy being the most obvious. We look forward to working with you on this, knowing we will be able to serve you more efficiently in the future.

12. **Reprints**. The senior author will receive two copies of the *Journal* issue and 25 complimentary reprints of his or her article. The junior author will receive two copies of the *Journal* issue. These are sent several weeks after the Journal issue is published and in circulation. An order form for the purchase of additional reprints will also be sent to all authors at this time. (Approximately 4-6 weeks are necessary for the preparation of reprints.) Please do not query the *Journal's* Editor about reprints. All such questions should be sent directly to The Haworth Press, Inc., Production Department, 21 East Broad Street, West Hazleton, PA 18201. To order additional reprints (minimum 50 copies), please contact The Haworth Document Delivery Center, 10 Alice Street, Binghamton, NY 13904-1580; 1-800-342-9678 or Fax (607) 722-6362.

13. **Copyright**. Copyright ownership of your manuscript must be transferred officially to The Haworth Press, Inc. before we can begin the peer-review process. A form fully explaining this will accompany the Editor's letter acknowledging receipt of the manuscript. All authors must sign the form and return the original to the Editor as soon as possible. Failure to return the copyright form in a timely fashion will result in a delay in review and subsequent publication.

Journal of Personal Selling & Sales Management

ADDRESS FOR SUBMISSION:

Greg W. Marshall, Editor
Journal of Personal Selling & Sales
Management
Rollins College
Crummer Craduate School of Business
1000 Holt Avenue - 2722
Winter Park, FL 32789-4499
USA
Phone: 407-691-1150
E-Mail: jpssm@rollins.edu
Web: http://mkt.cba.cmich.edu/jpssm

PUBLICATION GUIDELINES:

Manuscript Length: 26-30
Copies Required: Four
Computer Submission: No
Format: N/A
Fees to Review: 0.00 US$

Manuscript Style:
    See Manuscript Guidelines

CIRCULATION DATA:

Reader: Academics
Frequency of Issue: Quarterly
Sponsor/Publisher: Academy of Marketing
   Science / Pi Sigma Epsilon National
   Education Foundation

REVIEW INFORMATION:

Type of Review: Blind Review
No. of External Reviewers: 3
No. of In House Reviewers: 0
Acceptance Rate: 11-20%
Time to Review: 1 - 2 Months
Reviewers Comments: Yes
Invited Articles: 0-5%
Fees to Publish: 0.00 US$

MANUSCRIPT TOPICS:
Sales/Selling

MANUSCRIPT GUIDELINES/COMMENTS:

About the Journal
The *Journal of Personal Selling & Sales Management* is positioned as the premier journal internationally that is devoted exclusively to the publication of peer-reviewed articles in the field of selling and sales management.

Manuscript Preparation for Initial Submission
All manuscripts must be sent directly to the Editor. Do not send manuscripts to the Publisher or the Associate Editor. *JPSSM* is currently not set up to process electronic submission of manuscripts. Therefore, please submit four (4) non-returnable copies of manuscripts along with a cover letter to:
   Editor
   Journal of Personal Selling & Sales Management
   Phone: (573) 882-1039; Fax: (573) 884-5718
   E-mail: **jpssm@missouri.edu**

Order of Inclusion

A. Front Matter

First Page. Title of paper, name and position of author(s), each author(s)' complete contact information (complete postal address, phone number, fax number, and email address). Manuscripts received without complete contact information for each author will be desk rejected.

Second Page. A brief sketch for each author limited to only the following information: name, highest degree held and awarding school, current title or position, current organization or institution, and email address. Example: William L. Cron (Ph.D., Indiana University), Professor of Marketing, M.J. Neeley School of Business, Texas Christian University, b.cron@ tcu.edu.

Do not include information on prior publications, courses taught, organizations consulted, etc. (i.e., limit the information to only the above). The email address of each author must be included.

If you have any acknowledgements of assistance, please place these on the second page under the brief author sketches.

Third Page. Title of paper without names of the author(s) and a brief abstract of no more than 100 words summarizing the article. Be sure the abstract walks the reader through major aspects of the article. Begin page numbering on this page, placing the numbers at the bottom center. This page will be Page 1.

B. Body of Text

Text begins on the fourth page. The title of the paper should not appear again at the top of this page. First-level headings (major headings) are to be centered; second-level headings are to be flush left; third-level headings are to be indented, followed by a period and the related copy beginning immediately thereafter. Headings should be in boldface type, in upper/lower case. Font for the entire manuscript should be 12 point Times Roman or the equivalent (i.e., serif).

Do not begin with the heading "Introduction." Of course, the first several paragraphs will be your introduction, but do not label it as such.

Footnotes are to be avoided. In an extraordinary case in which a footnote is needed, number it in the body of the text and place the note text just before the references.

Manuscript length should normally not exceed 40 pages including all appendices, tables, figures, and references. Use standard 8 ½ X 11 white paper.

Throughout the manuscript, use only one space after punctuation -- not two. This includes after periods, colons, questions marks, and other types of punctuation.

C. Technical Appendices

Technical appendices may be used to include mathematical or highly technical material that supports the main text but is not critical to the reader's interpretation of the text. Label these appendices "Appendix 1," "Appendix 2," etc. They must be referred to in the text of the article, but are not to be designated for placement (unlike tables and figures -- see below).

D. Tables and Figures

Each table or figure should be placed on a separate page and numbered consecutively beginning with Table 1 and Figure 1. A table or figure should not be included unless it is referenced in the text of the article. In the paper, tables come first followed by figures. Placement in the text should be indicated as follows:

```
------------------------------------
         Place Table 2 about here
------------------------------------
```

Review a recent copy of *JPSSM* to see how to set up the format and titles for your tables and figures. Table or figure number and title should be typed on two separate lines in boldface type using upper/lower case. Example:

Table 1
Job Involvement Items

Footnotes in tables and figures should be designated by superscript numbers that correspond to notes at the bottom of the table or figure (outside the box or line).

E. References

References within the text should include the author(s)' last name(s) and year of publication with no comma immediately preceding the date, enclosed in parentheses. Example: (Brown and Peterson 1993). If practical, place the citation just before a punctuation mark, preferably at the end of a sentence. If the author(s)' names are used within the text sentence, place the year of publication in parentheses. Example: "The results reported by Brown and Peterson (1993) provide evidence of...." If a particular page or section is cited, it should be placed within the parentheses. Example: (Brown and Peterson 1993, p. 73) or Brown and Peterson (p. 73) depending on the context. For multiple authorship articles use up to three names in the citation. With four or more authors, use the first author's name and et al. Example: (Cravens et al. 1993) or Cravens et al. (1993) depending on the context.

A listing of references in alphabetical order should appear at the end of the manuscript (starting on a separate page), listed by the first author (last name/first name/middle initial), all other authors (first name/middle initial/last name), and then year of publication. Complete names of each author are to be cited. Do not use initials-only unless that author typically writes under initials-only. Example: list Cravens, David W. not Cravens, D.W. Articles by the same author(s) with the same publication year should be distinguished by a lower-case letter after the date. Example: 1992a and 1992b. For authors cited more than once, substitute six hyphens (dashes) for each repeated name in the reference list. Generally, within a series of articles by the same first author you will list any single-author papers first (ascending date order) followed by any two-author papers (also in ascending date order), then papers by three-authors, four-authors, etc.

Examples
Churchill, Gilbert A., Jr. (1996), "Better Measurement Practices are Critical to Better Understanding of Sales Management Issues," *Journal of Personal Selling & Sales Management*, 12 (Spring), 73-80.

------, Neil M. Ford, Steven W. Hartley, and Orville C. Walker,Jr. (1985), "The Determinants of Salesperson Performance: A Meta-Analysis," *Journal of Marketing Research*, 22 (May), 103-18.

Rackham, Neil and John DeVincintis (1999), *Rethinking the Sales Force: Redefining Selling to Create and Capture Customer Value*, 1st ed., New York: McGraw-Hill.

Walker, Orville C., Jr (1979), "Where Do We Go From Here? Selected Conceptual and Empirical Issues Concerning the Motivation and Performance of the Industrial Salesforce," in *Critical Issues in Sales Management: State-of-the-Art and Future Research Needs*, Gerald Albaum and Gilbert A. Churchill, Jr, eds., Eugene, OR: College of Business Administration/University of Oregon, 10-75.

The second in a pair of page numbers should be elided as follows: DO – 100-103, 125-37; 108-25; 150-59. DON'T – 100-3, 140-9.

Special Requirements: Methods
For empirical articles authors must systematically document information about the sample(s) utilized, as well as the relationships among variables. With regard to the sample(s), complete information should be provided (concisely in the text or a table) about the sampling procedure (type, selection method), method of contact, sponsorship (if applicable), incentives provided to participants, number in the sampling frame, response rate, industries from which the sample was drawn, company characteristics, geographic scope of the sampling frame, major activities/job responsibilities represented, as well as respondent characteristics including age, gender, length of service, experience level, and any other relevant characteristics. Authors with manuscripts based on research using student samples need to contact the Editor prior to submission to determine if their use of students is acceptable to *JPSSM*. It is expected that means, standard deviations, inter-correlations, and reliability/validity indices will be provided for measures in the study. Generally, all scale items not drawn from previously published literature should appear in a table or in an appendix (depending on how extensive the list).

Review Procedure
Manuscripts are reviewed independently by members of the *JPSSM* Editorial Review Board and by ad hoc reviewers chosen by the Editor. Typically, three reviewers assess each manuscript. The evaluations and recommendations of the reviewers guide the Editor in his decision. The reviews are double blind -- neither authors nor reviewers know the identity of the others.

It is the policy of *JPSSM* that manuscripts submitted for review must not have been published or be under consideration for publication elsewhere. Manuscripts that are substantially similar in content to articles already published or accepted for publication in *JPSSM* or elsewhere are ineligible for publication in *JPSSM*. It is the responsibility of the author(s) to abide by these provisions when submitting a manuscript to *JPSSM* for review.

JPSSM strives for a review process that is thorough and constructive, so that regardless of the ultimate decision about publication in *JPSSM* the author(s) can benefit from the feedback obtained on their work.

It is possible for a manuscript submitted to *JPSSM* to be desk rejected by the Editor. Although several reasons might precipitate this action, common reasons are: (1) the topic or type of submission does not fit the editorial positioning of *JPSSM*, or (2) the manuscript is not submitted according to the guidelines provided in this document.

Submitting Revised Manuscripts and Accepted Manuscripts
It is the responsibility of the author(s) to complete invited manuscript revisions in a timely manner. The maximum time allowed for resubmission of an invited revision is six months from the date of the invitation to revise. The procedure for submitting revised manuscripts is posted on the *JPSSM* web site: **mkt.cba.cmich.edu/jpssm**, as are instructions for preparing manuscripts that have been accepted for publication.

Call for Ad Hoc Reviewers
Individuals interested in serving as an ad hoc reviewer for *JPSSM* should contact the Editor at **jpssm@rollins.edu**.

Journal of Pharmaceutical Marketing & Management

ADDRESS FOR SUBMISSION:

E. M. Kolassa, Editor
Journal of Pharmaceutical Marketing &
 Management
Medical Marketing Economics, LLC
400 S. Lamar Blvd.
Suite A
Oxford, MS 38655
USA
Phone: 662-281-0502
E-Mail: mick@m2econ.com
Web: www.haworthpressinc.com

CIRCULATION DATA:

Reader: Academics, Business Persons
Frequency of Issue: Quarterly
Sponsor/Publisher: Haworth Press, Inc.

PUBLICATION GUIDELINES:

Manuscript Length: 20
Copies Required: Three
Computer Submission: Yes
Format: MS Word
Fees to Review: 0.00 US$

Manuscript Style:
 , ASHP Guidelines in AM J. Hosp.
Pharm.

REVIEW INFORMATION:

Type of Review: Blind Review
No. of External Reviewers: 2
No. of In House Reviewers: 1
Acceptance Rate: 25%
Time to Review: 1 - 2 Months
Reviewers Comments: Yes
Invited Articles: 0-5%
Fees to Publish: 0.00 US$

MANUSCRIPT TOPICS:

Advertising & Promotion Management; Marketing Research; Marketing Theory & Applications; Production/Operations

MANUSCRIPT GUIDELINES/COMMENTS:

About the Journal

The *Journal of Pharmaceutical Marketing & Management* is a valuable multidisciplinary journal devoted to solving the problems inherent in the management and marketing of pharmaceutical products and services. The journal maintains a vigorous policy of publishing quality research reports of interest to individuals involved in the manufacturing, wholesale, institutional, retail, regulatory, organizational, and academic components of the pharmaceutical industry.

In addition to valuable research and informative book reviews, each issue of the *Journal of Pharmaceutical Marketing & Management* regularly presents the "Poster Papers" section, providing succinct reports of pilot studies, early results, and provocative findings from investigations and similar applications. These brief reports provide early dissemination of new and valuable professional data, informing the reader of potentially important developments.

1. **Original Articles Only.** Submission of a manuscript to this *Journal* represents a certification on the part of the author(s) that it is an original work, and that neither this manuscript nor a version of it has been published elsewhere nor is being considered for publication elsewhere.

2. **Manuscript Length.** Your manuscript may be approximately 20 typed, double-spaced pages (including references). Long manuscripts may be considered at the discretion of the editor.

3. **Manuscript Style.** References, citations, and general style of manuscripts for this *Journal* should follow ASHP guidelines (as stated in the Am J of Hosp Pharm 1982; 39:1538-43 and Am J Hosp Pharm 1988; 45:177-8). References should appear at the end of the manuscript, numbered in order of appearance in the paper. Reference numbers in the text should appear in parentheses at the end of sentences.

If an author wishes to submit a paper that has been already prepared in another style, he or she may do so. However, if the paper is accepted (with or without reviewer's alterations), the author is fully responsible for retyping the manuscript in the correct style as indicated above. Neither the Editor nor the Publisher is responsible for re-preparing manuscript copy to adhere to the *Journal's* style.

4. **Manuscript Preparation**
Margins. Leave at least a 1" margin on all four sides.
Paper. Use clean, white 8½" x 11" bond paper.
Number of Copies. 4 (the original plus three photocopies)
Cover Page. Important—Staple a cover page to the manuscript, indicating only the article title (this is used for anonymous refereeing).
Second "Title Page." Enclose a regular title page but do not staple it to the manuscript. Include the title again, plus:
* Full authorship
* An ABSTRACT of about 100 words. (Below the abstract provide 3–10 key words for index purposes).
* A header or footer on each page with abbreviated title and pg number of total (e.g., pg 2 of 7)
* An introductory footnote with authors' academic degrees, professional titles, affiliations, mailing and e-mail addresses, and any desired acknowledgment of research support or other credit.

5. **Return Envelopes.** When you submit your four manuscript copies, also include:
* A 9" x 12" envelope, self-addressed and stamped (with sufficient postage to ensure return of your manuscript);
* A regular envelope, stamped and self-addressed. This is for the Editor to send you an "acknowledgement of receipt" letter.

6. Spelling, Grammar, and Punctuation. You are responsible for preparing manuscript copy which is clearly written in acceptable, scholarly English and which contains no errors of spelling, grammar, or punctuation. Neither the Editor nor the Publisher is responsible for correcting errors of spelling and grammar. The manuscript, after acceptance by the Editor, must be immediately ready for typesetting as it is finally submitted by the author(s).
Check your paper for the following common errors:

- Dangling modifiers
- Misplaced modifiers
- Unclear antecedents
- Incorrect or inconsistent abbreviations

Also, check the accuracy of all arithmetic calculations, statistics, numerical data, text citations, and references.

7. Inconsistencies Must Be Avoided. Be sure you are consistent in your use of abbreviations, terminology, and in citing references, from one part of your paper to another.

8. Preparation of Tables, Figures, and Illustrations. Any material that is not textual is considered artwork. This includes tables, figures, diagrams, charts, graphs, illustrations, appendices, screen captures, and photos. Tables and figures (including legend, notes, and sources) should be no larger than 4½" x 6½". Type styles should be Helvetica (or Helvetica narrow if necessary) and no smaller than 8 point. We request that computer-generated figures be in black and white and/or shades of gray (preferably no color, for it does not reproduce well). Camera-ready art must contain no grammatical, typographical, or format errors and must reproduce sharply and clearly in the dimensions of the final printed page (4½" x 6½"). Photos and screen captures must be on disk as a TIF file, or other graphic file format such as JPEG or BMP. For rapid publication we must receive black-and-white glossy or matte positives (white background with black images and/or wording) in addition to files on disk. Tables should be created in the text document file using the software's Table feature.

9. Submitting Art. Both a printed hard copy and a disk copy of the art must be provided. We request that each piece of art be sent in its own file, on a disk separate from the disk containing the manuscript text file(s), and be clearly labeled. We reserve the right to (if necessary) request new art, alter art, or if all else has failed in achieving art that is presentable, delete art. If submitted art cannot be used, the Publisher reserves the right to redo the art and to change the author for a fee of $35.00 per hour for this service. The Haworth Press, Inc. is not responsible for errors incurred in the preparation of new artwork. Camera-ready artwork must be prepared on separate sheets of paper. Always use black ink and professional drawing instruments. On the back of these items, write your article title and the journal title lightly in soft-lead pencil (please do not write on the face of art). In the text file, skip extra lines and indicate where these figures are placed. Photos are considered part of the acceptable manuscript and remain with the Publisher for use in additional printings.

10. Electronic Media. Haworth's in-house typesetting unit is able to utilize your final manuscript material as prepared on most personal computers and word processors. This will minimize typographical errors and decrease overall production time. Please send the first draft and final draft copies of your manuscript to the journal Editor in print format for his/her final review and approval. After approval of your final manuscript, please submit the final approved version both on printed format ("hard copy") and floppy diskette. On the outside of the diskette package write:

1. The brand name of your computer or word processor
2. The word processing program and version that you used
3. The title of your article, and
4. The file name.

Note. Disk and hard copy must agree. In case of discrepancies, it is The Haworth Press' policy to follow hard copy. Authors are advised that no revisions of the manuscript can be made after acceptance by the Editor for publication. The benefits of this procedure are many with speed and accuracy being the most obvious. We look forward to working with your electronic submission, which will allow us to serve you more efficiently.

11. **Alterations Required by Referees and Reviewers**. Many times a paper is accepted by the Editor contingent upon changes that are mandated by anonymous specialist referees and members of the Editorial Board. If the Editor returns your manuscript for revisions, you are responsible for retyping any sections of the paper to incorporate these revisions (if applicable, revisions should also be put on disk).

12. **Typesetting**. You will not be receiving galley proofs of your article. Editorial revisions, if any, must therefore be made while your article is still in manuscript. The final version of the manuscript will be the version you see published. Typesetter's errors will be corrected by the production staff of The Haworth Press. Authors are expected to submit manuscripts, disks, and art that are free from error.

13. **Reprints**. The senior author will receive two copies of the journal issue and 25 complimentary reprints of his or her article. The junior author will receive two copies of the journal issue. These are sent several weeks after the journal issue is published and in circulation. An order form for the purchase of additional reprints will also be sent to all authors at this time. (Approximately 4–6 weeks is necessary for the preparation of reprints.) Please do not query the *Journal's* Editor about reprints. All such questions should be sent directly to The Haworth Press, Inc., Production Department, 37 West Broad Street, West Hazleton, PA 18202. To order additional reprints (minimum 50 copies), please contact The Haworth Document Delivery Center, 10 Alice Street, Binghamton, NY 13904–1580; 1–800–342–9678 or Fax (607) 722–6362.

14. **Copyright**. Copyright ownership of your manuscript must be transferred officially to The Haworth Press, Inc. before we can begin the peer-review process. The Editor's letter acknowledging receipt of the manuscript will be accompanied by a form fully explaining this. All authors must sign the form and return the original to the Editor as soon as possible. Failure to return the copyright form in a timely fashion will result in a delay in review and subsequent publication.

Journal of Political Marketing

ADDRESS FOR SUBMISSION:

Bruce I. Newman, Editor
Journal of Political Marketing
DePaul University
1 East Jackson Boulevard
Chicago, IL 60604
USA
Phone: 312-362-5186
E-Mail: bnewman@depaul.edu
Web: http://www.haworthpress.com/store/
product.asp?sku=J199

CIRCULATION DATA:

Reader: Academics
Frequency of Issue: Quarterly
Sponsor/Publisher: Haworth Press, Inc.

PUBLICATION GUIDELINES:

Manuscript Length: 26-30
Copies Required: Three
Computer Submission: No
Format: N/A
Fees to Review: 0.00 US$

Manuscript Style:
    Chicago Manual of Style

REVIEW INFORMATION:

Type of Review:
No. of External Reviewers: 3
No. of In House Reviewers: 0
Acceptance Rate: 21-30%
Time to Review: 2 - 3 Months
Reviewers Comments: Yes
Invited Articles: 0-5%
Fees to Publish: 0.00 US$

MANUSCRIPT TOPICS:

Advertising & Promotion Management; Business Law, Public Responsibility & Ethics; Communication; Direct Marketing; E-Commerce; Global Business; Marketing Research; Marketing Theory & Applications; Non-Profit Organizations; Office Administration/Management; Public Administration; Services

MANUSCRIPT GUIDELINES/COMMENTS:

About the Journal

The new *Journal of Political Marketing*: political campaigns in the new millennium is vital reading for politicians and candidates at every level of office as well as political party officials, political consultants, corporate lobbyists, pollsters, media specialists, journalists, and students and educators in these and related fields. In comparison to competing publications, this journal puts exciting articles with a high level of sophistication and detail in your hands, keeping you on top of current developments in political marketing and campaign strategy. The journal's focus includes current and predicted future trends such as the application of Internet marketing techniques to politics, which may be at the forefront of future politics around the world.

The *Journal of Political Marketing* offers business executives, managers, and academics a new approach to the use of marketing in the commercial marketplace. For the first time, a journal has been developed to examine the use of marketing and business practices by candidates, politicians, political parties, lobbyists, political action committees and interest groups. This new stream of literature can be used to identify innovative strategies to use in the marketplace.

The *Journal of Political Marketing* brings you the expertise of academics and practitioners as well as professionals in related fields that fall under the umbrella of political marketing. Planned columns include:

- "Propaganda in Politics"-addresses the growing concerns of using propaganda to influence politics
- "Political Advertising"-a discussion of trends and predictions for the future
- "Cyber-Democracy"-devoted to the application of direct marketing and Internet technologies to politics
- "E-Government"-a column on the "customer service" attribute of political marketing
- "Strategic Corporate Lobbying"-an examination of the role lobbying plays in influencing government
- "Campaigns from Around the World"-deals with elections taking place in different countries
- "Direct Marketing and Marketing Research"-a commentary on how trends in the market significantly affect political marketing
- "Party Politics"-a look at campaigns and marketing strategies by the various parties

Instructions for Authors

1. **Original Articles Only.** Submission of a manuscript to this *Journal* represents a certification on the part of the author(s) that it is an original work, and that neither this manuscript nor a version of it has been published elsewhere nor is being considered for publication elsewhere.

2. **Manuscript Length.** Your manuscript may be approximately 5-50 typed, double-spaced pages (including references and abstract). Lengthier manuscripts may be considered, but only at the discretion of the Editor. Sometimes, lengthier manuscripts may be considered if they can be divided up into sections for publication in successive *Journal* issues.

3. **Manuscript Style.** References, citations, and general style of manuscripts for this *Journal* should follow the Chicago style (as outlined in the latest edition of the *Manual of Style* of the University of Chicago Press). References should be double-spaced and placed in alphabetical order.

If an author wishes to submit a paper that has been already prepared in another style, he or she may do so. However, if the paper is accepted (with or without reviewer's alterations), the author is fully responsible for retyping the manuscript in the correct style as indicated above. Neither the Editor nor the Publisher is responsible for re-preparing manuscript copy to adhere to the *Journal*'s style.

4. Manuscript Preparation
Margins. Leave at least a 1" margin on all four sides.
Paper. Use clean, white 8½" x 11" bond paper.
Number of Copies. 4 (the original plus three photocopies)
Cover Page. Important—Staple a cover page to the manuscript, indicating only the article title (this is used for anonymous refereeing).
Second "Title Page." Enclose a regular title page but do not staple it to the manuscript. Include the title again, plus:

- Full authorship
- An ABSTRACT of about 100 words. (Below the abstract provide 3-10 key words for index purposes).
- A header or footer on each page with abbreviated title and pg number of total (e.g., pg 2 of 7)
- An introductory footnote with authors' academic degrees, professional titles, affiliations, mailing and e-mail addresses, and any desired acknowledgment of research support or other credit.

5. Return Envelopes.
When you submit your four manuscript copies, also include:

- A 9" x 12" envelope, self-addressed and stamped (with sufficient postage to ensure return of your manuscript);
- A regular envelope, stamped and self-addressed. This is for the Editor to send you an "acknowledgement of receipt" letter.

6. Spelling, Grammar, and Punctuation.
You are responsible for preparing manuscript copy which is clearly written in acceptable, scholarly English and which contains no errors of spelling, grammar, or punctuation. Neither the Editor nor the Publisher is responsible for correcting errors of spelling and grammar. The manuscript, after acceptance by the Editor, must be immediately ready for typesetting as it is finally submitted by the author(s). Check your paper for the following common errors:

- Dangling modifiers
- Misplaced modifiers
- Unclear antecedents
- Incorrect or inconsistent abbreviations

Also, check the accuracy of all arithmetic calculations, statistics, numerical data, text citations, and references.

7. Inconsistencies Must Be Avoided.
Be sure you are consistent in your use of abbreviations, terminology, and in citing references, from one part of your paper to another.

8. Preparation of Tables, Figures, and Illustrations.
Any material that is not textual is considered artwork. This includes tables, figures, diagrams, charts, graphs, illustrations, appendices, screen captures, and photos. Tables and figures (including legend, notes, and sources) should be no larger than 4½"x 6½". Type styles should be Helvetica (or Helvetica narrow if necessary) and no smaller than 8 point. We request that computer-generated figures be in black and white and/or shades of gray (preferably no color, for it does not reproduce

well). Camera-ready art must contain no grammatical, typographical, or format errors and must reproduce sharply and clearly in the dimensions of the final printed page (4½"x 6½"). Photos and screen captures must be on disk as a TIF file, or other graphic file format such as JPEG or BMP. For rapid publication we must receive black-and-white glossy or matte positives (white background with black images and/or wording) in addition to files on disk. Tables should be created in the text document file using the software's Table feature.

9. **Submitting Art.** Both a printed hard copy and a disk copy of the art must be provided. We request that each piece of art be sent in its own file, on a disk separate from the disk containing the manuscript text file(s), and be clearly labeled. We reserve the right to (if necessary) request new art, alter art, or if all else has failed in achieving art that is presentable, delete art. If submitted art cannot be used, the Publisher reserves the right to redo the art and to change the author for a fee of $35.00 per hour for this service. The Haworth Press, Inc. is not responsible for errors incurred in the preparation of new artwork. Camera-ready artwork must be prepared on separate sheets of paper. Always use black ink and professional drawing instruments. On the back of these items, write your article title and the journal title lightly in soft-lead pencil (please do not write on the face of art). In the text file, skip extra lines and indicate where these figures are placed. Photos are considered part of the acceptable manuscript and remain with the Publisher for use in additional printings.

10. **Electronic Media.** Haworth's in-house typesetting unit is able to utilize your final manuscript material as prepared on most personal computers and word processors. This will minimize typographical errors and decrease overall production time. Please send the first draft and final draft copies of your manuscript to the journal Editor in print format for his/her final review and approval. After approval of your final manuscript, please submit the final approved version both on printed format ("hard copy") and floppy diskette. On the outside of the diskette package write:
1. The brand name of your computer or word processor
2. The word processing program and version that you used
3. The title of your article, and
4. The file name

Note. Disk and hard copy must agree. In case of discrepancies, it is The Haworth Press' policy to follow hard copy. Authors are advised that no revisions of the manuscript can be made after acceptance by the Editor for publication. The benefits of this procedure are many with speed and accuracy being the most obvious. We look forward to working with your electronic submission, which will allow us to serve you more efficiently.

11. **Alterations Required by Referees and Reviewers.** Many times a paper is accepted by the Editor contingent upon changes that are mandated by anonymous specialist referees and members of the Editorial Board. If the Editor returns your manuscript for revisions, you are responsible for retyping any sections of the paper to incorporate these revisions (if applicable, revisions should also be put on disk).

12. **Typesetting**. You will not be receiving galley proofs of your article. Editorial revisions, if any, must therefore be made while your article is still in manuscript. The final version of the manuscript will be the version you see published. Typesetter's errors will be corrected by the production staff of The Haworth Press. Authors are expected to submit manuscripts, disks, and art that are free from error.

13. **Reprints**. The senior author will receive two copies of the journal issue and 25 complimentary reprints of his or her article. The junior author will receive two copies of the journal issue. These are sent several weeks after the journal issue is published and in circulation. An order form for the purchase of additional reprints will also be sent to all authors at this time. (Approximately 4-6 weeks is necessary for the preparation of reprints.) Please do not query the Journal's Editor about reprints. All such questions should be sent directly to The Haworth Press, Inc., Production Department, 37 West Broad Street, West Hazleton, PA 18202. To order additional reprints (minimum: 50 copies), please contact The Haworth Document Delivery Center, 10 Alice Street, Binghamton, NY 13904-1580; 1-800-342-9678 or Fax (607) 722-6362.

14. **Copyright** ownership of your manuscript must be transferred officially to The Haworth Press, Inc. before we can begin the peer-review process. The Editor's letter acknowledging receipt of the manuscript will be accompanied by a form fully explaining this. All authors must sign the form and return the original to the Editor as soon as possible. Failure to return the copyright form in a timely fashion will result in a delay in review and subsequent publication.

Journal of Product and Brand Management

ADDRESS FOR SUBMISSION:

Richard C. Leventhal, Editor
Journal of Product and Brand Management
7678 Upham Street
Arvada, CO 80003
USA
Phone: 303-420-9067
E-Mail: rcleventhal@hotmail.com
Web: www.emeraldinsight.com/jpbm.htm

CIRCULATION DATA:

Reader: Academics, Business Persons
Frequency of Issue: 7 Times/Year
Sponsor/Publisher: Emerald Group
  Publishing Limited

PUBLICATION GUIDELINES:

Manuscript Length: 16-20
Copies Required: Three
Computer Submission: No
Format: N/A
Fees to Review: 0.00 US$

Manuscript Style:
  See Manuscript Guidelines

REVIEW INFORMATION:

Type of Review: Blind Review
No. of External Reviewers: 2
No. of In House Reviewers: 1
Acceptance Rate: 25%
Time to Review: 4-6 Weeks
Reviewers Comments: Yes
Invited Articles: 5-10%
Fees to Publish: 0.00 US$

MANUSCRIPT TOPICS:

Advertising & Promotion Management; Brand Equity; Brand Management; Direct Marketing; E-Commerce; Global Business; Marketing Research; Marketing Theory & Applications; Product Development; Production/Operations; Sales/Selling; Strategic Management Policy

MANUSCRIPT GUIDELINES/COMMENTS:

About the Journal

The *Journal of Product & Brand Management* featuring *Pricing Strategy & Practice* offers you a direct route to worldwide research at the cutting edge of product and brand management and pricing. This internationally respected journal examines critical issues, which need to be taken into consideration when determining brand and pricing strategies and policies. Offering expert analysis and practical recommendations to aid decision-making and stimulate further research activity, it provides an invaluable source of knowledge for academics and corporate practitioners. Every article published in the *Journal of Product & Brand Management* has been subject to a double blind review process to ensure its relevance and quality.

Coverage

- Brand management
- Consumer behaviour
- Pricing strategy
- Marketing research

- New product development
- International pricing
- Brand equity

Copyright

Articles submitted to the journal should be original contributions and should not be under consideration for any other publication at the same time. Authors submitting articles for publication warrant that the work is not an infringement of any existing copyright and will indemnify the publisher against any breach of such warranty. For ease of dissemination and to ensure proper policing of use, papers and contributions become the legal copyright of the publisher unless otherwise agreed. Submissions should be sent to the Editor.

Editorial Objectives

The *Journal of Product & Brand Management* is an academic journal written for both practitioners and scholars. The objective of the journal is to publish articles that enrich the practice of product and brand management while simultaneously making significant contributions to knowledge of product and brand issues. Manuscripts must offer meaningful implications and recommendations for practitioners, but also must be conceptually or theoretically sound and offer significant research findings or insights.

Further, if the manuscript reports the findings of original research, the methodology and findings not only should be scientifically defensible, but also should be presented clearly and to the extent possible in a nontechnical manner such that readers with limited backgrounds in research methods and statistical analyses are not discouraged from reading the article.

However it should be noted that research is not the only basis for an acceptable article. Case analyses, book reviews, and other thought-provoking manuscripts are encouraged. Article cases of an international nature are especially welcome. The editorial goal is to create a journal of relevance to an international audience. To do this we seek articles from all parts of the world. Particularly welcome are manuscripts which address product and brand issues from the perspective of comparative international markets.

Pricing Strategy & Practice Special Section

Prof. Hooman Estelami and Prof. Sarah Maxwell, Fordham Pricing Center, Fordham University, Graduate School of Business, 113 West 60th Street, New York, New York 10023

Editorial Policy

Pricing Strategy & Practice provides a forum for the discussion of the real implications of pricing decisions, and will cover such issues as:

- Developing and maintaining price differentials;
- Discounting and other price reduction strategies;
- Price and product positioning;
- Price bundling;
- Price comparison and advertising;
- International pricing;
- Value-oriented pricing;

- Organizing for price management;
- pricing for product launches;
- legal implications of pricing.

Editorial Scope
a. A brief description of the problems or issues the article will address, the basic premise of the paper, and/or the article's objective(s). This paragraph should be positioned near the front of the article.
b. Background and reference to existing, applicable literature. Articles should convince readers that authors have done their homework in reviewing and crediting relevant literature, and pointing interested readers to additional sources of information. Ordinarily, however, literature reviews need not be exhaustive. Where applicable, the background section should include an overview of the theory(ies) within which the article is couched.
c. Interesting examples that illuminate and reinforce the thrust of the article.
d. Clear presentation and discussion of the study's findings, if applicable.
e. A summary to wrap-up key ideas.
f. Practical implications

Reviewing Process
Each paper is reviewed by the editor and, if it is judged suitable for this publication, it is then sent to three referees for double blind peer review. Based on their recommendations, the editor then decides whether the paper should be accepted as is, revised or rejected.

Manuscript Requirements
Four copies of the manuscript should be submitted in double line spacing with wide margins. All authors should be shown and author's details must be printed on a separate sheet and the author should not be identified anywhere else in the article.

As a guide, articles should be between 3,000 and 6,000 words in length. A title of not more than eight words should be provided. A brief **autobiographical note** should be supplied including full name, affiliation, e-mail address and full international contact details. Authors must supply a **structured abstract** of 100-150 words. Up to six **keywords** should be included which encapsulate the principal subjects covered by the article.

Where there is a **methodology**, it should be clearly described under a separate heading. **Headings** must be short, clearly defined and not numbered. **Notes** or **Endnotes** should be used only if absolutely necessary and must be identified in the text by consecutive numbers, enclosed in square brackets and listed at the end of the article.

Figures, charts and **diagrams** should be kept to a minimum. They must be black and white with minimum shading and numbered consecutively using Arabic numerals with a brief title and labelled axes. In the text, the position of the figure should be shown by typing on a separate line the words "take in Figure 2". Good quality originals must be provided.

Tables should be kept to a minimum. They must be numbered consecutively with roman numerals and a brief title. In the text, the position of the table should be shown by typing on a separate line the words "take in Table IV".

Photos and **illustrations** must be supplied as good quality black and white original half tones with captions. Their position should be shown in the text by typing on a separate line the words "take in Plate 2".

References to other publications should be complete and in Harvard style. They should contain full bibliographical details and journal titles should not be abbreviated. For multiple citations in the same year use a, b, c immediately following the year of publication. References should be shown within the text by giving the author's last name followed by a comma and year of publication all in round brackets, e.g., (Fox, 1994). At the end of the article should be a reference list in alphabetical order as follows

For Books
Surname, initials and year of publication, title, publisher, place of publication, e.g. Casson, M. (1979), Alternatives to the Multinational Enterprise, Macmillan, London.

For Chapter in Edited Book
Surname, initials and year, "title", editor's surname, initials, title, publisher, place, pages, e.g., Bessley, M. and Wilson, P. (1984), "Public policy and small firms in Britain", in Levicki, C. (Ed.), Small Business Theory and Policy, Croom Helm, London, pp.111-26. Please note that the chapter title must be underlined.

For Journals
Surname, initials, year "title", journal, volume, number, pages, e.g. Fox, S. (1994) "Empowerment as a catalyst for change: an example from the food industry", Supply Chain Management, Vol 2 No 3, pp. 29-33

If there is more than one author list surnames followed by initials. All authors should be shown.

Electronic sources should include the URL of the electronic site at which they may be found, as follows:

Neuman, B.C.(1995), "Security, payment, and privacy for network commerce", IEEE Journal on Selected Areas in Communications, Vol. 13 No.8, October, pp.1523-31. Available (IEEE SEPTEMBER) http://www.research.att.com/jsac/.

Notes/Endnotes should be used only if absolutely necessary. They should, however, always be used for citing Web sites. They should be identified in the text by consecutive numbers enclosed in square brackets and listed at the end of the article. Please then provide full Web site addresses in the end list.

Final Submission of the Article
Once accepted for publication, the final version of the manuscript must be provided, (including a sturcutred abstract) accompanied by a 3.5" **disk** of the same version labelled with: disk format; author name(s); title of article; journal title; file name.

Each article must be accompanied by a completed and signed Journal Article Record Form available from the Editor or on http://www.literaticlub.co.uk/.

The manuscript will be considered to be the definitive version of the article. The author must ensure that it is complete, grammatically correct and without spelling or typographical errors. In preparing the disk, please use one of the following formats: Word, Word Perfect, Rich text format or TeX/LaTeX. Figures, which are provided electronically, must be in tif, gif or pic file extensions. All figures and graphics must also be supplied as good quality originals.

Final Submission Requirements
Manuscripts must be clean, good quality hard copy and;
- include an abstract and keywords
- have Harvard style references
- include any figures, photos and graphics as good quality originals
- be accompanied by a labelled disk
- be accompanied by a completed Journal Article Record Form

Technical assistance is available from MCB's World Wide Web Literati Club on http://www.literaticlub.co.uk/ or contact Mike Massey at MCB, e-mail mmassey@mcb.co.uk.

Journal of Promotion Management

ADDRESS FOR SUBMISSION:

Richard Alan Nelson, Editor
Journal of Promotion Management
Louisiana State University
Manship School of Mass Communication
211 Journalism Building
Baton Rouge, LA 70803-7202
USA
Phone: 225-578-6686
E-Mail: Rnelson@LSU.edu
Web: www.haworthpress.com/web/JPM

PUBLICATION GUIDELINES:

Manuscript Length: 10-20
Copies Required: Four
Computer Submission: Yes
Format: MS Word, WordPerfect
Fees to Review: 0.00 US$

Manuscript Style:
    American Psychological Association

CIRCULATION DATA:

Reader: Academics, Business Persons
Frequency of Issue: Quarterly
Sponsor/Publisher: Haworth Press, Inc.

REVIEW INFORMATION:

Type of Review: Blind Review
No. of External Reviewers: 2
No. of In House Reviewers: 1
Acceptance Rate: 21-30%
Time to Review: 1 - 2 Months
Reviewers Comments: Yes
Invited Articles: 6-10%
Fees to Publish: 0.00 US$

MANUSCRIPT TOPICS:

Advertising & Promotion Management; Direct Marketing; Global Business; Marketing Research; Marketing Theory & Applications; Non-Profit Organizations; Sales/Selling; Technology/Innovation

MANUSCRIPT GUIDELINES/COMMENTS:

The *Journal of Promotion Management* is a quality refereed publication dedicated to bridging the gap between practitioners in advertising, public relations, and personal selling, policymakers, and knowledgeable academics by publishing useful articles about innovations in planning and applied research. Besides public relations, the focus is on advertising, alternative promotional media, direct marketing, e-commerce, integrated communication, personal selling, promotional products/specialty advertising, reseller support, and sales promotions. A special emphasis is made to demonstrate promotion management in action. In addition to contemporary practice, theoretical concerns and historical studies are also welcomed.

Instructions for Authors

1. **Original Articles Only**. Submission of a manuscript to this *Journal* represents a certification on the part of the author(s) that it is an original work, and that neither this

manuscript nor a version of it has been published elsewhere nor is being considered for publication elsewhere. Discuss with the editor his policy on updated studies and new research that includes materials previously in the trade press. If any of the material in your manuscript has been previously published, please obtain the appropriate permission and attached the original written and signed form to the front of the manuscript.

2. Manuscript Length. Articles normally are 10-to-20 pages, including references, abstract and tables. If you have a shorter or longer study, contact the editor to discuss your project. Sometimes, lengthier manuscripts may be considered if they can be divided up into sections for publication in successive *Journal* issues. Recommended is use of the 11 point Times New Roman font size, including references and notes.

3. Manuscript Style. References, citations, and general style of manuscripts for this *Journal* should follow the APA style (as outlined in the latest edition of the *Publication Manual of the American Psychological Association*). References should be double-spaced and placed in alphabetical order.

If an author wishes to submit a paper that has been already prepared in another style, he or she may do so. However, if the paper is accepted (with or without reviewer's alterations), the author is fully responsible for retyping the manuscript in the correct style as indicated above. Neither the editor nor the publisher is responsible for re-preparing manuscript copy to adhere to the *Journal*'s style.

4. Manuscript Preparation.
Margins. Leave at least a 1-inch margin on all four sides.
Paper. Use clean white, 8½" x 11" bond paper.
Number of Copies. 4 (the original plus three photocopies)
Cover page. Important—Staple a cover page to the manuscript, indicating only the article title (this is used for anonymous refereeing).
Second "title page." Enclose a regular title page but do not staple it to the manuscript. Include the title again, plus:

• Full authorship
• An abstract of about 100 words (below the abstract provide 3-10 key words for index purposes)
• An introductory footnote with authors' highest academic degree and institution granting it, professional titles, affiliations, mailing and e-mail addresses, and any desired acknowledgment of research support or other credit
• A signed Manuscript Submission and Copyright Form. Download this from: http://www.haworthpress.com (see "Section 14: Copyright" below). Please attach the Manuscript Submission Form, signed by all authors to the front of the first copy of the manuscript. Please print name of author under signature in order to verify the signature. Re-list all addresses and phone numbers, faxes, e-mail etc., on a separate sheet of paper and attached to the back of the Manuscript Submission Form. This information is needed so as to send the printed copies of the journals to the authors.

5. Reference Linking. The Haworth Press is participating in reference linking for journal articles. (For more information on reference linking initiatives, please consult the CrossRef website at www.crossref.org.) When citing a journal article include the article's Digital Object Identifier (DOI), when available, as the last item in the reference. A Digital Object Identifier is a persistent, authoritative, and unique identifier that a publisher assigns to each article. Because of its persistence, DOIs will enable The Haworth Press and other publishers to link to the article referenced, and the link will not break over time. This will be a great resource in scholarly research. An example of a reference to a journal article which includes a DOI:

Vizine-Goetz, Diane (2002). Classification Schemes for Internet Resources Revisited. Journal of Internet Cataloging 5(4): 5:18. doi: 10.1300/J141v05n04_02

6. **Return Envelopes**. When you submit your four manuscript copies, also include a regular

- a 9" x 12" envelope, self-addressed and stamped (with sufficient postage to ensure return of your manuscript);
- a regular envelope, stamped and self-addressed. This is for the editor to send you an "acknowledgement of receipt" letter.

7. **Spelling, Grammar, and Punctuation**. You are responsible for preparing manuscript copy which is clearly written in acceptable scholarly English and which contains no errors of spelling, grammar, or punctuation. Neither the editor nor the publisher is responsible for correcting errors of spelling and grammar. The manuscript, after acceptance by the editor, must be immediately ready for typesetting as it is finally submitted by the author(s). Check your paper for the following common errors:

- Dangling modifiers
- Misplaced modifiers
- Unclear antecedents
- Incorrect or inconsistent abbreviations

8. **Inconsistencies Must be Avoided**. Be sure you are consistent in your use of abbreviations, terminology, and in citing references, from one part of your paper to another.

9. **Alterations Required by Referees and Reviewers**. Many times a paper is accepted by the editor contingent upon changes that are mandated by anonymous specialist referees and members of the Editorial Board. If the editor returns your manuscript for revisions, you are responsible for retyping any sections of the paper to incorporate these revisions. If applicable, please send the first draft and final draft copies of your manuscript to the journal editor in print format for his final review and approval. After approval of your final manuscript, please also submit the final approved version both on printed format ("hard copy") and floppy diskette or e-mail version (preferred) to the editor. However, e-mail is much faster and preferred: **Rnelson@LSU.edu**. If using a diskette rather than e-mail attachment, submit the computer disk with your article in either MS Word or Corel WordPerfect format for PC (not Mac). On the outside of the diskette package write the title of your article and file name. NOTE: Disk/e-mail and hard copy must agree. In case of discrepancies, it is The Haworth Press's policy to follow hard copy. Authors are advised that no revisions of the manuscript can be made after acceptance by the editor for publication. The benefits of this procedure are many with speed and accuracy being the most obvious. We look forward to working with you on this, knowing we will be able to serve you more efficiently in the future

10. **Submitting Art: Preparation of Tables, Figures, and Illustrations.** All tables, figures, illustrations, etc. must be "camera-ready." That is, they must be cleanly typed or artistically prepared so that they can be used either exactly as they are or else used after a photographic reduction in size. Both a printed hard copy and a disk copy of the art must be provided. We request that each piece of art be sent in its own file, on a disk separate from the disk containing the manuscript text file(s), and be clearly labeled. We reserve the right to (if necessary) request new art, alter art, or if all else has failed in achieving art that is presentable, delete art. If submitted art cannot be used, the publisher reserves the right to redo the art and to change the author for a fee of $55.00 per hour for this service. The Haworth Press, Inc. is not responsible for errors incurred in the preparation of new artwork. Camera-ready artwork must be prepared on separate sheets of paper. Always use black ink and professional drawing instruments. On the back of these items, write your article title and the journal title lightly in soft-lead pencil (please do not write on the face of art). In the text file, skip extra lines and indicate where these figures are placed. Photos are considered part of the acceptable manuscript and remain with the publisher for use in additional printings.

11. **Electronic Media.** Haworth's in-house typesetting unit is able to utilize your final manuscript material as prepared on most personal computers and word processors. This will minimize typographical errors and decrease overall production time lag. Please send the first draft and final draft copies of your manuscript to the *Journal* editor in print format for his/her final review and approval. **After approval of your final manuscript**, please submit the final approved version both on printed format ("hard copy") and floppy diskette. On the outside of the diskette package write:

A. The brand name of your computer or word processor
B. The word-processing program that you used
C. The title of your article, and
D. File name

Note. Disk and hard copy must agree. In case of discrepancies, it is The Haworth Press's policy to follow hard copy. Authors are advised that no revisions of the manuscript can be made after acceptance by the editor for publication. The benefits of this procedure are many with speed and accuracy being the most obvious. We look forward to working with you on this, knowing we will be able to serve you more efficiently in the future.

12. **Typesetting.** You will not be receiving galley proofs of your article. Editorial revisions, if any, must therefore be made while your article is still in manuscript. The final version of the manuscript will be the version you see published. Typesetter's errors will be corrected by the production staff of The Haworth Press. Authors are expected to submit manuscripts, disks, and art that are free from error. The disk must be the one from which the accompanying manuscript (finalized version) was printed out.

13. **Reprints.** The senior author will receive two copies of the *Journal* issue as well as complimentary reprints of his or her article. The junior author will receive two copies of the *Journal* issue. These are sent several weeks after the *Journal* issue is published and in circulation. An order form for the purchase of additional reprints will also be sent to all authors at this time. (Approximately 8 weeks is necessary for the preparation of reprints.)

652

Please do not query the *Journal*'s editor about reprints. All such questions should be sent directly to The Haworth Press, Inc., Production Department, 37 West Broad Street, West Hazleton, PA 18202. To order additional reprints (minimum 50 copies), please contact The Haworth Document Delivery Center, 10 Alice Street, Binghamton, NY 13904-1580, USA; Tel. 1-800-342-9678 or Fax 607-722-6362.

14. **Copyright** ownership of your manuscript must be transferred officially to The Haworth Press, Inc., before we can begin the peer-review process. The editor's letter acknowledging receipt of the manuscript will be accompanied by a form fully explaining this. All authors must sign the form and return the original to the editor as soon as possible. Either include the copyright form with your submission or mail/fax it to the editor. Failure to return the copyright form in a timely fashion will result in delay in review and subsequent publication. Authors are responsible for meeting applicable copyright laws and getting copyright permissions IN ADVANCE for any material originally created by others that they intend to reproduce. More information is available at **http://www.HaworthPress.com/web/JPM**.

Journal of Public Affairs

ADDRESS FOR SUBMISSION:

Journal of Public Affairs
Electronic Submission to Debbie Burns
dburns@business.otago.ac.nz
Phone:
E-Mail: dburns@business.otago.ac.nz
Web: www.interscience.wiley.com/
journal/pa

CIRCULATION DATA:

Reader: Academics, Public Affairs
Professionals
Frequency of Issue: Quarterly
Sponsor/Publisher: John Wiley & Sons

PUBLICATION GUIDELINES:

Manuscript Length: 16-20
Copies Required: Three
Computer Submission: Yes
Format: MS Word, WordPerfect, or TeX
Fees to Review: 0.00 US$

Manuscript Style:
Uniform System of Citation (Harvard
Blue Book)

REVIEW INFORMATION:

Type of Review: Blind Review
No. of External Reviewers: 2
No. of In House Reviewers: 1
Acceptance Rate: 40%
Time to Review:
Reviewers Comments: Yes
Invited Articles: 21-30%
Fees to Publish: 0.00 US$

MANUSCRIPT TOPICS:

Advertising & Promotion Management; Communication; Direct Marketing; Marketing Research; Marketing Theory & Applications; Political Marketing; Public Administration; Public Affairs

MANUSCRIPT GUIDELINES/COMMENTS:

Topics Include. Government relations and lobbying; issues management; community relations; corporate social responsibility and political strategy and marketing

Full guidelines for contributors can be found at the journal homepage:
www.interscience.wiley.com/journal/pa

Aims

Journal of Public Affairs provides an international forum for refereed papers, case studies and reviews on the latest developments, practice and thinking in government relations, public affairs and political marketing. The *Journal* is guided by the twin objectives of publishing submissions of the utmost relevance to the day-to-day practice of communication specialists, and promoting the highest standards of intellectual rigor.

The Editorial Board welcomes the submission of papers, briefings, case studies and reviews for publication. Authors submitting articles for publication should specify which section of the *Journal* they wish their paper to be considered for: Academic Papers or Practice Papers. An essential criterion for the publication of academic papers is that they add to the literature; for practice papers that they are of direct relevance and of use to those involved in the management of business and organizational communication. All articles submitted will be subject to double-blind refereeing. Full guidance notes for contributors can be found at the back of each issue or at www.interscience.wiley.com/journal/pa

Journal of Public Affairs is published quarterly. Subscription enquiries should be addressed to: John Wiley & Sons Ltd, Journals Fulfilment, 1 Oldlands Way, Bognor Regis, West Sussex, PO22 9SA, UK Tel: +44 1243 843335; Fax: +44 1243 843232; email: **cs-journals@wiley. co.uk**

Notes to Contributors

Initial manuscript submission. Submit the manuscript to Debbie Burns by e-mail to **dburns@ business.otago.ac.nz**.

Authors must also supply:

- an electronic copy of the final version (see section below);
- a Copyright Transfer Agreement with original signature(s) - without this we are unable to accept the submission; and
- permission grants - if the manuscript contains extracts, including illustrations, from other copyright works (including material from on-line or intranet sources) it is the author's responsibility to obtain written permission from the owner of the publishing rights to reproduce such extracts using the Wiley Permission Request Form. Permission grants should be submitted with the manuscript.

Submitted manuscripts should not have been previously published and should not be submitted for publication elsewhere while they are under consideration by Wiley. Submitted material will not be returned to the author unless specifically requested.

Electronic submission. The electronic copy of the final, revised manuscript must be sent to the Editor together with the paper copy. Disks should be PC or Mac formatted; write on the disk the software package used, the name of the author and the name of the journal. We are able to use most word processing packages, but prefer Word or WordPerfect, or TeX (or one of its derivatives).

Illustrations must be submitted in electronic format where possible. Save each figure as a separate file, in TIFF or EPS format preferably, and include the source file. Write on the disk the software package used to create them; we favour dedicated illustration packages over tools such as Excel or Powerpoint.

Manuscript style. The language of the journal is English. All submissions must have a title, be printed on one side of the paper, be double-line spaced and have a margin of 3cm all round. Illustrations and tables must be printed on separate sheets, and not be incorporated into the text.

- The title page must list the full title, short title and names and affiliations of all authors. Give the full address, including email, telephone and fax, of the author who is to check the proofs.
- Include the name(s) of any sponsor(s) of the research contained in the paper, along with grant number(s).
- Supply a one-paragraph summary for all articles, with bullet points of the main areas of interest. This should be a concise summary of the whole paper, not just the conclusions, and should be understandable without reference to the rest of the paper. It should contain no citation to other published work.

Practitioner papers. This section of the Journal welcomes contributions which can be more descriptive (and less analytical) of current business practice. They can be in the form of case studies, will be subject to less rigorous refereeing and need not display in-depth knowledge of previous academic work in the field. Practitioner papers should be 2000-5000 words.

Academic papers. This section of the Journal will publish traditionally styled academic articles subject to rigorous refereeing and will be expected, at a minimum, to display a sound knowledge of previous work in the area and some original research content. Academic papers can be up to 6000 words.

The Journal's Editors and Editorial Board particularly welcome submissions which present case study material, new approaches and techniques, empirical research or conceptual papers.

Reference style. References should be quoted in the text as name and year within brackets and listed at the end of the paper alphabetically. Where reference is made to more than one work by the same author published in the same year, identify each citation in the text as follows: (Collins, 1998a), (Collins, 1998b). Where three or more authors are listed in the reference list, please cite in the text as (Collins et al., 1998).

All references must be complete and accurate. Where possible the DOI for the reference should be included at the end of the reference. Online citations should include date of access. If necessary, cite unpublished or personal work in the text but do not include it in the reference list. References should be listed in the following style:

Stace D, Holtham C, Courtney N. 2004. Mapping opportunity space: options for a sustainable e-strategy. Strategic Change 13: 237–251. DOI: 10.1002/jsc.691
Ansoff HI, Declerck P, Hayes L. 1976. From Strategic Planning to Management. John Wiley: Chichester.
Morris PE. 1979. Strategies for learning and recall. In Applied Problems in Memory, Gruneberg MM, Morris PE (eds). Academic Press: London; 25–57.
The Geriatric Website. 1999. http://www.wiley.com/oap/ [1 April 1999].

Illustrations. Supply each illustration on a separate sheet, with the lead author's name and the figure number, with the top of the figure indicated, on the reverse. Supply original photographs; photocopies or previously printed material will not be used. Line artwork must be high-quality laser output (not photocopies). Tints are not acceptable; lettering must be of a reasonable size that would still be clearly legible upon reduction, and consistent within each figure and set of figures. Supply artwork at the intended size for printing.

The cost of printing colour illustrations in the journal will be charged to the author. If colour illustrations are supplied electronically in either TIFF or EPS format, they may be used in the PDF of the article at no cost to the author, even if this illustration was printed in black and white in the journal. The PDF will appear on the Wiley InterScience site.

Copyright. To enable the publisher to disseminate the author's work to the fullest extent, the author must sign a Copyright Transfer Agreement, transferring copyright in the article from the author to the publisher, and submit the original signed agreement with the article presented for publication. A copy of the agreement to be used (which may be photocopied) can be found in the first issue of each volume of the Journal of Public Affairs. Copies may also be obtained from the journal editor or publisher, or may be printed from the Wiley InterScience website.

Further information. Proofs will be sent to the author for checking. This stage is to be used only to correct errors that may have been introduced during the production process. Prompt return of the corrected proofs, preferably within two days of receipt, will minimise the risk of the paper being held over to a later issue. The publisher will supply the corresponding author of each article or review with 25 free offprints. Additional offprints and further copies of the journal may be ordered, prior to publication. There is no page charge to authors.

Journal of Public Policy & Marketing

ADDRESS FOR SUBMISSION:

Joel B. Cohen, Editor
Journal of Public Policy & Marketing
University of Florida
College of Business Administration
208 Bryan Hall
PO Box 117155
Gainesville, FL 32611-7155
USA
Phone: 352-392-2397 x1237
E-Mail: jppm@cba.ufl.edu
Web: www.cba.ufl.edu/jppm

PUBLICATION GUIDELINES:

Manuscript Length: 26-30
Copies Required: Five
Computer Submission: No
Format: N/A
Fees to Review: 0.00 US$

Manuscript Style:
    Chicago Manual of Style, 15th Edition

CIRCULATION DATA:

Reader: Academics, Government, Law
Frequency of Issue: 2 Times/Year
Sponsor/Publisher: American Marketing
    Association

REVIEW INFORMATION:

Type of Review: Blind Review
No. of External Reviewers: 3+
No. of In House Reviewers: 1
Acceptance Rate: 11-20%
Time to Review: 1 - 2 Months
Reviewers Comments: Yes
Invited Articles: 6-10%
Fees to Publish: 0.00 US$

MANUSCRIPT TOPICS:

Advertising & Promotion Management; Business Law, Public Responsibility & Ethics; Communication; Consumer Protection & Anti-trust; Direct Marketing; E-Commerce; Global Business; Marketing Regulation; Marketing Research; Marketing Theory & Applications; Non-Profit Organizations; Public Administration; Technology/Innovation

MANUSCRIPT GUIDELINES/COMMENTS:

Editorial Guidelines

Mission. *Journal of Public Policy & Marketing* (*JPP&M*) is the premier academic and professional journal that chronicles and analyzes the joint impact of marketing and governmental policies and actions on economic performance, consumer welfare, and business decisions. Written for concerned marketing scholars, policymakers, government officials, legal scholars, practicing attorneys, and executives, *JPP&M* examines the interface between marketing and public policy and the functioning and performance of the nation's economy. Articles encompass broad societal concerns that range from environmental and health-related issues to privacy and financial well-being. *JPP&M* is highly respected for its topical and insightful commentary.

Primary Reader Targets
The primary audiences for *JPP&M* are academic scholars interested in researching the issues, public policy decision makers at all levels of government, and marketing executive faced with public policy concerns.

Manuscript Guidelines
Manuscript and Disk Preparation. Send one stapled non-returnable copy and a 3.5 inch diskette formatted in either Microsoft Word or Adobe PDF to Joel B. Cohen, Editor, Journal of Public Policy & Marketing, 302 Bryan Hall, P.O. Box 117155, University of Florida, Gainesville, FL 32611-7155. Further information is available at http://www.cba.ufl.edu/jppm

Keep an extra exact copy for future reference.

Manuscripts, should be typed double-spaced using a 12 pt. font on 8 ½ x 11 inch white, non-erasable paper. Allow margins of at least one inch on all four sides. Type on one side of the paper only.

Please refer to the section "Preparing the Final Version and Editing Style Rules" when preparing the final version for publication.

What Goes Where
1. Name of author(s); title; and author(s) footnote, including present position, complete address, telephone number, fax number, e-mail address, and any acknowledgment of financial or technical assistance on the front page.
2. Title of paper and a brief abstract of no more than 50 words substantively summarizing the article on the second page. It should be informative, giving the reader a "taste" of the article.
3. The text with major headings centered on the page and subheadings flush with the left margin.
4. Technical appendices if applicable.
5. Footnotes numbered consecutively on a separate page.
6. Tables, numbered consecutively, each on a separate page. If tables appear in an appendix, they should be numbered separately and consecutively, as Table A1, A2, and so on.
7. Figures, numbered consecutively, each placed on a separate page. As with tables, if figures appear in an appendix, they should be numbered separately, as Figure A1, A2, and so on.
8. References, typed double-spaced in alphabetical order by author's last name (see Reference Style below).

Mathematical Notation
- Mathematical notation must be clear within the text.
- Equations should be centered on the page. If equations are numbered, type the number in parentheses flush with the left margin.
- If equations are too wide to fit in a single column, indicate appropriate breaks.
- Please include a list of all Greek characters or mathematical symbols used in the text, with their names written beside them.

- Please avoid using Equation Editor for simple in-line mathematical copy, symbols, and equations. Type these in Word instead. For display equations, using the Equation Editor is appropriate. In addition, please avoid stacking in-line equations. If the equation is difficult, place it as a display rather than in line and number it accordingly.

Tables

Tables should consist of at least four columns and four rows; otherwise, they should be left as in-text tabulations or their results should be integrated in the text.

- The table number and title should be typed on separate lines above the table, centered.
- Use only horizontal rules.
- Designate units (e.g., %, $) in column headings.
- Align all decimals.
- Refer to tables in text by number. Avoid using the words "above" and "below."
- If possible, combine closely related tables.
- Indicate placement of tables in text.
- Make sure the necessary measures of statistical significance are reported with the table.

Figures and Camera-Ready Artwork

- Figures should be prepared professionally on disk and as camera-ready copy.
- The figure number and title should be typed on separate lines above the figure, centered.
- Label both vertical and horizontal axes. The ordinate label should be centered above the ordinate axis; the abscissa label should be placed beneath the abscissa.
- Place all calibration tics as well as the values outside of the axis lines.
- Once a manuscript has been accepted, complex tables and all figures must be on disk and camera-ready. Table and figure headings should be typed on a separate page and attached to the appropriate camera-ready art. These titles will be set in *JPP&M's* typeface.
- Lettering should be large enough to read easily with 50% reduction. Any art not done on a computer graphics program should be professionally drafted, so that it reproduces nicely in the journal.
- Do not submit camera-ready art until your manuscript has been accepted. If the artwork is completed, submit photocopies.

Reference Citations within the Text

Citations in the text should be by the author's last name and year of publication enclosed in parentheses without punctuation; for example, (Kinsey 1960). If practical, the citation should stand by a punctuation mark. Otherwise insert it in a logical sentence break.

If the author's name is used within the sentence, there is no need to repeat the name in the citation; just use the year of publication in parentheses, as in "... The Howard Harris Program (1966)."

If a particular page, section, or equation is cited, it should be placed within the parentheses; for example, (Kinsey 1960, p. 112).

For multiple authors, the full citation should be used for up to three authors; for four or more, the first author's name followed by "et al." (no italics) should be used. If the authors' names are used within the sentence, the first author's name should be used, followed by "and colleagues."

A series of citations should be listed in alphabetical order and separated by semicolons: (Donnelly 1961; Kinsey 1960; Wensely 1981).

If a particular reference need not contain the date of the publication in order to be located readily, the reference may be given in the text only and not in the reference list. Examples of this include references to the U.S. Constitution, U.S. Code, and the Code of Federal Regulations.

Constitutional references may typically be made in the text only and should include identity of the constitution being cited if not obvious or other than the U.S. Constitution, the article or amendment number, and the section number, if any; for example, (Amendment XIV, Section 2).

Statutory references may be given in the text by statute name and citation in the U.S. Code, as in (Robinson-Patman Act, 15 U.S.C. sections 13-13b, 21a).

Regulatory references may be given parenthetically in the text, such as (FTC Credit Practices Rule, 16 C.F.R. section 444).

Reference List Style
Books and Journals
References are to be listed alphabetically, last name first, followed by publication date in parentheses. Use full first name, not just initials. The reference list should be typed double-spaced on a separate page. Do not use indents or tabs. Put two hard returns between each reference. Authors are responsible for the accuracy of their references. Check each item carefully.

Single- and multiple-author references for books:
Donnelly, James H. and William R. George (1981), Marketing of Services. Chicago: American Marketing Association.

Single- and multiple-author references for periodicals (include the author's name, publication date, article title, complete name of periodical, volume number, month of publication or issue number, and page numbers):
Petty, Ross D. (1991), "The Evolution of Comparative Advertising Law: Has the Lanham Act Gone Too Far?" Journal of Public Policy & Marketing, 10 (2), 161-81.

Single- and multiple-author references for an article in a book edited by another author(s):
Nevin, John R. and Ruth A. Smith (1981), "The Predictive Accuracy of a Retail Gravitation Model: An Empirical Evaluation," in The Changing Marketing Environment, Kenneth Bernhardt et al., eds. Chicago: American Marketing Association, 119-23.

If an author appears more than once, substitute four hyphens (this will appear as a one-inch line when typeset) for each author's name (do not use underlines):

Day, George (1981b), "The Product Life Cycle: Analysis and Applications Issues," Journal of Marketing, 45 (Fall), 60-67.

____ (1996), "Using the Past as a Guide to the Future: Reflections on the History of the Journal of Marketing," Journal of Marketing, 60 (January), 14-16.

If two or more works by the same author have the same publication date, they should be differentiated by letters after the date. The letter should also appear with the citation in the text:

Fornell, Claes and David F. Larcker (1981a), "Evaluating Structural Equation Models with Unobservable Variables and Measurement Error," Journal of Marketing Research, 18 (February), 39-50.

____ and ____ (1981b), "Structural Equation Models with Unobservable Variables and Measurement Error: Algebra and Statistics," Journal of Marketing Research, 18 (August), 382-88.

References to unpublished works, such as doctoral dissertations and working papers, should be included in the reference list. Please ensure that the department for which the paper was written is also included:

BenAkiva, Moshe (1977), "Choice Models with Simple Choice Set Generating Processes," working paper, Department of Civil Engineering, Massachusetts Institute of Technology.

Authors familiar with legal citation style should be aware that marketing reference format requires that journal article citations include the issue number or monthly date and the last page of the article as well as the first. For example:

Preston, Ivan L. (1987), "Extrinsic Evidence in Federal Trade Commission Deceptiveness Cases," Columbia Business Law Review, 1987 (3), 633-94.

Please note that because legal journals do not require citation to the issue date or number or the last page of the article, this information must be obtained before adapting legal periodical references to *JPP&M* reference list style.

Legislative, Executive, & Administrative Materials
Statutory references in which the date of enactment is important must be included in the reference list and provide name of the statute, year in parentheses, and citation to the public law or chapter number, followed by the session law citation:

WheelerLea Amendment (1938), Ch. 49, 52 Stat. 111.

Nutrition Labeling and Education Act (1990), Public Law No. 101535, 104 Stat. 2353.

Legislative reports should be treated as books:

U.S. Senate, Committee on Commerce, Science and Transportation (1980), Unfairness: Views on Unfair Acts and Practices in Violation of the Federal Trade Commission Act, Committee Print, 96th Cong., 2d sess., (April).

Newly proposed or enacted regulations may be referenced to citation to the Federal Register. Similarly, reference to material not appearing in the Code of Federal Regulation may be made to the Federal Register:

Unfair or Deceptive Advertising and Labeling of Cigarettes in Relation the Health Hazards of Smoking, Statement of Basis and Purpose (1964), 29 Fed. Reg. 8324.

Policy statements, guidelines, reports, and opinion letters should be cited to topical loose-leaf services if available:

Department of Justice and Federal Trade Commission (1994), Statement of Enforcement Policy and Analytical Principles Relating to Health Care Antitrust, 4 Trade Reg. Rep. (CCH) Paragraph 13,152 at 20,769.

Department of Justice and Federal Trade Commission (1994), Horizontal Merger Guidelines, 62 Antitrust & Trade Reg. Rep. (BNA) No. 1559 (Special Supp.).

Federal Trade Commission, Bureau of Consumer Protection (1986), Ophthalmic Practice Rules. Washington, DC: U.S. Government Printing Office.

Judicial and Administrative Decisions and Settlements
Judicial and administrative decisions should be cited in the text by case name and year followed by specific page number, if desired, within parentheses. Reference list citations should be made to the best source available for the decision being used as a reference. Subsequent resolutions of the same case on appeal also should be indicated, but lower-level decisions need not be cited unless relevant. For decisions by tribunals in which the reported citation does not indicate the identity of the tribunal, the identity should be given in parentheses with a specific date if needed to locate the decision. File numbers and parenthetical explanations also may be given:

FTC v. Sperry and Hutchinson Co. (1972), 405 U.S. 233.

Simeon Management Corp. v. FTC (1978), 579 F.2d 1137 (9th Cir.).

Avon Products, Inc. v. S.C. Johnson & Son, Inc. (1994), 1994 U.S. Dist. LEXIS 7950, 94 Civ. 3958 (AGS)(S.D.N.Y. June 15).

Thompson Medical Co., Inc. (1984), 104 F.T.C. 648, affirmed, 791 F.2d 189 (D.C.Cir 1986), cert. denied, 107 S.Ct. 1289 (1987).

US v. Delta Dental Plan of Arizona, Inc. (1994), 67 Antitrust & Trade Reg. Rep. (BNA) 277, No. CIV. 941793 PHXPGR (D.C. Ariz.)(August 30)(proposed consent decree).

References to the Bluebook
The Bluebook: A Uniform System of Citation (15th ed.) may be consulted regarding legal references for technical advice on form, abbreviations, and so on. Authors are advised that abbreviations should be used only when they are likely to be familiar to *JPP&M* readers with a non-legal background.

Readability
JPP&M manuscripts are judged not only on the depth and scope of the ideas presented and their contributions to the field, but also on their clarity and whether they can be read and understood. Readers have varied backgrounds. Hence, write in an interesting, readable manner with varied sentence structure and use as little passive voice as possible. Also, avoid using technical terms few readers are likely to understand. If you do use such terms, be sure that their meaning is clear the first time they are used.

Review Procedure

The procedure guiding the selection of articles for publication in *JPP&M* requires that no manuscript be accepted until after it has been reviewed by the editor and at least two members of the Editorial Review Board. The decision of the editor to publish the manuscript is influenced considerably by the judgments of these advisors, who are experts in their respective fields. The author's name and credentials are removed prior to forwarding a manuscript to reviewers to maximize objectivity and ensure that a manuscript is judged solely on the basis of its content and contribution to the field.

Acceptance Criteria

All manuscripts are judged on their contributions to the advancement of the science and/or practice of marketing and public policy.

All articles are expected to follow the rules for scholarly work, namely:

- Use references to previous work when developing your model or theory. Do not assume other works on the subject do not exist, thus giving yourself credit for all the ideas in your manuscript.
- When data collection is discussed, consider the relevance of the sample to the subject matter. Carefully chosen sample groups are preferable to haphazardly chosen subjects who have little knowledge of or relevance to the subject being studied.
- Give as much information as possible about the characteristics of the sample and its representativeness of the population being studied.
- Do not ignore the nonrespondents. They might have different characteristics than the respondents.
- Give consideration to the limitations of your study, model, and/or concepts and discuss them explicitly in your manuscript. Be objective.
- Use appropriate statistical procedures.
- Address the reliability and validity of any empirical findings.

Preparing the Final Version and Editing Style Rules

After a manuscript is accepted for publication, the final version must be submitted on a 3.5 inch disk. The disk copy should contain the entire manuscript, including tables, figures, footnotes, and references, as well as author bios and executive summaries. Although authors may prepare the disk copy using almost any word processing software that is Macintosh or IBM compatible, submission of the disk copy using Word (any version) for Windows is preferred. LaTex, PCTex, OzTeX, Scientific Word, or any other form of TeX is incompatible with AMA's publishing software and therefore is not accepted. Please note the following guidelines when preparing the final version:

- The AMA follows its own supplementary house style so that articles in the same issue will not have conspicuously different styles. However, the AMA uses its style in accordance with the *Chicago Manual of Style: The Essential Guide for Authors, Editors, and Publishers*, 14th ed., Chicago: University of Chicago Press, 1993. In addition, *Merriam Webster's Collegiate Dictionary*, 11th edition, is used.
- The abstract should be written in third person.

- Whenever possible, authors should use active voice, as the passive voice is wordier and often comparatively clumsy. When passive voice is used excessively, it can make expression seem vague and evasive. If an author prefers passive voice, then the article setup should be in active voice only, for example, "In the next section, we compare two theoretically based message design strategies." For a single author, however, passive voice is acceptable; use active voice sparingly except for article setup. For single authors, the royal "we" is not acceptable.
- Per *Webster's*, the AMA distinguishes between words such as enable vs. allow, whereas and although vs. while, due to vs. because of, based on vs. on the basis of, believe vs. feel, and so on. If you have specific questions about this style, please contact the journal's technical editor.
- Italics should only be used for emphasis, definition of a term or set of terms, and for certain statistical abbreviations (p). Foreign words that are familiar and/or can be found in the main part of Webster's, such as a priori, are not italicized.
- Always spell out acronyms on first use, unless universally known (e.g., IBM, AIDS, AT&T).
- At all times, an author's meaning should be upheld. During copy editing, if the author's meaning has been changed, it is the journal's policy to respect the author's desire to change back to the original wording. To assist the copy editor in ensuring the accuracy of the article, please make note of any technical terms or field-specific jargon that should not be modified during the editing process. This can be done on the second page of the document, directly following the abstract.
- Footnotes should not be used for reference purposes and should be avoided if possible. If necessary to improve the readability of the text, a few footnotes may be included. They should appear double-spaced on a separate page and be numbered consecutively throughout the text.
- Write the name of the software program used on the disk submitted.

Other Information

All published material is copyrighted by the American Marketing Association with future-use rights reserved. However, this does not limit the author's right to use his or her own material in future works.

For details on manuscript preparation not covered here, see *Chicago Manual of Style: The Essential Guide for Authors, Editors, and Publishers*, 14th ed., Chicago: University of Chicago Press, 1993. For specific questions on content or editorial policy, contact the journal's managing editor.

Journal of Public Procurement

ADDRESS FOR SUBMISSION:

Dr. Khi V. Thai, Editor-in-Chief
Journal of Public Procurement
Florida Atlantic University
111 E. Las Olas Blvd.
Fort Lauderdale, FL 33301
USA
Phone: 954-762-5650
E-Mail: thai@fau.edu
Web: www.pracademics.com

CIRCULATION DATA:

Reader: Academics, Practioners
Frequency of Issue: Quarterly
Sponsor/Publisher: Pracademics Press, Inc.

PUBLICATION GUIDELINES:

Manuscript Length: 20+
Copies Required: Electronic
Computer Submission: Yes Email
Format:
Fees to Review: 0.00 US$

Manuscript Style:
    American Psychological Association

REVIEW INFORMATION:

Type of Review: Blind Review
No. of External Reviewers: 3
No. of In House Reviewers: 0
Acceptance Rate: 20-30%
Time to Review: 2 - 3 Months
Reviewers Comments: Yes
Invited Articles: 5-10%
Fees to Publish: 0.00 US$

MANUSCRIPT TOPICS:
Management Control; Public Administration; Purchasing/Materials Management

MANUSCRIPT GUIDELINES/COMMENTS:

Editorial Policy
Published three times a year, the *Journal of Public Procurement* seeks to further the understanding of public procurement by exploring theories and practices of public procurement keyed to:

- Functional areas, including but not limited to procurement policy, procurement strategic planning and scheduling, contract formation, contract administration, evaluation, and procurement methods and techniques;
- Substantive areas such as government procurement laws and regulations, procurement economics and politics, and procurement ethics; and
- Topical issues such as e-Procurement, procurement transparency, and green procurement.

JoPP covers not only procurement at the federal, state and local government levels in the United States and Canada, but also government procurement in developed and developing nations. It will include research studies, narrative essays, exemplar cases--both good or bad-- from past experiences, commentaries, book reviews, and occasionally, reprints of informative published government reports.

Directions for Submission

1. Manuscripts can be submitted electronically to **thai@fau.edu** or in printed form (three copies) to the Editor.

2. A cover letter must accompany each submission indicating the name, e-mail address of the corresponding author.

3. Only original papers will be accepted, and copyright of published papers will be vested in the publisher. The general format of the manuscript should be as follows: title of article, names of author, abstract, and text discussion.

4. The abstract should not have more than 120 words. Whenever possible, the text discussion should be divided into such major sections as introduction, methods, results, discussion, acknowledgments, and references. Manuscripts should be submitted typed, double-spaced, on one side only. The entire typing area on the title page should be four and one-half inches wide by five and one-half inches long. The major headings should be separated from the text by two lines of space above and one line of space below. Each heading should be in capital letters, centered, and in bold. Secondary headings, if any, should be flushed with the left margin, in bold characters, and have the first letter of all main words capitalized. Leave two lines of space above and one line of space below secondary headings. All manuscripts should be left- and right-hand margin justified.

Acknowledgements of collaboration, sources of research funds, and address changes for an author should be listed on a separate section at the end of the paper after the section on References.

Explanatory footnotes should be kept to a minimum and be numbered consecutively throughout the text and aggregated in sequence under the heading notes, at the end of the text but before references.

References should be in the APA manuscript style of citation, and aggregated in the alphabetical order at the end of the manuscript under the heading, **References**.

For detailed guidelines, please visit **www.pracademics.com**.

Journal of Public Transportation

ADDRESS FOR SUBMISSION:

Gary Brosch, Editor
Journal of Public Transportation
University of South Florida
Center for Urban Transportation Research
4202 E Fowler Ave, CUT 100
Tampa, FL 33620-5375
USA
Phone: 813-974-3120
E-Mail: jpt@cutr.usf.edu
Web: www.nctr.usf.edu/jpt/journal.htm

PUBLICATION GUIDELINES:

Manuscript Length: 16-20
Copies Required: Electronic
Computer Submission: Yes Disk, Email
Format: MS Word, ASCII
Fees to Review: 0.00 US$

Manuscript Style:
  Chicago Manual of Style

CIRCULATION DATA:

Reader: Academics
Frequency of Issue: Quarterly
Sponsor/Publisher: National Center for
  Transit Research / USDOT/ Research &
  Special Programs Administration

REVIEW INFORMATION:

Type of Review: Editorial Review
No. of External Reviewers: 2
No. of In House Reviewers: 1
Acceptance Rate: 60%
Time to Review: 4 - 6 Months
Reviewers Comments: Yes
Invited Articles:
Fees to Publish: 0.00 US$

MANUSCRIPT TOPICS:

Business Law, Public Responsibility & Ethics; Marketing Theory & Applications; Operations Research/Statistics; Organizational Behavior & Theory; Production/Operations; Public Administration; Services; Technology/Innovation; Transportation/Physical Distribution

MANUSCRIPT GUIDELINES/COMMENTS:

Submission of Manuscripts

The *Journal of Public Transportation* is a quarterly, international journal containing original research and case studies associated with various forms of public transportation and related transportation and policy issues. Topics are approached from a variety of academic disciplines, including economics, engineering, planning, and others, and include policy, methodological, technological, and financial aspects. Emphasis is placed on the identification of innovative solutions to transportation problems.

All articles should be approximately 4,000 words in length (18-20 double-spaced pages). Manuscripts not submitted according to the journal's style will be returned. Submission of the manuscript implies commitment to publish in the journal. Papers previously published or under review by other journals are unacceptable. All articles are subject to peer review. Factors considered in review include validity and significance of information, substantive

668

contribution to the field of public transportation, and clarity and quality of presentation. Copyright is retained by the publisher, and, upon acceptance, contributions will be subject to editorial amendment.

All manuscripts must be submitted electronically, double-spaced in Word file format, containing only text and tables. If not created in Word, each table must be submitted separately in Excel format, and all charts and graphs must be in Excel format. All supporting illustrations and photographs must be submitted separately in an image file format, such as TIF, JPG, AI or EPS, having a minimum 300 dpi. Each chart and table must have a title and each figure must have a caption.

All manuscripts should include sections in the following order, as specified:
- Cover Page – title (12 words or less) and complete contact information for all authors
- First Page of manuscript – title and abstract (up to 150 words)
- Main Body – organized under section headings
- References – Chicago Manual of Style, author-date format
- Biographical Sketch – of each author

Submit manuscripts to:
Lisa Maitland, Assistant to the Editor
Center for Urban Transportation Research
University of South Florida
Phone: 813-974-6423
Fax: 813-974-5168
Email: **jpt@cutr.usf.edu**
Web: **www.nctr.usf.edu/jpt/journal.htm**

Journal of Quality Assurance in Hospitality & Tourism

ADDRESS FOR SUBMISSION:

Hailin Qu, Editor
Journal of Quality Assurance in Hospitality
& Tourism
Oklahoma State University
School of Hotel and Restaurant
Administration
Stillwater, OK 74078
USA
Phone: 405-744-6711
E-Mail: h.qu@okstate.edu
Web: www.haworthpress.com

PUBLICATION GUIDELINES:

Manuscript Length: 21-25
Copies Required: Three
Computer Submission: Yes Email
Format: MS Word for Windows
Fees to Review: 0.00 US$

Manuscript Style:
American Psychological Association

CIRCULATION DATA:

Reader: Academics, Business Persons,
Graduate Students
Frequency of Issue: Quarterly
Sponsor/Publisher: Haworth Press, Inc

REVIEW INFORMATION:

Type of Review: Blind Review
No. of External Reviewers: 2
No. of In House Reviewers: 0
Acceptance Rate: 60%
Time to Review: 2 - 3 Months
Reviewers Comments: Yes
Invited Articles: 0-5%
Fees to Publish: 0.00 US$

MANUSCRIPT TOPICS:

Advertising & Promotion Management; Direct Marketing; E-Commerce; Global Business; Labor Relations & Human Resource Mgt.; Marketing Research; Marketing Theory & Applications; Operations Research/Statistics; Organizational Development; Production/Operations; Sales/Selling; Services; Small Business Entrepreneurship; Strategic Management Policy; Tourism, Hospitality & Leisure

MANUSCRIPT GUIDELINES/COMMENTS:

1. **Manuscripts**. Manuscripts should be submitted in triplicate to the Editor:
   Hailin Qu, PhD
   Professor and William E. Davis Distinguished Chair
   School of Hotel and Restaurant Administration
   Oklahoma State University
   Stillwater, OK 74078; USA
   Phone: (405) 744-6711; Fax: (405) 744-6299
   E-mail: **h.qu@okstate.edu**

Electronic submission is encouraged and a manuscript can be submitted as an email attachment file to the editor.

All editorial inquiries should be directed to the Editor.

2. **Original Articles Only.** Submission of a manuscript to this journal represents a certification on the part of the author(s) that it is an original work, and that neither this manuscript nor a version of it has been published elsewhere nor it is being considered for publication elsewhere.

3. **Copyright.** Copyright ownership of your manuscript must be transferred officially to The Haworth Press, Inc. before we can begin the peer-review process. The Editor's letter acknowledging receipt of the manuscript will be accompanied by a form fully explaining this. All authors must sign the form and return the original to the Editor as soon as possible. Failure to return the copyright form in a timely fashion will result in delay in review and subsequent publication. [SEE "MANUSCRIPT SUBMISSION FORM"]

4. **Manuscript Length.** The journal publishes two main classes of articles: full-length articles of approximately 5,000 words (15-25 pages, double-spaced), and shorter opinion/reports/viewpoint pieces of about 1,500 words (5-10 pages, double-spaced). Longer manuscripts will be considered at the discretion of the Editor who may recommend publication as a monograph edition of the journal or division into sections for publication in successive journal issues.

5. **Manuscript Style.** References, citations, and general style of manuscripts for this journal should follow the APA style (as outlined in the latest edition of the *Publication Manual of the American Psychological Association*). References should be double spaced and placed in alphabetical order. The use of footnotes within the text is discouraged. Words should be underlined only when it is intended that they be typeset in italics. If an author wishes to submit a paper that had been already prepared in another style, he or she may do so. However, if the paper is accepted (with or without reviewer's alterations), the author is fully responsible for retyping the manuscript in the correct style as indicated above. Neither the Editor nor the Publisher is responsible for re-preparing manuscript copy to adhere to the journal's style.

6. **Digital Object Identifier (Doi) Linking.** The Haworth Press is participating in reference linking for journal articles. (For more information on reference linking initiatives, please consult the Cross Ref Web site at www.crossref.org.) When citing a journal article include the article's Digital Object Identifier (DOI), when available, as the last item in the reference. A Digital Object Identifier is a persistent, authoritative, and unique identifier that a publisher assigns to each article. Because of its persistence, DOIs will enable The Haworth Press and other publishers to link to the article referenced, and the link will not break overtime. This will be great resource in scholarly research.

An example of a reference to a journal article which includes a DOI:
Vizine-Goetz, Diane (2002). Classification Schemes for Internet Resources Revisited. *Journal of Internet Cataloging* 5(4): 5:18. doi: 10.1300/J14lv05n04_02

7. **Manuscript Preparation.** Margins: leave at least a one-inch margin on all four sides. Paper: use clean, white, 8½" x 11" bond paper. Number of copies: 3 (the original plus two photocopies). Cover page: Important-staple a cover page to the manuscript, indicating only the article title (this is used for anonymous refereeing) and the ABSTRACT. Second "title page": enclose a regular title page but do not staple it to the manuscript. Include the title again, plus:

- full authorship credits in order of seniority;
- an ABSTRACT of about 100 words;
- 5 or 6 keywords that identify article content;
- an introductory footnote with authors' academic degrees, professional titles, affiliations, mailing and e-mall addresses, and any desired acknowledgment of research support or other credit;
- a header or footer on each page with abbreviated title and pg number of total (e.g., pg 2 of 7).

8. **Return Envelopes.** When submitting manuscripts in print format, it is required that you also include:

- a regular self-addressed envelope. This is for the Editor to send you an "acknowledgment of receipt" letter.

9. **Spelling, Grammar, Punctuation, and Inconsistencies.** You are responsible for preparing manuscript copy which is clearly written in acceptable, scholarly English, and which contains no errors of spelling, grammar, or punctuation. Neither the Editor nor the Publisher is responsible for correcting errors of spelling and grammar. The manuscript, after acceptance by the Editor, must be immediately ready for typesetting as it is finally submitted by the author(s). The *APA Publication Manual* gives explicit instructions on punctuation, spelling, abbreviations, statistical formulae, etc. Check your paper for the following common errors:

- dangling modifiers
- misplaced modifiers
- unclear antecedents
- incorrect or inconsistent abbreviations

Also, check the accuracy of all arithmetic calculations, statistics, numerical data, text citations, and references. All cited references must be given in full, including the volume, issues and page numbers. INCONSISTENCIES MUST BE AVOIDED. Be sure you are consistent in your use of abbreviations, terminology, and in citing references, from one part of your paper to another.

10. **Preparation of Tables, Figures, and Illustrations.** Any material that is not textual is considered artwork. This includes tables, figures, diagrams, charts, graphs, illustrations, appendices, screen captures, and photos. Tables and figures (including legend, notes, and source) should be no larger than 4½ x 6½ inches. Type style should be Helvetica (or Helvetica Narrow if necessary) and no smaller than 8 point. We request that computer-generated figures be in black and white and/or shades of gray (preferably no color, for it does not reproduce well). Camera-ready art must contain no grammatical, typographical, or format errors and must reproduce sharply and clearly in the dimensions of the final printed page (4½ x 6½

inches). Photos and screen captures must be on a disk as a TIFF file, or other graphic File format such as JPEG or BMP. For rapid publication we must receive black-and-white glossy or matte positives (white background with black images and/or wording) in addition to files on disk. Tables should be created in the text document file using the software's Table feature.

11. Submitting Art. Both a printed hard copy and a disk copy of the art must be provided. We request that each piece of art be sent in its own file, on a disk separate from the disk containing the manuscript text file(s), and be clearly labeled. We reserve the right to (if necessary) request new art, alter art, or if all else has failed in achieving art that is presentable, delete art. If submitted art cannot be used, the Publisher reserves the right to redo the art and to charge the author a fee of $55.00 per hour for this service. The Haworth Press, Inc. is not responsible for errors incurred in the preparation of new artwork. Camera-ready artwork must be prepared on separate sheets of paper. On the back of these items, write your article title and the journal title lightly in soft-lead pencil (please do not write on the face of art). In the text file, skip extra lines and indicate where these figures are to be placed. Photos are considered part of the acceptable manuscript and remain with the Publisher for use in additional printings.

12. Examples of Format
Examples of References to Periodicals:
- Journal Article: One Author
  Zins, Andreas H. (1999). Destination portfolios using a European vacation style typology. *Journal of Travel & Tourism Marketing*, 8(1), 1-23.
- Journal Article: Multiple Authors
  Kaynak, E. & Mitchell, L. A. (1981). Analysis of marketing strategies used in diverse cultures. *Journal of Advertising Research*, (June), 2 1(3), 25-32.
- Magazine Article
  Tinnin, D. B. (1981, Novensber 16). The heady success of Holland's Heineken. *Fortune*, pp. 158-164.
- Newspaper Article: No Author
  The opportunity of world brands. (1984, June 3). *The New York Times*, p.6.
- Monograph
  Franko, L. G. (1979). A survey of the impact of manufactured exports from industrializing countries in Asia and Latin America. *Changing International Realities [Monograph] No. 6.*

Examples of References to Books:
- References to an Entire Book
  Holloway, J. C. & Plant, R. V. (1993). *Marketing for Tourism* (2nd ed.). London: Pitman Publishing.
- Book with a Corporate Author
  Committee for Economic Development. (1981). *Transitional corporations and developing countries*. New York: Author.
- Edited: Book
  Chon, K. 5. (1991). *The Management of Hotel Sales and Marketing*. Washington, D.C.: Hotel Sales and Marketing Association International Foundation.

- Book with No Author or Editor
  Marketing opportunities in Japan. (1978). London: Deotsu.
- Article or Chapter in an Edited Book
  Shostack, G. L. (1986). *Breaking free from product marketing.* In C. W. L. Hart & D. A. Tray (Eds.), Strategic Hotel-Motel Marketing (pp. 42-50). East Lansing, MI: Educational Institute of the AHMA.

Proceedings of Meetings and Symposia:
- Published Proceedings, Published Contributions to a Symposium
  Hoistius, K. (1985). Organizational buying of airline services. In S. Shaw, L. Sparks & E. Kaynak (Eds.). *Marketing in the 1990's & Beyond* (pp. 262-272). Second World Marketing Congress, held at University of Stirling. Scotland. (August 28-31)
- Unpublished Paper Presented at a Meeting
  Yucelt, U. (1987). *Tourism marketing planning in developing economies.* Paper presented at the annual meeting of the Academy of Marketing Science, Bal Harbour, Florida.

Doctoral Dissertations:
- Published Doctoral Dissertation
  Czinkota, M. F. (1980). An analysis of export development strategies in selected U.S. industries. *Dissertation Abstracts International, Vol* (issue). (University Microfilms No. 80-1 5, 865).
- For references to unpublished manuscripts, publications of limited circulation, reviews and interviews, and non-print media, please refer to the latest edition of the *Publication Manual of the American Psychological Association.*

13. **Alterations Required by Referees and Reviewers**. A paper may be accepted by the Editor contingent upon changes that are mandated by anonymous specialist referees and members of the Editorial Board. If the Editor returns your manuscript for revisions, you are responsible far retyping any sections of the paper to incorporate these revisions (if applicable, revisions should also be put on disk).

14. **Typesetting**. You will not receive galley proofs of your article. Editorial revisions, if any, must therefore be made while your article is still in manuscript. The final version of the manuscript will be the version you see published. Typesetting errors will be corrected by the production staff of The Haworth Press, Inc. Authors are expected to submit manuscripts, disks, and art that are free from error.

15. **Electronic Media**. Haworth's in-house typesetting unit is able to utilize your final manuscript material as prepared an most personal computers and word processors. This will minimize typographical errors and decrease overall production time. Please send the first draft and final draft copies of your manuscript to the journal Editor in print format for his final review and approval. After approval of your final manuscript, please submit the final approved version both on printed format ("hard copy") and floppy diskette. On the outside of the diskette package write: 1. the brand name of your computer or word processor, 2. the word processing program and version that you used, 3. the title of your article, and 4. the file name.

Note. Disk and hard copy must agree. In case of discrepancies, it is The Haworth Press' policy to follow hard copy. Authors are advised that no revisions of the manuscript can be made after acceptance by the Editor for publication. The benefits of this procedure are many with speed and accuracy being the most obvious. We look forward to working with your electronic submission which will allow us to serve you more efficiently.

16. **Reprints**. The senior author will receive two copies of the journal issue as well as complimentary reprints several weeks after the issue has been published. The junior author will receive two copies of the journal issue. An order form will be sent to the corresponding author for the purchase of additional reprints at this time. (Approximately 4-6 weeks is necessary for the preparation of reprints.) Please do not query the journal's Editor about reprints. All such questions should be sent directly to The Haworth Press, Inc., Print Journal Production Department, 37 West Broad Street. West Hazleton, PA 18202 USA. To order additional reprints, please contact Document Delivery Service, The Haworth Press, Inc., 10 Alice Street. Binghamton, NY 13904-1580 USA, 1-800-HAWORTH or FAX 1-607-722-6362.

17. **Copyright and Permissions**. For permission to reprint articles that have appeared in Haworth journals, please contact: Copyright & Permissions Department, The Haworth Press, Inc., 10 Alice Street, Binghamton, NY 13904-1580.

18. **Library Photocopying. Attention Librarians**: If your library subscribes to this journal, Haworth® waives all photocopying fees or any royalty payments for multiple internal library use. By "internal library use" we mean:

- photocopying multiple copies of any article for your reserve room or reference area
- photocopying of articles for routing to either students or faculty members
- multiple photocopying by students for coursework
- multiple photocopying by faculty members for passing out to students at no charge or for their own files
- other traditional internal library multiple use of journal articles

Journal of Radio Studies

ADDRESS FOR SUBMISSION:

Douglas Ferguson, Editor
Journal of Radio Studies
College of Charleston
Department of Communication
5 College Way
Charleston, SC 29401
USA
Phone: 843-953-7854
E-Mail: fergusond@cofc.edu
Web: www.beaweb.org/publications

PUBLICATION GUIDELINES:

Manuscript Length: 21-25
Copies Required: Four
Computer Submission: Yes Email
Format: MS Word
Fees to Review: 0.00 US$

Manuscript Style:
American Psychological Association

CIRCULATION DATA:

Reader: Academics
Frequency of Issue: Bi-Monthly
Sponsor/Publisher: Broadcast Education
Association with Lawrence Erlbaum
Associates, Inc.

REVIEW INFORMATION:

Type of Review: Blind Review
No. of External Reviewers: 3
No. of In House Reviewers: 0
Acceptance Rate: 21-30%
Time to Review: 1 - 2 Months
Reviewers Comments: Yes
Invited Articles: 6-10%
Fees to Publish: 0.00 US$

MANUSCRIPT TOPICS:
Communication; Radio

MANUSCRIPT GUIDELINES/COMMENTS:

Submitted articles undergo a blind review. Manuscripts should be sent to the Editor in four high-quality photocopies, and should conform to the stylistic guidelines of the APA. Manuscripts may also be sent electronically. Mailing address and brief biographical summaries of authors should be provided on a separate page. Another page should include an abstract of no more than 100 words. Manuscripts should not exceed 6500 words (about 25 pages). Articles appearing in *JRS* are evaluated according to their conceptualization, importance to radio studies and mass communication theory, contribution to the mass media literature, interest to *JRS* readers, soundness of research and methodological procedures, and the clarity of presentation.

Journal of Relationship Marketing

ADDRESS FOR SUBMISSION:

David Bejou, Editor
Journal of Relationship Marketing
Virginia State University
School of Business
PO Box 9398
Petersburg, VA 23806-9388
USA
Phone: 804-524-5166
E-Mail: dbejou@vsu.edu
Web: www.haworthpress.com

PUBLICATION GUIDELINES:

Manuscript Length: 16-20
Copies Required: Two
Computer Submission: Yes Email
Format: MS Word
Fees to Review: 0.00 US$

Manuscript Style:
 American Psychological Association

CIRCULATION DATA:

Reader: Academics, Business Persons
Frequency of Issue: Quarterly
Sponsor/Publisher: Haworth Press, Inc. /
 Bill Cohen

REVIEW INFORMATION:

Type of Review: Blind Review
No. of External Reviewers: 3
No. of In House Reviewers: 1
Acceptance Rate: 11-20%
Time to Review: 1 Month or Less
Reviewers Comments: Yes
Invited Articles: 0-5%
Fees to Publish: 0.00 US$

MANUSCRIPT TOPICS:
Business Information Systems (MIS); E-Commerce; Marketing Research; Marketing Theory & Applications; Organizational Behavior & Theory; Relationship Marketing; Sales/Selling; Services; Strategic Management Policy

MANUSCRIPT GUIDELINES/COMMENTS:

About the Journal
The *Journal of Relationship Marketing* is a quarterly journal that publishes peer-reviewed (double-blind) conceptual and empirical papers of original works that make serious contributions to the understanding and advancement of relationship marketing theory, research, and practice. This academic journal is interdisciplinary and international in nature.

Topics of interest (not limited to):
• Evolution and life cycle of RM
• Theoretical and methodological issues in RM
• Types of RM, networks and strategic alliances
• Internal and external customer relationship management strategies
• Psychological underpinning of RM

- Ethics, communication, quality, trust, commitment, satisfaction, loyalty, and dissolution in RM
- Applications of RM in different disciplines and industries
- International perspectives in RM
- RM strategies in Services economy, Higher education, and e-commerce
- RM, technology, and the web
- Profitability and RM
- Case studies and best practices in RM

If you are interested in becoming an ad hoc reviewer for *JRM*, please send or email a brief statement indicating your areas of expertise and interest along with a copy of your CV. *JRM* will be accepting submissions effective immediately. For information on submission guidelines please contact:

David Bejou, Founding Editor
Dean of School of Business
Virginia State University
P.O. Box 9398
Petersburg, Virginia 23806
USA
804-524-5166
Email: **dbejou@vsu.edu**

Submission Checklist
Your package must be mailed using FedEx, UPS, or other similar carriers.
1. Signed cover letter
2. APA manuscript style
3. Abstract of about 100 words
4. 3-10 keywords at the end of abstract
5. Author information about 80 words (on a separate sheet)
6. 2 copies of paper (1 original and 1 copy), double-spaced and printed on one side only (8½ X 11) White paper. Average length of an article is about 15-20 pages (This does not apply to special issues and agreements between the editor and authors).
7. Completed manuscript submission form with original signatures by all authors. (This form must be completed and submitted before the review process begins).
8. Completed Art/Photo Release Form for all tables, figures, charts, graphs, photos, illustrations, etc. (if applicable).
9. Complete mailing address, telephone numbers, fax, and email for all authors.
10. Two computer disk copies for each article. Label Disk A & B (backup copy). On the outside of the diskette package please write:
    A. the brand name of your computer or word processor
    B. the word-processing program that you used
    C. the title of your article, your name, and
    D. file name

Please mail the completed package to David Bejou at the address above.

Journal of Research in Marketing and Entrepreneurship

ADDRESS FOR SUBMISSION:

Robert G. Schwartz, Executive Editor
Journal of Research in Marketing and
    Entrepreneurship
Eastern Washington University
College of Business and
    Public Administration
668 N. Riverpoint Blvd.
Spokane, WA 99203
USA
Phone: 509-358-2254
E-Mail: rschwartz@ewu.edu
Web: www.ewu.edu/jrme

PUBLICATION GUIDELINES:

Manuscript Length: 21-25
Copies Required: One
Computer Submission: Yes Disk, Email
Format: MS Word
Fees to Review: 0.00 US$

Manuscript Style:
    American Psychological Association

CIRCULATION DATA:

Reader: Academics, Business Persons
Frequency of Issue: 1-2 Times/Year
Sponsor/Publisher: UK Academy of
    Marketing, UIC Special Interest
    Group/Entrepreneurial & Small Bus.
    Marketing/EWU

REVIEW INFORMATION:

Type of Review: Blind Review
No. of External Reviewers: 40
No. of In House Reviewers: 3+
Acceptance Rate: 11-20%
Time to Review: 1 - 2 Months
Reviewers Comments: Yes
Invited Articles: 21-30%
Fees to Publish: 0.00 US$

MANUSCRIPT TOPICS:
Business Education; E-Commerce; Intrapreneurship; Marketing Research; Marketing Theory & Applications; Organizational Behavior & Theory; Small Business Entrepreneurship; Strategic Management Policy; Technology/Innovation

MANUSCRIPT GUIDELINES/COMMENTS:

About the Journal
The objective of this *Journal* is to encourage and disseminate work that is truly at the marketing entrepreneurship Interface. The Interface historically is rooted in the study of SME behavior, however in line with its development - work covering other organizational forms and ownership is encouraged. We have no wish to force on authors a singular view of what constitutes the Interface but articles submitted must defend a coherent and robust definition of what their author(s) believe to constitute the Interface. One of the tenets of the Interface is that we need to understand better the relationship between marketing and entrepreneurship and its practice in organizations, and for this to inform our work as teachers, researchers and consultants. Therefore authors must draw out the practical lessons from their work. The

Editorial Board will ensure the coherence of the *Journal* theme by not selecting articles that are solely about entrepreneurship or solely about, say, the SME.

Shaw and Carson (1995) argue that for the Interface to be a paradigm it needs to address new realities, raise and answer new questions, embrace new themes and legitimize new research methods. Thus:

- Work that does this will be particularly welcomed.
- Case study and qualitative methodology will be particularly valued.
- Work that transfers best practice into the arenas of teaching (including teaching cases) and SME performance will be especially welcomed.
- An acceptance of valid research methodologies from traditional positivist to post modernist.

While not wishing to predispose prospective authors to a particular view of the Interface, we now turn to some more specific guidance. One might consider that the Interface is concerned with making good the deficit of well perceived methodological work on marketing and the smaller enterprise, particularly the entrepreneurial enterprise.

One might consider the following notions about the Interface:

- **A particular organizational form**: the particular application of marketing to the SME, or the micro business. However, studies concerned with intrapreneurship, whole nations or the public sector would be of interest to the Editors.
- **Putting entrepreneurship into marketing**: marketing & entrepreneurship are not necessarily one and the same, so what constitutes the art and practice of entrepreneurial marketing? Putting marketing into entrepreneurship - how do successful entrepreneurs market their product and services? "Good marketing is inherently entrepreneurial. It is coping with uncertainty, assuming calculated risks, being proactive and offering attractive innovations relative to competitors ... and good entrepreneurship is inherently marketing orientated. A customer focus by everyone in the enterprise is a way of life. And the implementation of marketing strategies that generate customer satisfaction is essential to survival. "(Hills)
- **Relevant competencies**: Authors such as Hills and Carson would argue that at the heart of both marketing and entrepreneurship are common competencies. Although one can then proceed to distinguish entrepreneurial from non-entrepreneurial competencies outside of that core.
- **Similar and dissimilar characteristics and behavior**: "There are similarities and dissimilarities between entrepreneurial decision making and formal marketing planning and management competencies and contact networks. Entrepreneurial decisions are inherently informal, haphazard, creative, opportunistic and reactive whereas marketing decisions are formal, sequential, systems orientated, disciplined and structured. On the other hand there are similarities in the construction and employment of personal contact networks between entrepreneurs and marketing managers. Equally some of the skills required by entrepreneurs are those required by the competent marketing manager, for example, analytical, judgmental and positive thinking, innovation and creativity." Carson, (1993)

In addition to the above the Interface seeks also to understand many issues that are of general concern to SME researchers, for example, we are comfortable with, and keen to promote debate on views such as:

- Addressing appropriate competencies for the entrepreneur
- The role of entrepreneurship (and as appropriate intrapreneurship) in organizational development
- Organizational life cycles; firm growth stages and the distinguishing, and under-standing, of critical episodes
- External help, support and personal contact networks
- Relationships between SMEs and larger firms that will inform the debate about how SMEs can deal successfully with larger firms and how they in turn can manage their relationships with SMEs.
- Strategic and management issues related to marketing as tactics, management or culture.
- Cultural & sociological perspectives on the entrepreneur
- Cross cultural studies & work on developing economies
- Opportunity recognition
- Appropriate research methodology

In considering the above list we would appreciate authors recognizing as Hills (1993) that small business is simply the 'enterprise size variable' and that to understand SMEs and entrepreneurship we must consider those constraints (or opportunities) that are unique to the SME itself. Papers about larger concerns should pay due regard to those factors have made them grow and/or what is the actual entrepreneurial context that sets them apart. If the paper is dealing with other organizational forms, such as the public sector, then what is the entrepreneurial behavior that merits reporting and discussing and/or in what sense is the marketing function entrepreneurial?

Call for Papers

We are seeking high quality papers for the *Journal of Research in Marketing and Entrepreneurship*. Submitted papers will be subject to double blind review to ensure rigour and fairness in the review process. For a number of years, the journal has been closely associated with the Academy of Marketing special interest group in Entrepreneurial and Small Business Marketing and the group of researchers associated with the University of Illinois at Chicago's Research at the Marketing/Entrepreneurship interface. The journal seeks contributions from around the world which contribute to knowledge generation in relation to entrepreneurial and small business marketing. Although many papers may focus on the small and medium sized enterprise, papers which consider relevant issues in the larger firm are also welcome.

The relationship between Marketing and Entrepreneurship has had, to date, an exciting, innovative, thought provoking existence. Although research in the area is still relatively young, critical thinking has progressed by leaps and bounds. In order to ensure that this innovative research continues to stimulate both existing researchers in the area, as well as attracting those new to the area, the journal welcomes contributions which adopt tried and tested methodologies but also approaches new to marketing and entrepreneurship which are capable of building a critical knowledge base.

681

Although there is no tightly defined limit to contribution themes, the following are deemed central to entrepreneurial marketing. Previous papers have focused on networking, word of mouth marketing, creativity, marketing/entrepreneurship orientation, SME marketing and entrepreneurship, corporate entrepreneurship and educational issues. Any contribution which endeavours to stimulate thinking and ultimately strives to build on existing entrepreneurial marketing theories and concepts is encouraged.

The hard work of the founding editors, Professor David Carson and Professor Gerry Hills and the editors to date John Day and Paul Reynolds should be gratefully acknowledged. The journal now has a new Executive Editor, Robert. G. Schwartz, Eastern Washington University Foundation Chairholder and Distinguished Professor of Entrepreneurship. Professor Schwartz has been a frequent and valuable participant in the various symposia associated with the journal on both sides of the Atlantic Ocean and beyond. The journal is also capably served by its new Senior Editor, Professor Ian Fillis of the University of Stirling in Scotland.

From time to time, the journal will focus on specific themes. Although we welcome papers from the broad field of marketing and entrepreneurship, we are currently seeking papers and cases for 2005. Of special interest are:
- Cases related to entrepreneurial firms (8-10 single spaced pages preferred)
- Opportunity recognition
- Strategy and performance relationships in entrepreneurial firms
- Methodologies for analyzing entrepreneurial firms

Of particular importance are single and multi-industry studies with data not being agglomerated across all firm types. Point in time studies over periods of time are also of importance.

To sum up, the journal is truly international in both its readership and in the published papers. We welcome your interest in the journal and look forward to receiving your submissions. If you have any questions regarding the journal please contact executive editor Robert Schwartz at (509) 358-2254 or **rschwartz@mail.ewu.edu**

Author and Journal Relationship
This journal seeks unpublished manuscripts that are not currently under consideration by another publication. It is a condition of publication that the author(s) formally state that the work does not infringe any existing copyright and that they will indemnify the *Journal* and the publishers against any breach of that warranty. On publication, the copyright of the work passes to the *Journal*. Our understanding is that accepted papers will not have been, nor will be published elsewhere other than copy written proceedings.

Following assignment of the copyright authors will be provided free of charge with either an electronic (disk) offprint of their article or a limited number of hard copy offprints. The choice of media being with the Editor. The assignment of copyright will allow the Editor to properly manage the use of the papers and the journal issues and is in no way intended to diminish Authors' normal and reasonable rights. No restriction is sought over Authors' academic freedom to use arguments and data in other works.

All prospective manuscripts will be acknowledged within a short time after being received and the *Journal* aims to manage the review process in a timely, efficient and effective manner. The Editor will review initially the papers for general suitability, and if judged suitable will process them for blind double review. Authors should not in their writing or citation style seek to identify themselves to the reviewers through unnecessarily referencing their own prior work. The Editor will then on the recommendations of the reviewers decide whether the work should be accepted as it is, have revisions requested or be rejected. Where revisions are asked for it would be appreciated if authors would add a separate commentary demonstrating how they believe that they have addressed substantive review points.

Format and Style
Clearly putting your manuscript into print is a collaborative and iterative effort but it would help us both, and speed up the time to publication, if, manuscripts are as close as they can be to being ready for publication from the very start of the process. The following are thus some required basic manuscript features and styles.

Footnotes
Authors are not to use footnotes.

Tables, Figures etc.
Tables, Figures, Charts should have a title and be numbered consecutively using Arabic numerals. Please insert at the end of the manuscript, each on a separate sheet. Our preferred word processing package is Microsoft Word and authors should be using the 'Table' command in Word. Tables, figures, charts, and graphs should have the same font and size as the body (Times New Roman, 12pt.). The source and table notes should be the same font but 10 pt.

Table layout should be:
* Exhibit X: Title
* (space)
* headings
* data
* (space)
* source:
* table notes:

Photographs, Illustrations and Complex Charts
The production process will be to set the journal electronically and then to produce the paper copy, hence, we would prefer any such material in electronic format. If that is not possible then camera-ready format that will scan is acceptable.

Would authors please ensure that the maximum width of all exhibits is 6 inches.

Headings
Headings should be at two levels - main in UPPERCASE, bold and center justified and Second Level in upper and lower case, bold, and right justified. If you wish to emphasize words please do so sparingly and use italics not bold. There should be two spaces above the main heading and one space between the heading and the text. Second level headings should have one space above it and one space between it and the text.

Order of Work
1. **Title Page**. Title, Author Name(s), Affiliation, Mailing Address, Telephone, Fax, e-mail, if multiple authors, the contact author.
2. **Second Page**. Title and then Abstract of 100-150 words - the abstract should cover the article and findings and allow a reader to make an informed judgment about whether they would wish to read the whole article. Up to four significant keywords for abstracting and indexing purposes.
3. **Third Page**. (onwards) Text single-spaced, 1" margins, 12pt Times New Roman for the main text. Left and right justify. Single space between each paragraph. Early on in the paper - a clear statement as to why the author(s) perceive this as an 'Interface' paper and a clear statement of methodology, dataset and theoretical underpinning as appropriate. Prior to your conclusions - a statement drawing out practical implications of the work - these may be any, or all of, theoretical, methodological, practical or practitioner as appropriate.
4. **Final Page**. Conclusions and on a new page References. Biographical notes on the author(s) would be appreciated, say, about 100 words.

For questions on formatting please contact Courtney Jensen at **cea@mail.ewu.edu**

Referencing
Please use the APA style.

In the text the conventional placement e.g. Jerome (1999) .... (Jerome, 1999) .... (Jerome & Lewis, 1999) ... (Jerome, Davey, & Peters, 1999) ... (Jerome et al., 1999). Electronic Internet references should be as detailed as possible in order to allow the reader to access that particular site and page(s).

References at end in alphabetical order following the style below:
Journals
Surname, Initial/s. (Year). Title. *Journal, Volume*, pages.

Sivakumar, K. (1996). Trade-off Between Frequency and Depth of Price Promotions: Implications for High- and Low-priced Brands. *Journal of Marketing Theory and Practice, Winter*, 4, 1-8.

For multiple authors list all by surnames followed by initial/s.
Books
Surname, Initial/s. (Year), *Title*, edition, Place of Publication: Publisher.

Casson, M. (1979), *Alternatives to Multinational Enterprise*, London: Macmillan.

Chapter or paper in edited book or proceedings:
Surname, Initial/s. (Year). Title of chapter. In editor/s (Eds.), *Title of book* (pages of chapter). Place of Publication: Publisher.

Doyle, P. (1990). Managing the Marketing Mix. In Baker, M. J., (2), *The Marketing Book* (pp. 227-267).London: William Heinemann Ltd., 227-267.

When you list the pages of the chapter in parentheses after the book title use "pp." before the number. This abbreviation, however, does not appear before the page numbers in periodical references.

Technical Details
We will be publishing using Microsoft Word (and associated packages) and using Adobe Acrobat for the actual journal files. Hence our preference has to be for manuscripts initially in Word format. Please let us have a 3.5" disk or 100mb Zip disk clearly labeled with author, title, file names, operating system and word processing system used, and information on graphics files if appropriate. The disk should be accompanied by three copies of the article, double-spaced, single sided with approximately 1" margins all around. Typeface should be Times New Roman 12pt. Sensible and practical adjustments being made for tables, charts etc. Please left and right justify. Single space between words except between sentences which should be two spaces.

Word length should be between 3-6000. All submissions should be emailed to **rschwartz@ mail.ewu.edu**

Final Submission and Publication
Upon acceptance and final revision, the article should be submitted as detailed above with one paper copy of the article. You are responsible for ensuring that the hard-copy and the disk versions are identical. The Editor will consider this to be the definitive version and you are responsible for ensuring that it is without spelling, grammatical, typing errors and is complete in all respects.

Disclaimers
Unless stated to the contrary opinions and conclusions stated in the journal are those of their Authors and are not those of the Publisher, the Editor (s), the Editorial Board and any Co-sponsors of this Journal. The information in this *Journal* is believed to be correct and offered in good faith but it is not intended as a substitute for appropriate detailed individual advice and no responsibility is taken for the outcomes of readers acting, or not acting upon, the information and ideas in this *Journal*. Nor should any advertisement or publicity about events and opportunities be considered an endorsement by the Publisher, Editor(s), the Editorial Board and any Co-sponsors of this *Journal*.

Journal of Retailing

ADDRESS FOR SUBMISSION:

Michael Levy & Dhruv Grewal, Co-Editors
Journal of Retailing
Babson College
Malloy Hall
231 Forest Street
Babson Park, MA 02457-0310
USA
Phone: 781-239-4381
E-Mail: jr@babson.edu
Web: www.babson.edu/jr

CIRCULATION DATA:

Reader: Academics, Business Persons
Frequency of Issue: Quarterly
Sponsor/Publisher: Stern School of
  Business, New York University / Elsevier
  Inc.

PUBLICATION GUIDELINES:

Manuscript Length: 20-50 Maximum
Copies Required: Electronic Only
Computer Submission: Yes Required
Format: See Guidelines
Fees to Review: 0.00 US$

Manuscript Style:
  Chicago Manual of Style

REVIEW INFORMATION:

Type of Review: Blind Review
No. of External Reviewers: 2-3
No. of In House Reviewers: 1
Acceptance Rate: 10-15%
Time to Review: 2 Months
Reviewers Comments: Yes
Invited Articles: 0-5%
Fees to Publish: 0.00 US$

MANUSCRIPT TOPICS:

Advertising & Promotion Management; Business Information Systems (MIS); Business Law, Public Responsibility & Ethics; E-Commerce; Global Business; Marketing Research; Operations Research/Statistics; Organizational Behavior & Theory; Purchasing/Materials Management; Sales/Selling; Services; Small Business Entrepreneurship; Strategic Management Policy; Technology/Innovation; Transportation/Physical Distribution

MANUSCRIPT GUIDELINES/COMMENTS:

Topics Include. Consumer Behavior; Location Analysis; Logistics; Marketing Channels; Marketing Mix; Merchandise Management; Real Estate; Relationship Management; Retail Strategy; Retailing; Store Atmospheric Issues; Supply Chain Management

Unlike other general marketing journals such as *Journal of Marketing* and *Journal of the Academy of Marketing Science*, *JR* has traditionally been bound by the confines of its name, both because of its explicit editorial policy set by previous editors and by the perception of its contributors and readers. During our tenure as Editors, we wish to continue the tradition of publishing articles that appeal to academics and practitioners with an interest in retailing and related topics. To clearly delineate *JR*'s domain, we must first define retailing—a business that sells products and/or services to consumers for their personal or family use. This definition includes the interface of retailers with vendors and consumers as well as other topics that impact retailers. *JR*'s domain **does not** include topics or data sets where retailers are not involved or are only superficially involved. Prospective authors may find this position unnecessarily restricting. We believe, however, that the practice and study of retailing is replete with topics and data that are just begging to be examined.

What encompasses research in retailing? To answer this question, we must look at the retailer, and ask what a retailer does.

- They analyze their customers
- They develop strategies.
- They choose markets and channels in which to compete.
- They make location decisions.
- They find, design, purchase, price, and promote merchandise and services.
- They organize their operations and manage their employees and stores.
- They create an atmosphere that is inviting to customers and conducive for buying.

The above topics have been, and will continue to be, within the domain of research in retailing, and by extension, *Journal of Retailing*. Other topics that go beyond the operational walls of a typical retailer are also appropriate for *JR*, so long as retailing is the focus of the paper. This does not mean, however, that every article has to be explicitly about retailers per se. Examples include: emerging technologies, multiple channel retailing, supply chain management, measurement and marketing science issues, relationships with third-party service providers, public policy issues. Consider the following topics that have appeared in recent *JR*s and are therefore appropriate:

- Emerging technologies are enabling conventional retailers to better integrate multiple channels to create and deliver value to customers. Manuscripts that examine this increasingly important topic are encouraged.
- Supply chain management articles, whose findings impact retailers or should be of relevance to retailers are appropriate.
- Articles that deal with a measurement issue, such as service quality, that should be important to retailers are welcomed.
- There is little substantive difference between research in retailing and services. Indeed, much of what distinguishes retailers is service based. Further, *JR* has supported two special issues on Services research in recent years, and will continue to do so in the future. Papers submitted to *JR*, however, should be limited to those examining vendor-to-retailer or retailer-to-customer service issues.
- Relationships with service suppliers, such as third party logistics providers (transportation and public warehousing), site selection (GIS) firms, and promotion/advertising agencies are welcome as long as the focus of the paper is to improve the operations, efficiency, or innovative abilities of the retailer.
- Public policy issues, such as consumer rights, retailer ethics, green-marketing, purchasing from firms utilizing child labor or other human rights violations, deceptive price promotions, Americans with Disabilities Act violations, anti-trust, competitive and environmental issues, are just a few of many potentially interesting topics.

- In addition, we continue to reach out to marketing scientists.
- The topics chosen for exposition here represent only a partial sampling. We welcome your comments, either by email or phone, regarding any submission issue.

Submission of Manuscripts and the Review Process
The Editorial Office encourages authors to submit manuscripts—electronically as PDF or Word format—to the Editors.

The procedures for the selection of articles for *JR* is similar to other refereed journals. The manuscripts are generally sent to three reviewers who are either members of the review board or ad hoc reviewers who are experts in one or more of the domains covered in the paper. The review process is "double-blind." All identification of authors and reviewers are removed prior to correspondence to insure that the paper is judged based solely on its contribution.

We are very motivated to facilitate the review process. Reviewers are chosen carefully on the basis of their expertise, insight, constructive comments, and timely reviews. The length of our review process compares favorably with other leading marketing journals. Reviewers are asked to return their completed manuscripts within 30 days.

We act decisively once the review process is complete. If a revision is requested, our instructions to authors are designed to move the authors toward a successfully published manuscript. In our notes to authors, we will emphasize reviewers' comments that we believe are most important to address. Every effort will be made to mediate conflicting reviewer comments. Our goal is not to send papers back to reviewers' for third round decisions.

In submitting a manuscript to *JR*, the author(s) vouch that the manuscript has neither been published, accepted for publication, nor currently under review at any other location. The author(s) also agree that the manuscript will not be placed under review elsewhere while the review process at *JR* is ongoing. If the manuscript is accepted for publication, the author(s) further guarantee not to withdraw it for submission elsewhere. If the manuscript is based upon data or other materials that have been published elsewhere, or under review elsewhere, the author(s) should submit for the editor's consideration a copy of these materials.

Publication Format
In preparing the manuscript for submission, the following format should be followed.

Title Page. The title page should include the name, title, institutional affiliation, address, phone number, and e-mail address of each author. The date of the manuscript and any acknowledgments should appear on this page.

Abstract. The title of the manuscript and a 100-word summary summarizing the article should begin the numbered pages (page 1).

Text. The main text begins on the second page. A brief orientation to the focus and intended contribution of your study should introduce your paper. Standard articles should be no longer than 40 pages in length; notes should be no more than 20, including reference and graphics. Manuscripts over 50 pages in length may be immediately returned to authors for trimming.

Headings. Primary headings are centered in upper case. Secondary headings are flush left in upper and lower case. With the exception of initial paragraphs in primary sections, the first line of each paragraph should be indented.

Style. A concise style and minimal redundancy another enhance presentations. An emphasis upon the active tense is preferred. Issues set forth in literature review or methodology sections should be referenced subsequently only in abbreviated form. Data presented in a table or figure need not be described in detail within the text.

Equations. Special care should be taken in the presentation of equations, the capitalization and italicization of algebraic symbols in order to be clear to the typesetter. Equations should be numbered on the far right with an even margin.

Spelling. The manuscript should be subjected to both computer-based grammatical and spelling review. Where spelling and hyphenation is optional, be consistent. Avoid the use of such expressions as operationalize and generalizability. Spell out numbers one through twenty in the text as well as the word percent.

References. Reference citations should be placed in the text and consist of the cited author's last name and the year of publication, enclosed in parentheses, and without punctuation, for example (Hendon 1989). If the author's name appears in the sentence, only the year of publication should appear in parentheses, for example, "...as suggested by Markin, Lillis, and Narayana (1976)."

References to multiple works should occur within one set of parentheses, separated by semicolons, as in: (Mathis and Jackson 1979; Megginson 1985; Hershey 1971).

Where possible, references should appear immediately before a punctuation mark.

Reference List. The list of references begins on a separate page and typed double-spaced. The first line of each entry is even with the left margin, and subsequent lines are indented five spaces. Sort references by the first author's last name; multiple papers by the same author should be listed in chronological order. Use the examples below as a guide to reference style.

Book
Hall, Margaret, John Knapp and Christopher Winston (1961). *Distribution in Great Britain and North America.* Oxford, England: Oxford University Press.

Journal Article
Cummings, Thomas and Susan Manning (1977). "The Relationship between Worker Alienation and Work-Related Behavior," *Journal of Vocational Behavior*, 10 (April). 167-179.

Book Chapter
Katona, George and Eva Muller (1963). "A Study of Purchasing Decisions." Pp. 30-87 in *Consumer Behavior: A Study of Purchasing Decisions.* Lincoln Clark (Ed.), New York: New York University Press, 30-87.

Conference Proceedings Paper
Westbrook, R.A. and Richard Oliver (1980). "Developing Better Measures of Consumer Satisfaction: Some Preliminary Results." Pp. 150-165 in *Advances in Consumer Research*, IX(A). Kent Monroe ed. Ann Arbor, MI: Association for Consumer Research.

Unpublished Work or Working Paper
Rein, Martin and S.M. Miller, (April 30, 1984), "The Demonstration Project as a Strategy of Change: Mobilization for Youth Training Institute Workshop," Columbia University, New York, NY.

Footnotes should be used sparingly and only for the purpose of extending or clarifying the main text with respect to an interesting, but somewhat tangential topic. Otherwise, the material should be included in the main text. Footnotes, numbered consecutively throughout the manuscript, should be typed, doubled-spaced, and attached as a separate page.

Tables and Figures. Each table and figure is numbered consecutively in Arabic numerals. The title should be centered and in upper and lower case. Table footnotes should be indicated by a, b, c, and so forth. Tables should be limited in size while still serving the purpose of the authors. Where used, it should be as simple as possible. For example, it usually is not necessary to include both frequencies and percentages. Numerous statistical findings, such as means, t-scores, and significance symbols of other sorts, are best relegated to the tables.

Graphics. Authors are responsible for completing professional-looking graphics. For materials such as graphs, charts, line drawings or illustrations, we prefer that authors provide camera-ready copy. You may obtain such copy using suitable office suite programs such as PowerPoint and a clean, 600dpi printer and the use of a lightly coated paper. The preparation of graphics by use of simple symbols available on word processors produces inadequate results. If you do not wish to submit camera-ready copy, a separate graphic file written in either EPS (encapsulated postscript), TIFF (tagged image file format) or PS (PostScript) file may be submitted. A print from a graphics file must still be provided.

Final Manuscript. If a manuscript is accepted for publication, authors should send two paper copies of their final version. These manuscripts must be printed, double-spaced on one side of 8½ x 11-inch paper using 1-inch margins on all sides, and 12-point type. An electronic image on diskette in either Word for Windows or WordPerfect is required.

Executive Summary. Authors must also provide an executive summary. However, this need not be included upon with the initial submission. This summary serves as an extended abstract for readers who wish to gain the flavor of an article prior to investing additional time in reading it. The review should highlight the major contributions of the article in an easily readable manner. The summary is ideally suited to point out interesting managerial, policy or social implications not touched upon within the main text. Executive summaries for all articles are printed at the front of the issue and will also appear on the *Journal's* Web page. They should be about two or three manuscript pages long.

Journal of Retailing and Consumer Services

ADDRESS FOR SUBMISSION:

Harry Timmermans, Editor
Journal of Retailing and Consumer Services
Eindhoven Univesrity of Technology
EIRASS Faculty of Architecture
Building and Planning
Postvak 20, PO Box 513
5600 MB Eindhoven,
The Netherlands
Phone: 31 (0) 402-472594
E-Mail: eirass@bwk.tue.nl
Web:

PUBLICATION GUIDELINES:

Manuscript Length: 21-25
Copies Required: Three
Computer Submission: Yes Email
Format:
Fees to Review: 0.00 US$

Manuscript Style:
    See Manuscript Guidelines

CIRCULATION DATA:

Reader: Academics
Frequency of Issue: Quarterly
Sponsor/Publisher: Elsevier Inc.

REVIEW INFORMATION:

Type of Review: Blind Review
No. of External Reviewers: 3
No. of In House Reviewers: 0
Acceptance Rate: 11-20%
Time to Review: 2 - 3 Months
Reviewers Comments: Yes
Invited Articles: 0-5%
Fees to Publish: 0.00 US$

MANUSCRIPT TOPICS:

Advertising & Promotion Management; Business Information Systems (MIS); Consumer Behavior; Direct Marketing; Global Business; Labor Relations & Human Resource Mgt.; Marketing Research; Marketing Theory & Applications; Operations Research/Statistics; Organizational Behavior & Theory; Production/Operations; Public Administration; Purchasing/Materials Management; Sales/Selling; Services; Small Business Entrepreneurship; Strategic Management Policy; Technology/Innovation; Transportation/Physical Distribution

MANUSCRIPT GUIDELINES/COMMENTS:

Description

The journal is an international and interdisciplinary forum for research and debate in the rapidly developing—and converging—fields of retailing and services studies. Published quarterly, it focuses particularly on consumer behaviour and on policy and managerial decisions, encouraging contributions both from practitioners in the forefront of new developments in retailing and services, and from academics across a wide range of relevant disciplines. The *Journal of Retailing and Consumer Services* covers:

- The distribution and selling of goods
- The retailing of professional services such as health and law

- The retailing of consumer services such as transportation, tourism, leisure, and personal financial services.

For employers and course providers, it also addresses issues of education and training.
In addition to the main refereed articles and detailed case studies, the journal features short viewpoint pieces and state-of-the-art surveys, book and software reviews, and a calendar of events.

GUIDE FOR AUTHORS
Submission of Papers
Authors are requested to submit their manuscripts and figures to the Editor electronically. Please send manuscripts via email to: **eirass@bwk.tue.nl**

Submission of a paper implies that it has not been published previously, that it is not under consideration for publication elsewhere, and that if accepted it will not be published elsewhere in the same form, in English or in any other language, without the written consent of the publisher. Translated material, which has not been published in English, will also be considered. All articles are refereed to ensure accuracy and relevance, and amendments to the script may be required before final acceptance.

Types of Contribution
The journal publishes full-length research papers, case studies and book reviews. There is also a viewpoint section which exists for the expression of opinion, and allows authors to submit material not suitable for a full-length article but containing ideas worthy of publication. Full-length articles should be 4,000-6,000 words long, although articles longer than 6,000 words will be accepted on an occasional basis, if the topic demands this length of treatment. Book reviews should be 800-1,200, and viewpoints 1,500-2,000 words in length.

Manuscript Preparation
General. Manuscripts must be typewritten, double-spaced with wide margins on one side of white A4 paper. Good quality printouts with a font size of 12 or 10 pt are required. The corresponding author should be identified (include a Fax number and E-mail address). Full postal addresses must be given for all co-authors. Authors should consult a recent issue of the journal for style if possible. An electronic copy of the paper should accompany the final accepted version. The Editors reserve the right to adjust style to certain standards of uniformity. Authors should retain a copy of their manuscript since the Publisher cannot accept responsibility for damage or loss of papers. Original manuscripts are discarded one month after publication unless the Publisher is asked to return original material after use.

Text. Follow this order when typing manuscripts: Title, Authors, Affiliations, Abstract, Keywords, Main text, Acknowledgements, Appendix, References, Vitae, Figure Captions and then Tables. Do not import the Figures or Tables into your text. The corresponding author should be identified with an asterisk and footnote. All other footnotes (except for table footnotes) should be identified with superscript Arabic numerals. Footnotes should be grouped together in a section at the end of the text in numerical order, and double spaced. The text should be organized under appropriate section headings which, ideally, should not be more than 600 words apart. All headings should be placed on the left-hand side of the text.

692

Abstract. Include a self-contained abstract up to 100 words outlining in a single paragraph the aims, scope and conclusions of the paper.

Keywords. Up to three keywords or phrases (maximum 10 words in total) to facilitate access and indexing should be included.

Units. All measurements should be given in metric (SI) units.

References. All publications cited in the text should be presented in a list of references following the text of the manuscript. In the text refer to the author's name (without initials) and year of publication, e.g. "Since Peterson (1993) has shown that..." or "This is in agreement with results obtained later (Kramer, 1994)". For three or more authors use the first author followed by "et al." in the text. The list of references should be arranged alphabetically by authors' names. The manuscript should be carefully checked to ensure that the spelling of authors' names and dates are exactly the same in the text as in the reference list. References should be given in the following form:

Ratchford, B.T., Norton, D.P., 1988. A model and measurement approach for studying retail productivity. Journal of Retailing 64 (3), 241-263.

Kaplan, R.S., Norton, D.P., 1996. The Balanced Scorecard: Translating Strategy into Action. Harvard Business School Press, Boston, MA.

Sealy, K., 1992. International air transport. In: Hoyle, B.S., Knowles, R.D. (Eds.), Modern Transport Geography. Belhaven Press, London, pp. 233-256.

Illustrations. All illustrations should be provided in camera-ready form, suitable for reproduction (which may include reduction) without retouching. Photographs, charts and diagrams are all to be referred to as Figure(s) and should be numbered consecutively in the order to which they are referred. They should accompany the manuscript, but should not be included within the text. Their position should be indicated in the text. All illustrations should be clearly marked on the back with the figure number and the author's name. All figures are to have a caption. Captions should be supplied on a separate sheet.

Line drawings. Good quality printouts on white paper produced in black ink are required. All lettering, graph lines and points on graphs should be sufficiently large and bold to permit reproduction when the diagram has been reduced to a size suitable for inclusion in the journal. Dye-line prints or photocopies are not suitable for reproduction. Do not use any type of shading on computer-generated illustrations.

Photographs. Original photographs must be supplied as they are to be reproduced (e.g. black and white or colour). If necessary, a scale should be marked on the photograph. Please note that photocopies of photographs are not acceptable.

Colour. Where colour figures are required, the author will be charged accordingly.

Tables. Tables should be numbered consecutively and given a suitable caption and each table typed on a separate sheet. Footnotes to tables should be typed below the table and should be referred to by superscript lowercase letters. No vertical rules should be used. Tables should not duplicate results presented elsewhere in the manuscript, e.g. in graphs.

Electronic Submission

Authors should submit an electronic copy of their paper with the final version of the manuscript. The electronic copy should match the hardcopy exactly. Always keep a backup copy of the electronic file for reference and safety. For authors using LaTeX, the document style files, as well as the instructions "Preparing articles with LaTeX" in the form of a dvi file, can be obtained free of charge from any host on the Comprehensive TeX Archive Network (CTAN) using anonymous ftp. The primary CTAN hosts are ftp.dante.de and ftp.tex.ac.uk. The Elsevier macros are in /pub/tex/macros/latex/contrib/supported/elsevier. These can also be downloaded from the Internet site: http://www.tex.ac.uk. Full details of electronic submission and other formats can be obtained from http://www.elsevier.nl/locate/disksub or from Author Services at Elsevier Science.

Proofs

Proofs will be sent to the author (first named author if no corresponding author is identified of multi-authored papers) and should be returned within 48 hours of receipt. Corrections should be restricted to typesetting errors; any others may be charged to the author. Any queries should be answered in full. Please note that authors are urged to check their proofs carefully before return, since the inclusion of late corrections cannot be guaranteed. Proofs are to be returned to the Log-in Department, Elsevier Science, Stover Court, Bampflyde Street, Exeter, Devon EX1 2AH, UK.

Offprints

Fifty offprints will be supplied free of charge. Additional offprints and copies of the issue can be ordered at a specially reduced rate using the order form sent to the corresponding author after the manuscript has been accepted. Orders for reprints (produced after publication of an article) will incur a 50% surcharge.

Copyright

All authors must sign the "Transfer of Copyright" agreement before the article can be published. This transfer agreement enables Elsevier Science Ltd to protect the copyrighted material for the authors, without the author relinquishing his/her proprietary rights. The copyright transfer covers the exclusive rights to reproduce and distribute the article, including reprints, photographic reproductions, microfilm or any other reproductions of a similar nature, and translations. It also includes the right to adapt the article for use in conjunction with computer systems and programs, including reproduction or publication in machine-readable form and incorporation in retrieval systems. Authors are responsible for obtaining from the copyright holder permission to reproduce any material for which copyright already exists.

694

Author Services

For queries relating to the general submission of manuscripts (including electronic text and artwork) and the status of accepted manuscripts, please contact Author Services, Log-in Department, Elsevier Science, The Boulevard, Langford Lane, Kidlington, Oxford OX5 1GB, UK. E-mail: authors@elsevier.co.uk, Fax: +44 (0) 1865 843905, Tel: +44 (0) 1865 843900. Authors can also keep a track of the progress of their accepted article through our OASIS system on the Internet. For information on an article go to this Internet page and key in the corresponding author's name and the Elsevier reference number.

Journal of Selling and Major Account Management

ADDRESS FOR SUBMISSION:

Dan C. Weilbaker, Editor
Journal of Selling and Major Account
    Management
Northern Illinois University
Department of Marketing
DeKalb, IL 60115
USA
Phone: 815-753-6216
E-Mail: dweilbak@niu.edu
Web: www.cob.niu.edu/jsmam

PUBLICATION GUIDELINES:

Manuscript Length: 21-25
Copies Required: Four
Computer Submission: Yes Email Preferred
Format: MS Word, English
Fees to Review: 0.00 US$

Manuscript Style:
    Chicago Manual of Style

CIRCULATION DATA:

Reader: Academics, Business Persons,
    Sales People & Managers, Account
    Managers
Frequency of Issue: Quarterly
Sponsor/Publisher: Northern Illinois
    University, Department of Marketing

REVIEW INFORMATION:

Type of Review: Blind Review
No. of External Reviewers: 3
No. of In House Reviewers: 1
Acceptance Rate: 21-30%
Time to Review: 1 - 2 Months
Reviewers Comments: Yes
Invited Articles: 21-30%
Fees to Publish: 50.00 US$
1 year Subscription fee

MANUSCRIPT TOPICS:
Account Management; Communication; Global Business; Sales Management; Sales/Selling

MANUSCRIPT GUIDELINES/COMMENTS:

Editorial Policy
The main objective of the journal is to provide a focus for collaboration between practitioners and academics for the advancement of education and research in the areas of selling , sales management and major account management. Our audience is comprised of both practitioners in industry and academics researching in sales.

The *Journal* strives to enhance best practice in the field of selling, sales management and major account management. Articles that promote this will be given priority for publication. In particular, we see this as being achieved through two distinct forms of contribution: empirical papers reporting research which is concerned with developing, testing or validating theories of sales management or selling activities and practitioner articles which provide commentaries, best practices and case studies that address key sales, sales management or major accout management issues.

All academic papers published must have a well defined and extensive managerial implications section reflecting the research findings.

Notes to Contributors

1. Articles for consideration should be sent to Editor: Dan C. Weilbaker, Department of Marketing Northern Illinois University, DeKalb, IL 60115 by Email to **dweilbak@niu.edu (preferred method)** or by fax: 001 815-753-6014.

2. Articles in excess of 6000 words will not normally be accepted. The Editor welcomes shorter articles, case studies and reviews. Contributors should specify the length of their articles.

3. The manuscript should be submitted by email if possible in Microsoft Word format, author's name(s) and short title of the article. Alternatively, the contribution may be mailed with four copies to the above address. Neither the editor nor Northern Illinois University, Department of Marketing accepts any responsibility for loss or damage of any contributions submitted for publication in the *Journal*.

Biographical note. Supply a short biographical note giving the author(s) full name, appointment, institutions or organization / company and recent professional attainments.

Synopsis. An abstract or resume not exceeding 100 words should be included.

Diagrams / text boxes / tables should be submitted without shading although a copy of how the authors wishes the diagram to appear shaded may be submitted by way of illustrative example. These should be numbered consecutively and typed on separate pages at the end of the article with an indication in the text where it should appear.

References should be cited using the Harvard method. No footnotes should be used for references or literature citations. Wherever possible, full bibliographic details (e.g., volume number issue number or date, page numbers publisher year of publication) should be included.

Footnotes for clarification or elaboration should be used very sparingly - they may be indicated in the text and at the beginning of the footnote by the use of asterisks and / or daggers.

4. Any article or other contribution submitted must be the original unpublished work of the author(s) not submitted for publication elsewhere.

5. Manuscripts should be typewritten using one side of 8 ½" X 11" with all margins of 1" and double-spaced. Font style should be Times New Roman in 12 pitch. Footnotes should be typed at the bottom of the page and numbered consecutively throughout the text.

6. Cross references should not be to page numbers but to the text accompanying a particular footnote.

7. An address for correspondence (including Email address) should be supplied as well as a telephone and fax number at which the author(s) may be contacted.

8. Authors undertake to check proofs and to return them within the specified date. They should be free from grammatical, syntax or spelling errors. Failure to return proofs will result in the publication of the article at the editor's discretion in which event the editor does not accept liability for any changes made to grammar syntax, spelling or other changes deemed necessary. The editor reserve the right not to accept any alterations or corrections made.

Ethics and the Blind Review Process
The Journal uses a double-blind review process. Neither the author nor the reviewer should know the others identify. These identities, known only to the editorial staff, are never released, even after the article has been published. If you recognize the author from something in the manuscript, have reviewed this manuscript for another journal, or have read a substantially identical version in another journal, please return the manuscript to the Editor with a note to that effect. If you have seen the article in conference proceedings please notify the editor when you return your review. While we will not publish extant papers, we realize that conference presentations are one means by which authors test their ideas before seeking full publication and the editor will insist on a substantial difference from the proceedings paper.

Upon receipt, the Editor reviews a manuscript to ensure that its topic is within the editorial scope of the *Journal* and that it meets accepted professional standards as outlined in the Notes to Contributors. The Editor then selects three reviewers on the basis of their expressed interests and expertise. If the Editor has misinterpreted your knowledge, as related to the manuscript topic, please send the manuscript back to be reassigned. Under no circumstances should you turn the manuscript over to another individual for review. Certainly feel free to consult with a colleague on an issue raised in the manuscript, or for help with a technical point or two, but be sure the review represents your thoughts.

Feedback
Please feel free to contact the Editor, Dan C. Weilbaker, Ph.D. by email to **dweilbak@ niu.edu** or by phone at 001 815 753 6216 about these guidelines or any concerns you might have about other aspects of the *Journal*.

Copyright in all contributions is with Northern Illinois University, Department of Marketing.

Journal of Service Research

ADDRESS FOR SUBMISSION:

A. Parasuraman, Editor
Journal of Service Research
University of Miami
School of Business
Department of Marketing
PO Box 248147
Coral Gables, FL 33124-6554
USA
Phone: 301-284-3160
E-Mail: jsr@miami.edu
Web: http://jsr.sagepub.com/

PUBLICATION GUIDELINES:

Manuscript Length: 26-35
Copies Required: Electronic
Computer Submission: Yes Email
Format: MS Word
Fees to Review: 0.00 US$

Manuscript Style:
    See Manuscript Guidelines

CIRCULATION DATA:

Reader: Academics, Business Persons
Frequency of Issue: Quarterly
Sponsor/Publisher: Center for Excellence in
    Service, Univerity of Maryland / Sage
    Publications, Inc.

REVIEW INFORMATION:

Type of Review: Blind Review
No. of External Reviewers: 3
No. of In House Reviewers: 0
Acceptance Rate: 20%
Time to Review: 1 - 2 Months
Reviewers Comments: Yes
Invited Articles: 0-5%
Fees to Publish: 0.00 US$

MANUSCRIPT TOPICS:

Business Information Systems (MIS); Direct Marketing; E-Commerce; Global Business; Health Care Administration; Marketing Research; Marketing Theory & Applications; Non-Profit Organizations; Operations Research/Statistics; Organizational Behavior & Theory; Organizational Development; Production/Operations; Public Administration; Services; Strategic Management Policy; Technology/Innovation; Tourism, Hospitality & Leisure

MANUSCRIPT GUIDELINES/COMMENTS:

About the Journal

The purpose of the *Journal of Service Research* is to be a first-rate outlet for the best service research. The journal is international in scope, in keeping with the increasing globalization of business, multi-disciplinary, in keeping with how the best management is done, and relevant to the business world, in a majority of its articles. The mission of *JSR* is to be the leading outlet for the most advanced research in service marketing, e-Service, service operations, service human resources and organizational design, service information systems, customer satisfaction and service quality, and the economics of service.

Manuscript Submission Guidelines

The objective of the *Journal of Service Research* is to publish articles in service marketing, service operations, service human resources and organizational design, service information systems, service innovation, customer satisfaction and service quality, electronic commerce, and the economics of service. Its purpose is to serve as a medium through which those with research interests can exchange ideas and keep abreast of the latest developments pertaining to service research.

The journal strives to be international in scope, in keeping with the increased globalization of business; multidisciplinary, in keeping with how the best management is done; and relevant to the business world in a majority of its articles.

Articles are encouraged from industry practitioners as well as academics. No particular research ideology is preferred, and quantitative, qualitative, managerial, and behavioral approaches are welcome. Articles of any length will be considered, as long as the contribution to length ratio remains high.

The procedures guiding the selection of articles for publication in the journal require that no manuscript be accepted until it has been reviewed in a double-blind review process and sent to three reviewers. The editor's decision to publish a manuscript is influenced considerably by the judgments of these reviewers, who are experts in their respective fields of travel. It is journal policy to remove the author's name and credentials prior to forwarding a manuscript to a reviewer to maximize objectivity and ensure that manuscripts are judged solely on the basis of their content.

Two principal criteria are used by the editor and reviewers in the judgment of a manuscript: (a) Does it make a significant and substantive contribution to the literature of service research? and (b) Does it convey its message clearly and concisely? Does it communicate technical information so that it is easily understood by most readers?

Manuscript Preparation

Manuscripts should be created in MS Word format and should be typed double-spaced, including references. Do not use single spacing anywhere. Page numbers are to be placed in the upper right-hand corner of every page. A tab indent should begin each paragraph.

Please group all sections of the article in one file; do not use separate files for tables, references or figures. The author's name should not appear anywhere except on the cover page. The author should keep an extra exact copy for future reference. Manuscripts are reviewed simultaneously by several different reviewers who are geographically separated.

For details of manuscript preparation not covered in the following sections, see *The Chicago Manual of Style* (15th edition), Chicago and London: University of Chicago Press, 2003.

1. What Goes Where?

- **First Page.** Name of author(s), title, and 4-5 keywords; author(s) note, including present position, complete address, telephone/fax numbers, e-mail address, and any acknowledgment of financial or technical assistance. (This page will not be sent to the reviewers.)
- **Second Page.** Title of paper (without author's name) and a brief abstract of no more than 150 words substantively summarizing the article. This should be informative, giving the reader a "taste" of the article.
- **Body.** The text, with major headings centered on the page and subheadings flush with the left margin. Major headings should use all uppercase letters; side subheadings should be typed in upper and lowercase letters. The percent sign (%) should be used.
- **Tables and Figures.** Each table or figure should be prepared on a separate page and grouped together at the end of the manuscript. The data in tables should be arranged so that columns of like materials read down, not across. Nonsignificant decimal places in tabular data should be omitted. The tables and figures should be numbered in Arabic numerals, followed by brief descriptive titles. Additional details should be footnoted under the table, not in the title. In the text, all illustrations and charts should be referred to as figures. Figures must be clean, crisp, black-and-white, camera-ready copies. Please avoid the use of gray-scale shading; use hatch marks, dots, or lines instead.
- **References.** References should be typed double-spaced in alphabetical order by author's last name (see 3).

2. Reference Citations Within Text

Citations in the text should include the author's last name, and year of publication enclosed in parentheses without punctuation, for example (Kinsey 1960). If practical, the citation should be placed immediately before a punctuation mark. Otherwise, insert it in a logical sentence break.

If a particular page, section, or equation is cited, it should be placed within the parentheses, for example, (Kinsey 1960, p.112). For multiple authors, use the full, formal citation for up to three authors, but for four or more use the first author's name with "et al." For example, use (White and Smith 1977) and (Brown, Green, and Stone 1984). For more than three authors, use (Hunt et al. 1975) unless another work published in that year would also be identified as (Hunt et al. 1975); in that case, list all authors, for example, (Hunt, Bent, Marks, and West 1975).

3. Reference List Style

Journal Article

Dwyer, F. Robert (1989), "Customer Lifetime Valuation to Support Marketing Decision Making," *Journal of Direct Marketing*, 3 (Autumn), 8-15.

Schneider, Benjamin and David E. Bowen (1985), "Employee and Customer Perceptions of Service in Banks: Replication and Extension," *Journal of Applied Psychology*, 70, 423-33.

------, Jill K. Wheeler, and Jonathan F. Cox (1992), "A Passion for Service: Using Content Analysis to Explicate Service Climate Themes," *Journal of Applied Psychology*, 77 (October), 705-16.

Wensley, Jim (1988), "Analyzing the Effect of Strategic Marketing," *Journal of Marketing*, 42 (Fall), 173-88.

Newspaper Article, Magazine Article
Schwartz, J. (1993), "Obesity Affects Economic, Social Status," *The Washington Post*, September 30, A1.

Book
Becker, H. (1964), *Human Capital: A Theoretical and Empirical Analysis with Specific Reference to Education*. New York: Columbia University Press.

Donnelly, James H. and Brad P. Jones (1982), *Marketing of Services*. New York: American Marketing Association.
Book, Edition

Corey, Raymond E. (1991), *Industrial Marketing Cases and Concepts*, 4th ed. Englewood Cliffs, NJ: Prentice Hall.

Chapter in an Edited Book
Isen, Alice M. (1984), "Toward Understanding the Role of Affect in Cognition," in *Handbook of Social Cognition*, Vol. 3, R. S. Wyer and Thomas K. Srull, eds. Hillsdale, NJ: Lawrence Erlbaum, 101-9.

Unpublished Manuscripts, Doctoral Dissertations, Working Papers
Berger, A. and G. Humphrey (1997), "Efficiency of Financial Institutions: International Survey and Directions for Future Research," working paper, Federal Reserve Board, Washington, DC.

Roos, Inger (1998), "Customer Switching Behavior in Retailing," doctoral dissertation, Swedish School of Economics and Business Administration, Helsingfors, Finland.

Manuscript Submission
Please e-mail all manuscripts as attachments in MS Word format to A. Parasuraman, Editor, Journal of Service Research; e-mail: **jsr@miami.edu**; phone: 305-284-3160; fax: 305-284-2758 (Department of Marketing, P.O. Box 248147, University of Miami, Coral Gables, FL 33124).

Journal of Services Marketing

ADDRESS FOR SUBMISSION:

Charles L. Martin, Editor
Journal of Services Marketing
Wichita State University
Campus Box 84
Wichita, KS 67260
USA
Phone: 316-978-7104
E-Mail: charles.martin@wichita.edu
Web: www.emeraldinsight.com/jsm.htm

CIRCULATION DATA:

Reader: Academics, Business Persons
Frequency of Issue: 7 Times/Year
Sponsor/Publisher: Emerald Group
   Publishing Limited

PUBLICATION GUIDELINES:

Manuscript Length: 8,000 Word Maximum
Copies Required: Four
Computer Submission: No
Format: N/A
Fees to Review: 0.00 US$

Manuscript Style:
   See Manuscript Guidelines

REVIEW INFORMATION:

Type of Review: Blind Review
No. of External Reviewers: 3
No. of In House Reviewers: 1
Acceptance Rate: 21-30%
Time to Review: 2 - 3 Months
Reviewers Comments: Yes
Invited Articles: 0-5%
Fees to Publish: 0.00 US$

MANUSCRIPT TOPICS:

Advertising & Promotion Management; Communication; Direct Marketing; E-Commerce; Global Business; Human Resource Management; Marketing Research; Marketing Theory & Applications; Non-Profit Organizations; Organizational Behavior & Theory; Sales/Selling; Services; Small Business Entrepreneurship; Tourism, Hospitality & Leisure; Transportation/Physical Distribution

MANUSCRIPT GUIDELINES/COMMENTS:

The objective of this *Journal* is to provide the practitioners of marketing with new ideas that will be applicable to their daily work. Each article must put forth recommendations as to how the material contained in the article can be utilized in business practice. The *Journal* should also provide teachers of marketing with actual business examples of how the theories taught in the classroom work in the "real world". We would expect that this will add meaning and "flavor" to their lectures.

The basis of an article may be research, but it is not intended that the actual research be printed. If the methodology is so unique as to warrant inclusion, it will be added as an appendix. But, research is not the only basis of an article. Cases, concepts, and industry reviews and practices may be put forth with equal acceptability. In addition, we have provided a section for Commentary, which need be little more than personal opinion.

Article Content
Each article should contain:
1. Background and short references to previous articles, if they are pertinent. Specifically omit endless strings of quotations by other authors, especially if the ideas are currently well accepted. This is particularly true of citations in the literature that are five or more years old. They have generally lost their uniqueness. If previous material is pertinent, please paraphrase it and eliminate endnotes and authors. Citations should be used only for significant and timely contributions. Also, standard textbooks should not be used as references. Note: With the advent of databases, it is not possible, within the twinkling of an electronic lash, to call forth everything that has ever been written on a subject. Some authors think that all such material should be quoted and end noted. Our readers don't. Such material may be recommended for additional reading.

2. Based premise, major thought, problem or concept.

3. A discussion of the theory incorporating any research (but not the actual research which may be added in an appendix).

4. A case example or clear argument supporting the basic premise or concept.

5. A summary to wrap-up the key ideas. Then, a section title Managerial Implications and Recommendations - that is, the practical applications for the information presented in the article.

The Managerial Implications and Recommendations are the key to the entire article. Without such a section, or a comparable one, no manuscript can be accepted.

Article Length
Articles should be under 8,000 words, including abstract, exhibits, references, etc. Half that amount, with a few charts, graphs or sidebars will also do nicely. Also, articles in the section for Commentary can be as little as one or two pages in length, or about 800-1,600 words. Here we would like to encourage very creative writing.

Do not prepare final artwork. We will do this. Of course, if you already have artwork that can be reproduced, please advise. We would like to use it. Just make sure that what you submit is very clear.

Footnotes, Endnotes, and References
This journal does not follow the standard format of most other journals.

Important. References to an author's work should be handled via a number corresponding to the author's work in the alphabetized End Notes. The author's name and date (e.g., Kotler, 1984), as is the custom, should not be used; only the reference number (superscript). Thus, the reference numbers in the text will be out of numerical sequence. Other constructions such as "According to Smith..." or "(See Smith, 1983)" or "Jones describes sales as..." are not to be used. The purpose is to eliminate authors' names and extraneous words in the text that might slow down the reader's quest for the heart of the article. Other references or reading recommendations should be listed after End Notes under the title of References.

Note. Articles using the format above will be processed and reviewed in a much more expeditious manner.

Footnotes should only be used for clarification such as a definition of a term that might not be in common use, e.g., cognitive dissonance* or clarification of a point that some readers might need.

Prior Exposure

Articles that have been published elsewhere or have been submitted concurrently to other publications are generally not acceptable. However, there are exceptions such as foreign publications, conference proceedings, obscure journals, or significantly different exposure, which may mitigate our policy. We are striving to have the best possible material and will, therefore, be flexible. Copyright permission for previously printed material is the responsibility of the author. On submission, we assume that such permission, where required, has been granted. (Note: Many of our authors now find that the best way to avoid copyright problems is copyright the material presented at conferences themselves. Then they can grant permission to any publication they deem worthy.)

Speeches that are rewritten into article form are generally quite acceptable.

Review Process

The editor reviews all articles for general acceptability upon receipt. If major revisions are required at that point, the manuscript will be returned to the author with appropriate comments. If the topic is acceptable, it will be sent to as many as three external reviewers for comments. The process is double-blind. We ask these reviewers to return the manuscript in about six weeks, but as a practical matter it generally takes a few weeks longer – especially during June, July, August and during the Christmas holiday season.

Among other issues, the reviewers are asked to review for acceptability on these four points:
- Applicability to a practicing marketer
- Strong on conceptual basis or interesting case study
- Clarity of thought
- Solid summary

Authors may request from the Editor a copy of the list of questions many reviewers refer to when they review manuscripts.

The last phrase, after final revision, is copy-edited for grammar, syntax, etc., which we do. Thus, a final proofing and, depending on the timing, it is always our intention to have the author see a final proof before typesetting.

The process may seem long and tedious at times but the author and we both have the same goal - excellence. Viewed from that perspective each review provides new insights and opportunities to achieve that goal. When the article is finally printed, all will agree that it was worth the trouble.

Copyright Policy

Manuscript Submission

A manuscript, abstract, and brief author's biography should be double spaced, with a margin on each side to facilitate comments. Also, please submit FOUR copies. Authors of articles accepted for publication may be asked to revise their references and abstracts to conform to our style guidelines. It will be our pleasure to provide reprints of the published article and a subscription to each author.

Send material directly to the editor at his address in the USA. Paper copies are preferred for the initial review.

Thank you for your interest.
Charles L. Martin, Ph.D., Editor

Journal of Services Research

ADDRESS FOR SUBMISSION:

Vinnie Jauhari, Editor
Journal of Services Research
Inst For International Mgmt & Technology
336, Phase - IV
Udyog Vihar
Gurgaon
Haryana - 122001,
India
Phone: 91-124-2397783
E-Mail: jsr@iimtobu.ac.in
Web: www.jsr-iimt.net

PUBLICATION GUIDELINES:

Manuscript Length: 26-30
Copies Required: Two
Computer Submission: Yes Email
Format: MS Word
Fees to Review: 0.00 US$

Manuscript Style:
Uniform System of Citation (Harvard
Blue Book)

CIRCULATION DATA:

Reader: Business Persons, Academics
Frequency of Issue: 2 Times/Year
Sponsor/Publisher: Institute for
International Management and
Technology (IIMT)

REVIEW INFORMATION:

Type of Review: Blind Review
No. of External Reviewers: 2
No. of In House Reviewers: 3
Acceptance Rate: 21-30%
Time to Review: 2 - 3 Months
Reviewers Comments: Yes
Invited Articles: 6-10%
Fees to Publish: 0.00 US$

MANUSCRIPT TOPICS:

Advertising & Promotion Management; Business Education; Business Information Systems (MIS); E-Commerce; Global Business; Health Care Administration; Marketing Research; Services; Small Business Entrepreneurship; Strategic Management Policy; Technology/Innovation; Tourism, Hospitality & Leisure

MANUSCRIPT GUIDELINES/COMMENTS:

Overview

The service sector is a dominant contributor to GDP in most developed and developing nations. A large segment of the population is involved in this sector for their livelihood. It is a requisite that focused academic attention is directed at it. This is an imperative if the sector has to grow in a planned manner in the future. The on-line economy or new age businesses, most of which are service companies, had started with great fanfare but the life cycle of the 'dotcom' companies, hordes of which have gone bust, have proven at least one thing amongst others – that, the business modelling of these companies were not thought out in their entirety and that the assumptions and benchmarks that were used in strategy formulation were faulty at best. This is obviously going to be there when a sunrise sector opens up but the kind of chaos that it has led-to the world over, especially in the stock markets, indicates that the thinkers, researchers and analysts were not able to see through the consequences and were not able to provide guidelines and propose relevant business models. This is avoidable (if at all partially) only when there is a corpus of research and analytical work to base decisions upon or to at least lend some objectivity to decision making.

The *Journal of Services Research* is an effort in this direction to help build and document such a corpus by promoting researchers from India and abroad to focus on issues related to services management and provide well researched and tested benchmarks for industry, and also to provide new directions for further research.

IIMT as an institution focuses on the emerging sectors of service businesses and we feel that it is relevant for us to take an initiative in harnessing academic and industry effort in order to further the boundaries of knowledge in our chosen area of endeavour. We look forward to inputs from relevant quarters-suggesting, criticising and contributing to the increased awareness and understanding of this sector.

Scope
The journal publishes research in the areas outlined below. The research could have a focus on marketing, finance, production, HR, strategy or policy in any of the outlined induction group.

Guidelines for Authors
Journal of Services Research invites original, research based papers and cases in the area of services management. This journal publishes papers of interest to academicians and to practitioners of business. The papers range widely over different areas of services. It is a condition for publication that the material sent is original work which has not been previously published or submitted for publication elsewhere. The guidelines for contributors are listed below:

1. **Manuscripts** should normally be of up to 10,000 words (20-40 A-4 size pages, typed double space and 11-point font). Microsoft Word for windows and WordPerfect are the preferred softwares for submission. Manuscripts must be submitted in duplicate with the cover page bearing only the title of the paper and authors' names, designations, official addresses and phone/fax numbers.

2. **Abstract**. Submit an abstract of about 150 words.

3. **Tables and Figures**. Their location in the text should be indicated as follows:

Table –1 about here

4. **End notes**. All notes should be indicated by serial numbers in the text and literature cited should be detailed under Notes at the end of the paper bearing corresponding numbers, before the references.

5. **References**. Place the references at the end of the manuscript following the endnotes. Arrange the reference list in alphabetical order of author's surnames, and chronologically for each author where more than one work by that author is cited. The author's surname is placed

first, followed by initials, then the year of publication is given followed by details of the publication. The name of the publication (usually a book or journal) appears in italics. Following examples will illustrate the style used in the journal.

Book (first edition)
Surname, Initials, and Surname, Initials. (date) *Title*, Place of publication, Publisher
Saunders, M.N.K and Cooper, S.A. (1993) *Understanding Business Statistics*, London, DP Publications Ltd.

Book (other than first edition)
Surname, Initials. and Surname, Initials. (date) Title (?edn), Place of publication, Publisher
Morris, C. (1999) Quantitative *Approaches to Business Studies* (5th edn), London, Financial Times Pitman Publishing.

Journal article
Surname, Initials. and Surname, Initials. (date) 'Title of article', *Journal name*, volume number, part number, pages.
Storey, J., Cressey, P., Morris, T. and Wilkinson, A. (1997) 'Changing employment practices in UK banking: case studies', *Personnel Review*, 28:1, 24-42.

Journal article (no obvious author)
Corporate name or Publication name (date) 'Title of article', *Journal name*, volume number, part number, pages.
Local Government Chronicle (1993) 'Westminster poised for return to AMA fold', *Local Government Chronicle*, 5 November, p.5.

[Other examples can be found at **www.jsr-iimt.net**.]

6. Follow **British spellings** throughout (programme, not program).

7. Universal "s" in "ise" "isation" words.

8. **Use of numerals**. One to twelve in words, thirteen and above in figures , unless the reference is to percentages (5 percent), distance (5 km) or age (10 years old). Use 1900s and 19th century.

9. No stops after abbreviations (UK, MBA). Use stops after initials (V.P.Singh).

10. Use single quotes throughout. however in case of use of double quotes for example, "In the words of Szell, the 'the economic question' is today ......" the quotation can be encased within single quote in the double quotes. Quotations in excess of 45 words should be separated from the text with a line space above and below and indented on the left. Quotes should be cited accurately from the original source, should not be edited, and should give the page numbers of the original publication.

11. Italicization and use of diacriticals is left to the contributors, but must be consistent. When not using diacriticals, English spelling should be followed.

12. Capitalization should be kept to the minimum and should be consistent.

13. An author will receive 5 off prints and a complimentary copy of the issue in which his/her paper appears.

14. Book reviews must provide the following details, and in this order: Name of author/title of book reviewed/place of publication/publisher/year of publication/number of pages, in Roman and Arabic figures to include preliminary pages/and price, with binding specifications such as paperback or hardback. For example:

Brian K. Julyan, *Sales and Service for the Wine Professional*. London and New York: Cassell, 1999. ix+214pp. £16.99 paper.

15. If papers are accepted for publication, contributors are requested to send floppy disks containing the full text of the paper including notes, references, tables, charts and maps.

16. Manuscripts which do not conform to these guidelines will not be considered for publication.

17. Manuscripts not considered for publication will not be sent back. Those submitting papers should also certify that the paper has not been published or submitted for publication elsewhere.

18. Manuscripts and all editorial correspondence should be addressed to: Editor, Journal of Services Research, Institute for International Management & Technology, 336, Udyog Vihar Phase IV, Gurgaon 122 001. Ph: (0124) 239 7783/85/86, 5014165; Fax: (0124) 239 7288 Email: **jsr@iimtobu.ac.in** Website: **www.iimtobu.ac.in**

Journal of Sport Management

ADDRESS FOR SUBMISSION:

Laurence Chalip, Editor
Journal of Sport Management
University of Texas at Austin
Kinesiology and Health - BEL
1 University Station - D3700
Austin, TX 78712-0360
USA
Phone: 512-471-1273
E-Mail: lchalip@mail.utexas.edu
Web: www.humankinetics.com

CIRCULATION DATA:

Reader: Academics
Frequency of Issue: Quarterly
Sponsor/Publisher: Human Kinetics

PUBLICATION GUIDELINES:

Manuscript Length: 30 Maximum
Copies Required: Four
Computer Submission: Yes
Format: MS Word
Fees to Review: 0.00 US$

Manuscript Style:
    American Psychological Association

REVIEW INFORMATION:

Type of Review: Blind Review
No. of External Reviewers: 3
No. of In House Reviewers: 0
Acceptance Rate: 18-22%
Time to Review: 2 - 3 Months
Reviewers Comments: Yes
Invited Articles: 0-5%
Fees to Publish: 0.00 US$

MANUSCRIPT TOPICS:
All in Relation to Sport Management; Labor Relations & Human Resource Mgt.; Marketing; Organizational Behavior & Theory; Organizational Development; Public Administration; Sport Policy

MANUSCRIPT GUIDELINES/COMMENTS:

Mission Statement
The *Journal of Sport Management* (*JSM*) publishes articles that focus on the theoretical and applied aspects of management related to sport, exercise, dance, and play. Articles are evaluated on their merit for contributing to the understanding of sport management through theory development and application.

JSM publishes research and scholarly review articles; short reports on replications, test development, and data reanalysis (Research Notes); editorials that focus on significant issues pertaining to sport management (Sport Management Perspectives); journal abstracts (Sport Management Digest); book reviews (Off the Press); and news items of interest to professionals in sport management (Management Memos). Manuscripts focusing on topics such as leadership, motivation, communication, organization, professional preparation, ethics, marketing, economics, and financial administration related to sport and exercise are appropriate. Papers written from historical, psychological, philosophical, sociological, and other perspectives are encouraged. Papers focusing on sport management in a variety of settings are also desired-professional sport, intercollegiate and interscholastic sports, health/sport clubs, sport facilities, sport events, and community recreational sports.

JSM accepts articles that are derived from both experimental and experiential methodologies. Laboratory and highly controlled field experiments may be appropriate for the study of certain sport management issues, as are field studies, surveys, case studies, observational methods, and field evaluation approaches. Articles submitted to *JSM* are judged on the appropriateness of the methods for the problem being studied rather than prescribing that certain methods are the only ones suitable for the study of sport management.

Papers investigating theoretical constructs, research that moves toward theory development, and articles that link theory with practice are especially encouraged. *JSM* invites papers presenting new and/or controversial ideas as well as those applying traditional concepts. Articles without a theoretical base are also invited to the extent that they contribute to an understanding of sport management.

Submission Guidelines
JSM publishes articles focusing on the theoretical and applied aspects of management related to sport, broadly defined. We welcome submissions on a wide range of managerial topics dealing with voluntary, public, and commercial sport organizations and the complex social, cultural, political, economic, and technological environments in which they are located. As the goal is to advance the body of knowledge in sport management, articles must be theoretically grounded and must contribute new insights, explanations, or methodological approaches. In addition, the implications for sport managers should be fully developed based on the findings.

Sport management is a multi-disciplinary field. Submissions are welcomed from all relevant disciplines including kinesiology, management, marketing, economics, communications, tourism, law, psychology, sociology, and cultural studies. International submissions are encouraged.

In addition to regular research articles, *JSM* publishes position papers on significant issues pertaining to sport management (Sport Management Perspectives), short reports on replications or new methodological applications (Research Notes), book reviews (Off the Press), article abstracts (Sport Management Digest), and conferences (Management Memos). Individuals interested in submitting book reviews should contact the Section Editor, Karen Danylchuk, EdD, Associate Professor, School of Kinesiology, 3M Centre, The University of Western Ontario, London, ON, Canada N6A 3K7.

In preparing manuscripts for publication in the *Journal of Sport Management*, authors should follow the guidelines in the *Publication Manual of the American Psychological Association* (5th ed.). All articles must be preceded by an abstract of no more than 150 words. Manuscripts must be submitted in English and must be double-spaced, including references and blocked quotations, on standard 8½ x 11-in. white paper with approximately 1½ -in margins (or A4). Regular articles should typically not exceed 30 manuscript pages, and Research Notes should not exceed 15 pages. If footnotes are used, they should not exceed 6 lines each. Figures submitted on disk should be saved in Excel or TIFF formats. All tables, figure captions, and footnotes must be grouped together on pages separate from the body of the text. Reference citations in the text must be accurate concerning dates of publication and spelling of author names, and they must cross-check with those in the reference list. Copies of manuscripts are not returned to the authors.

The original manuscript and three copies should be sent to the Editor. Manuscripts must not be submitted to another journal while they are under review by *JSM*, nor should they have been previously published. All manuscripts are evaluated by blind review and comments from reviewers along with the editorial decision are made available to the authors. The name(s) of the author(s) should not appear on the manuscript proper. The first page of the original should include the title of the paper and the name and affiliation of each author, as well as the full mailing and e-mail addresses and fax number of the author who is to receive the galley proofs if the manuscript is accepted. The title page on the three copies should show only the title at the top of the page and the running head at the bottom. Authors of manuscripts accepted for publication must transfer copyright to Human Kinetics Publishers, Inc.

Journal of Strategic E-Commerce

ADDRESS FOR SUBMISSION:

Current Editor / Check Website
Journal of Strategic E-Commerce
Digital Submission Through Website
Address other questions to:
 Jim or JoAnn Carland at # below
USA
Phone: 828-293-9151
E-Mail: info@alliedacademies.org
Web: www.alliedacademies.org

CIRCULATION DATA:

Reader: Academics
Frequency of Issue: Yearly
Sponsor/Publisher: Allied Academies, Inc.

PUBLICATION GUIDELINES:

Manuscript Length: 16-20
Copies Required: Submit Through Web
Computer Submission: Yes ˙
Format: MS Word, WordPerfect
Fees to Review: 0.00 US$

Manuscript Style:
 American Psychological Association

REVIEW INFORMATION:

Type of Review: Blind Review
No. of External Reviewers: 3
No. of In House Reviewers: 2
Acceptance Rate: 21-30%
Time to Review: 3 - 4 Months
Reviewers Comments: Yes
Invited Articles: 0-5%
Fees to Publish: 75.00 US$ Membership

MANUSCRIPT TOPICS:

E-Commerce; E-Government; Public Administration; Strategic Management of E-Commerce

MANUSCRIPT GUIDELINES/COMMENTS:

The journal publishes theoretical or empirical research on any of the Manuscript Topics.

Comments. All authors of published manuscripts must be members of the appropriate academy affiliate of Allied Academies. The current membership fee is US$75.00.

Editorial Policy Guidelines

The primary criterion upon which manuscripts are judged is whether the research advances the discipline. Key points include currency, interest and relevancy.

In order for a theoretical manuscript to advance the discipline, it must address the literature to support conclusions or models which extend knowledge and understanding. Consequently, referees pay particular attention to completeness of literature review and appropriateness of conclusions drawn from that review.

In order for an empirical manuscript to advance the discipline, it must employ appropriate and effective sampling and statistical analysis techniques, and must be grounded by a thorough literature review. Consequently, referees pay particular attention to the research methodology and to the conclusions drawn from statistical analyses and their consistency with the literature.

Journal of Strategic International Business

ADDRESS FOR SUBMISSION:

Tahi J. Gnepa, Editor
Journal of Strategic International Business
983 Woodland Drive
Turlock, CA 95382-7281
USA
Phone: 209-667-3448
E-Mail: Review@iabe.org
Web: www.iabe.org; www.aibe.org

CIRCULATION DATA:

Reader: Business Persons, Academics
Frequency of Issue: 2 Times/Year
Sponsor/Publisher: Academy of
  International Business and Economics
  (AIBE)

PUBLICATION GUIDELINES:

Manuscript Length: 11-15
Copies Required: One
Computer Submission: Yes Disk, Email
Format: MS Word
Fees to Review: 0.00 US$

Manuscript Style:
  Chicago Manual of Style

REVIEW INFORMATION:

Type of Review: Blind Review
No. of External Reviewers: 2
No. of In House Reviewers: 1
Acceptance Rate: 11-20%
Time to Review: 1 - 2 Months
Reviewers Comments: Yes
Invited Articles: 0-5%
Fees to Publish: 0.00 US$

MANUSCRIPT TOPICS:

Advertising & Promotion Management; E-Commerce; Global Business; International Marketing; Marketing Research; Marketing Theory & Applications; Purchasing/Materials Management; Sales/Selling; Services; Strategic Management Policy; Technology/Innovation; Tourism, Hospitality & Leisure

MANUSCRIPT GUIDELINES/COMMENTS:

Please use following manuscript Guidelines for submission of your papers for the review. Papers are reviewed on a continual basis throughout the year. Early Submissions are welcome! Please email your manuscript to **Review@iabe.org**.

Copyright. Articles, papers, or cases submitted for publication should be original contributions and should not be under consideration for any other publication at the same time. Authors submitting articles/papers/cases for publication warrant that the work is not an infringement of any existing copyright, infringement of proprietary right, invasion of privacy, or libel and will indemnify, defend, and hold AIBE or sponsor(s) harmless from any damages, expenses, and costs against any breach of such warranty. For ease of dissemination and to ensure proper policing of use papers/articles/cases and contributions become the legal copyright of the AIBE/IABE unless otherwise agreed in writing.

716

General Information. These are submission instructions for review purpose only. Once your submission is accepted you will receive submission guidelines with your paper acceptance letter. The author(s) will be emailed result of the review process in about 6-8 weeks from submission date. Papers are reviewed and accepted on a continual basis. Submit your papers early for full considerations!

Typing. Paper must be laser printed/printable on 8.5" x 11" white sheets in Arial 10-point font single-spaced lines justify style in MS Word. All four margins must be 1" each.

First Page. Paper title not exceeding two lines must be CAPITALIZED AND CENTERED IN BOLD LETTERS. Author name and university/organizational affiliation of each author must be printed on one line each. Do NOT include titles such as Dr., Professor, Ph.D., department address email address etc. Please print the word "ABSTRACT" in capitalized bold letters left justified and double-spaced from last author's name/affiliation. Abstract should be in italic. Please see the sample manuscript.

All other Headings. All other section headings starting with INTRODUCTION must be numbered in capitalized bold letters left justified and double-spaced from last line above them. See the subsection headings in the sample manuscript.

Tables Figures and Charts. All tables figures or charts must be inserted in the body of the manuscripts within the margins with headings/titles in centered CAPITALIZED BOLD letters.

References and Bibliography. All references listed in this section must be cited in the article and vice-versa. The reference citations in the text must be inserted in parentheses within sentences with author name followed by a comma and year of publication. Please follow the following formats:

Journal Articles
Khade Alan S. and Metlen Scott K. "An Application of Benchmarking in Dairy Industry" *International Journal of Benchmarking* Vol. III (4) 1996 17

Books
Harrison Norma and Samson D. Technology Management: Text and Cases McGraw-Hill Publishing New York 2002

Internet
Hesterbrink C. E-Business and ERP: Bringing two Paradigms together October 1999; PricewaterhouseCoopers *www.pwc.com*.

Author Profile(s). At the end of paper include author profile(s) not exceeding five lines each author including name highest degree/university/year current position/university and major achievements. For example:

Author Profile:
Dr. Tahi J. Gnepa earned his Ph.D. at the University of Wisconsin Madison in 1989. Currently he is a professor of international business at California State University Stanislaus and Managing Editor of Journal of International Business Strategy (JIBStrategy).

Manuscript. Absolutely no footnotes! Do not insert page numbers for the manuscript. Please do not forget to run spelling and grammar check for the completed paper. Save the manuscript on your diskette/CD or hard drive.

Electronic Submission. Send your submission as an MS Word file attachment to your Email to **Review@iabe.org**.

Journal of Strategic Marketing

ADDRESS FOR SUBMISSION:

Carolyn A. Strong, Editor
Journal of Strategic Marketing
Cardiff University
Cardiff Business School
Colum Drive
Cardiff, CF1 3EU
UK
Phone: +44 (0) 122-875-559
E-Mail: strong@cardiff.ac.uk
Web: www.routledge.co.uk

CIRCULATION DATA:

Reader: Academics
Frequency of Issue: Quarterly
Sponsor/Publisher: Routledge (Taylor &
    Francis Ltd.)

PUBLICATION GUIDELINES:

Manuscript Length: 30+
Copies Required: Three
Computer Submission: Yes
Format: All formats, prefer MS Word
Fees to Review: 0.00 US$

Manuscript Style:
    Chicago Manual of Style

REVIEW INFORMATION:

Type of Review: Blind Review
No. of External Reviewers: 2
No. of In House Reviewers: 2
Acceptance Rate: 21-30%
Time to Review: 1 - 2 Months
Reviewers Comments: Yes
Invited Articles: 0-5%
Fees to Publish: 0.00 US$

MANUSCRIPT TOPICS:
Marketing Theory & Applications

MANUSCRIPT GUIDELINES/COMMENTS:

Aims and Scope
Journal of Strategic Marketing publishes papers on key aspects of the interface between marketing and strategic management. It is a vehicle for discussing long-range activities where marketing has to play in managing the long-term objectives and strategies of companies. The objectives of the *Journal* are as follows:
1. To bridge the disciplines of marketing and strategic management, and to address the development of knowledge concerning the role that marketing has to play in the management of strategy.
2. To provide a vehicle for the advancement of knowledge in the field of strategic marketing and to stimulate research in this area.
3. To consider the role of marketing as an orientation of management at the strategic level of organizations.
4. Explore the overall management of the marketing function within total corporate management, with particular focus on issues of concern to marketing managers, directors and vice presidents.

5. To publish state of the art papers, empirical research results, practical aspects of theory, case studies, new methodological developments, conceptual developments, and to encourage published discussion on articles.

Issues that the *Journal* covers include:
- Marketing philosophy in corporate management.
- The role of marketing in strategic planning.
- Marketing information systems in relation to company wide needs.
- Market and industry stakeholder needs.
- International strategies.
- SBU analysis and decision making.
- Marketing related synergies.
- Integrating marketing planning with strategic planning.
- The management of marketing-led change.
- The development and utilization of marketing plans.
- Resource allocation in strategic and marketing plans.
- HRM related to marketing personnel.
- The implementation of strategic and marketing plans.
- Marketing effectiveness at the operational and strategic levels.
- The utilization and development of control systems.
- Relationship Marketing

Articles should be between 4000-6000 words. Three copies should be sent to one of the Editors at Cardiff Business School, Colum Drive, Cardiff, CF1 3EU, UK

Submission of Papers on Disk
We are able to accept most common forms of disks. However, authors must also submit three hard copies of the paper for copyediting purposes. If for some reason we are unable to use the disk, the paper will be typeset in the usual manner.

Presentation
Contributions should be typed on A4 paper with double-line spacing and wide margins (at least 2.5€cm). Each article should be presented as follows:
1. Title page: title, authors' names and addresses and the name, address, and telephone and fax numbers of the author to whom all correspondence concerning the article should be sent.
2. Second page: title, abstract of about 150 words and up to six keywords for indexing purposes.
3. Main body of the paper: presented as given below.

References
The Harvard system should be used; that is the name of the author and date of publication are cited in the text. The references are listed in alphabetical order at the end of the article in the following style:

Journal Articles
Hutt, M.D., Reigen, P.H. and Ronchetto, J.R. (1988) Tracing emergent processes in marketing strategy formulation. Journal of Marketing 52, 4--19.

Articles in Books, Conference Proceedings etc.
Wensley, J.R.C. (1987) Marketing strategy. In: M.J. Barker (ed) The Marketing Book, London: Heinemann.

Books
Jain, S.C. (1985) Marketing Planning and Strategy, 2nd Edn, Cincinnati: South-Western.

Tables and Figures
Each should be numbered in the order in which they are referred to in the text and cited as Fig. 1, Figs 2--5, Table 1, Tables 1 and 2 etc.

Figures and tables should not be included in the text but accompany the manuscript on separate pages.

Figures should be originals (not photocopies), printed from a laser printer or drawn in black ink on white card. The size of any labelling should be sufficient to allow for reductions of up to 50%. Figure captions should be grouped together on a separate sheet.

Footnotes
These should not be used unless absolutely essential. If included they should be kept to a minimum, and numbered consecutively on separate sheets.

Copyright
Submission of an article to the *Journal of Strategic Marketing* is taken to imply that it presents original unpublished work which is not under consideration for publication elsewhere.

On acceptance of a paper the authors will be asked to assign copyright to the publishers, Routledge, by signing a copyright form.

Refereeing
All articles will be double-blind refereed, and comments will be communicated to the authors. Articles will only be accepted for publication when they have been modified in line with the referees' comments.

Proofs
Proofs will be sent to the corresponding author (unless otherwise specified) for correction. The author should return the proofs within three days of receipt to avoid delay to publication. Extensive alterations which were not in the original manuscript are strongly discouraged.

Journal of Sustainable Tourism

ADDRESS FOR SUBMISSION:

Bill Bramwell & Bernard Lane, Co-Editors
Journal of Sustainable Tourism
c/o Multilingual Matters Ltd
Frankfurt Lodge
Clevedon Hall
Victoria Road
Clevedon, BS21 7HH
England
Phone: +44 (0) 1275 876519
E-Mail: info@channelviewpublications.com
Web: www.channelviewpublications.com

CIRCULATION DATA:

Reader: Academics
Frequency of Issue: Bi-Monthly
Sponsor/Publisher: Multilingual Matters /
  Channel View Publications

PUBLICATION GUIDELINES:

Manuscript Length: 16-20
Copies Required: Four
Computer Submission: Yes Preferred
Format: RTF, DOC Files
Fees to Review: 0.00 US$

Manuscript Style:
  American Psychological Association

REVIEW INFORMATION:

Type of Review: Blind Review
No. of External Reviewers: 3
No. of In House Reviewers: 2
Acceptance Rate: 60%
Time to Review: 4 - 6 Months
Reviewers Comments: Yes
Invited Articles: 0-5%
Fees to Publish: 0.00 US$

MANUSCRIPT TOPICS:
Business Education; Global Business; Organizational Development; Services; Tourism, Hospitality & Leisure

MANUSCRIPT GUIDELINES/COMMENTS:

Topics Include. Sustainable Tourism, Tourism and Environment, Tourism Policy and Planning, Tourism and Culture, Tourism and Business

Editors. Bill Bramwell (Sheffield Hallam University) and Bernard Lane (University of Bristol)

NB. Subscription includes On-line access.
Library/Institutional £240.00 or US$520.00 or Euro €420.00
Individual/Schools £55.00 or US$99.00 or Euro €80.00

1. Articles should not normally exceed 7,000 words. Note that it is our policy not to review papers that are currently under consideration by other journals.

2. They should be typed, double-spaced on A4 paper, with ample left- and right-hand margins, on one side of the paper only, and every page should be numbered consecutively. A cover page should contain only the title, thereby facilitating anonymous reviewing by two independent assessors. Authors may also wish to take precautions to avoid textual references, which would identify themselves to the referees. In such cases the authors of accepted papers will have the opportunity to include any such omitted material before the paper is published.

3. Submissions for Work in Progress/Readers' Response/Letters to the Editor sections should be approximately 500 words in length.

4. Main contact author should also appear in a separate paragraph on the title page.

5. An abstract should be included. This should not exceed 200 words (longer abstracts are rejected by many abstracting services).

6. A short version of the title (maximum 45 characters) should also be supplied for the journal's running headline.

7. To facilitate the production of the annual subject index, a list of key words (not more than six) should be provided, under which the paper may be indexed.

8. Footnotes should be avoided. Essential notes should be numbered in the text and grouped together at the end of the article. Diagrams and figures, if they are considered essential, should be clearly related to the section of the text to which they refer. The original diagrams and figures should be submitted with the top copy.

9. References should be set out in alphabetical order of the author's name in a list at the end of the article. They should be given in standard form, as in the Appendix below.

10. References in the text of an article should be by the author's name and year of publication, as in these examples: Jones (1987) in a paper on... [commonest version]; Jones and Evans (1997c: 22) state that... [where page number is required]; Evidence is given by Smith et al. (1984)... [for three or more authors]. Further exploration of this aspect may be found in many sources (e.g., Brown & Green, 1982; Jackson, 1983; White, 1981a) [note alphabetical order, use of & and semicolons].

11. Articles may be submitted electronically or by hard copy. If sent electronically, text should be saved in the author's normal word processor format (please give name of the program used). Any Figures or Tables should be saved in a separate file from the rest of the text.

Electronic submissions should be sent by e-mail attachment to **submissions@channelview publications.com**, with the covering message clearly stating the name of the journal concerned; on CD-ROM, or on disc (IBM compatible or high-density AppleMac) to the Editor, Journal Name, c/o Channel View Publications, Frankfurt Lodge, Clevedon Hall, Victoria Road, Clevedon BS21 7HH, England.

If hard copies are provided, four copies of the manuscript should be sent, together with a CD-Rom or disc as above, to this same address.

12. The author of an article accepted for publication will receive page proofs for correction, if there is sufficient time to do so. This stage must not be used as an opportunity to revise the paper, because alterations are extremely costly; extensive changes will be charged to the author and will probably result in the article being delayed to a later issue. Speedy return of corrected proofs is important.

Appendix 1: References
A very large majority of authors' proof-corrections are caused by errors in references. Authors are therefore requested to check the following points particularly carefully when submitting manuscripts:

- Are all the references in the reference list cited in the text?
- Do all the citations in the text appear in the reference list?
- Do the dates in the text and the reference list correspond?
- Do the spellings of authors' names in text and reference list correspond, and do all authors have the correct initials?
- Are journal references complete with volume and pages numbers?
- Are references to books complete with place of publication and the name of the publisher?

It is extremely helpful if references are presented as far as possible in accordance with our house style. A few more typical examples are shown below. Note, especially, use of upper and lower case in paper titles, use of capital letters and italic (underlining can be used as an alternative if italic is not available) in book and journal titles, punctuation (or lack of it) after dates, journal titles, and book titles. The inclusion of issue numbers of journals, or page numbers in books, is optional but if included should be as per the examples below.

Department of Education and Science (DES) (1985) *Education for All* (The Swann Report). London: HMSO.

Evans, N.J. and Ilbery, B.W. (1989) A conceptual framework for investigating farm-based accommodation and tourism in Britain. *Journal of Rural Studies* 5 (3), 257–266.

Evans, N.J. and Ilbery, B.W. (1992) Advertising and farm-based accommodation: A British case study. *Tourism Management* 13 (4), 415–422.

Laufer, B. (1985) Vocabulary acquisition in a second language: The hypothesis of 'synforms'. PhD thesis, University of Edinburgh.

Mackey, W.F. (1980) The ecology of language shift. In P.H. Nelde (ed.) *Languages in Contact and in Conflict* (pp. 35–41). Wiesbaden: Steiner.

724

Marien, C. and Pizam, A. (1997) Implementing sustainable tourism development through citizen participation in the planning process. In S. Wahab and J. Pigram (eds) *Tourism, Development and Growth* (pp. 164–78). London: Routledge.

Morrison, D. (1980) Small group discussion project questionnaire. University of Hong Kong Language Centre (mimeo).

Zahn, C.J. and Hopper, R. (1985) The speech evaluation instrument: A user's manual (version 1.0a). Unpublished manuscript, Cleveland State University.

Zigler, E. and Balla, D. (eds) (1982) *Mental Retardation: The Developmental-Difference Controversy.* Hillsdale, NJ: Lawrence Erlbaum.

Appendix 2: Figures, Diagrams, and Graphics
Illustrations, diagrams, and other graphics should be supplied separately from the text, not embedded within it. The position of artwork relative to the text should be indicated by (e.g.) 'Figure 2 near here.' It is rarely possible to place figures on the printed page exactly as in the manuscript, so a cross-reference (e.g. 'see Figure 2') normally needs to appear as part of the text.

Figure captions should not normally form part of the figure, but should be supplied as part of the text. However, keys should normally be included as part of the artwork.

Unless arranged otherwise, all illustrations will be printed in black-and-white, so artwork incorporating colours is not normally appropriate, and may be rejected. It is normally better to use shading or hatching rather than tints, if at all possible. Coloured tints will all come out as grey, and even grey tints should normally be separated by at least 20% (i.e., 20% black, 40% black, etc.).

The size of figures, and the type sizes used in them, should be appropriate to the *Journal* in which they are to be printed (normally 120mm wide and 200mm high). Artwork larger than this is acceptable, but will be reduced to fit these dimensions.

Figures and diagrams, if not supplied electronically, should be supplied as clean black-and-white prints, suitable as camera-ready copy for scanning.

For artwork supplied electronically, our preferred formats are EPS or TIFF formats. Most art programs give 'Save As' or 'Export' options into one or other or both of these formats. Other formats (e.g., those built into word processors such as Word) normally do not produce such reliable results, and it is usually preferable for authors to supply camera-ready copy for scanning if neither EPS nor TIFF is possible. In all cases, we need a printout supplied by the author for references purposes.

Electronic artwork must be supplied in black-and-white, as we cannot guarantee that figures will reproduce correctly if supplied in colour.

The EPS format is usually the most appropriate one for line drawings. However, file sizes may be very large, and in which case files should be supplied on CD-ROM, rather than sent by e-mail, as large e-mails may be rejected.

The TIFF format is more appropriate for figures containing tones or grey-scales, and for photographs. The resolution is an important consideration, as this needs to be at least 300dpi for printing purposes. The default resolution in many programs is 72dpi, and the default format is JPEG, but although these give acceptable results when viewed on a computer screen, they are rarely good enough when transferred to the printed page. To cut down on file size, the LZW compression is often acceptable. Files should be saved with a preview, if at all possible.

For more details, please e-mail us on **info@multilingual-matters.com**.

Journal of Targeting, Measurement, and Analysis for Marketing

ADDRESS FOR SUBMISSION:

Mariam Hasan, Publisher
Journal of Targeting, Measurement, and
  Analysis for Marketing
Palgrave Macmillan
Houndmills
Basingstoke, RG21 6XS
UK
Phone:
E-Mail: submissions@palgrave.com
Web: http://www.palgrave-journals.com/
  jt/index.html

PUBLICATION GUIDELINES:

Manuscript Length: 2,000-5,000 Words
Copies Required: One + Electronic Copy
Computer Submission: Yes Email
Format:
Fees to Review: 0.00 US$

Manuscript Style:
, Vancouver

CIRCULATION DATA:

Reader: Business Persons, Academics
Frequency of Issue: Quarterly
Sponsor/Publisher: Palgrave Macmillan

REVIEW INFORMATION:

Type of Review: Blind Review
No. of External Reviewers: 3
No. of In House Reviewers: 2
Acceptance Rate: 50%
Time to Review: 1 - 2 Months
Reviewers Comments: Yes
Invited Articles: 31-50%
Fees to Publish: 0.00 US$

MANUSCRIPT TOPICS:

Advertising & Promotion Management; Business Education; Business Information Systems (MIS); Communication; Direct Marketing; Global Business; Marketing Research; Marketing Theory & Applications; Non-Profit Organizations; Operations Research/Statistics; Organizational Behavior & Theory; Organizational Development; Strategic Management Policy

MANUSCRIPT GUIDELINES/COMMENTS:

Under the guidance of its expert Editor and an eminent international Editorial Board, *Journal of Targeting, Measurement and Analysis for Marketing* has developed into one of the world's leading forums for the latest thinking, techniques and developments on the measurement, analysis and targeting of marketing activities. *Journal of Targeting, Measurement and Analysis for Marketing* has established itself as a key bridge between applied academic research and commercial best practice, globally.

Instructions for Authors

1. Papers should be between 2,000 and 5,000 words in length. Authors are requested to submit a hard copy of their manuscript as well as an electronic copy by email. Submissions should be addressed to:

Mariam Hasan
Publisher
Palgrave Macmillan
Houndmills
Basingstoke RG21 6XS, UK
E-mail: **submissions@palgrave.com**

Please clearly state for which journal you are contributing.

2. All papers should be accompanied by a short abstract, outlining the aims and subject matter of the paper.

3. Papers should be accompanied by a short (about 50 words) description of the author and, if appropriate, the organisation of which he or she is a member. This will be published.

4. Papers should be supported by actual or hypothetical examples, wherever possible and appropriate. Authors should not seek to use the *Journal* as a vehicle for marketing any specific product or service.

5. Authors should avoid the use of personal pronouns or language or slang which is not in keeping with the academic and professional style of the *Journal*.

6. Titles of organisations etc. should be written out first in full followed by the organisation's initials in brackets, e.g. Direct Marketing Association (DMA), and thereafter the initials only should be used.

7. Papers should be supported by references. References should be set out in accordance with the Vancouver style - that is, they should be numbered consecutively in the text and then set out in full in a corresponding numbered list at the end of the text in the following form: [for journal articles] Author (year) 'Title of article', *Journal name*, Vol., No., pp.; [for books] Author (year) 'Title of chapter' in 'Editor' (ed.), 'Book title', Publisher, place of publication.

8. Photographs and illustrations supporting papers should be submitted where appropriate. Photographs should be good-quality positives, printed from the original negatives and in black and white only. They should be 8x13 cm or larger. Figures and other line illustrations should be submitted both electronically and in good quality originals and electronic copy of the data should also be included.

9. Authors are asked to ensure that references to named people and/or organisations are accurate and without libellous implications.

10. All contributions sent to the Publisher, whether invited or not, will be subjected to double blind refereeing and will be reviewed by at least two referees. Any such contribution must bear the author's full name and address, even if this is not for publication. Contributions, whether published pseudonymously or not, are accepted on the strict understanding that the author is responsible for the accuracy of all opinion, technical comment, factual report, data, figures, illustrations and photographs. Publication does not necessarily imply that these are the opinions of the Editorial Board or of the Publisher, nor does the Board accept any liability for the accuracy of such comment, report and other technical and factual information. The Publisher will, however, strive to ensure that all opinion, comments, reports, data, figures, illustrations and photographs are accurate, insofar as it is within its abilities to do so. The Publisher reserves the right to edit, abridge or omit material submitted for publication.

11. **Copyright**. Authors are responsible for obtaining permission from copyright holders for reproducing through any medium of communication those illustrations, tables, figures or lengthy quotations previously published elsewhere. Add your acknowledgements to the typescript, preferably in the form of an "Acknowledgements" section at the end of the paper. Credit the source and copyright of photographs or figures in the accompanying captions.

The journal's policy is to own copyright in all contributions. Before publication, authors assign copyright to the Publishers, but retain their rights to republish this material in other works written or edited by themselves, subject to full acknowledgement of the original source of publication.

The journal mandates the Copyright Clearance Center in the USA and the Copyright Licensing Agency in the UK to offer centralised licensing arrangements for photocopying in their respective territories.

12. No contribution will be accepted which has been published elsewhere, unless it is expressly invited or agreed by the Publisher. Authors should be aware that papers submitted to the Journal should not be simultaneously submitted for review to any other publications.

13. All reasonable efforts are made to ensure accurate reproduction of text, photographs and illustrations. The Publisher does not accept responsibility for mistakes, be they editorial or typographical, nor for consequences resulting from them.

14. Authors will be given the opportunity to purchase offprints of their paper once typesetting has been finalised. The Publishers will send first-named authors up to three free copies of the issue containing their paper.

Journal of Teaching in Travel & Tourism

ADDRESS FOR SUBMISSION:

Cathy Hsu, Editor-in-Chief
Journal of Teaching in Travel & Tourism
Hong Kong Polytechnic University
School of Hotel & Tourism Management
Hung Hom
Kowloon,
Hong Kong
Phone: +852 2766 4682
E-Mail: hmhsu@polyu.edu.hk
Web: www.istte.org/journal.asp

CIRCULATION DATA:

Reader: Academics
Frequency of Issue: Quarterly
Sponsor/Publisher: International Society of
    Travel & Tourism Educators (ISTTE) /
    Haworth Press

PUBLICATION GUIDELINES:

Manuscript Length: 21-25
Copies Required: Three
Computer Submission: Yes ·
Format: MS Word
Fees to Review: 0.00 US$

Manuscript Style:
    American Psychological Association

REVIEW INFORMATION:

Type of Review: Blind Review
No. of External Reviewers: 2
No. of In House Reviewers: 1
Acceptance Rate: 50%
Time to Review: 1 - 2 Months
Reviewers Comments: Yes
Invited Articles: 11-20%
Fees to Publish: 0.00 US$

MANUSCRIPT TOPICS:
Business Education; Tourism, Hospitality & Leisure

MANUSCRIPT GUIDELINES/COMMENTS:

About the Journal
The *Journal of Teaching in Travel & Tourism* is the professional journal of the International Society of Travel & Tourism Educators (ISTTE). *JTTT* serves as an international interdisciplinary forum and reference source for travel and tourism education. The readership of *JTTT* is international in scope, with a good representation in college and university libraries as well as high schools and professional schools offering courses in travel and tourism.

Here is a sample of what you'll find in *JTTT*.
* Cutting-edge topics for inclusion in travel and tourism courses
* The latest developments in travel and tourism teaching methods and/or technology
* International travel and tourism course curriculum
* Teaching and learning evaluation issues
* Careers for travel and tourism students

The *Journal of Teaching in Travel and Tourism* publishes quality manuscripts relating to travel and tourism education at various levels, ranging from professional schools to degree-granting universities.

Instructions for Authors

1. **Original Articles Only.** Submission of a manuscript to the *Journal* represents a certification on the part of the author(s) that it is an original work, and that neither this manuscript nor a version of it has been published elsewhere nor is being considered for publication elsewhere.

Electronic submissions are accepted. When submitting manuscripts via email attachments, only Microsoft Word for Windows format is accepted. All information should be included in one file (i.e., cover page, text, references, and tables/figures). The separate page should be in the email message.

For inquiries on submissions, contact the Editor.

2. **Manuscript Length.** Your manuscript may be approximately 5,000 words (15-25 double-spaced pages, including references, tables, and figures). Lengthier manuscripts or shorter viewpoint/opinion pieces will be considered at the discretion of the Editor. Sometimes, lengthier manuscripts may be considered if they can be divided up into sections for publication in successive *Journal* issues.

3. **Manuscript Style.** References, citations, and general style of manuscripts for this *Journal* should follow the APA style, as outlined in the latest edition of the *Publication Manual of the American Psychological Association*. References should be double-spaced and placed in alphabetical order. The use of footnotes within the text is discouraged. Words should be underlined only when it is intended that they be typeset in italics.

If an author wishes to submit a paper that has been already prepared in another style, he or she may do so. However, if the paper is accepted (with or without reviewer's alterations), the author is fully responsible for retyping the manuscript in the correct style as indicated above. Neither the Editor nor the Publisher is responsible for re-preparing manuscript copy to adhere to the *Journal*'s style.

4. **Manuscript Preparation**
Margins. Leave at least a 1" margin on all four sides.
Paper. Use clean, white 8½" x 11" bond paper.
Number of Copies. 4 (the original plus 3 photocopies)
Cover Page. Important—Staple a cover page to the manuscript, indicating only the article title (this is used for anonymous refereeing).
Second "Title Page". Enclose a regular title page but do not staple it to the manuscript. Include the title again, plus:
- Full authorship
- An ABSTRACT of about 100 words. (Below the abstract provide 3-10 key words for index purposes).

- A header or footer on each page with abbreviated title and pg number of total (e.g., pg 2 of 7)
- An introductory footnote with authors' academic degrees, professional titles, affiliations, mailing and e-mail addresses, and any desired acknowledgment of research support or other credit.

5. Return Envelopes. When you submit your four manuscript copies, also include:
- A 9" x 12" envelope, self-addressed and stamped (with sufficient postage to ensure return of your manuscript);
- A regular envelope, stamped and self-addressed. This is for the Editor to send you an "acknowledgement of receipt" letter.

6. Spelling, grammar, and punctuation. You are responsible for preparing manuscript copy which is clearly written in acceptable, scholarly English and which contains no errors of spelling, grammar, or punctuation. Neither the Editor nor the Publisher is responsible for correcting errors of spelling and grammar. The manuscript, after acceptance by the Editor, must be immediately ready for typesetting as it is finally submitted by the author(s).

Check your paper for the following common errors:
- Dangling modifiers
- Misplaced modifiers
- Unclear antecedents
- Incorrect or inconsistent abbreviations

Also, check the accuracy of all arithmetic calculations, statistics, numerical data, text citations, and references.

7. Inconsistencies must be avoided. Be sure you are consistent in your use of abbreviations, terminology, and in citing references, from one part of your paper to another.

8. Preparation of Tables, Figures, and Illustrations. Any material that is not textual is considered artwork. This includes tables, figures, diagrams, charts, graphs, illustrations, appendices, screen captures, and photos. Tables and figures (including legend, notes, and sources) should be no larger than 4½ x 6½". Type styles should be Helvetica (or Helvetica narrow if necessary) and no smaller than 8 point. We request that computer-generated figures be in black and white and/or shades of gray (preferably no color, for it does not reproduce well). Camera-ready art must contain no grammatical, typographical, or format errors and must reproduce sharply and clearly in the dimensions of the final printed page (4½ x 6½"). Photos and screen captures must be on disk as a TIF file, or other graphic file format such as JPEG or BMP. For rapid publication we must receive black-and-white glossy or matte positives (white background with black images and/or wording) in addition to files on disk. Tables should be created in the text document file using the software's Table feature.

9. Submitting Art. Both a printed hard copy and a disk copy of the art must be provided. We request that each piece of art be sent in its own file, on a disk separate from the disk containing the manuscript text file(s), and be clearly labeled. We reserve the right to (if necessary) request new art, alter art, or if all else has failed in achieving art that is presentable, delete art. If submitted art cannot be used, the Publisher reserves the right to redo the art and to change the author for a fee of US$35 per hour for this service. The Haworth Press, Inc. is not responsible for errors incurred in the preparation of new artwork. Camera-ready artwork must be prepared on separate sheets of paper. Always use black ink and professional drawing instruments. On the back of these items, write your article title and the journal title lightly in soft-lead pencil (please do not write on the face of art). In the text file, skip extra lines and indicate where these figures are placed. Photos are considered part of the acceptable manuscript and remain with the Publisher for use in additional printings.

10. **Electronic Media.** Haworth's in-house typesetting unit is able to utilize your final manuscript material as prepared on most personal computers and word processors. This will minimize typographical errors and decrease overall production time. Please send the first draft and final draft copies of your manuscript to the *Journal* Editor in print format for his/her final review and approval. After approval of your final manuscript, please submit the final approved version both on printed format ("hard copy") and floppy diskette. On the outside of the diskette package write:

a.   The brand name of your computer or word processor
b.   The word processing program and version that you used
c.   The title of your article, and
d.   The file name.

Note. Disk and hard copy must agree. In case of discrepancies, it is The Haworth Press' policy to follow hard copy. Authors are advised that no revisions of the manuscript can be made after acceptance by the Editor for publication. The benefits of this procedure are many with speed and accuracy being the most obvious. We look forward to working with your electronic submission which will allow us to serve you more efficiently.

11. **Alternations Required by Referees and Reviewers.** Many times a paper is accepted by the Editor contingent upon changes that are mandated by anonymous specialist referees and members of the Editorial Board. If the Editor returns your manuscript for revisions, you are responsible for retyping any sections of the paper to incorporate these revisions (if applicable, revisions should also be put on disk).

12. **Typesetting.** You will not be receiving galley proofs of your article. Editorial revisions, if any, must therefore be made while your article is still in manuscript. The final version of the manuscript will be the version you see published. Typesetter's errors will be corrected by the production staff of The Haworth Press. Authors are expected to submit manuscripts, disks, and art that are free from error.

13. **Reprints.** The senior author will receive two copies of the *Journal* issue and complimentary reprints of his or her article. The junior author will receive two copies of the *Journal* issue. These are sent several weeks after the *Journal* issue is published and in circulation. An order form for the purchase of additional reprints will also be sent to all authors at this time. (Approximately 4–6 weeks is necessary for the preparation of reprints.) Please do not query the *Journal*'s Editor about reprints. All such questions should be sent directly to The Haworth Press, Inc., Production Department, 37 West Broad Street, West

Hazleton, PA 18202. To order additional reprints (minimum: 50 copies), please contact The Haworth Document Delivery Center, 10 Alice Street, Binghamton, NY 13904–1580; 1-800-429-6784 or Fax (607) 722–6362.

14. **Copyright**. Copyright ownership of your manuscript must be transferred officially to The Haworth Press, Inc. before we can begin the peer-review process. The Editor's letter acknowledging receipt of the manuscript will be accompanied by a form fully explaining this. All authors must sign the form and return the original to the Editor as soon as possible. Failure to return the copyright form in a timely fashion will result in a delay in review and subsequent publication.

Journal of the Academy of Business Education

ADDRESS FOR SUBMISSION:

J. Kline Harrison, Editor
Journal of the Academy of Business
 Education
Wake Forest University
The Wayne Calloway School of Business
 and Accountancy
PO Box 7285, Reynolda Station
Winston-Salem, NC 27109-7285
USA
Phone: 336-758-4907
E-Mail: harrisjk@wfu.edu
Web: www.abe.villanova.edu/

PUBLICATION GUIDELINES:

Manuscript Length:
Copies Required: Four
Computer Submission: No
Format: See Website
Fees to Review: 0.00 US$

Manuscript Style:
 See Manuscript Guidelines

CIRCULATION DATA:

Reader: Academics
Frequency of Issue: Quarterly
Sponsor/Publisher: Academy of Business
 Education

REVIEW INFORMATION:

Type of Review: Blind Review
No. of External Reviewers: 3
No. of In House Reviewers: 0
Acceptance Rate: 11-20%
Time to Review: 2 - 3 Months
Reviewers Comments: Yes
Invited Articles:
Fees to Publish: 50.00 US$

MANUSCRIPT TOPICS:
Accounting, Economics, & Finance; Business Education; Business Information Systems (MIS); Business Law, Public Responsibility & Ethics; Global Business; Marketing Theory & Applications; Office Administration/Management; Production/Operations; Sales/Selling

MANUSCRIPT GUIDELINES/COMMENTS:

The *Journal of Business Education* is a multi-disciplinary journal seeking the following kinds of papers:
1. Educational Research - empirical research that tests teaching practices, student performance and learning environments
2. Pedagogy - papers offering interesting or unique approaches to teaching or delivering business education
3. Curriculum - papers addressing interesting or unique approaches to curriculum development and discipline integration
4. Literature Reviews - papers that offer extensive reviews of current relevant research and thought

5. Multi-Disciplinary - papers emphasizing multi-disciplinary/inter-disciplinary approaches to business education
6. Ethics and Moral Values - papers offering guidance in the integration of ethics and moral values in business education

Submission Guidelines

There are few strict layout requirements for submitting a manuscript for review. Specific style instructions for publication will be provided upon acceptance of manuscript. Style and format requirements that are important for publication are often not suitable for reviewing. However, the following are guidelines helpful in preparing your manuscript for submission:

1. **Manuscripts** should be typed, double-spaced in an easy to read font; e.g., Times Roman (12-point) or Courier (10-point).

2. **Cover page** should include paper title, authors' names and affiliations, phone number, and email address of manuscript contact person. Authors' names should appear nowhere else in manuscript.

3. **First page** of manuscript should begin with paper title, followed by an abstract of no more than 100 words, then followed by the first section of the paper that should be called "INTRODUCTION."

4. **Sections.** There should be no more than three levels of headings in body of paper:
*   Level One headings should be left justified and all caps.
*   Level Two headings should begin each word with capital letter and left justified.
*   Level Three headings same as Level Two, but italicized.

5. **Endnotes.** Use endnotes only, not footnotes. Number them consecutively throughout the manuscript with superscripted Arabic numerals. Place all endnotes together at end of manuscript before the REFERENCES section.

6. **Equations.** Number all equations consecutively and place number in parentheses at the right margin of equation. If you use equation editor, place equation number outside of equation box.

7. **Tables.** Except for very small tables, tables should be placed at end of manuscript. Make very effort to avoid "landscape" orientations, but we understand this is not always possible. Tables should have centered headings as: Table 1: Title of Table Should Look Like This Note in body of paper approximately where table or figure should be placed, as:

Place Table 1 about here
----

8. **Figures**. All figures should be headed as in the tables described above, except use the word "Figure" in place of "Table." Each figure must ultimately be provided in camera ready form on a separate sheet.

9. **References**. References should appear alphabetically by author's last name at end of paper. Citations in body of paper should be in [brackets]. Only include references actually cited in paper.

Examples:
Smith, R. J. "Learning by Doing: Teaching Can Be Fun," *Journal of Business Education*, 22 (Spring, 1994),77-81.

Jones, R. R., Carol King and Sidney Slack. "Team Teaching Via the Internet," *Journal of Educational Design*, 7 (No. 2, 1993), 123-144.

In the body of the paper show citations like this [Smith, 1994] or [Jones et al., 1993].

10. There is no submission fee for members (only one author need be an ABE member). For non-ABE members there is a US$50 submission fee. Submit four (4) copies of the manuscript, along with the submission fee (for non-members) payable to the "Academy of Business Education," to the Editor.

Journal of the Academy of Business Research

ADDRESS FOR SUBMISSION:

Dawn Valentine, Editor
Journal of the Academy of Business
    Research
PO Box 41
Birmingham, AL 35080
USA
Phone: 205-665-6557
E-Mail: aobusiness@bellsouth.net
Web:

PUBLICATION GUIDELINES:

Manuscript Length: 1-15
Copies Required: One
Computer Submission: Yes Email
Format: MS Word
Fees to Review: 95.00 US$

Manuscript Style:
    American Psychological Association

CIRCULATION DATA:

Reader: Academics
Frequency of Issue: 2 Times/Year
Sponsor/Publisher:

REVIEW INFORMATION:

Type of Review: Blind Review
No. of External Reviewers: 2
No. of In House Reviewers: 0
Acceptance Rate: 80%
Time to Review: 1 Month or Less
Reviewers Comments: Yes
Invited Articles: 11-20%
Fees to Publish: 0.00 US$

MANUSCRIPT TOPICS:

Advertising & Promotion Management; Business Law, Public Responsibility & Ethics; Communication; Direct Marketing; E-Commerce; Global Business; Marketing Research; Marketing Theory & Applications; Public Administration; Sales/Selling; Services; Small Business Entrepreneurship; Strategic Management Policy; Tourism, Hospitality & Leisure

MANUSCRIPT GUIDELINES/COMMENTS:

American Psychological Association guidelines are followed; for more information regarding manuscript guidelines, please contact the editor at the above address.

Journal of the Academy of Marketing Science

ADDRESS FOR SUBMISSION:

George M. Zinkhan, Editor
Journal of the Academy of Marketing
   Science
University of Georgia
Terry College of Business
Dept of Marketing & Distribution
Brooks Hall
Athens, GA 30602-6258
USA
Phone: 706-542-2123
E-Mail: gzinkhan@terry.uga.edu
Web: www.j-ams.org

PUBLICATION GUIDELINES:

Manuscript Length: 50
Copies Required: Five
Computer Submission: No
Format: N/A
Fees to Review: 0.00 US$

Manuscript Style:
   See Manuscript Guidelines

CIRCULATION DATA:

Reader: Academics
Frequency of Issue: Quarterly
Sponsor/Publisher: Academy of Marketing
   Science / Sage Publications

REVIEW INFORMATION:

Type of Review: Blind Review
No. of External Reviewers: 2-4
No. of In House Reviewers: 0
Acceptance Rate: 10-15%
Time to Review: 2 - 3 Months
Reviewers Comments: No Reply
Invited Articles: 0-5%
Fees to Publish: 0.00 US$

MANUSCRIPT TOPICS:

Advertising & Promotion Management; Business Law, Public Responsibility & Ethics; Communication; Direct Marketing; E-Commerce; Global Business; Marketing Research; Marketing Theory & Applications; Non-Profit Organizations; Sales/Selling; Services; Strategic Management Policy; Technology/Innovation; Transportation/Physical Distribution

MANUSCRIPT GUIDELINES/COMMENTS:

About the Journal. The *Journal of the Academy of Marketing Science* (*JAMS*) is devoted to the study and improvement of marketing and serving as a vital link between scholarly research and practice by publishing research-based articles in the substantive domain of marketing. *JAMS* has a long-standing tradition of publishing articles that:

- Address "leading-edge" issues
- Are thought-provoking
- Challenge or shift dominant conceptual and methodological paradigms
- Attempt to change perspectives and/or cause a phenomenon to be viewed in a different light
- Extend, in one fashion or another, the boundaries of the discipline

Instructions to Contributors

Manuscripts must be double-spaced on 8½" x 11" non-erasable bond, leaving margins of at least 1". Manuscript length should be reasonable for the contribution offered. Please proofread the manuscript very carefully.

Manuscripts are reviewed by the editor and at least two members of the *JAMS* Editorial Review Board or by occasional reviewers. The cover page of the manuscript showing the author's name and affiliation is removed before the manuscript is sent to reviewers in order to ensure objectivity. If at all possible, please do not identify the author(s) in the body of the paper either directly or by citation.

Articles accepted for publication should be accompanied by a copy of the article saved on an IBM-compatible disk, preferably in Word, and information about the author(s) up to 100 words each, including terminal degree and e-mail address, written as a paragraph on a separate sheet to appear at manuscript end.

With the submission of a manuscript, the following three items should be included:
1. Cover page showing title, key words, each author's name, affiliation, complete address, telephone and fax numbers, and e-mail address.
2. Abstract of up to 150 words.
3. Manuscript information and reviewers suggestion form. This is optional. The form can be downloaded from the Website: **www.j-ams.org/**

Mathematical Notation

Notations should be clearly explained within the text. Equations should be centered on the page. If equations are numbered, type the number in parentheses flush with the right margin. Unusual symbols and Greek letters should be identified. For equations that may be too wide to fit in a single column, indicate appropriate breaks.

Tables and Figures

Indicate table and figure placement within text. Each table should be typed on a separate page at the end of the article. Tables should be typed flush with the left-hand margin and have proper labeling of axes, column headings, and other notations. The table number and title should be typed on separate lines. Tables on disk should be free of cells or other dividing elements.

Figures and artwork must be high quality and camera ready, such as clean, black-and-white laser printouts. Each figure should appear on a separate page. Do not send glossies.

Endnotes and References

Use endnotes only if absolutely necessary. Endnotes should be numbered consecutively and double-spaced on a separate, attached sheet.

Reference citations within the text should consist of the author's last name and date of publication, without punctuation, enclosed within parentheses, and should be inserted before punctuation and/or at a logical break in the sentence. If several citations are needed, separate them with semicolons, and list alphabetically. Give the page number only if necessary for a direct quote. If the author's name has just been listed in the text, the date in parentheses is sufficient. If two or more works by an author have the same year, distinguish them by placing a, b, etc. after the year. Use et al. for works by four or more authors.

For example:
Jones' latest proposal (1979) has been questioned by some (Boston 1981; Brown 1990), but is generally accepted by others (Fritz 1979; Lang 1979; Rotwang 1984). Investigators (Cockburn et al. 1985; Hodges McCollum, and Hall 1981; Lee and King 1983) have found that...

References should be double-spaced and attached on a separate page. Works by a single author, list chronologically; two authors, alphabetically and then chronologically; three authors, the same; four or more, list chronologically. References should be in the following format:

Books
Bagozzi, Richard P. 1980. *Causal Models in Marketing.* New York: Wiley

Journals
Singh, Jagdip. 1991. "Understanding the Structure of Consumers' *Marketing Science 19* (Summer): 223-244

Three or More Authors
Zeithaml, Valarie A., Leonard L. Berry, and A. Parasuraman. 1993. "The Nature and Determinants of Customer Experiences of Service." *Journal of the Academy of Marketing Science 21* (Winter): 1-12.

Article in a Book Edited by Another Author
Levitt, Theodore. 1988. "The Globalization of Markets." In *Multinational Marketing Management.* Eds. Robert D. Buzzell and John A. Quelch, Reading MA: Addison-Wesley, 186-205.

Unpublished Dissertations
Paterson, Karen S. 1985. "The Effects of Bilingual Labels in Buyer Behavior." Dissertation. University of California at Irvine.

Submit five (5) clear, letter-quality copies to the editor. Additional information, including *JAMS's* Editorial Policies can be found under AMS publications on the Website.

Journal of the Association of Marketing Educators

ADDRESS FOR SUBMISSION:

S.M. (Steve) Walsh, Associate Editor
Journal of the Association of Marketing
    Educators
SUNY Oneonta
Division of Economics & Business
Ravine Parkway
Oneonta, NY 13820
USA
Phone: 607-433-1878
E-Mail: walshsm@oneonta.edu
Web: www.amarked.org

CIRCULATION DATA:

Reader: Academics
Frequency of Issue: 2 Times/Year
Sponsor/Publisher: The Association of
    Marketing Educators, An International
    Organization

PUBLICATION GUIDELINES:

Manuscript Length: 21-25
Copies Required: Four
Computer Submission: Yes Disk or Email
Format: WordPerfect
Fees to Review: 0.00 US$

Manuscript Style:
    American Psychological Association

REVIEW INFORMATION:

Type of Review: Blind Review
No. of External Reviewers: 0
No. of In House Reviewers: 3
Acceptance Rate: 6-10%
Time to Review: 2 - 3 Months
Reviewers Comments: Yes
Invited Articles: 0-5%
Fees to Publish: 50.00 US$

MANUSCRIPT TOPICS:

Advertising & Promotion Management; Business Education; Business Law, Public Responsibility & Ethics; Direct Marketing; Global Business; Marketing Research; Marketing Theory & Applications; Sales/Selling

MANUSCRIPT GUIDELINES/COMMENTS:

The *Journal of the Association of Marketing_Educators* is a semiannual scholarly journal published by The Association of Marketing Educators, an International organization, now beginning its fifth decade of professional service as a non-profit organization.

Journal submissions are welcomed from anyone interested in any a part of Marketing or Marketing Education including, but not restricted to Marketing Theory and its diverse applications; Marketing Research; International Marketing; Advertising and Promotion Marketing; Direct Marketing; Sales and Sales Management; Consumer Behavior; Business Law, Public Responsibility and Ethics as they relate to the field of Marketing; Marketing Management; Retailing; Relationship Marketing; and Marketing related Business Education.

All submitted manuscripts should be original and should not be under consideration for publication elsewhere. Submitted materials should adhere to the style and format practices outlined in the *Publication Manual of The American Psychological Association*. While the approximate length of articles is 21 to 25 double-spaced pages, both longer and shorter submissions will be considered if they are of exceptional quality.

Please include a separate title page that lists the names and institutional affiliations of all authors and their phone numbers, email addresses, and fax numbers. Specific references to the names of the authors of submitted materials should be omitted from all subsequent pages to facilitate an impartial review process: When the four requisite copies are received (along with a diskette using WordPerfect 5.3 or a compatible language format), the identification will be removed by the recipient editor. It will then be sent to the other two editors as part of a double-blind, refereed process.

Views stated in the various articles published in The *Journal of the Association of Marketing Educators* are those of the individual authors and are not necessarily those of The Association of Marketing Educators or of the editors of this Journal.

Manuscripts may be submitted to:

Thaddeaus Mounkurai, Senior Editor
Daytona Beach Community College
P O Box 2811
Daytona Beach, FL 32120-2811

Mick Harrington, Associate Editor
SUNY Canton
12 Hillside Road
Canton, NY 13617

Steve Walsh, Associate Editor
SUNY Oneonta
Oneonta, NY 13820

Journal of the International Academy for Case Studies

ADDRESS FOR SUBMISSION:

Current Editor / Check Website
Journal of the International Academy for
   Case Studies
Digital Submission Through Website
Address other questions to:
   Jim or JoAnn Carland at # below
USA
Phone: 828-293-9151
E-Mail: info@alliedacademies.org
Web: www.alliedacademies.org

CIRCULATION DATA:

Reader: Academics
Frequency of Issue: 6 Times/Year
Sponsor/Publisher: Allied Academies, Inc.

PUBLICATION GUIDELINES:

Manuscript Length: 25
Copies Required: Submit Through Web
Computer Submission: Yes
Format: MS Word, WordPerfect
Fees to Review: 0.00 US$

Manuscript Style:
   American Psychological Association

REVIEW INFORMATION:

Type of Review: Blind Review
No. of External Reviewers: 2
No. of In House Reviewers: 2
Acceptance Rate: 25%
Time to Review: 3 - 4 Months
Reviewers Comments: Yes
Invited Articles: 0-5%
Fees to Publish: 75.00 US$ Membership

MANUSCRIPT TOPICS:

Advertising & Promotion Management; Business Education; Business Information Systems (MIS); Business Law, Public Responsibility & Ethics; Communication; Direct Marketing; E-Commerce; Global Business; Marketing Research; Marketing Theory & Applications; Non-Profit Organizations; Sales/Selling; Services; Small Business Entrepreneurship; Teaching Cases - Any Discipline or Area; Tourism, Hospitality & Leisure; Transportation/Physical Distribution

MANUSCRIPT GUIDELINES/COMMENTS:

Editorial Comment on Manuscript Topics

- Our scope is broader than the topics listed above. The journal publishes Teaching Cases in any discipline area. Cases must be accompanied by an Instructor's Note.
- All authors of published manuscripts must be members of the appropriate academy affiliate of Allied Academies. The current membership fee is $75.00 US.

Editorial Policy Guidelines

The primary criterion upon which cases are judged is whether the case, together with its instructor's note, can be an effective teaching tool.

Cases need not conform to any guideline and may be in any discipline. Narrative cases are acceptable as well as disguised field cases, library cases or illustrative cases. Each case must be accompanied by an instructor's note and the note MUST conform to the editorial policy. This policy may be found on the website.

Referees require a decision point in a case and pay particular attention to readability and potential for student interest and involvement. Consequently, cases which DESCRIBE action are NOT generally acceptable. The important point is the use of a case in classroom teaching.

Journal of the International Society of Business Disciplines

ADDRESS FOR SUBMISSION:

Jason T. White, Editor
Journal of the International Society of
  Business Disciplines
24670 Interlude Road
Maryville, MO 64468
USA
Phone: 660-562-1764
E-Mail: jwhite@mail.nwmissouri.edu
  jwhite@isobd.org
  cacker@isobd.org
Web: www.isobd.org

PUBLICATION GUIDELINES:

Manuscript Length: 1-15
Copies Required: Three
Computer Submission: Yes Disk, Email
Format: MS Word
Fees to Review: 0.00 US$

Manuscript Style:
  See Manuscript Guidelines

CIRCULATION DATA:

Reader: Academics
Frequency of Issue: Semi-annually
Sponsor/Publisher: International Society of
  Business Disciplines

REVIEW INFORMATION:

Type of Review: Blind Review
No. of External Reviewers: 2
No. of In House Reviewers: 1
Acceptance Rate: 21-30%
Time to Review: 2 - 3 Months
Reviewers Comments: No
Invited Articles: 0-5%
Fees to Publish: 3.00 US$ per page to
  15, then $5 per page

MANUSCRIPT TOPICS:

Advertising & Promotion Management; Business Education; Business Law, Public Responsibility & Ethics; Direct Marketing; E-Commerce; Global Business; Marketing Research; Marketing Theory & Applications; Non-Profit Organizations; Office Administration/Management; Organizational Behavior & Theory; Organizational Development; Public Administration; Sales/Selling; Services; Small Business Entrepreneurship; Technology/Innovation

MANUSCRIPT GUIDELINES/COMMENTS:

The *Journal of the International Society of Business Disciplines* (*JISOBD*) seeks both theoretical and practitioner papers to be considered for publication. *JISOBD* is an international, refereed and double-blind reviewed scholarly journal. We seek articles promoting scholarship in applied, theoretical and practitioner research in all areas of business and economics. Case studies will also be considered for publication.

Articles presented at the semi-annual meeting of the International Society of Business Disciplines (ISOBD) received priority placement consideration in *JISOBD*, once accepted by the review team.

Submission Criteria
Articles should follow standard MLA citation guidelines. All articles must be double-spaced and not exceed 15 pages in length, including cover page and citations. If accepted, *JISOBD* charges $3.00 per page for compilation and distribution of the journal. An additional $5.00 per page surcharge will be assessed on those submissions in excess of 15.

The title page should include the article's title; author's names, affiliations and ranks; email address of primary contact person; and phone number for same.

All papers must be submitted in an electronic format that is readable by Microsoft Word. Tables, graphs and figures must be properly formatted within the Word submission, or they will not be accepted.

Only electronic submissions are accepted. For consideration, email your paper to **cacker@isobd.org**

Editorial Review Process
To complete the double-blind review referee process takes approximately 8-12 weeks. Once that process is complete, the submitting author will receive an email indicating whether the article has been: 1) accepted for publication without change; 2) provisionally accepted for publication pending certain changes; 3) rejected for publication. We do require a signed binding copyright agreement from all authors, once the article has been accepted for publication in *JISOBD*. Electronic submission of these signatures is acceptable.

Journal of Transport Economics and Policy

ADDRESS FOR SUBMISSION:

Steve Morrison, Managing Editor
Journal of Transport Economics and Policy
University of Bath
School of Management
Claverton Down
Bath, BA2 7AY
UK
Phone: +44 (0) 1225-386302
E-Mail: jtep@management.bath.ac.uk
Web: www.jtep.org   and   www.jtep.com

CIRCULATION DATA:

Reader: Academics, Professionals, Business
  Persons
Frequency of Issue: 3 Times/Year
Sponsor/Publisher: University of Bath /
  London School of Economics

PUBLICATION GUIDELINES:

Manuscript Length: 30+
Copies Required: Two
Computer Submission: Yes Email
Format: MS Word, PDF, English
Fees to Review: 0.00 US$

Manuscript Style:
  See Manuscript Guidelines

REVIEW INFORMATION:

Type of Review: Editorial Review
No. of External Reviewers: 2
No. of In House Reviewers: 2
Acceptance Rate: 0-30%
Time to Review: 4 - 6 Months
Reviewers Comments: Yes
Invited Articles: 0-5%
Fees to Publish: 0.00 US$

MANUSCRIPT TOPICS:
Transportation/Physical Distribution

MANUSCRIPT GUIDELINES/COMMENTS:

1. Articles range from fundamental studies making original contributions to analysis, to those exploring innovations in policy. All articles are refereed by appropriate experts, and editorial policy is assisted by a distinguished international Editorial Board. The *Journal* takes no sides on transport issues; the interest and academic merit of articles are the sole criteria for acceptance.

2. The *Journal* is distributed worldwide; it has subscribers from over 70 countries. This is reflected in its coverage, with transport practices in over 30 countries and every continent forming the basis for articles. Many aspects of urban traffic have been examined both in general and in the context of particular cites, though invariably with universal application. Topics include rail, air and motor vehicle modes, as well as shipping and infrastructure. There are regular notes on developments in government policy.

3. Contributors range from mathematicians and theoretical economists to practicing consultants, administrators and people involved in business. Their nationalities are varied as the countries about which they write.

4. Manuscripts should be submitted electronically in pdf or Word format, supported by two hard copies. If the articles are submitted in pdf format and accepted for publication, a non-pdf format will be required for typesetting.

An abstract of not more than 200 words, detailing the main points of the article, must be submitted with the article.

5. Articles should contain a final section in which the author sets out his or her main conclusions in a way which will be at least broadly intelligible to the non-specialist reader.

6. Camera-ready copy of diagrams must be provided with the manuscript; otherwise, if the article is accepted, a charge will be made to cover the cost of artwork. Diagrams should be clearly drawn and accompanied by the basic statistics that were required for their preparation; the axes must be clearly labelled; the reader must be able to understand the diagrams without hunting in the text for explanations.

7. Where mathematical arguments are used, the full working necessary for justifying each step of the argument should accompany the article, in order to assist the referee. The detailed workings will not be published. Care should be taken to ensure that all signs and symbols are clear and to avoid any possible confusion between, for example, figure 1 and letter 1.

8. Statistical tables should be clearly headed and the reader should be able to understand the meaning of each row or column without hunting in the text for explanations of symbols, etc. Units of measurement, base-dates for index numbers, geographical area covered and sources should be clearly stated. Authors are fully responsible for the accuracy of the data and for checking their proofs; whenever they feel that the referee would have difficulty in testing the derivation of their statistics, they should provide supplementary notes on the methods used, which will not be published.

9. Footnotes should be brief, as they are placed at the foot of the page. Any explanation requiring more than a very few lines should be either included in the text or placed in an appendix at the end of the article.

10. References should be carefully checked, and complete in respect of the place and year of publication. If a bibliographical list is given, it should follow the style used in the current issue. Only these works cited in the text should be included.

11. Authors are expected to read proofs expeditiously and to keep corrections down to a very low level. If alterations are made at the proof stage, the editors reserve the right either not to give effect to them or to make a charge.

12. Because of the heavy pressure on space, the editors will give preference to articles which deal succinctly with an issue which is both important and clearly defined. The editors will not consider articles which have been submitted elsewhere.

13. **Comments on published articles**. Anyone wanting to submit comments on a *Journal* article is asked first to send a copy to the author, inviting him to send the commentator his observations and in particular to explain any points on which the commentator has misunderstood what the author was saying. The commentator is asked to allow the author a reasonable time to reply before he sends anything to the editors, and to enclose any reply which he may have received, so that the convent and rejoinder may be published together.

Journal of Transportation and Statistics

ADDRESS FOR SUBMISSION:

Marsha Fenn, Managing Editor
Journal of Transportation and Statistics
RITA BTS USDOT
Room 4117
400 Seventh Street SW
Washington, DC 20590
USA
Phone: 202-366-1845
E-Mail: marsha.fenn@dot.gov
Web: www.bts.gov/publications/jts

PUBLICATION GUIDELINES:

Manuscript Length: 15-30
Copies Required: One
Computer Submission: Yes Email
Format: See Manuscript Guidelines
Fees to Review: 0.00 US$

Manuscript Style:
    Chicago Manual of Style

CIRCULATION DATA:

Reader: Academics, Researchers
Frequency of Issue: 3 Times/Year
Sponsor/Publisher: Bureau of
    Transportation Statistics, Research &
    Innovative Tech. Admin., U.S. Dept. of
    Trans.

REVIEW INFORMATION:

Type of Review: Peer Review
No. of External Reviewers: 2
No. of In House Reviewers: 1
Acceptance Rate: 31-50%
Time to Review: Over 6 Months
Reviewers Comments: Yes
Invited Articles: 0-5%
Fees to Publish: 0.00 US$

MANUSCRIPT TOPICS:
Transportation/Physical Distribution

MANUSCRIPT GUIDELINES/COMMENTS:

The *Journal of Transportation and Statistics* (*JTS*) is a scholarly, peer-reviewed journal sponsored by the Bureau of Transportation Statistics (BTS) of the U.S. Department of Transportation (DOT). Its 28-member Editorial Board is made up of prominent individuals in academia and DOT. The journal serves the transportation community by increasing the understanding of the role of transportation in society, its function in the economy, and its interactions with the environment. In addition, the *JTS* provides a forum for the latest developments in transportation information and data, theory, concepts, and methods of analysis relevant to all aspects of the transportation system.

The *JTS* publishes original research using planning, engineering, statistical, and economic analysis to improve public and private mobility and safety in transportation. We are soliciting contributions that broadly support this objective. Examples of the type of material sought include:

- analyses of transportation planning and operational activities and the performance of transportation systems

- advancement of the science of acquiring, validating, managing, and disseminating transportation information
- analyses of the interaction of transportation and the economy
- analyses of the environmental impacts of transportation

JTS will continue to focus on data, description and analysis and will explicitly avoid policy studies. Recognizing that transportation systems are increasingly interconnected on a global level, the *JTS* seeks articles on both domestic and international subjects.

The views presented in the articles in this journal are those of the authors and not necessarily the views of the Bureau of Transportation Statistics. All material contained in this journal is in the public domain and may be used and reprinted without special permission; citation as to sources is required.

Guidelines for Manuscript Submission

Please note. Submission of a paper indicates the author's intention to publish in the *Journal of Transportation and Statistics (JTS)*. Submission of a manuscript to other journals is unacceptable. Previously published manuscripts, whether in an exact or approximate form, cannot be accepted. Check with the managing editor if in doubt.

Scope of *JTS*. *JTS* publishes articles original research planning, engineering, statistical, and economic analyses to improve public and private mobility and safety in all modes of transportation.

Manuscripts must be double spaced, including quotations, abstract, reference section, and any notes. All figures and tables should appear at the end of the manuscript with each one on a separate page. Do not embed them in your manuscript.

Because the *JTS* audience works in diverse fields, please **define terms** that are specific to your area of expertise.

Electronic submissions via email to the Managing Editor are strongly encouraged. We can accept PDF, Word, WordPerfect, Excel, and Adobe Illustrator files. If you cannot send your submission via email, you may send a disk or CD by overnight delivery service or send a hardcopy by the U.S. Postal Service (regular mail; see below). Do not send disks or CDs through regular mail.

Hardcopy submissions delivered to BTS by the U.S. Postal service are irradiated. Do not include a disk in your envelope; the high heat will damage it.

The **cover page** of your manuscript must include the title, author name(s) and affiliations, and the telephone number and surface and email addresses of all authors.

Put the **Abstract** on the second page. It should be about 100 words and briefly describe the contents of the paper including the mode or modes of transportation, the research method, and the key results and/or conclusions. Please include a list of **keywords** to describe your article.

752

Graphic elements (figures and tables) must be called out in the text. Graphic elements must be in black ink. We will accept graphics in color only in rare circumstances.

References follow the style outlined in the *Chicago Manual of Style*. All non-original material must be sourced.

International papers are encouraged, but please be sure to have your paper edited by someone whose first language is English and who knows your research area.

Accepted papers must be submitted electronically in addition to a hard copy (see above for information on electronic submissions). Make sure the hard copy corresponds to the electronic version.

Page Proofs. As the publication date nears, authors will be required to return article page proofs to the Managing Editor within 48 hours of receipt.

Acceptable software for text and equations is limited to Word and LaTeX. Data behind all figures, maps, and charts must be provided in Excel, Word, or DeltaGraph (unless the data are proprietary). Data in American Standard Code for Information Interchange (ASCII) text will be accepted but is less desirable. Acceptable software for graphic elements is limited to Excel, DeltaGraph, or Adobe Illustrator. If other software is used, the file supplied must have an .eps or .PDF extension. We do not accept PowerPoint.

Maps are accepted in a variety of Geographic Information System (GIS) programs. Files using .eps or .pdf extensions are preferred. If this is not possible, please contact the Managing Editor. Send your files on a CD-ROM via overnight delivery service.

Send all submission materials to:
Marsha Fenn
Managing Editor, Journal of Transportation and Statistics
Bureau of Transportation Statistics
U.S. Department of Transportation
400 7th Street, SW, Room 4117
Washington, DC 20590
E-mail: **marsha.fenn@dot.gov**

Journal of Transportation Law, Logistics and Policy

ADDRESS FOR SUBMISSION:

Frank N. Wilner, Editor-in-Chief
Journal of Transportation Law, Logistics
  and Policy
606 Tivoli Passage Alley
Alexandria, VA 22314
USA
Phone: 703-304-7022
E-Mail: frw.rail@att.net
Web: atllp.com

CIRCULATION DATA:

Reader: Business Persons
Frequency of Issue: Quarterly
Sponsor/Publisher: Professional Association
  and Non-Profit Corporation, Association
  of Transportation Practitioners

PUBLICATION GUIDELINES:

Manuscript Length:
Copies Required: One
Computer Submission:
Format:
Fees to Review: 0.00 US$

Manuscript Style:
  Uniform System of Citation (Harvard
  Blue Book)

REVIEW INFORMATION:

Type of Review: Editorial Review
No. of External Reviewers: 0
No. of In House Reviewers: 2
Acceptance Rate:
Time to Review: 1 - 2 Months
Reviewers Comments: No
Invited Articles:
Fees to Publish: 0.00 US$

MANUSCRIPT TOPICS:
Transportation/Physical Distribution

MANUSCRIPT GUIDELINES/COMMENTS:

The *Journal of Transportation Law, Logistics and Policy* is published by the Association of Transportation Practitioners, 931 N. Paxton St., Alexandria, VA 22304 USA. The *Journal* is published quarterly in the fall, winter, spring, and summer, and is directed toward the needs of transportation professionals (attorney and non-attorney, traffic and distribution managers, members of faculty of post secondary educational institutions, and students) interested in transportation law, regulation, practice, and procedure.

Editorial Policy
The editorial policy of the *Journal of Transportation Law, Logistics And Policy* is to publish articles of a scholarly nature on any subject having to do with transportation—law, practice, legislation, regulation, history, theory, economics, statistics, or any other aspect—including non-transportation subjects of interest to practitioners. Our principal concern is transportation in the United States and Canada, but we welcome also articles about transportation in other countries.

Manuscripts Accepted/Denied

No manuscript can be accepted for publication in the *Journal* until it has been reviewed by the Editor in Chief and Executive Editor. The Editor in Chief, in conjunction with the editorial office, will ultimately make the decision of publication.

Manuscripts are received by the *Journal* editorial office and, when accepted for publication, are for the "exclusive" use of the *Journal of Transportation Law, Logistics and Policy*. A manuscript that has been accepted by or that has already appeared in a book or in another periodical of general circulation, is ordinarily not acceptable for publication. There can be some exceptions, i.e., material from a forthcoming book. Publication of a series of articles to appear in successive issues of the *Journal* is not usual, and special permission is made with the Editor in Chief.

The *Journal* must be cautious against articles that are designed too directly to influence on-going litigation, as this violates ethical rules and distorts the *Journal* from its purpose of serving only the cause of scholarship. This concern, however, by no means prevents us from publishing articles on subjects regarding pending cases where we are satisfied that the author(s) are not acting as counsel or are not otherwise improperly attempting to influence the court or agency in the pending case.

Speeches, as such, are not published in the *Journal*. However, a speech may serve as the basis for an article and will be accepted when it follows the guidelines set forth in the "Manuscripts Preparation" section of this style sheet.

Manuscript Submission

All correspondence regarding submission of manuscripts should be directed to Frank N. Wilner, Editor in Chief, *Journal of Transportation Law, Logistics and Policy*.

Manuscript Preparation

Contact Editor-in-Chief.

Journal of Transportation Management

ADDRESS FOR SUBMISSION:

Jerry W. Wilson, Editor
Journal of Transportation Management
Georgia Southern University
College of Business Administration
Dept of Management Marketing & Logistics
PO Box 8154
Stateboro, GA 30460-8154
USA
Phone: 912-681-0257
E-Mail: jwwilson@georgiasouthern.edu
Web: www.deltanualpha.org

PUBLICATION GUIDELINES:

Manuscript Length: 25 Maximum
Copies Required: Four
Computer Submission: Yes
Format: MS Word, WordPerfect
Fees to Review: 0.00 US$

Manuscript Style:
    See Manuscript Guidelines

CIRCULATION DATA:

Reader: Academics, Professional
Frequency of Issue: 2 Times/Year
Sponsor/Publisher: Delta Nu Alpha,
    International Transportation Fraternity

REVIEW INFORMATION:

Type of Review: Blind Review
No. of External Reviewers: 2
No. of In House Reviewers: 1
Acceptance Rate: 30%
Time to Review: 4 - 6 Months
Reviewers Comments: Yes
Invited Articles: 20%
Fees to Publish: 0.00 US$

MANUSCRIPT TOPICS:
Logistics; Purchasing/Materials Management; Transportation/Physical Distribution

MANUSCRIPT GUIDELINES/COMMENTS:

The *Journal of Transportation Management* (*JTM*) is sponsored by Delta Nu Alpha International Transportation Fraternity and published by the College of Business Administration at Georgia Southern University.

Editorial Policy
The primary purpose of the *JTM* is to serve as a channel for the dissemination of information relevant to the management of transportation and logistics activities in any and all types of organizations. Articles accepted for publication will be of interest to both academics and practitioners and will specifically address the managerial implications of the subject matter. Articles that are strictly theoretical in nature, with no direct application to the management of transportation and logistics activities, would be inappropriate for the *JTM*.

Acceptable topics for submission include, but are not limited to carrier management, modal and intermodal transportation, international transportation issues, transportation safety, marketing of transportation services, domestic and international transportation policy, transportation economics, customer service, and the changing technology of transportation. Articles from related areas, such as third party logistics and purchasing and materials management, are acceptable as long as they are specifically related to the management of transportation and logistics activities.

Submissions from industry practitioners and from practitioners co-authoring with academics are particularly encouraged in order to increase the interaction between the two groups. Authors considering the submission of an article to the *JTM* are encouraged to contact the editor for help in determining relevance of topic and material.

The opinions expressed in published articles are those of the authors and do not necessarily reflect the opinions of the editor, the Editorial Review Board, Delta Nu Alpha International Transportation Fraternity, or Georgia Southern University.

GUIDELINES FOR SUBMISSION/PUBLICATION
Front Matter
1. **First page**. Title of the paper, name and position of the author(s), author(s) complete address(es) and telephone number(s), e-mail address(es), and any acknowledgement of assistance.

2. **Second page**. A brief biographical sketch of each author including name, degree(s) held, title or position, organization or institution, previous publications and research interests.

3. **Third page**. Title of the paper without author name(s) and a brief abstract of no more than 100 words summarizing the article. The abstract, which precedes the body of the article, serves to generate reader interest in the full article.

Formatting
1. Manuscripts should be typed, double-spaced (body of text only), on white 8½ by 11-inch paper.

2. You may either submit four (4) paper copies of the manuscript for review or email the manuscript directly to the Editor The article should be prepared using either: WordPerfect 9.0 or lower or Microsoft Word 2000 or lower.

3. Accepted articles, in final form, are to be submitted on disk or via email (in WordPerfect or Microsoft Word format as described above) and in hardcopy. Note: Macintosh versions of WordPerfect and Microsoft Word are **not** acceptable.

4. The entire manuscript should have 1" margins on all sides in Times 10-point font. Times New Roman or Century Schoolbook are both acceptable.

5. The entire manuscript must be typed **left-justified**, with the exception of tables and figures.

Title Page and Abstract

1. The manuscript title should be printed in Times 11-point and in all capital letters and bold print.

2. Author(s) affiliations(s) are to be printed in upper and lower case letters below the title. Author(s) are to be listed with affiliation(s) only.

3. The abstract should be 100 words or less.

Body of Manuscript

1. Main headings are bolded and in all caps.

2. First level headings are upper/lower case and bolded.

3. Second level headings are upper/lower case.

4. The body is NOT indented. A full blank line is left between paragraphs.

5. A full blank line should be left between all headings and paragraphs.

6. Unnecessary hard returns should not be used at the end of each line.

Tables and Figures

1. **Only** Tables and Figures are to appear in camera-ready format! Each table or figure should be numbered in Arabic style (i.e., Table 1, Figure 2).

2. All tables **must** be typed in WordPerfect table or Microsoft Word table functions. Tables should **not** be tabbed or spaced to align columns. Column headings should not be created in separate tables. Table titles should not be created as part of the table.

3. All figures **must** be created in one of the following formats: TIFF, CGM, or WPG.

4. Tables and figures are **not** to be included unless directly referred to in the body of the manuscript.

5. Remember that the *JTM* is printed in black and white. Use of color and/or shading should be avoided.

6. Unless included in the proper text location, placement of tables and figures in the manuscript should be indicated as follows:

Table or Figure About Here

Equations and Citations
1. Equations are placed on a separate line with a blank line both above and below, and numbered in parentheses, flush right. Examples:

$$y = c + ax + bx \qquad (1)$$
$$y = a + 1x + 2x + 3x + ax \qquad (2)$$

2. References within the text should include the author's last name and year of publication enclosed in parentheses, e.g., (Wilson 2005; Rakowski and Southern 2004). For more than one cite in the same location, references should be in chronological order, as above. For more than one cite in the same year, alphabetize by author name, such as (Wilson 2001; Novak 2002; Rakowski 2003; Wilson 2004). If practical, place the citation just ahead of a punctuation mark. If the author's name is used within the text sentence, just place the year of publication in parentheses, e.g., "According to Monrodt and Rutner (2005)... ,". For multiple authors, use up to three names in the citation. With four or more authors, use the lead author and et al., (Wilson et al. 2004).

3. Footnotes may be used where necessary. Footnotes are in 8-point font and should appear at the bottom of the page using numbers (1, 2, etc.). Note: footnotes should be explanatory in nature if used, not for reference purposes.

4. All references should be in block style. Hanging indents are not to be used.

5. Appendices follow the body of the text but do not precede references.

6. The list of references cited in the manuscript should immediately follow the body of the text in alphabetized order, with the lead author's surname first and the year of publication following all author names. Work by the same author with the same year of publication should be distinguished by lower case letters after the date (e.g., 2005a). For author names that repeat, in the same order, in subsequent cites, substitute a .5-inch underline for each name that appears. A blank line should separate each reference in the list. Do not number references.

7. All references to journals, books, etc., are *italicized*, **not** underlined. Examples are as follows:

Journal Article
Pohlen, Terrance L. (2003), "A Framework for Evaluating Supply Chain Performance," *Journal of Transportation Management*, 14(2): 1-21.

Book Chapter
Manrodt, Karl (2003), "Drivers of Logistics Excellence: Implications for Carriers," in J. W. Wilson (Ed.), *Logistics and Transportation Yearbook 2005* (pp. 126-154) Englewood Cliffs, NJ: Prentice-Hall, Inc.

Book
Coyle, John J., Bardi, Edward J., and Novack, Robert A. (2006), *Transpotation*, 6th ed., Mason, OH: Thomson South-Western College Publishing.

Wilson, J. W. (2004), "Adapting to the Threat of Global Terrorism: Redefining the Process of Outsourcing," [On-line]. Available: http://georgiasouthern.edu/coba/centers/lit/threat.doc Accessed: 04/21/05.

Manuscript Sample
TECHNOLOGY BASED SUPPLY CHAIN TRAINING: ITS USE AND EFFECTIVENESS

Brian J. Gibson, Auburn University
Jonathan D. Whitaker, Accenture LLC

ABSTRACT

Employee training is a huge business in the United States with spending in the neighborhood of $51 billion dollars. Over the last five years a growing proportion of the training dollars have been committed to technology based training involving distance learning and e-learning. This article reports on the use of these innovative training methods in supply chain management and their impact on organizations in terms of cost effectiveness, time efficiency, skill development, and return on investment.

INTRODUCTION

Training presents a vexing challenge for businesses. On one hand, it's viewed as a necessary tool for building employee competency, improving productivity, and establishing competitive advantage (Buhler, 2001). Tom Peters, best selling author and quality guru, goes so far as to recommend that companies, "train everyone lavishly, you can't overspend on training" (2004). However, training consumes critical resources (time and money) and organizations find it difficult to measure the return on investment (ROI) of training. Despite its intrinsic value, these realities make training a cost cutting target in times of economic instability.

TBT Adoption [upper/lower case and bolded]

The initial questions of the survey focused on the training methods used by each organization for supply chain training. Overall, 62.9 percent of the respondents use some form of TBT. The use of TBT methods across the five business groups ranged from 55 percent to 67 percent, with manufacturers and logistics service providers leading the way (See Table 1).

Table 1 About Here

References
Buhler, Patricia M. (2001), "Managing in the New Millennium," *Supervision*, 62(10): 13-15.

760

Byrne, Patrick M. (2004), "Outsourcing and Supply Chain Management: A Natural Marriage," *Logistics Management*, 43(4): 34.

Ellram, Lisa M., and Easton, Liane (1997), "The Internet: A New Forum for Teaching Supply Management," *Proceedings of the Twenty-Sixth Annual Transportation and Logistics Educators Conference*, Oak Brook, IL: Council of Logistics Management.

Journal of Travel & Tourism Marketing

ADDRESS FOR SUBMISSION:

K. S. (Kaye) Chon, Editor
Journal of Travel & Tourism Marketing
Hong Kong Polytechnic University
School of Hotel & Tourism Management
Hung Hom
Kowloon,
Hong Kong
Phone: 852-2766-6382
E-Mail: hmkchon@poly.edu.hk
Web: www.haworthpress.com

PUBLICATION GUIDELINES:

Manuscript Length: 15-25
Copies Required: Four or 1 Electronic
Computer Submission: Yes Email
Format:
Fees to Review: 0.00 US$

Manuscript Style:
American Psychological Association

CIRCULATION DATA:

Reader: Administrators
Frequency of Issue: Quarterly
Sponsor/Publisher: Haworth Press, Inc.

REVIEW INFORMATION:

Type of Review: Blind Review
No. of External Reviewers: 3
No. of In House Reviewers: 0
Acceptance Rate: 21-30%
Time to Review: 1 - 2 Months
Reviewers Comments: Yes
Invited Articles: 0-5%
Fees to Publish: 0.00 US$

MANUSCRIPT TOPICS:
Advertising & Promotion Management; Business Information Systems (MIS); Communication; Direct Marketing; E-Commerce; Global Business; Marketing Research; Marketing Theory & Applications; Sales/Selling; Services; Small Business Entrepreneurship; Tourism, Hospitality & Leisure

MANUSCRIPT GUIDELINES/COMMENTS:

About the Journal
The *Journal* publishes empirical and conceptual articles related to research and management practice of travel and tourism marketing services. Topics could include traveler behavior, tourism industry marketing, hotel and resort industry marketing, airline industry marketing, etc.

The *Journal of Travel & Tourism Marketing* is a managerially oriented and applied journal which will serve as a medium through which researchers and managers in the field of travel and tourism can exchange ideas and keep abreast with the latest developments in the field. The journal will publish articles on travel and tourism related to marketing management practices, applied research studies, critical reviews on major issues, and business and government policies affecting travel and tourism marketing.

As an international journal, the *Journal of Travel & Tourism Marketing* will place special emphasis on submissions reflecting the perspectives of contributors from other countries and will include articles treating North American perspectives as well. Travel and tourism educators, consultants and business researchers with interests in travel and tourism marketing, and government policymakers will benefit from the timely information presented in this innovative journal.

Instructions for Authors

1. Original articles only. Submission of a manuscript to this Journal represents a certification on the part of the author(s) that it is an original work, and that neither this manuscript nor a version of it has been published elsewhere nor is being considered for publication elsewhere.

Manuscripts can be submitted in electronic format or in hard copies. Submit to Editor-in-Chief, K. S. (Kaye) Chon, PhD, CHE (e-mail: **hmkchon@polyu.edu.hk**), School of Hotel & Tourism Management, The Hong Kong Polytechnic University, Hung Hom, Kowloon, Hong Kong SAR, PRC. In case of submission in hard copies, submit four (4) copies of the manuscript printed only one side of the paper and stapled. Indicate clearly either in an e-mail message or cover letter accompanying the manuscript submission that the manuscript is intended for publication consideration in *JTTM*.

2. Manuscript Length. The *Journal* publishes two main classes of articles: full-length articles of approximately 5,000 words (15-25 pages, double-spaced), and shorter opinion/reports/ viewpoint pieces of about 1,500 words (5-10 pages, double-spaced). Longer manuscripts will be considered at the discretion of the Editor who may recommend publication as a monograph edition of the *Journal* or division into sections for publication in successive *Journal* issues.

3. Manuscript Style. References, citations, and general style of manuscripts for this Journal should follow the APA style (as outlined in the latest edition of the *Publication Manual of The American Psychological Association*). References should be double-spaced and placed in alphabetical order. The use of footnotes within the text is discouraged. Words should be underlined only when it is intended that they be typeset in italics.

If an author wishes to submit a paper that has been already prepared in another style, he or she may do so. However, if thepaper is accepted (with or without reviewer's alternation), the author is fully responsible for retyping the manuscript in the correct style as indicated above. Neither the Editor nor the Publisher is responsible for re-preparing manuscript copy to adhere to the Journal's style.

4. Manuscript Preparation
Margins. Leave at least a one-inch margin on all four sides.
Paper. Use clean white, 8 ½ " x 11" bond paper.
Number of Copies. 4 (the original plus three photocopies).
Cover Page. Important--staple a cover page to the manuscript, indicating only the article title (this is used for anonymous refereeing).

Second "Title Page". Enclose a regular title page but do not staple it to the manuscript. Include the title again, plus:

- full authorship
- an introductory footnote with authors' academic degrees, professional titles, affiliations, mailing and e-mail addresses, and any desired acknowledgement of research support or other credit.

Abstract. Include an abstract of about 100 words accompanied by three to six keywords at the beginning of the manuscript after the "title page".

5. **Reference Linking**. The Haworth Press is participating in reference linking for journal articles. (For more information on reference linking initiatives, please consult the CrossRef Web site at www.crossref.org.) When citing a journal article include the article's Digital Object Identifier (DOI), when available, as the last item in the reference. A Digital Object Identifier is a persistant, authoritative, and unique indentifier that a publisher assigns to each article. Because of its persistence, DOIs will enable The Haworth Press and other publishers to link to the article referenced, and the link will not break over time. This will be a great resource in scholarly research.

An example of a reference to a journal article which includes a DOI:
Vizine-Goetz, Diane (2002).
Classification Schemes for Internet Resources Revisited.
Journal of Internet Cataloging 5(4): 5:18. doi: 10.1300/J141v05n04_02

6. **Spelling, Grammar, and Punctuation**. You are responsible for preparing manuscript copy which is clearly written in acceptable, scholarly English and which contains no errors of spelling, grammar, or punctuation. Neither the Editor nor the Publisher is responsible for correcting errors of spelling and grammar. The manuscript, after acceptance by the Editor, must be immediately ready for typesetting as it is finally submitted by the author(s).

Check your paper for the following common errors:
- dangling modifiers
- misplaced modifiers
- unclear antecedents
- incorrect or inconsistent abbreviations

Also, check the accuracy of all arithmetic calculations statistics numerical data, text citations, and references.

7. **Return Envelopes**. When you submit your four manuscript copies, also include:
- a 9" x 12" envelope, self-addressed and stamped (with sufficient postage to ensure return of your manuscript)
- a regular envelope, stamped and self-addressed. This is for the Editor to send you an "acknowledgement of receipt" letter.

8. **Inconsistencies Must be Avoided**. Be sure you are consistent in your use of abbreviations, terminology, and in citing references, from one part of your paper to another.

9. **Preparation of Tables, Figures, and Illustrations**. Any material that is not textual is considered artwork. This includes tables, figures, diagrams, charts, graphs, illustrations, appendices, screen captures, and photos. Tables and figures (including legend, notes and sources) should be no larger than 4 ½ x 6 ½ inches. Type styles should be Helvetica (or Helvetica narrow if necessary) and no smaller than 8 point. We request that computer-generated figures be in black and white and/or shades of gray (perferably no color, for it does not reproduce well). Camera-ready art must contain no grammatical, typographical, or format errors and must reproduce sharply and clearly in the dimensions of the final printed page (4 ½ x 6 ½ inches). Photos and screen captures must be on disk as a TIF file, or other graphic file format such as JPEG or BMP. For rapid publication we must receive black-and-white glossy or matte positives (white background with blace images and/or wording) in addition to files on disk. Tables should be created in the text document file using the software's Table feature.

10. **Submitting Art**. Both a printed hard copy and a disk copy of the art must be provided. We request that each piece of art be sent in its own file, on a disk separate from the disk containing the manuscript text file(s), and be clearly labeled. We reserve the right to (if necessary) request new art, alter art, or if all else has failed in achieving art that is presentable, delete art. If submitted art cannot be used, the Publisher reserves the right to redo the art and to change the author for a fee of $35.00 per hour for this service. The Haworth Press, Inc. is not responsible for errors incurred in the preparation of new artwork. Camera-ready artwork must be prepared on separate sheets of paper. Always use black ink and professional drawing instruments. On the back of these items, write your article title and the journal title lightly in soft-lead pencil (please do not write on face of art). In the text file, skip extra lines and indicate where these figures are placed Photos are considered part of the acceptable manuscript and remain with Publisher for use in additional printings.

11. **Electronic Media**. Haworth's in-house typesetting unit is able to utilize your final manuscript material as prepared on most personal computers and word processors. This will minimize typographical errors and decrease overall production time. Please send the first draft and final draft copies of your manuscript to the journal editor in print format for his/her final review and approval. After approval of your final manuscript, please submit the final approved version both on printed format ("hard copy") and floppy diskette or CD-rom. On the outside of the diskette package write:
A.   the brand name of your computer or word processor
B.   the word processing program and version that you used
C.   the title of your article, and
D.   the file name.

Note. Disk and hard copy must agree. In case of discrepancies, it is The Haworth Press's policy to follow the electronic copy. Authors are advised that no revisions of the manuscript can be made after acceptance by the editor for publication. The benefits of this procedure are many with speed and accuracy being the most obvious. We look forward to working with your electronic submission which will allow us to serve you more efficiently.

12. Alterations Required By Referees and Reviewers. Many times a paper is accepted by the Editor contingent upon changes that are mandated by anonymous specialist referees and members of the Editorial Board. If the Editor returns your manuscript for revisions, you are responsible for retyping any sections of the paper to incorporate these revisions (if applicable, revisions should also be put on disk).

13. Typesetting. You will not be receiving galley proofs of your article. Editorial revisions, if any, must therefore be made while your article is still in manuscript. The final version of the manuscript will be the version you see published. Typesetter's errors will be corrected by the production staff of The Haworth Press. Authors are expected to submit manuscripts, disks, and art that are free from error.

14. Reprints. The senior author will receive two copies of the journal issue as well as complimentary reprints of his or her article. The junior authors will receive two copies of the journal issue. These are sent several weeks after the journal issue is published and in circulation. An order form for the purchase of additional reprints will also be sent to all authors at this time. (Approximately 8 weeks is necessary for the preparation of reprints.) Please do not query the journal's editor about reprints. All such questions should be sent directly to The Haworth Press, Inc., Production Department, 37 West Broad Street, West Hazleton, PA 18202. To order additional reprints (minimum: 50 copies), please contact The Haworth Document Delivery Center, 10 Alice Street, Binghamton, New York 13904-1580; 1-800-342-9678 or Fax (607) 722-6362.

15. Copyright. Copyright ownership of your manuscript must be transferred officially to The Haworth Press, Inc. before we can begin the peer-review process. The Editor's letter acknowledging receipt of the manuscript will be accompanied by a form fully explaining this. All authors must sign the form and return the original to the Editor as soon as possible. Failure to return the copyright form in a timely fashion will result in delay in review and subsequent publication.

Journal of Travel Research

ADDRESS FOR SUBMISSION:

Richard R. Perdue, Editor
Journal of Travel Research
Virginia Tech
Department of Hospitality & Tourism Mgmt
362 Wallace Hall
Blacksburg, VA 24061
USA
Phone: 540-231-5515
E-Mail: rick.perdue@vt.edu
Web: www.sagepub.com

PUBLICATION GUIDELINES:

Manuscript Length: 21-25
Copies Required: One Electronic
Computer Submission: Yes Email
Format: MS Word
Fees to Review: 0.00 US$

Manuscript Style:
    Chicago Manual of Style

CIRCULATION DATA:

Reader: Academics
Frequency of Issue: Quarterly
Sponsor/Publisher: Travel and Tourism
    Research Association

REVIEW INFORMATION:

Type of Review: Blind Review
No. of External Reviewers: 3
No. of In House Reviewers: 1
Acceptance Rate: 11-20%
Time to Review: 1 - 2 Months
Reviewers Comments: Yes
Invited Articles: 0-5%
Fees to Publish: 0.00 US$

MANUSCRIPT TOPICS:
Services; Tourism, Hospitality & Leisure

MANUSCRIPT GUIDELINES/COMMENTS:

Author's Checklist
Manuscripts submitted for publication consideration in the *Journal of Travel Research* must include four hard copies. To be considered, the following standards must be met.

Hard Copy
- Everything is double-spaced: text, abstract, biographical paragraph, endnotes, author's notes / acknowledgements, references, appendices, tables, etc.
- Everything is left-justified, with a ragged right-hand margin (no full justification).
- Format is one-inch margins on all sides. Minimum print size is 12 point, except in tables and figures, where 10 pt type may be used.
- Each section begins on a separate page: title, abstract, text, appendices, notes, references, each table, and each figure. Tables and figures are not embedded in the manuscript.
- Title page includes ALL authors' names, addresses, telephone numbers, fax numbers, e-mail addresses, original submission date, revised submission dates.
- Authors' names are only on the cover page.

- Title Page also includes 4 to 5 keywords
- Abstract is 150 words or less
- Endnotes are grouped on a separate page; there are no footnotes.
- All in-text citations are included in the reference list; all references have in-text citations
- Reference list follows Journal's style, *Chicago Manual of Style* (14th ed). See the following examples:

Journal article. Snepender, David and Laura Milner (1990). "Demographic and Situational Correlates of Business Travel," Journal of Travel Research, 28 (Spring): 27-32

Book Chapter. Miller, Kenneth E. (1975). "A Situational Multiattribute Model." In Advances in Consumer Research, Vol. 2. edited by Mary Jane Schlinger. Chicago: Association for Consumer Research. Pp455-463

Book. Gee, Chuck Y., Dexter J.L. Choy, and James C. Makens (1984). The Travel Industry. Westport, CT: AVI.

- Figures are camera-ready: they appear exactly as they should in the journal, including being close top the trim size of the journal.
- Tables do not have cells or lines dividing the different elements. Preferably each element is separated by a tab.
- Written, signed permission for copyrighted material had been obtained where necessary.
- For each submission (original, revisions, etc.) four copies of the manuscript are submitted.

If Accepted, Authors must submit: (1) an electronic disk copy meeting the following standards, (2) a completed Author / Co-Author information sheet and (3) Sage publication copyright agreement must be received before the paper can officially enter the publication queue. The author / co-author information sheet and publication agreement forms will be sent with the letter of acceptance.

Disk Copy
- Disk is clearly labeled with:
  a. Name of lead author
  b. Name of journal
  c. File name
  d. Software and version used, also whether MacIntosh or PC format.
- The disk version is exactly the same as the hard copy version.
- Everything except figures is in one file (no separate files for biographical paragraph, abstract, references, tables.)
- Figures are in separate file, not embedded in the article (even if figures are included on the disk, you must still provide a camera-ready hard copy).
- Each and every author has signed the Sage Publications agreement (no exceptions)

Journal of Vacation Marketing

ADDRESS FOR SUBMISSION:

Julie Glass, Editorial Manager
Journal of Vacation Marketing
Southern Cross University
School of Tourism & Hospitality Mgmt.
PO Box 157
Lismore, NSW 2480
Australia
Phone: +61 (02) 6620 3257
E-Mail: jglass@scu.edu.au
Web:

PUBLICATION GUIDELINES:

Manuscript Length: 2,500-5,000 Words
Copies Required: Three
Computer Submission: Yes
Format: MS Word
Fees to Review: 0.00 US$

Manuscript Style:
, Cambridge

CIRCULATION DATA:

Reader: Academics, Business Persons
Frequency of Issue: Quarterly
Sponsor/Publisher: Sage Publications

REVIEW INFORMATION:

Type of Review: Blind Review
No. of External Reviewers: 2
No. of In House Reviewers: 2
Acceptance Rate: 50%
Time to Review: 1 - 2 Months
Reviewers Comments: Yes
Invited Articles: 30%
Fees to Publish: 0.00 US$

MANUSCRIPT TOPICS:

Advertising & Promotion Management; Business Education; Direct Marketing; E-Commerce; Global Business; Marketing Research; Marketing Theory & Applications; Organizational Behavior & Theory; Sales/Selling; Services; Technology/Innovation; Tourism, Hospitality & Leisure

MANUSCRIPT GUIDELINES/COMMENTS:

Description

The *Journal of Vacation Marketing* provides an international forum for applied research papers, case studies, briefings and reviews on the latest techniques, thinking and practice in the marketing of hotels, travel, tourism attractions, conventions and destinations.

Its objective is to provide a forum for the publication of refereed academic papers and reviewed practitioner papers which are of direct relevance to industry, while meeting the highest standards of intellectual rigour.

In doing so, the *Journal* seeks to encourage communication and the sharing of expertise between all those concerned with the marketing of tourism services including practitioners in both the commercial and non-commercial sectors, relevant government and local government agencies, academics, researchers and consultants.

The main sectors covered by the *Journal of Vacation Marketing* are:

- Accommodation: Hotels, Apartments, Condominiums, Holiday Villages, Holiday Parks
- Destinations: Tourist Boards, Tourist Offices and Tourist Associations
- Holiday/Travel Organisers: Tour Operators, Tour Wholesalers and Brokers, Travel Agents, Conference Organisers etc
- Transport: Airlines, Shipping, Car Rental, Railways, Coaches etc
- Attractions: Theme and Amusement Parks, Museum, National/Wildlife Parks, Heritage Sites etc

The Editorial Board welcomes papers, case studies and briefings in addition to book reviews, conference reports and current issues papers from both academic and practitioner authors for publication.

New Authors

The *Journal of Vacation Marketing* actively encourages new authors, particularly practitioners, to submit a paper to the Journal. Additional 'Guidelines for Practitioners' are available directly from Perry Hobson, the Editor-in-Chief at the address below. In particular, he welcomes preliminary contact from both new and emerging practitioner and academic authors to discuss in initial ideas for a paper submission. Utilising the resources of the Editors and the Editorial Board, the *Journal* aims actively to encourage and help new authors by providing additional feedback and comments:

J.S. Perry Hobson PhD, Editor-in-Chief,
School of Tourism & Hospitality Management,
Southern Cross University,
PO Box 157, Lismore, NSW 2480,
Australia
Tel: +61 2 6620 3259; Fax: +61 2 6622 2208
E-mail: **phobson@scu.edu.au**

Manuscript Submission Guidelines

Manuscripts should be submitted in electronic format to: **jglass@scu.edu.au**

1. Each paper should come with the following information on a separate sheet:
a. title of paper, date and word count;
b. author's full name, affiliation, institutional & email address, telephone and fax numbers;
c. an abstract of up to 150 words;
d. up to 5 key words;
e. a biographical note of 25 to 50 words.

2. The typescript should be carefully checked for errors before it is submitted for publication. Authors are responsible for the accuracy of quotations, for supplying complete and correct references, and for obtaining permission where needed to cite another author's material.

3. **Tables**. These should be typed (double line-spaced) on separate sheets and their position within the text clearly indicated. All tables should have short descriptive captions with footnotes and their source(s) typed below the tables.

4. **Illustrations**. All line diagrams and photographs are termed 'Figures' and should be referred to as such in the manuscript. They should be numbered consecutively. Line diagrams should be presented in a form suitable for immediate reproduction (i.e. not requiring redrawing), each on a separate A4 sheet and in b/w only. Please provide a disk version as EPS files (all fonts embedded) or TIFF files, 800 dpi. Photographs should preferably be submitted as TIFF files, 300 dpi. For scanning they should be clear, glossy, unmounted b/w prints with a good range of contrast. All figures should have short descriptive captions typed on a separate sheet.

5. **References**. These should be indicated by superscript numbers in the text, and presented at the end of the text. Please use the following style:

Book
Surname, X. and Surname,Y. (year) *Title with Initial Caps: Subtitle with Initial Caps*. Place: Publisher.

Article in book
Surname, X. (year) 'Title of Chapter', in X. Surname and Y. Surname (eds) Title of Book, pp. xxx-xxx. Place: Publisher.

Journal article
Surname, X. (year) 'Title of Article', *Name of Journal* vol. no.(issue no.): xx-xxx [page range].

Paper
Surname, X. (year) 'Title of Paper', paper presented at Name of Conference, City, Month of presentation.

Website
Surname, X. (year) 'Title of Article', *Name of Journal* vol.no.(issue no.), URL (consulted Month,Year): http:/xxxx.xxxx.xx.xx/xxxx/xxxx

6. **Spelling**. UK or US spellings may be used with '-ize' spellings as given in the *Oxford English Dictionary* (e.g. organize, recognize).We also endorse the guidelines provided by the American Psychological Association and the British Sociological Association for non-sexist and non-racist language.

7. **Other style points**. Italics should be indicated by underlining; single quotation marks should be used, with double inside single, where necesssary; dates should be in the form 24 November 1997; delete points from abbreviations, hence UK, USA etc.; when referring to pagination and dates use the smallest number of numerals possible (e.g. 10-19, 42-5, 116-35, 1961-4).

8. **Offprints**. Authors are sent proofs for checking and correction, and will receive 25 offprints of their article plus one copy of the journal by the end of the month of publication.

9. **Copyright**. Before publication authors are requested to assign copyright to Sage Publications, subject to retaining their right to reuse the material in other publications written or edited by themselves and due to be published at least one year after initial publication in this journal.

Journal of Website Promotion

ADDRESS FOR SUBMISSION:

Richard Alan Nelson, Editor
Journal of Website Promotion
Louisiana State University
Manship School of Mass Communication
211 Journalism Building
Baton Rouge, LA 70803-7202
USA
Phone: 225-578-6686
E-Mail: Rnelson@LSU.edu
Web: www.haworthpress.com/web/JWP

PUBLICATION GUIDELINES:

Manuscript Length: 10-20
Copies Required: Four
Computer Submission: Yes
Format: MS Word, WordPerfect
Fees to Review: 0.00 US$

Manuscript Style:
American Psychological Association

CIRCULATION DATA:

Reader: Academics, Business Persons
Frequency of Issue: Quarterly
Sponsor/Publisher: Haworth Press, Inc.

REVIEW INFORMATION:

Type of Review: Blind Review
No. of External Reviewers: 2
No. of In House Reviewers: 1
Acceptance Rate: 21-30%
Time to Review: 1 - 2 Months
Reviewers Comments: Yes
Invited Articles: 6-10%
Fees to Publish: 0.00 US$

MANUSCRIPT TOPICS:
Advertising & Promotion Management; Business Law, Public Responsibility & Ethics; Communication; Direct Marketing; E-Commerce; Global Business; Marketing Theory . & Applications; Sales/Selling; Strategic Management Policy; Technology/Innovation

MANUSCRIPT GUIDELINES/COMMENTS:

The *Journal of Website Promotion* is a major new journal devoted to bridging the gap between practitioners and knowledgeable academics by publishing useful articles about the field. The broad depth of coverage provides professional communicators and faculty with a useful tool for understanding and applying the website promotion management to their careers. Organizations invest a great deal of resources in the effort to create and host their websites, but often neglect to effectively promote them. This failure to take full advantage of the web unfortunately can have real negative impacts on profits and/or the bottom line. Effective site promotion is the most vital step in conducting e-business and leading new visitors to a website. Successful web promotion then is all about influence and impact, whether for the corporation or non-profit organization. While website hits, number of unique visitors, search site indexing and rankings all have a part to play in web promotion, the most important web statistic remains the sale. Focusing on sales typically defines the method and the implementation for web promotion.

Web promotion managers develop and implement plans that make it easier for potential customers to find their client's web pathways. Internet marketing is also about attracting the right traffic, creating a user-friendly atmosphere, and developing content relevant to customers. Website promotion is the exposure generated for a website via the internet or any other means. Promotion is first done online usually through search engines and directories as well as newsgroups and email lists. It is important to ensure that the text summary that describes the site on a search engine compellingly encourages customers to visit "you" rather than the site of a competitor. More standard promotional methods such as radio, television, billboard, magazine, and newspaper advertising are also widely used and accepted. Some examples of printed materials include brochures, news releases, URL business cards, letterheads, calendars, etc.

Instructions for Authors

1. **Original Articles Only**. Submission of a manuscript to this *Journal* represents a certification on the part of the author(s) that it is an original work, and that neither this manuscript nor a version of it has been published elsewhere nor is being considered for publication elsewhere. Discuss with the editor his policy on updated studies and new research that includes materials previously in the trade press. If any of the material in your manuscript has been previously published, please obtain the appropriate permission and attached the original written and signed form to the front of the manuscript.

2. **Manuscript Length**. Articles normally are 10-to-20 pages, including references, abstract and tables. If you have a shorter or longer study, contact the editor to discuss your project. Sometimes, lengthier manuscripts may be considered if they can be divided up into sections for publication in successive *Journal* issues. Recommended is use of the 11 point Times New Roman font size, including references and notes.

3. **Manuscript Style**. References, citations, and general style of manuscripts for this *Journal* should follow the APA style (as outlined in the latest edition of the *Publication Manual of the American Psychological Association*). References should be double-spaced and placed in alphabetical order.

If an author wishes to submit a paper that has been already prepared in another style, he or she may do so. However, if the paper is accepted (with or without reviewer's alterations), the author is fully responsible for retyping the manuscript in the correct style as indicated above. Neither the editor nor the publisher is responsible for re-preparing manuscript copy to adhere to the *Journal*'s style.

4. **Manuscript Preparation**.
Margins. Leave at least a 1-inch margin on all four sides.
Paper. Use clean white, 8½" x 11" bond paper.
Number of Copies. 4 (the original plus three photocopies)
Cover page. Important—Staple a cover page to the manuscript, indicating only the article title (this is used for anonymous refereeing).

Second "title page." Enclose a regular title page but do not staple it to the manuscript. Include the title again, plus:

- Full authorship
- An abstract of about 100 words (below the abstract provide 3-10 key words for index purposes)
- An introductory footnote with authors' highest academic degree and institution granting it, professional titles, affiliations, mailing and e-mail addresses, and any desired acknowledgment of research support or other credit
- A signed Manuscript Submission and Copyright Form. Download this from: http://www.haworthpress.com (see "Section 14: Copyright" below). Please attach the Manuscript Submission Form, signed by all authors to the front of the first copy of the manuscript. Please print name of author under signature in order to verify the signature. Re-list all addresses and phone numbers, faxes, e-mail etc., on a separate sheet of paper and attached to the back of the Manuscript Submission Form. This information is needed so as to send the printed copies of the journals to the authors.

5. **Reference Linking.** The Haworth Press is participating in reference linking for journal articles. (For more information on reference linking initiatives, please consult the CrossRef website at www.crossref.org.) When citing a journal article include the article's Digital Object Identifier (DOI), when available, as the last item in the reference. A Digital Object Identifier is a persistent, authoritative, and unique identifier that a publisher assigns to each article. Because of its persistence, DOIs will enable The Haworth Press and other publishers to link to the article referenced, and the link will not break over time. This will be a great resource in scholarly research. An example of a reference to a journal article which includes a DOI:

Vizine-Goetz, Diane (2002). Classification Schemes for Internet Resources Revisited. Journal of Internet Cataloging 5(4): 5:18. doi: 10.1300/J141v05n04_02

6. **Return Envelopes.** When you submit your four manuscript copies, also include a regular

- a 9" x 12" envelope, self-addressed and stamped (with sufficient postage to ensure return of your manuscript);
- a regular envelope, stamped and self-addressed. This is for the editor to send you an "acknowledgement of receipt" letter.

7. **Spelling, Grammar, and Punctuation.** You are responsible for preparing manuscript copy which is clearly written in acceptable scholarly English and which contains no errors of spelling, grammar, or punctuation. Neither the editor nor the publisher is responsible for correcting errors of spelling and grammar. The manuscript, after acceptance by the editor, must be immediately ready for typesetting as it is finally submitted by the author(s). Check your paper for the following common errors:

- Dangling modifiers
- Misplaced modifiers
- Unclear antecedents
- Incorrect or inconsistent abbreviations

8. **Inconsistencies Must be Avoided.** Be sure you are consistent in your use of abbreviations, terminology, and in citing references, from one part of your paper to another.

9. **Alterations Required by Referees and Reviewers.** Many times a paper is accepted by the editor contingent upon changes that are mandated by anonymous specialist referees and members of the Editorial Board. If the editor returns your manuscript for revisions, you are responsible for retyping any sections of the paper to incorporate these revisions. If applicable, please send the first draft and final draft copies of your manuscript to the journal editor in print format for his final review and approval. After approval of your final manuscript, please also submit the final approved version both on printed format ("hard copy") and floppy diskette or e-mail version (preferred) to the editor. However, e-mail is much faster and preferred: **Rnelson@LSU.edu.** If using a diskette rather than e-mail attachment, submit the computer disk with your article in either MS Word or Corel WordPerfect format for PC (not Mac). On the outside of the diskette package write the title of your article and file name. NOTE: Disk/e-mail and hard copy must agree. In case of discrepancies, it is The Haworth Press's policy to follow hard copy. Authors are advised that no revisions of the manuscript can be made after acceptance by the editor for publication. The benefits of this procedure are many with speed and accuracy being the most obvious. We look forward to working with you on this, knowing we will be able to serve you more efficiently in the future

10. **Submitting Art: Preparation of Tables, Figures, and Illustrations.** All tables, figures, illustrations, etc. must be "camera-ready." That is, they must be cleanly typed or artistically prepared so that they can be used either exactly as they are or else used after a photographic reduction in size. Both a printed hard copy and a disk copy of the art must be provided. We request that each piece of art be sent in its own file, on a disk separate from the disk containing the manuscript text file(s), and be clearly labeled. We reserve the right to (if necessary) request new art, alter art, or if all else has failed in achieving art that is presentable, delete art. If submitted art cannot be used, the publisher reserves the right to redo the art and to change the author for a fee of $55.00 per hour for this service. The Haworth Press, Inc. is not responsible for errors incurred in the preparation of new artwork. Camera-ready artwork must be prepared on separate sheets of paper. Always use black ink and professional drawing instruments. On the back of these items, write your article title and the journal title lightly in soft-lead pencil (please do not write on the face of art). In the text file, skip extra lines and indicate where these figures are placed. Photos are considered part of the acceptable manuscript and remain with the publisher for use in additional printings.

11. **Electronic Media.** Haworth's in-house typesetting unit is able to utilize your final manuscript material as prepared on most personal computers and word processors. This will minimize typographical errors and decrease overall production time lag. Please send the first draft and final draft copies of your manuscript to the *Journal* editor in print format for his/her final review and approval. After approval of your final manuscript, please submit the final approved version both on printed format ("hard copy") and floppy diskette. On the outside of the diskette package write:
A.   The brand name of your computer or word processor
B.   The word-processing program that you used
C.   The title of your article, and
D.   File name

Note. Disk and hard copy must agree. In case of discrepancies, it is The Haworth Press's policy to follow hard copy. Authors are advised that no revisions of the manuscript can be made after acceptance by the editor for publication. The benefits of this procedure are many with speed and accuracy being the most obvious. We look forward to working with you on this, knowing we will be able to serve you more efficiently in the future.

12. **Typesetting**. You will not be receiving galley proofs of your article. Editorial revisions, if any, must therefore be made while your article is still in manuscript. The final version of the manuscript will be the version you see published. Typesetter's errors will be corrected by the production staff of The Haworth Press. Authors are expected to submit manuscripts, disks, and art that are free from error. The disk must be the one from which the accompanying manuscript (finalized version) was printed out.

13. **Reprints**. The senior author will receive two copies of the *Journal* issue as well as complimentary reprints of his or her article. The junior author will receive two copies of the *Journal* issue. These are sent several weeks after the *Journal* issue is published and in circulation. An order form for the purchase of additional reprints will also be sent to all authors at this time. (Approximately 8 weeks is necessary for the preparation of reprints.) Please do not query the *Journal*'s editor about reprints. All such questions should be sent directly to The Haworth Press, Inc., Production Department, 37 West Broad Street, West Hazleton, PA 18202. To order additional reprints (minimum 50 copies), please contact The Haworth Document Delivery Center, 10 Alice Street, Binghamton, NY 13904-1580, USA; Tel. 1-800-342-9678 or Fax 607-722-6362.

14. **Copyright** ownership of your manuscript must be transferred officially to The Haworth Press, Inc., before we can begin the peer-review process. The editor's letter acknowledging receipt of the manuscript will be accompanied by a form fully explaining this. All authors must sign the form and return the original to the editor as soon as possible. Either include the copyright form with your submission or mail/fax it to the editor. Failure to return the copyright form in a timely fashion will result in delay in review and subsequent publication. Authors are responsible for meeting applicable copyright laws and getting copyright permissions IN ADVANCE for any material originally created by others that they intend to reproduce. More information is available at **http://www.HaworthPress.com/web/JWP**.

Journal of World Business

ADDRESS FOR SUBMISSION:

John W. Slocum, Jr., Editor-in-Chief
Journal of World Business
Southern Methodist University
Cox School of Business
Dallas, TX 75275-0333
USA
Phone: 214-768-3157
E-Mail: jslocum@mail.cox.smu.edu
Web:

CIRCULATION DATA:

Reader: Academics, Business Persons
Frequency of Issue: Quarterly
Sponsor/Publisher: Elsevier Inc.

PUBLICATION GUIDELINES:

Manuscript Length: 28 Maximum
Copies Required: Four
Computer Submission: Yes
Format: MS Word, WordPerfect
Fees to Review: 0.00 US$

Manuscript Style:
    See Manuscript Guidelines

REVIEW INFORMATION:

Type of Review: Blind Review
No. of External Reviewers: 2
No. of In House Reviewers: 3
Acceptance Rate: 11-20%
Time to Review: 1 - 2 Months
Reviewers Comments: Yes
Invited Articles: 15%
Fees to Publish: 0.00 US$

MANUSCRIPT TOPICS:
Labor Relations & Human Resource Mgt.; Marketing Theory & Applications; Organizational Behavior & Theory; Strategic Management Policy

MANUSCRIPT GUIDELINES/COMMENTS:

Description
Formerly the *Columbia Journal of World Business*, the journal's editors are committed to build on the past strengths to make the all-new *Journal of World Business* the premier source of information on international business going into the 21st century. The scope and perspective will be to use sound theory and basic research findings as a point of departure for exciting new breakthroughs in the development and practice of international management and marketing.

With specifically designated editorial boards to recognize the importance of both the Pacific Rim and European contributions to world business, the structure of the editorial team and the new domain of *JWB* focuses on international HRM, marketing and strategic issues, broadly defined.

Mission

Journal of World Business seeks to publish manuscripts in the domains of international business strategy, human resource management, and marketing. Manuscripts should have relevant and concise theoretical foundations. They also need to translate their findings to professional practitioners seeking to improve their practice of management.

1. **Length**. Maximum of 28 pages total, double-spaced, 1½-inch margins, and 12-point type font. Microsoft Word for Windows and WordPerfect are the preferred software for submission. Upon final acceptance of your manuscript, you will be supplied with more specific guidelines and you will need to submit a diskette of your work.

2. The **cover letter** should indicate the title and the names, addresses, phone and fax numbers and e-mail address (if applicable) of two or three relevant reviewers for your paper. These may or may not be selected by the editor.

3. The **title page** should include the title and the names, addresses, fax, phone and e-mail of all authors. The corresponding author should be designated. A 100-word **abstract** should be the second page.

4. **Referencing** should be generally held to a minimum and follow the *Journal of World Business* format:

In Text. Put parentheses around the citation(s), use author's last name and correct date (Spender, 1995) or (Spender & Kessler, 1995). If the authors have more than one publication in a year, use the following notation (Spender, 1995, 1995a). When a work is in press, please use (Ford, in press).

End of Text

For articles

   Dewar, R.D., & Dutton, J.E. (1986) The adoption of radical and incremental innovations: An empirical analysis. *Management Science*, 32: 1422-1433

   Dougherty, D. (1990) Understanding new markets for products. *Strategic Management Journal*, 11:59-78.

For articles when cited journal does not publish sequential page numbers throughout a year

   Foker, L.B. (1991). Quality: American, Japanese, and Soviet perspectives. *Academy of Management Executive*, 5(4): 63-74.

   Gupta, A.K., & Wilemon, D.L. (1990). Accelerating development of technology-based new products. *California Management Review*, 32(2):24-44.

For books

   Hall, E.T. (1983). *The dance of life: The other dimension of time*. Garden City, NY: Anchor Press.

   Jones, J.W. (1993). *High-speed management*. San Francisco, CA: Jossey-Bass.

For articles in books
 Katz, R. (1980). Time and Work: Toward an integrated perspective. Pp. 81-127 in L.L. Cummings & B.M. Staw (Eds.), *Research in organizational behaviour*, Vol. 3. Greenwich, CT: JAI Press.

5. Send a self-addressed, stamped return card to acknowledge receipt of the manuscript.

6. Send four copies to editor-in-chief.

If From Pacific Rim/Asian countries send four copies to Tan Hwee Hoon, Editor, Pacific Rim, The National University of Singapore, 10 Kent Ridge Crescent, Singapore 119260.

If from Europe, send four copies to Susan C. Schneider, Editor, Europe, HEC University of Geneva, 102 Blvd. Carl Vogt, CH 1211 Geneva, Switzerland.

If from Latin America, send four copies to Frank Hoy, Editor, Latin America, College of Business Administration, University of Texas-El Paso, El Paso, TX 79968-0544

Management Science

ADDRESS FOR SUBMISSION:

Wallace J. Hopp, Editor-in-Chief
Management Science
ELECTRONIC SUBMISSION ONLY
Northwestern University
Department of Industrial Engineering
and Management Science
Evanston, IL 60208
USA
Phone: 847-491-3669
E-Mail: hopp@northwestern.edu
Web: http://mc.manuscriptcentral.com/ms

PUBLICATION GUIDELINES:

Manuscript Length: 32 double spaced
Copies Required: Submit Online
Computer Submission: Yes Required
Format: MS Word, PDF, TeX
Fees to Review: 0.00 US$

Manuscript Style:
　　See Manuscript Guidelines

CIRCULATION DATA:

Reader: Academics
Frequency of Issue: Monthly
Sponsor/Publisher: INFORMS

REVIEW INFORMATION:

Type of Review: Editorial Review
No. of External Reviewers: 3
No. of In House Reviewers: 0
Acceptance Rate: 11-20%
Time to Review: 4 - 6 Months
Reviewers Comments: Yes
Invited Articles: 0-5%
Fees to Publish: 0.00 US$

MANUSCRIPT TOPICS:

Advertising & Promotion Management; E-Commerce; Global Business; Marketing Research; Marketing Theory & Applications; Operations Research/Statistics; Production/Operations; Strategic Management Policy; Technology/Innovation; Transportation/Physical Distribution

MANUSCRIPT GUIDELINES/COMMENTS:

Editorial Statement

Management Science is a scholarly journal that publishes scientific research into the problems, interests and concerns of managers. Our scope includes articles that address management issues with tools from traditional fields such as operations research, mathematics, statistics, industrial engineering, psychology, sociology and political science, as well as cross-functional, multidisciplinary research that reflects the diversity of the management science professions. We also publish relevant articles and seek to stimulate research in emerging domains, such as those created by economic globalization, public policy shifts, technological improvements and trends in management practice.

Abridged Statement of Editorial Policies

Management Science seeks to publish articles that identify, extend, or unify scientific knowledge pertaining to management. Scientific paradigms can be drawn from a broad range of disciplines, as reflected by the departmental structure of the journal. However, the unifying thread of all Management Science articles is a fundamental focus on improving our understanding of the practice of management. Within this scope, theoretical, empirical, prescriptive and descriptive contributions are welcome. In addition to managerial relevance, articles must meet high standards of originality and rigor. More detailed descriptions of editorial policies are given in the editorial statements of the individual departments. Authors seeking up-to-date information about specific department editorial objectives should send their requests to the appropriate department editor or to the editor-in-chief.

Clear exposition is an important criterion for publication in *Management Science*. Articles must be readable, well-organized, and exhibit good writing style. As much as possible, papers suitable for *Management Science* should be readable by those comfortable with undergraduate mathematics. We accept the use of graduate level mathematics only if it is essential for understanding. All articles and notes, if judged potentially suitable for Management Science, will be refereed by at least two competent readers.

The submission of a paper to *Management Science* for refereeing means that the author certifies the manuscript is not copyrighted; nor has it been accepted for publication (or published) by any refereed journal; nor is it being refereed elsewhere. If the paper (or any version of it) has appeared, or will appear in a non-refereed publication, the details of such publication must be made known to the editor at the time of submission, so that the suitability of the paper for *Management Science* can be assessed. *Management Science* requires that at least one of the authors of each accepted article sign a Copyright Transfer Agreement form. For further information write: Professor Wallace J. Hopp, Northwestern University, Department of Industrial Engineering and Management Science, Evanston, IL 60208-3119.

Management Science is dedicated to publishing papers that scientifically address the problems, interests and concerns of managers.

Manuscript Preparation

1. **Do innovative research** that generates insights of interest to a practicing manager. (The research itself need not be directly accessible to managers, but the motivation and results should be of interest to them.)

2. **Write a good paper** that:
- is consistent with *Management Science* length and style requirements.
- complies with ethical guidelines for academic publishing.
- has not been published elsewhere in violation with INFORMS copyright policy.
- includes full cover page with names of all authors and an abstract.

3. **Select a department** to review your manuscript. To do this, you should carefully examine the current Department Editorial Objectives. If you have any questions about fit, you may contact the appropriate Department Editor or the Editor-in-Chief. If you feel your paper falls

between departments, you may note that on your submission. Departments Editors are being encouraged to handle interdisciplinary papers jointly.

Manuscript Submission

All submissions must be made electronically at **http://mc.manuscriptcentral.com/ms**. Details on how to do this are given in a PowerPoint tutorial. The basic steps are:

4. **Log in.** If you have not registered, you will be prompted to generate a new account that includes your personalized user ID. Please fill in the entire form; the email address is used for all correspondence related to your submission.

5. **Submit your paper on line**: Once logged in, the site walks you through ten steps for submitting a paper. The system accepts most word-processing formats, although MS Word or PDF are preferred. In addition to uploading your manuscript, you will be asked for an abstract, key words and a list of suggested referees who do not have any conflict of interest with you or your co-authors. All submissions to Management Science are expected to comply with INFORMS ethics and copyright guidelines.

6. **Get a manuscript tracking number** at the end of the submission. Please include this number in all subsequent correspondence regarding the paper.

Review Process

7. **Review for fit** is made by a Department Editor. Only if the paper is deemed consistent with journal and department objectives is it sent on for further review. This step should take less than two weeks.

8. **Review for significance** is made by an Associate Editor. If the paper is not judged to have the potential to make a significant contribution to the literature, it will be returned to the authors. This step should take less than two weeks.

9. **Detailed review** will be made by at least two qualified reviewers. Based on Referee and Associate Editor recommendations, the Department Editor will decide whether the paper should be accepted as is, revised or rejected.

10. **Timeline.** Our goal is to provide feedback to 75% of authors within 90 days and feedback to all authors within 180 days. If the paper goes beyond six months in the review process it is considered LATE. The on-line submission program is set up with automatic reminders to department Editors and Associate Editors to keep your manuscript moving through the system. But you are within your rights to inquire of the Department Editor concerning the status of a late paper.

Decision

11. **Email notification** will be sent to the corresponding author announcing that a decision has been made. You can access the decision and the supporting documents (e.g., referee reports) through your author center. The possible decisions are: Reject, Major Revision Required, Minor Revision Required, Accept.

12. **Revisions**, if suggested, will cause the manuscript to show up in the "Manuscripts to be Revised" area of your Author Center.

Post Acceptance

13. **Final submission**. If the paper is conditionally accepted for publication you will be requested to submit the final version of your manuscript in Word, Tex, Latex or WordPerfect format, along with a signed copyright form. Your paper will be transmitted directly to the Production editor at INFORMS. If any additional information is needed, you will be contacted.

As a condition of final acceptance of the paper for publication in *Management Science*, the author(s) must indicate if the paper is posted on a working paper website, other than their own. The author(s) are responsible for assuring that, if any part of the paper has been copyrighted for prepublication as a working paper, the copyright can and will be transferred to INFORMS when the paper has been accepted. This includes both print and electronic forms of the paper. On acceptance, the text, or any link to full text, must be removed from working paper websites, other the author(s)'s own website.

More Information. If you have any questions, are unable to access the ManuscriptCentral site, or are having trouble getting information on the status of your paper, please contact the Managing Editor.

Marketing Education Review

ADDRESS FOR SUBMISSION:

Pookie Sautter, Editor
Marketing Education Review
New Mexico State University
College of Business
Box 30001, MSC 5280
Las Cruces, NM 88003
USA
Phone: 505-646-6027
E-Mail: mer@nmsu.edu
Web: www.marketingeducationreview.com

PUBLICATION GUIDELINES:

Manuscript Length: 15-30
Copies Required: Five
Computer Submission: Yes
Format:
Fees to Review: 0.00 US$

Manuscript Style:
    See Manuscript Guidelines

CIRCULATION DATA:

Reader: Academics
Frequency of Issue: 3 Times/Year
Sponsor/Publisher: CtC Press

REVIEW INFORMATION:

Type of Review: Blind Review
No. of External Reviewers: 3
No. of In House Reviewers: 0
Acceptance Rate: 30%
Time to Review: 2 - 3 Months
Reviewers Comments: Yes
Invited Articles: 9%
Fees to Publish: 0.00 US$

MANUSCRIPT TOPICS:

Business Education; Communication; E-Commerce; Global Business; Marketing Education; Marketing Research; Marketing Theory & Applications; Sales/Selling; Services; Transportation/Physical Distribution

MANUSCRIPT GUIDELINES/COMMENTS:

Coverage

Following topics applied directly to study of marketing education: curriculum design and development, distance education, learning technologies, learning tools and techniques, outcomes assessment, pedagogy, program administration, and student recruitment and retention.

The focus of the *Marketing Education Review* is positioned as the journal for the scholarship of teaching in marketing education. The content promotes innovative approaches to curricular development, course content and delivery systems, student learning, career development and other issues which are important to marketing faculty.

Manuscript Preparation and Submission
Submit 2 electronic files either in Word or pdf file format to Pookie Sautter at **mer@nmsu.edu** The first file should contain the front matter of the article (part A below), and the second should contain the abstract and manuscript body of the text (parts B-D below).

All manuscripts should be typed, 12 pitch, double-spaced (including references) on 8½ by 11-inch white paper with margins of at least one inch on all four sides. Manuscripts typically range from 12-30 typed pages in length.

Order of Material
A. Front Matter
First Page. Title of paper, name and position of author(s), authors' complete mailing address(es), e-mail addresses, telephone number(s), and any acknowledgment of assistance.

Second Page. A brief biographical sketch of each author including name, degree(s) held, title or position, organization or institution, previous publications, and areas of research interest.

B. Manuscript Text
Begin this section with the ABSTRACT PAGE for the paper. The ABSTRACT PAGE includes the title of the paper without authors' name(s) and a brief abstract of no more than 100 words summarizing the article. The body of the paper begins on the fourth page, with major headings centered on the page and subheadings flush with the left margin. All headings and titles should be typed with upper and lower case. (Do not use all capitals.)

Footnotes are not used for reference purposes. In general, footnotes are seldom needed because the text itself should be clearly written. Thus, footnotes should be avoided. In the extreme case that a footnote is needed, it will be referred to as an endnote at the end of the article and must be approved by the editor before final submission.

C. Technical Appendices
Technical appendices may be used to include mathematical or highly technical material, which supports the main text but is not critical to the reader's interpretation of the text.

D. Tables and Figures
Each table or figure should be placed on a separate page and numbered consecutively beginning with Table 1 and Figure 1. A table or figure should not be included unless it is referred to in the text of the article. Placement in the text should be indicated as follows:

Table 1 about here

Footnotes in tables or figures should be designated by lower case letters. Table or figure number and title should be typed on two separate lines, using upper and lower case, as follows:

Table 1
Prospecting Methods and Sales Force Earnings

In the event that complicated tables or figures are used within the text, please submit a high-resolution printout (preferably a ≥600 dot-per-inch laser copy) as the original may need to be used for printing purposes.

E. References
References within the text should include the author's last name and year of publication enclosed in parentheses, e.g., (Meddaugh 1976). If practical, place the citation just ahead of a punctuation mark. If the author's name is used within the text sentence, just place the year of publication in parentheses, e.g., "According to Meddaugh (1976)..." If a particular page or section is cited, it should be placed within the parentheses, e.g., (Meddaugh 1976, p. 48). For multiple authors, use up to three names in the citation. With four or more authors, use the first author's name and et al. (Meddaugh et al. 1979).

An alphabetical listing of references should appear at the end of the manuscript, with the first author's surname first, and year of publication following all authors' names. Work by the same author with the same publication year should be distinguished by lowercase letters after the date (e.g., 1983a). For authors cited more than once, substitute a 1-inch line for each name that repeats. Examples are as follows:

Crissy, William J.E. and Robert M. Kaplan (1969), Salesmanship: The Personal Force in Marketing, New York: John Wiley & Sons.
Enis, Ben M. and Lawrence B. Chonko (1979), "A Review of Personal Selling: Implications for Managers and Researchers," in Review of Marketing: 1978, Gerald Zaltman and Thomas V. Bonoma, eds., Chicago: American Marketing Association, 23-32.
Ingram, Thomas N. and Danny N. Bellenger (1983), "Personal and Organizational Variables: Their Relative Effect on Reward Valences of Industrial Salespeople," Journal of Marketing Research, 20 (May), 198-205.

Acceptance Procedure
MER manuscripts are reviewed independently by members of the editorial review board, and their recommendations guide the Editor in his decision. The reviews are blind-neither authors nor reviewers know the identity of each other. Neither names which identify the authors or institutions should appear in the manuscript.

It is the policy of *MER* that manuscripts submitted to this journal must not be under publication consideration by another journal at the same time. Manuscripts, which are substantially similar in content to articles already published or accepted for publication in this journal or elsewhere, are ineligible for publication. It is the author's responsibility to abide by these provisions when submitting a manuscript for consideration to *MER*.

Marketing Health Services

ADDRESS FOR SUBMISSION:

Bill Gombeski, Editor
Marketing Health Services
UK Health Care
Marketing Department N113
800 Rose Street
Lexington, KY 40536
USA
Phone: 859-257-2296
E-Mail: gombeski@uky.edu
Web: www.marketingpower.com/live

PUBLICATION GUIDELINES:

Manuscript Length: 11-20
Copies Required: Five + 1 Disk
Computer Submission: Yes
Format: Prefer MS Word
Fees to Review: 0.00 US$

Manuscript Style:
    Chicago Manual of Style

CIRCULATION DATA:

Reader: , Health Care Marketers
Frequency of Issue: Quarterly
Sponsor/Publisher: American Marketing
    Association

REVIEW INFORMATION:

Type of Review: Blind Review
No. of External Reviewers: 3+
No. of In House Reviewers: 2
Acceptance Rate: 21-40%
Time to Review: 1 - 3 Months
Reviewers Comments: Yes
Invited Articles: 11-30%
Fees to Publish: 0.00 US$

MANUSCRIPT TOPICS:

Advertising & Promotion Management; Direct Marketing; Marketing Research; Various Marketing Areas in Health Care Field

MANUSCRIPT GUIDELINES/COMMENTS:

Mission Statement

Marketing Health Services magazine is tailored specifically to marketers and managers working in the healthcare field and is written primarily to serve their informational needs. *MHS* focuses on emerging issues that affect real-world decision making. It provides useful information, practical strategies, and research on important issues to help healthcare organizations compete and market themselves to enhance their viability and profitability.

Editorial Approach

MHS covers topics such as strategic planning, consumer attitudes and behavior, competitor analysis, product development, pricing, distribution, promotion, health care policy, and other management issues as they relate to marketing. A literature review is not acceptable, nor are promotional pieces for a product, person, or company. Because *MHS* seeks to inform our readers about cutting-edge thought and practice in health care marketing, only original material will be considered for publication.

Style and Submission Guidelines
Please submit article via e-mail. Include name, address, company, title, and e-mail address.
Manuscripts (including sidebars and exhibits):
- Feature articles: 3,500 words maximum, three exhibits and/or sidebars maximum
- Columns: 1,600 words maximum, no exhibits and/or sidebars
- Departments: 2,500 words maximum, two exhibits and/or sidebars maximum
- Bios: At the end of the article the author biography should consist of name, position, affiliation, and an e-mail address where the author can be reached for more information.
- Exhibits: Limit of three exhibits or sidebars. Please send exhibits separately in a TIFF, EPS, or JPEG file with 300-dpi resolution. Exhibits should not be used to validate methodology used to conduct a study, but rather to illustrate the findings (e.g., percentage of respondents who were enrolled in managed-care plans). If detailed data would enhance comprehension of the topic, please direct the reader to other publications or Web sites rather than reproducing the information in an exhibit. Exhibits might be cut, depending on space availability and usefulness to the reader.
- *MHS* articles do not include reference lists. If detailed attributions are necessary, please incorporate them into the text.

Readability
MHS articles are judged not only on the depth and cope of the ideas presented, but also on their clarity and whether they can be read and understood. Keep in mind that our readers have cried backgrounds. Avoid using technical terms hat few are likely to understand; if you must use such terms, include a brief definition. Spell out acronyms on first use. Remember: *MHS* is designed to be read, not deciphered.

Articles Based on Studies
Articles based on studies should present original pinking without relying heavily on other people's research, and the study must have been conducted within the prior two years. Interpret the findings, don't just report them; authors must clearly establish their position 'on an issue, even when presenting all sides of a debate. In general, the article should emphasize the findings and implications for marketers, not the methodology used to conduct the study. Some specific tips include:
- Don't wait until the end of the article to draw conclusions about a study. Create a lead using the five Ws—who, what, where, when, and why—and summarize major conclusions within the first three paragraphs.
- Use a narrative writing style and avoid excessive use of passive voice. Instead of "A study was conducted on patient perceptions of hospital advertising," say, "We conducted a study on..." Passive voice often obscures the subject of the sentence, opening the door to ambiguity and possible confusion for the reader. It is also boring to read.
- Don't reference everything you've ever read on the subject. Given your background and professional standing, a certain level of knowledge and expertise is assumed. For example, citing other sources for general statements such as "Health care marketers have witnessed dynamic changes in the industry over the past decade" is like saying "The sky is blue, according to my kindergarten teacher."

Give attribution only when:
1. **Quoting someone directly**. Good quotes liven up an article if used sparingly. Write the attribution into the article as follows: "Marketing health care is no longer a 'we vs. them' approach," according to Gerald McManis and Lisa Frey in their Fall 1994 Journal of Health Care Marketing article. Whenever possible, cite the original source, not an anthology.

2. **Citing statistics**. This can be very general. Use "according to government statistics" (or press reports) when statistics are in the public domain or likely to have been widely reported. Be sure to update such data to keep the information timely. If you found Direct Marketing Association estimates in a book, cite the source, not the book, and call the DMA for an update if possible.

3. **Introducing proprietary or classic techniques**. This is often a judgment call. Give credit to A. Parasuraman, Valarie Zeithaml, and Leonard Berry for their SERVQUAL model, for example, but not if you just mention it as one of several techniques. Give the credit only once, however, and don't reference statistical methods such as LISREL.
- Use percentages when reporting survey results, rather than significance scores, eigenvalues, canonical loadings, etc. Ordinary people—not just statisticians—should be able to understand the results. Remember: Statistics should be used to make your point, not to show how thorough your research was.

References
Any necessary attribution should be written into the text (see instructions on giving attribution). Do not use reference numbers, bracketed or parenthetical notes. The goal is to have *MHS* read like a magazine; not like an academic journal. However, authors may provide an "Additional Reading" list of no more than 8-10 items to be included at the end of the article. The purpose of this bibliography is to steer readers to other important works on the same topic. Please follow the *Journal of Marketing* style when creating the list.

Review Procedures
The review process for a submitted article generally is completed within six to eight weeks, barring unusual circumstances. High editorial standards are maintained through use of targeted procurement of articles, an active double-blind review process, commissioned articles, and communication with members of the marketing community.

General Information
All authors must sign the copyright release form that will be sent out when a paper is accepted for publication. All *MHS* material, including exhibits, is copyrighted by the AMA with future-use rights reserved. Articles are edited by the AMA's staff of professional editors, who generally rewrite all titles, subtitles, and subheads to conform to the magazine's style. We will not accept responsibility in case of loss.

Each author will receive a complimentary copy of the issue in which his/her article appears, and reprints will be available for purchase.

Send articles and correspondence to the Editor.

Marketing Intelligence & Planning

ADDRESS FOR SUBMISSION:

Keith Crosier, Editor
Marketing Intelligence & Planning
University of Strathclyde
Stenhouse Building
Department of Marketing
173 Cathedral Street
Glasgow, G4 0RQ
UK
Phone: 141-548-3234 or 141-959-1013
E-Mail: keithc@strath.ac.uk
Web: www.emeraldinsight.com/mip.htm

PUBLICATION GUIDELINES:

Manuscript Length:
Copies Required: Electronic
Computer Submission: Yes
Format: MS Word
Fees to Review: 0.00 US$

Manuscript Style:
    See Manuscript Guidelines

CIRCULATION DATA:

Reader: Academics, Business Persons
Frequency of Issue: 7 Times/Year
Sponsor/Publisher: Emerald Group
    Publishing Limited

REVIEW INFORMATION:

Type of Review: Blind Review
No. of External Reviewers: 2
No. of In House Reviewers: 3
Acceptance Rate: 40%
Time to Review: Over 6 Months
Reviewers Comments: Yes
Invited Articles: 0-5%
Fees to Publish: 0.00 US$

MANUSCRIPT TOPICS:

Advertising & Promotion Management; Business Information Systems (MIS); Direct Marketing; Global Business; Marketing Research; Marketing Theory & Applications; Organizational Development; Sales/Selling; Strategic Management Policy

MANUSCRIPT GUIDELINES/COMMENTS:

About the Journal

Marketing Intelligence & Planning offers in-depth analysis of the intricate relationship between planning and implementation, plus informed opinion and critical analysis from international experts in the field. As marketing techniques and technology increase in sophistication, it is essential that marketing professionals and academics understand how to apply them effectively. As such *Marketing Intelligence & Planning* aims to provide the practical implications that will help bridge the gap between academic research and practice. Every article published in *Marketing Intelligence & Planning* has been subject to a double blind review process to ensure its relevance and quality.

AUTHOR GUIDELINES

Copyright

Articles submitted to the journal should be original contributions and should not be under consideration for any other publication at the same time. Authors submitting articles for publication warrant that the work is not an infringement of any existing copyright and will indemnify the publisher against any breach of such warranty. For ease of dissemination and to ensure proper policing of use, papers and contributions become the legal copyright of the publisher unless otherwise agreed. Submissions should be sent to:

The Editor. Keith Crosier, Honorary Senior Research Fellow, Department of Marketing, University of Strathclyde, Stenhouse Building, 173 Cathedral Street, Glasgow, G4 0RQ, UK E-mail: **keithc@market.strath.ac.uk**

The Assistant Editor. David Pickton, Head of Department of Marketing, De Montfort University, Bosworth House, The Gateway, Leicester LE1 9BH, UK E-mail: **dpmar@dmu. ac.uk**

Editorial Objectives

To provide a vehicle that will help practising managers translate conceptual models and market place information into usable marketing plans. Users of research need to communicate with those who undertake research about their problems. They need to know how to process that information and translate it into action plans.

General Principles

It is our intention to encourage communications between marketing managers and researchers, to be positioned right at the academic practitioner interface. Contributors are encouraged to spell out the planning implications of their work for those involved in marketing. Articles based on experiences and evidence - rather than just philosophical speculation - will receive particular encouragement. A series of short articles on a linked theme appearing in successive issues would be particularly welcome.

The Reviewing Process

Each paper is reviewed prior to publication by the Editor and Assistant Editor. The Editor and Assistant Editor may, on occasions, choose to submit papers for further review by external referees.

Emerald Literati Editing Service

The Literati Club can recommend the services of a number of freelance copy editors, all themselves experienced authors, to contributors who wish to improve the standard of English in their paper before submission. This is particularly useful for those whose first language is not English. http://www.emeraldinsight.com/literaticlub/editingservice.htm

Manuscript Requirements

Three copies of the manuscript should be submitted in double line spacing with wide margins, accompanied by two 3.5" disks of the same version. This should facilitate speedier reviewing. All authors should be shown and author's details must be printed on a separate sheet and the author should not be identified anywhere else in the article.

As a guide, articles should be between 3,000 and 6,000 words in length. A title of not more than eight words should be provided. A brief autobiographical note should be supplied including full name, affiliation, e-mail address and full international contact details. Authors must supply a structured abstract set out under 4-6 sub-headings: Purpose; Methodology/ Approach; Findings; Research limitations/implications (if applicable); Practical implications (if applicable); and, the Originality/value of paper. Maximum is 250 words in total. In addition provide up to six keywords which encapsulate the principal topics of the paper and categorise your paper under one of these classifications: Research paper, Viewpoint, Technical paper, Conceptual paper, Case study, Literature review or General review. For more information and guidance on structured abstracts visit: http://www.emeraldinsight.com/literaticlub/editors/ editorialadmin/abstracts.htm

Where there is a **methodology**, it should be clearly described under a separate heading. **Headings** must be short, clearly defined and not numbered. **Notes** or **Endnotes** should be used only if absolutely necessary and must be identified in the text by consecutive numbers, enclosed in square brackets and listed at the end of the article.

Figures, charts and **diagrams** should be kept to a minimum. They must be black and white with minimum shading and numbered consecutively using Arabic numerals with a brief title and labelled axes. In the text, the position of the figure should be shown by typing on a separate line the words "take in Figure 2". Good quality originals must be provided.

Tables should be kept to a minimum. They must be numbered consecutively with roman numerals and a brief title. In the text, the position of the table should be shown by typing on a separate line the words "take in Table IV".

Photos and **illustrations** must be supplied as good quality black and white original half tones with captions. Their position should be shown in the text by typing on a separate line the words "take in Plate 2".

References to other publications should be complete and in Harvard style. They should contain full bibliographical details and journal titles should not be abbreviated. For multiple citations in the same year use a, b, c immediately following the year of publication. References should be shown within the text by giving the author's last name followed by a comma and year of publication all in round brackets, e.g. (Fox, 1994). At the end of the article should be a reference list in alphabetical order as follows:

(a) *for books*
surname, initials and year of publication, title, publisher, place of publication, e.g. Casson, M. (1979), Alternatives to the Multinational Enterprise, Macmillan, London.

(b) *for chapter in edited book*
surname, initials and year, "title", editor's surname, initials, title, publisher, place, pages, e.g. Bessley, M. and Wilson, P. (1984), "Public policy and small firms in Britain", in Levicki, C. (Ed.), Small Business Theory and Policy, Croom Helm, London, pp.111-26. Please note that the chapter title must be underlined.

(c) *for articles*
surname, initials, year "title", journal, volume, number, pages, e.g. Fox, S.(1994) "Empowerment as a catalyst for change: an example from the food industry", Supply Chain Management, Vol 2 No 3, pp. 29-33

If there is more than one author list surnames followed by initials. All ·authors should be shown.

Electronic sources should include the URL of the electronic site at which they may be found, as follows:
Neuman, B.C.(1995), "Security, payment, and privacy for network commerce", IEEE Journal on Selected Areas in Communications, Vol. 13 No.8, October,pp.1523-31. Available (IEEE SEPTEMBER) http://www.research.att.com/jsac/

Notes/Endnotes should be used only if absolutely necessary. They should, however, always be used for citing Web sites. They should be identified in the text by consecutive numbers enclosed in square brackets and listed at the end of the article. Please then provide full Web site addresses in the end list.

Final Submission of the Article
Once accepted for publication, the final version of the manuscript must be provided, accompanied by a 3.5" disk of the same version labelled with: disk format; author name(s); title of article; journal title; file name.

Each article must be accompanied by a completed and signed Journal Article Record Form available from the Editor or on http://www.emeraldinsight.com/literaticlub

The manuscript will be considered to be the definitive version of the article. The author must ensure that it is complete, grammatically correct and without spelling or typographical errors.

In preparing the disk, please use one of the following formats: Word, Word Perfect, Rich text format or TeX/LaTeX. Figures which are provided electronically must be in tif, gif or pic file extensions. All figures and graphics must also be supplied as good quality originals.

Final Submission Requirements
Manuscripts must be clean, good quality hard copy and;
* include an abstract and keywords
* have Harvard style references
* include any figures, photos and graphics as good quality originals
* be accompanied by a labelled disk
* be accompanied by a completed Journal Article Record Form

Technical assistance is available from the Literati Club on http://www.emeraldinsight.com/literaticlub or contact Mike Massey e-mail mmassey@emeraldinsight.com

Marketing Letters

ADDRESS FOR SUBMISSION:

Charles Weinberg & Bart Weitz, Editors
Marketing Letters
Springer
Journals Editorial Office
101 Phillip Drive
Norwell, MA 02061
USA
Phone: 781-871-6600
E-Mail: weinberg@commerce.ubc.ca
Web: http://MARK.Edmgr.com

CIRCULATION DATA:

Reader: Academics
Frequency of Issue: Quarterly
Sponsor/Publisher: Springer

PUBLICATION GUIDELINES:

Manuscript Length: 15-20
Copies Required: Five
Computer Submission: Yes Electronic
Format:
Fees to Review: 0.00 US$

Manuscript Style:
   See Manuscript Guidelines

REVIEW INFORMATION:

Type of Review: Editorial Review
No. of External Reviewers: 2
No. of In House Reviewers: No Reply
Acceptance Rate: 21-30%
Time to Review: 1 - 2 Months
Reviewers Comments: Yes
Invited Articles: 0-5%
Fees to Publish: 0.00 US$

MANUSCRIPT TOPICS:
Advertising & Promotion Management; Direct Marketing; E-Commerce; Empirical Studies in Marketing; Marketing Research; Marketing Theory & Applications; Non-Profit Organizations; Sales/Selling; Services

MANUSCRIPT GUIDELINES/COMMENTS:

Aims & Scope
Marketing Letters: A Journal of Research in Marketing publishes high-quality, shorter papers on marketing, the emphasis being on immediacy and current interest. The journal offers a medium for the truly rapid publication of research results. The focus of *Marketing Letters* is on empirical findings, methodological papers, and theoretical and conceptual insights across areas of research in marketing. *Marketing Letters* is required reading for anyone working in marketing science, consumer research, methodology, and marketing strategy and management. The key subject areas and topics covered in *Marketing Letters* are: choice models, consumer behavior, consumer research, management science, market research, sales and advertising, marketing management, marketing research, marketing science, psychology, and statistics.

Instructions for Authors

Authors submitting to *Marketing Letters* should use our fully web-enabled online manuscript submission and review system. Our online manuscript submission and review system offers authors the option to track the progress of the review process of manuscripts in real time. Manuscripts should be submitted to **http://MARK.edmgr.com**

The online manuscript submission and review system for *Marketing Letters* offers easy and straightforward login and submission procedures. This system supports a wide range of submission file formats: for manuscripts—Word, WordPerfect, RTF, TXT, and LaTex; for figures—TIFF, GIF, JPEG, EPS, PPT, and PostScript. PDF is not an acceptable format.

Authors are requested to download the Consent to Publish and Transfer of Copyright form from the journal's website. Please send a completed and duly signed form either by mail or fax to the Editorial Office of *Marketing Letters*. Authors should still follow the regular instructions for authors when preparing their manuscripts (see below).

Note. In case you encounter any difficulties while submitting your manuscript on line, please get in touch with the responsible Editorial Assistant by clicking on "CONTACT US" from the tool bar.

Manuscript Preparation

Submitted papers should typically be less than 20 double-spaced typewritten pages, including bibliographies, tables, etc. Final versions of accepted manuscripts (including notes, references, tables, and legends) should be typed double-spaced on 8½" x 11" (22cm x 29cm) white paper with 1" (2.5cm) margins on all sides. Sections should appear in the following order: title page, abstract, text, notes, references, tables, figure legends, and figures. Comments or replies to previously published articles should also follow this format with the exception of abstracts, which are not required.

Title Page. The title page should include the article title, authors' names and permanent affiliations, and the name, current address, and telephone number of the person to whom page proofs and reprints should be sent.

Abstract. The following page should include an abstract of not more than 100 words and a list of two to six keywords.

Text. The text of the article should begin on a new page. The introduction should have no heading or number. Subsequent section headings (including appendices) should be designated by Arabic numerals (1, 2, etc.), and subsection headings should be numbered 1.1, 1.2, etc. Figures, tables, and displayed equations should be numbered consecutively throughout the text (1, 2, etc.). Equation numbers should appear flush left in parentheses and running variables for equations (e.g. $i = 1, ...,n$) flush right in parentheses.

Notes. Acknowledgments and related information should appear in a note designated by an asterisk after the last author's name, and subsequent notes should be numbered consecutively and designated by superscripts (1, 2, etc.) in the text. All notes should be typed double-spaced beginning on a separate page following the text.

References. References in the text should follow the author-date format (e.g., Brown (1986). Jones (1978a, 1978b). Smith and Johnson (1983)). References should be typed double-spaced beginning on a separate page following the notes, according to the following samples (journal and book titles may be underlined rather than italicized). References with up to three authors should include the names of each author; references with four or more authors should cite the first author and add "et al." It is the responsibility of authors to verify all references.

Tables. Tables should be titled and typed double-spaced, each on a separate sheet, following the references. Notes to tables should be designated by superscripted letters (a, b, etc.) within each table and typed double-spaced on the same page as the table. Use descriptive labels rather than computer acronyms, and explain all abbreviations. When tables are typed on oversized paper, please submit both the original and a reduced copy.

Figures. Figures for accepted manuscripts should be submitted in camera-ready form, i.e. clear glassy prints or drawn in India ink on drafting paper or high quality white paper. Lettering in figures should be large enough to be legible after half size reduction. Authors should submit one 5" x 7" (13cm x 18cm) original and two photocopies of each figure, with authors names, manuscript title, and figure number on the back of each original and copy (use gummed labels if necessary to avoid damaging originals). Figures should be enclosed in a separate envelope backed by cardboard and without staples or paper clips. Figure legends should be typed double-spaced on a separate sheet following the tables.

Page Proofs and Reprints

Corrected page proofs must be returned within three days of receipt, and alterations other than corrections may be charged to the authors. Authors will receive 25 free reprints, and may order additional copies when returning the corrected proofs.

Any questions about the above procedures please send e-mail to **dthelp@springer-sbm.com**

Marketing Management

ADDRESS FOR SUBMISSION:

Carolyn Pollard Neal, Editor
Marketing Management
 ELECTRONIC SUBMISSION ONLY
Phone:
E-Mail: crpneal@bellsouth.net
Web: www.ama.org

PUBLICATION GUIDELINES:

Manuscript Length: See Guidelines
Copies Required: Electronic
Computer Submission: Yes Email Required
Format: See Guidelines
Fees to Review: 0.00 US$

Manuscript Style:
 See Manuscript Guidelines

CIRCULATION DATA:

Reader: Business Persons, Senior
 Marketing Executives
Frequency of Issue: Bi-Monthly
Sponsor/Publisher: American Marketing
 Association

REVIEW INFORMATION:

Type of Review: Blind Review
No. of External Reviewers: 2+
No. of In House Reviewers: 2+
Acceptance Rate: 21-30%
Time to Review: 2 - 3 Months
Reviewers Comments: Yes
Invited Articles: 85%
Fees to Publish: 0.00 US$

MANUSCRIPT TOPICS:
Advertising & Promotion Management; Global Business; Marketing Theory & Applications; Sales/Selling; Strategic Management Policy

MANUSCRIPT GUIDELINES/COMMENTS:

Topics Include. Assessing Marketing Effectiveness; Branding and Brand Management; Global Marketing; Growth, Innovation, & New Products; Managing Competitive Opportunity; Managing and Understanding Customers; Managing Marketing Information; Marketing Leadership; Marketing's Role in the Organization; Marketing ROI/Metrics; Pricing; Strategic Marketing and Management Practice

Mission Statement. *Marketing Management (MM)* packages and clearly communicates the best strategic thinking to meet the decision-making needs of knowledgeable executives managing real-world businesses.

Editorial Approach. *MM* provides thoughtful, timely, and useful information to senior marketing executives and other business executives whose interests lie in a compatible area. It publishes in-depth articles on functional areas of marketing, marketing management, and marketing as a philosophy of business. To help fulfill readers' professional development needs, *MM* provides the cutting edge of marketing thought and presents marketing as a vital and an important element of business.

High editorial standards are maintained through the use of targeted procurement of manuscripts, an active double-blind referee process, commissioned manuscripts, solicited interviews, and communication with members of the marketing community. Whenever possible, *MM* takes a unique approach to the editorial product by pairing academic and practitioner authors to broaden the perspectives on a topic.

In addition to feature articles, *MM* publishes a variety of regular columns and departments, interviews with prominent executives, book reviews, and letters to the Editor.

MM publishes only original manuscripts. A conference speech, if edited to conform with our style, also will be considered for publication.

Review Procedure

MM employs a double-blind referee process for all except columns, commissioned manuscripts, interviews, and some departments.

MM has two editorial boards: the Editorial Policy Board and the Editorial Review Board. In addition, ad hoc reviewers are enlisted for select subject matter.

After reading the reviews, the editor makes all final decisions on publication. The review process should be completed within six to eight weeks, barring unusual circumstances.

Writing for *MM*

As senior executives, *MM* readers have many demands on their time. All manuscripts must, therefore, contain information essential to their professional development and/or corporate or personal interests. Try to convey that information so readers can easily and rapidly comprehend it.

All manuscripts not specifically procured by the Editor will be subject to the review process. Procured manuscripts will be reviewed in a preliminary statement, as in the form of a detailed outline, and advice given for further development.

Manuscripts should comply with the style guidelines that follow.

In general, editorial content should have actual business applications and significance to the marketing profession.

Manuscripts are evaluated on a number of criteria. Generally, the manuscript must:

- Look at cutting-edge issues or topics that will affect executives in the conduct of business.
- Discuss such issues or topics in-depth, preferably with the inclusion of actual corporate experiences that point out the relevance to the reader.
- Challenge readers to look at new ideas, or perhaps old ideas in a new light and stimulate and extend their thinking, awaken their interest in, and awareness of, new approaches and options.
- Present original thinking. Avoid extensive reliance on other people's research.

- Interpret the findings of a research study, not just report them. Authors must clearly establish their position on an issue, even when presenting all sides of a debate.
- Extend ideas that are industry- or service-specific, geographically or demographically focused, or otherwise limited in scope or applicability. The information must be of value to a broad readership.
- Include a detailed description of how proposed marketing strategies can be implemented.
- Not promote a product, person, or company. Not discuss a trademarked idea or process. If a corporate story is translatable into direct benefit to other corporations, it should be written as such, not as a public relations promotion. The PR benefit is more effective when readers view the author as an expert.

In addition, reviewers will address a series of specific questions, including the following:
- Is the subject of current interest to *MM*'s readership of senior marketing executives?
- Do you perceive any inaccuracies in the facts or data presented?
- Is the main argument clearly expressed and does the manuscript flow smoothly and logically?
- Is the writing style clear and interesting?
- Are there any new concepts or techniques presented? Are they valid and worthy of discussion?
- Does this manuscript have practical application for the business community?
- Does the supportive material—charts , graphs, and sidebars—enhance understanding of the material?

Style Guidelines
Submission Format. Please submit via electronic mail. Please use double or 1.5 spacing, and do not embed graphic elements in text such as table of contents, bookmarks, and tables or boxed inserts.

Length of Manuscripts (including bio, title, deck, executive briefing, sidebars and exhibits)
- Feature Articles—3,000 to 3,500 words maximum
- Departments—1,800 to 2,000 words maximum, two exhibits and/or sidebars maximum

Cover Sheet and Bios. Include a separate page with author(s) name, position, and affiliation. Include address, phone, fax, and electronic mail address. This information should appear **only** on the cover page. Include a very short bio for each author on a separate sheet.

Titles and Abstracts. Titles of papers should be short and concise. Executive Briefings of no more than 75 words should provide a substantive summary of the manuscript, giving the readers a good understanding of the main points.

Attribution. *MM* is a magazine, not a journal. Avoid use of reference citation, i.e., bracketed or parenthetical notes, in the text. If attribution is absolutely necessary, such as for quoted material and statistics, write it into the text. Footnotes also should be incorporated into the text. If citations are absolutely necessary, list no more than 5 alphabetically by author on a separate page called Additional Reading at the end of the manuscript (use *Journal of Marketing* style to create this list).

Methodology. If the manuscript is based on a study, present only enough explanation of the methodology to establish the credibility of the study (sample frame and size, type of survey conducted, response rate); include a more detailed, but short, explanation in a separate section, possibly for use as a sidebar to the text, or, better yet, supply a Web site link so interested readers can find the information themselves. That also goes for additional exhibits, and other information the author(s) wishes to supply.

Exhibits. Limit of three exhibits and/or sidebars for each article. Label all charts, figures, and tables as "exhibits." Please create all exhibits in PPT, tiff, or eps files. Please submit all exhibits in a separate file from the text; do not incorporate exhibits into the text file. Note that exhibits may have to be cut, depending on applicability and space constraints. (Again, authors may refer readers to a Web site for additional material.)

Readability. Do not assume that our readers are completely familiar with the concepts and terminology of the specific subject under discussion. Define acronyms and industry-specific terms. Make your text direct and clear, and use a narrative style with limited use of passive voice.

General Information
All authors must sign the copyright release form that will be sent out when a paper is accepted for publication. All *MM* material, including exhibits, is copyrighted by the AMA with future-use rights reserved. Articles are edited by the AMA's staff of professional editors, who generally rewrite all titles, subtitles, and subheads to conform to the magazine's style. Even though care will be taken with returnable material, manuscripts, photographs, and so on, we can accept no responsibility in case of loss.

Each author will receive a complimentary copy of the issue in which his or her article appears as well as information on purchasing reprints. E-mail all manuscripts and correspondence to the Editor.

Marketing Management Journal

ADDRESS FOR SUBMISSION:

Mike D'Amico & Charles Pettijohn, Co-Eds
Marketing Management Journal
University of Akron
Department of Marketing
Akron, OH 44325-4804
USA
Phone: 330-972-7024
E-Mail: mdamico@uakron.edu
 cep288f@missouristate.edu
Web: mmaglobal.org

CIRCULATION DATA:

Reader: Academics, Business Persons
Frequency of Issue: 2 Times/Year
Sponsor/Publisher: Marketing Management
 Association

PUBLICATION GUIDELINES:

Manuscript Length: 30 Pages Maximum
Copies Required: Four
Computer Submission: Hardcopy Preferred
Format: MS Word
Fees to Review: 0.00 US$

Manuscript Style:
 See Manuscript Guidelines

REVIEW INFORMATION:

Type of Review: Blind Review
No. of External Reviewers: 3
No. of In House Reviewers: 0
Acceptance Rate: 21-30%
Time to Review: 2 - 3 Months
Reviewers Comments: Yes
Invited Articles: 0-5%
Fees to Publish: 15.00 US$
 per typeset page

MANUSCRIPT TOPICS:

Advertising & Promotion Management; Communication; Direct Marketing; E-Commerce; Global Business; Marketing Research; Marketing Theory & Applications; Non-Profit Organizations; Sales/Selling; Services; Strategic Management Policy; Transportation/Physical Distribution

MANUSCRIPT GUIDELINES/COMMENTS:

Co-Editor. Charles Pettijohn, Missouri State University, Springfield, MO 65804-0089 Phone: (417) 836-4188; Email: **cep288f@missouristate.edu**

Submission Guidelines

Manuscripts which do not conform to submission guidelines will be returned to authors for revision. Only submissions in the form required by the Editorial Board of the *Marketing Management Journal* will be distributed for review. Authors should submit four copies (4) of manuscripts and should retain the original. Photocopies of the original manuscript are acceptable. Upon acceptance, authors must submit a final manuscript in both hard copy and diskette form.

Manuscripts must not include any authorship identification with the exception of a separate cover page which should include authorship, institutional affiliation, manuscript title, acknowledgments where required, and the date of the submission. Manuscripts will be reviewed through a triple-blind process. Only the manuscript title should appear prior to the abstract.

Manuscripts must include an informative and self-explanatory abstract which must not exceed 250 words on the first page of the manuscript body. It should be specific, telling why and how the study was made, what results were, and why the results are important. The abstract will appear on the first page of the manuscript immediately following the manuscript title. Tables and figures used in the manuscript should be included on a separate page and placed at the end of the manuscript. Authors should insert a location note within the body of the manuscript to identify appropriate placement. Tables and figures should be constructed in table mode of Word or column parallel.

Final revision of article accepted for publication in the *Marketing Management Journal* must include a diskette in Word format in addition to two printed copies of the manuscript. Authors will receive a "final" typeset version of their article shortly before publication for a final check. The *JMM* requests fast turnaround on this final (author's) review.

The *Journal of Marketing* should be consulted for clarification of style related questions. Manuscripts must be submitted on 8½ by 11 inch, bond paper. Margins must be one inch. Manuscripts should be submitted on 12 point Times Roman and should not exceed thirty typewritten pages inclusive of body, tables and figures, and references.

References used in the text should be identified at the appropriate point in the text by the last name of the author, the year of the referenced publication, and specific page identity where needed. The style should be as follows: "...Wilkie (1989)" or "...Wilkie (1989, p.15)." Each reference cited must appear alphabetically in the reference appendix titled "REFERENCES." References should include the author(s) full names. The use of "et al.," is not acceptable in the reference section. The references should be attached to the manuscript on a separate page. The *JMM* prefers this style in the references: Kotler, Phillip, Paul Thisthlewhaite and Noam Chomsky, etc.

The Editorial Board of the *Marketing Management Journal* interprets the submission of a manuscript as a commitment to publish in the *Marketing Management Journal*. The Editorial Board regards concurrent submission of manuscripts to any other professional publication while under review by the *Marketing Management Journal* as unprofessional and unacceptable. Editorial policy also prohibits publication of a manuscript that has already been published in whole or in substantial part by another journal. Authors will be required to authorize copyright protection for the *Marketing Management Journal* prior to manuscripts being published. Manuscripts accepted become the copyright of the *Marketing Management Journal*.

The Editorial Board reserves the right for stylistic editing of manuscripts accepted for publication in the *Marketing Management Journal*.

Marketing Review (The)

ADDRESS FOR SUBMISSION:

Jim Blythe, Editor
Marketing Review (The)
University of Glamorgan
Business School
Pontypridd, Wales, CF37 1DL
UK
Phone: 01443 483 575
E-Mail: jwblythe@glam.ac.uk
Web: www.westburn.co.uk/tmr

CIRCULATION DATA:

Reader: Business Persons, Academics,
    Students
Frequency of Issue: Quarterly
Sponsor/Publisher: Westburn Publishers
    Ltd.

PUBLICATION GUIDELINES:

Manuscript Length: 11-15
Copies Required: One
Computer Submission: Yes Email
Format: MS Word, PDF, UK English
Fees to Review: 0.00 US$

Manuscript Style:
    Uniform System of Citation (Harvard
    Blue Book)

REVIEW INFORMATION:

Type of Review:
No. of External Reviewers: 0
No. of In House Reviewers: 1
Acceptance Rate:
Time to Review: 1 Month or Less
Reviewers Comments: Yes
Invited Articles: 31-50%
Fees to Publish: 0.00 US$

MANUSCRIPT TOPICS:

Advertising & Promotion Management; Communication; Direct Marketing; E-Commerce; Global Business; Marketing Research; Marketing Theory & Applications; Non-Profit Organizations; Organizational Behavior & Theory; Organizational Development; Purchasing/Materials Management; Sales/Selling; Services; Small Business Entrepreneurship; Strategic Management Policy; Tourism, Hospitality & Leisure

MANUSCRIPT GUIDELINES/COMMENTS:

Submissions (2 copies) should be of 4000-6000 words (excluding display material and references) typed double-spaced on A4 paper. The first page should consist of the title, authors' names, addresses and an indication of author for correspondence with his/her telephone/fax number. The second page should comprise an abstract of the paper (c. 150 words) and a biography (c. 150 words) detailing the authors' background, affiliations and interests. Display material must be numbered, captioned and cited in the text. Authors should avoid identifying themselves in the main body of the text.

Please note that authors must include a contact e-mail address / phone number in case there are any difficulties converting the electronic file of their paper. If the author wishes to receive a copy of their paper for proofing, please let us know when submitting the electronic copy.

804

References
References are indicated in the text by either "Recent work (Smith, 1970; Jones et al, 1990)" or "Recently Smith (1970) has found.". All such references should then be listed in alphabetical order at the end of the paper in accordance with the following conventions:

Books
Baker, Michael J. and Hart, Susan J. (1989), *Marketing and Competitive Success*, Hemel Hempstead, Philip Allen.

Journal Articles
Star, Steven H. (1989), "Marketing and its Discontents", *Harvard Business Review*, November/December 1989 No.6, pp. 148-154.

Contributions in books, proceedings, etc.
Doyle, Peter (1990), "Managing the Marketing Mix". In: *The Marketing Book* 2nd Edition. (Ed.)Baker, Michael J. (London), William Heinemann Ltd, pp. 227-267.

Copyright
Authors submitting a manuscript do so on the understanding that if it is accepted for publication, copyright in the paper exclusive shall be assigned to the Publisher. In consideration of the assignment of copyright each author shall receive a copy of the Review in which their paper appears, and electronic access to that year's online Review. A fee of £250 is payable on publication, to be shared equally among all the authors involved. Reprints of the paper may be purchased from our web site at extra cost. The Publisher will not put any limitations on the personal freedom of the author to use material contained in the paper in other works. Papers are accepted for the Review on the understanding that they have not been or will not be published elsewhere in the same form, in any language.

The Editor's contact details are:
Dr Jim Blythe
Business School
University of Glamorgan
Pontypridd
Wales
CF37 1DL

Submission of Accepted Papers
When supplying the final version of your article please email the paper to: **journals@ westburn.co.uk**

The accompanying email should clearly state the contents of the attachment which must fulfill the following requirements. Please follow these guidelines carefully:
- Include one copy of the word processed article in MS Word including figures and tables. (If using an alternative word processing package please save into Word when possible and also send in original format)

- If the article includes a figure which is a photograph, or a particularly complex illustration, this should be saved in a separate .png file. All diagrams and figures should be in black and white. All figures should be at 300dpi quality minimum. If prepared on an Apple, include the file in ASCII format.
- Ensure that the files are not saved as read-only. Virus check all files before sending them.
- The directives for preparing the paper in the style of the journal as set out in the Instructions to Authors must be followed; i.e. ensure the document is in the following order: Title; Authors; Addresses; Abstract; Running heads; Introduction; Materials and methods; Results; Discussion; Acknowledgements; References; Appendices; Figure legends; Tables; Footnotes; Abbreviations.
- It is the responsibility of the author to ensure that all these points are fulfilled, and that the material on the disk is correct. References MUST be presented in the manner given in the guidelines.

Additional points to note
- Use two carriage returns to end headings and paragraphs.
- Type text without end of line hyphenation, except for compound words.
- Be consistent with punctuation and only insert a single space between words and after punctuation.

Final Formatting
All authors will be sent a PDF of their paper in proof format for their approval. Papers will not be published without the return to the publishers of the signed copyright assignment form, which must be signed by all authors involved in the paper. It is the author's responsibility to obtain clearance if they wish to use copyright material within their paper.

All other enquiries and accepted papers and accompanying disks should be directed to:
Westburn Publishers Ltd
Westburn
Helensburgh
Argyll
G84 9NH
Scotland
Tel: +44 (0) 1436 678 699; Fax: +44 (0) 1436 670 328
Email: **tmr@westburn.co.uk**

Marketing Theory

ADDRESS FOR SUBMISSION:

Barbara Stern & Pauline Maclaran, Co-Eds
Marketing Theory
De Montfort University
Bosworth House
The Gateway
Leicester, LE1 9BH
UK
Phone: 44 116 2506428
E-Mail: marketingtheory@dmu.ac.uk
Web: www.sagepub.co.uk

PUBLICATION GUIDELINES:

Manuscript Length: 21-25
Copies Required: Five
Computer Submission: Yes Email Preferred
Format: MS Word
Fees to Review: 0.00 US$

Manuscript Style:
    See Manuscript Guidelines

CIRCULATION DATA:

Reader: Academics
Frequency of Issue: Quarterly
Sponsor/Publisher: Sage Publications, Ltd.

REVIEW INFORMATION:

Type of Review: Blind Review
No. of External Reviewers: 3
No. of In House Reviewers: 2
Acceptance Rate: 11-20%
Time to Review: 2 - 3 Months
Reviewers Comments: Yes
Invited Articles: 0-5%
Fees to Publish: 0.00 US$

MANUSCRIPT TOPICS:
Marketing Theory & Applications

MANUSCRIPT GUIDELINES/COMMENTS:

Marketing Theory provides a specialised academic medium and main reference for the development and dissemination of alternative and critical perspectives on marketing theory.

There are a growing number of researchers and management practitioners who believe that conventional marketing theory is often ill suited to the challenges of the modern business environment. *Marketing Theory* creates a high-quality, specialist outlet for management and social scientists who are committed to developing and reformulating marketing as an academic discipline by critically analysing existing theory. In so doing, it promotes an ethos that is explicitly theory driven; international in scope and vision; open, reflexive, imaginative and critical; and interdisciplinary.

Wide-Ranging Scope
The journal encompasses the full range of key theoretical, methodological and substantive debates and developments in marketing theory, broadly conceived. *Marketing Theory* publishes articles covering any aspect of theory, including strategy, consumer behaviour, new

product development and more. Research that builds on different methodological and disciplinary positions is particularly welcome. It is not the intention to promote any particular research or normative position. Literature reviews, theoretical and empirical papers are all equally encouraged. The editors particularly encourage contributions from academics at the start of their career as a positive strategy to create more interest in theory among new generations of the marketing academy.

Themes

Marketing Theory does not promote any particular research or normative position. The journal will not be limited to specific areas of marketing. It brings you a whole range of theoretical, methodological, and substantive debates and developments in marketing theory, covering such marketing issues as:

- Radical assessments of contemporary marketing theory and practice
- Modern and post-modern representations of marketing
- The ethics of marketing and the marketing of ethics
- Gender and marketing
- Ethnicity, cultural identity and marketing
- Critical consumer discourse
- 'Green' marketing philosophy and practice
- Competing histories of marketing thought
- Marketing and inequality
- Marketing as a political process
- Critical accounts of marketing in society
- Information technology and marketing

Submissions

The journal publishes theory papers and speculative essays, review articles and theoretically grounded methodology and empirical articles. Thematic symposia (typically comprising three or four papers) on a particular theme will be published from time to time.

Articles should be written in English and should not have been published nor be currently under review elsewhere. *Marketing Theory* will consider papers that have been published elsewhere in languages other than English, if they are submitted with an accompanying English translation.

Refereeing Procedures

Refereeing will be on an anonymous basis. *Marketing Theory* makes every effort to match papers with referees of appropriate theoretical backgrounds. Where the subject of a paper is interdisciplinary it may be sent to reviewer outside of the marketing academy. Referees are encouraged to provide prompt and constructive critiques of papers, and, where revision is required, to highlight potential avenues for further development..

The journal aims to keep contributors informed of the progress of their submissions on a regular basis, and, in recognition of this commitment, provides a first indication of a paper's progress within 10-12 weeks of the initial acknowledgement of receipt, and informs them of developments thereafter. It is the editors' intention, by these means, to deal fairly and in good faith with potential contributors and readers.

Paper Presentation
Manuscripts should be typewritten, double-spaced throughout (this includes Notes and References sections) on one side of A4 or US standard size white paper with generous margins. Reviewing is anonymous, so authors should supply two title pages, one with full identifying information (plus fax and e-mail numbers), one with title only.

Extent. Full papers should be between 5-7,000 words in length with shorter 'think pieces' of between 2,000 and 3,000 words.

Abstract. All papers require an abstract of 100-150 words and five to eight Keywords. Abstracts should be typed double-spaced on a separate sheet at the beginning of the manuscript.

Notes. Keep them to a minimum; number them consecutively through the text and present them typed as a double-spaced list before the References at the end of the manuscript. Do not present them as footnotes to the individual citation; this is not the style used by this journal.

References. Represent these in the text by author and date [typically: ... as Foxall (1999) and Saren (2000) comment...; ... as demonstrated (Stern, 2001; Gummerson, 2000)] and collate into an alphabetical (double-spaced) date-order list at the end of the manuscript, in the following style.

Books
Eden, C. and Ackermann, F. (1998) *Making Strategy: The Journey of Strategic Management.* London: Sage.

Journal Articles
Tsoukas, H. (1991) 'The Missing Link', *Academy of Management Review* 16(3): 566-85.

Chapters in Books
Gray, B. (1994) 'Women-only Management Training', in M. Tanton (ed.) *Women in Management: A Developing Presence*, pp. 33-56.

Conference and Other Papers
Thorne, M.L. (1996) 'The Sounds of Silence: New University Business Schools', paper presented at the annual conference of the British Academy of Management, University of Aston, April.

Tables and Figures. Supply on separate pages from the text, complete with captions and any source details (figures to be clear black and white originals, preferably suitable for direct reproduction). Indicate in the text where they are to be incorporated. [Note that authors are responsible for obtaining permission from copyright holders for reproducing any illustrations, tables, figures—or lengthy quotations—previously published elsewhere.]

Proofs

All article authors will see a set of proofs prior to publication.

Offprints

On publication, article authors will receive a printed copy of the journal, and offprints (25) will be sent to the first author of the article.

Mailing Your Manuscript

Please submit your work by email if possible. If not, five copies of the manuscript should be sent to Professor Pauline Maclaran at the above address.

Midwestern Business and Economic Review

ADDRESS FOR SUBMISSION:

James R. Owen, Editor
Midwestern Business and Economic
   Review
College of Business Administration
3410 Taft Blvd.
Wichita Falls, TX 76308
USA
Phone: 940-397-4149
E-Mail: james.owen@mwsu.edu
Web:

PUBLICATION GUIDELINES:

Manuscript Length: 16-25 Pages
Copies Required: Four
Computer Submission: Yes
Format: MS Word, RTF
Fees to Review: 0.00 US$

Manuscript Style:
   American Psychological Association

CIRCULATION DATA:

Reader: Academics, Business Bersons
Frequency of Issue: 2 Times/Year
Sponsor/Publisher: Midwestern State
   University College of Business
   Administration

REVIEW INFORMATION:

Type of Review: Blind Review
No. of External Reviewers: 2
No. of In House Reviewers: 1
Acceptance Rate: 35-40%
Time to Review: 2 - 3 Months
Reviewers Comments: No
Invited Articles: 0-5%
Fees to Publish: 0.00 US$

MANUSCRIPT TOPICS:

Advertising & Promotion Management; Business Education; Business Information Systems (MIS); Business Law, Public Responsibility & Ethics; Communication; Direct Marketing; E-Commerce; Global Business; Health Care Administration; Labor Relations & Human Resource Mgt.; Marketing Research; Marketing Theory & Applications; Non-Profit Organizations; Office Administration/Management; Operations Research/Statistics; Organizational Behavior & Theory; Organizational Development; Production/Operations; Public Administration; Purchasing/Materials Management; Sales/Selling; Services; Small Business Entrepreneurship; Strategic Management Policy; Technology/Innovation; Tourism, Hospitality & Leisure; Transportation/Physical Distribution

MANUSCRIPT GUIDELINES/COMMENTS:

The *Midwestern Business and Economic Review* invites submissions of original manuscripts and research by individuals in the public and private sector in the areas of economics and business administration Of particular interest are topics dealing with issues relevant to Texas and the Southwestern United States. Each manuscript submitted is anonymously reviewed by members of the Editorial Review Board and ad hoc reviews as needed. To meet the interest of a broad spectrum of the academic and business community, readability and expository clarity are considered essential in the review process.

All manuscripts submitted for review must meet the following guidelines:

- The manuscript should be double spaced, with 1" margins, and should not exceed twenty pages, including tables, figures, and references
- The first page should include the title of the article and an abstract not exceeding 100 words
- Endnotes are preferred over footnotes
- References should follow the American Psychological Association
- All tables and figures should be included on separate pages

A cover letter should be included with the submission containing the following:

- Title of manuscript
- Name, degree, rank, and affiliation of each author
- Contact information for each author (mailing address, telephone number, and email address)
- A brief biographical sketch of each author

It is preferred that each manuscript be accompanied by an electronic copy of the manuscript on a 3 ½" diskette, formatted in Microsoft Word or rich-text (RTF) formats. If an electronic copy is not submitted with the manuscript, one will be requested if the manuscript is selected for publication.

All manuscripts should be submitted to: Editor, Midwestern Business and Economic Review, Bureau of Business and Government Research, Midwestern State University, 3410 Taft Boulevard, Wichita Falls, Texas 76308-2099.

MIT Sloan Management Review

ADDRESS FOR SUBMISSION:

Editorial Submissions Department
MIT Sloan Management Review
Massachusetts Institute of Technology
Sloan School of Management
E60-100
77 Massachusetts Avenue
Cambridge, MA 02139-4307
USA
Phone: 617-253-9634
E-Mail: smrsubmissions@mit.edu
Web: www.mit-smr.com

PUBLICATION GUIDELINES:

Manuscript Length: 5,000 Words
    Maximum
Copies Required: One
Computer Submission: Yes
Format: MS Word, Excel, PowerPoint
Fees to Review: 0.00 US$

Manuscript Style:
    See Manuscript Guidelines

CIRCULATION DATA:

Reader: Academics, Business Persons,
    Management Consultants
Frequency of Issue: Quarterly
Sponsor/Publisher: MIT

REVIEW INFORMATION:

Type of Review: Blind Review
No. of External Reviewers: 2
No. of In House Reviewers: 1
Acceptance Rate: 7%
Time to Review: 2 - 3 Months
Reviewers Comments: Yes
Invited Articles: 11-20%
Fees to Publish: 0.00 US$

MANUSCRIPT TOPICS:

Business Ethics; Business Information Systems (MIS); Business Law, Public Responsibility & Ethics; Corporate Strategy; Financial Management; Global Business; Labor Relations & Human Resource Mgt.; Leadership & Organizational Studies; Management of Technology & Innovation; Managerial Economics; Marketing Theory & Applications; Operations Management & Research; Public Policy; Service & Quality

MANUSCRIPT GUIDELINES/COMMENTS:

Manuscript Guidelines for authors on the *MIT SMR* Website:
    www.mit-smr.com/author.html

Editorial Mission
The mission of *MIT Sloan Management Review* is to be the most trusted source of useful and innovative ideas for business leaders.

SMR Readers
* Circulation: 50,000
* Readership: 150,000

- 70% are business executives
- 10% are business professionals
- 10% are management consultants
- 10% are academics
- About 25% of subscribers live outside the United States

How We Edit an Article

Because the majority of *SMR*'s readers are business executives, we work with authors to ensure that research-based articles with complex technical ideas have the greatest possible influence on actual management practice. We help authors move from insider terminology to quickly accessible language. We work collaboratively, but we do edit and rewrite substantially in order to reach *SMR*'s primary audience.

We clarify phrases, make the passive voice active, invent engaging heads and subheads, devise ways to highlight the main points (perhaps with a bulleted list in a box) and delete redundant references. In short, we help authors tackle anything that might hinder widespread appreciation of their ideas. We delete or reword any language that promotes a business, service or product. Our readers will take an article more seriously if they don't perceive it to be thinly veiled marketing material.

SMR Content Areas

SMR covers all general-management topics, with a particular emphasis on strategic leadership and innovation.

Editorial Policy

SMR reserves the right to decide at any point in the process not to publish an article.

For questions about other policies, contact Managing Editor Beth Magura at (617) 253-0822 Correspondence accompanying submissions must state that the submitted work is original, has not been published elsewhere and will not be sent to another journal or magazine unless it has been declined by *SMR*.

We will consider articles based on research previously published in a purely academic journal if the new treatment develops managerial perspectives thoroughly. If an article is based on an author's recent book, the *SMR* submission must differ significantly.

Editorial Processing

All manuscripts undergo an internal review process involving *SMR* editors and may include members of the editorial advisory board. This process can take as long as 6 to 8 weeks, after which manuscripts are either rejected or sent into peer review pursuant to possible publication. (Unfortunately, we cannot provide detailed comments on rejected manuscripts.)

Peer review may take an additional 3 to 4 weeks. The decision to publish is ultimately predicated upon the outcome of peer review, the judgment of *SMR* editors, and, if necessary, a satisfactory editing and/or revision process that meets *SMR* standards. Articles usually appear in print within three to six months of acceptance.

Editorial Tips
Manuscripts are limited to 5,000 words, including references and text sidebars.

Include a summary of the research methodology (as an appendix to the paper, not included in the word count) to assist the peer reviewers in article assessment. If the article is accepted for publication in the journal, an *SMR* editor will help reduce the research methodology section to a short sidebar relevant to practicing managers.

Avoid generalizations. Be specific.

Authors are responsible for all facts, including dates and correct spellings of people's and organizations' names.

Authors have one opportunity to give reactions to *SMR's* editing and to make comments and changes—that opportunity comes after the content editing. Our process deadlines do not permit repeated rounds of revision.

SMR editors put articles into Associated Press style. They determine the article's placement in the journal as well as the final titles and illustrations.

What *SMR* Seeks From the Peer Review Process
- Is the paper essentially correct? If not, what changes are necessary to make it so?
- Does the paper offer something innovative or provide a new insight?
- Is the research sound and adequate to back up the authors' points?
- Would a practicing manager find the paper useful? Are there concepts, suggestions or techniques that could be implemented immediately? If not, what changes to the paper would you recommend?
- What parts of this paper, if any, improve your understanding of the subject matter? What principles, applications or ideas does the paper add to the field? Suggest ways to improve the clarity or focus of the discussion.
- How familiar is the author with the existing literature on this topic? What other sources would anchor, balance or enhance a discussion on this topic?

***MIT SMR*'s Intelligence Section**
SMR's Intelligence section, found at the beginning of the publication, allows readers to quickly access interesting new research and ideas from academia, industry and the consulting world - ideas that have potentially significant implications for managers.

SMR's editors sometimes choose to cover research in the Intelligence section rather than in a longer article for reasons such as:
- The findings (and management implications) can be effectively summarized in a brief report.
- The research is too preliminary for a full-length article or must be reported quickly because it is time sensitive.

- The research is on a vertical market or topic and therefore more appropriate for *SMR* as a brief summary than as a full-length article.

What makes an Intelligence item interesting to *SMR*?

- Research, that is useful to a wide range of management readers, is based on hard data and is methodologically sound.
- A new practice that's just emerging as a trend. Trends might be either positive or negative: new management practices or new management problems.
- General-management subjects. We run a large number of marketing, finance, leadership, entrepreneurship, e-business and operations pieces in this section. Strategy is covered less frequently because it is handled in more depth in other sections of the journal.
- Impact. Will the study change the way businesspeople think and act? Is it relevant and important to executives, managers and consultants? Is it engaging, interesting?
- Newness. We promise to provide readers with new and innovative ideas. The more novel and counter-the-conventional-wisdom a piece is, the more we like it.
- Depth. We prefer studies with solid research behind them. Authors presenting an original, innovative concept for which there is little available research will have to compensate by offering in-depth analysis to support the idea's practicality.
- Timeliness. The item should be from an unpublished or recently published study.

Endnotes

Although scholars often do, *SMR* does not identify references by date and author's last name in parentheses in the text, with a bibliography at the end of the article. Instead, *SMR* asks that authors place in the text superscripted numbers that refer to a list of endnotes assembled at the end of the article. These endnotes should be presented in *SMR* style (described below).

Each enumerated endnote may contain several related items (below see "*SMR* Special Style: Multiple Citations in One Reference"). It may be possible to group several citations or explanatory notes that occur in a single paragraph under one number.

We use *The Chicago Manual of Style* (*CMS*), 14th ed., as our guide for endnotes, but because we adhere to the *Associated Press Stylebook* for everything other than endnotes, there are some exceptions:

- Do not spell out the first name of authors in endnotes.
- Do not italicize book or magazine titles. Enclose book titles in quotation marks.
- Do not place within quotes or italicize magazine names.
- Other AP style conventions apply as well. For example, the AP abbreviates most months when used with a specific day (Jan. 1, 2004; but January 2010).

As a rule of thumb, AP trumps Chicago, and our AP-approved dictionary is *Webster's New World College Dictionary*, 4th ed.

Books
G. Hollenback and W. Vestal, eds., "Developing Leaders at All Levels" (Houston: American Productivity and Quality Center, 1999).

816

J. March and H.J. Simon, "Organizations," 2nd ed. (New York: John Wiley & Sons, 1966), 4-13.

Usage note: "The *Chicago Manual of Style*" advises against the use of **op. cit.** and **loc. cit.** (See 15.256, p. 583, in CMS.) If another page from a previously cited book is mentioned several endnotes later, follow the short-title approach:
March, "Organizations," 23.

Usage note: The use of ibid. is acceptable when referring to a single work cited in the endnote immediately preceding.

Article Cited in Anthology; Chapter Cited in Book
M. Shaw, "Communication Networks," in "Advances in Experimental Social Psychology," ed. L. Berkowitz (New York: Academic Press, 1964), 131-153.

S.M. McKinnon and W.J. Bruins, Jr., "Information for the Longer View," chap. 3 in "The Information Mosaic" (Boston: Harvard Business School Press, 1992).

Newspapers
W. Robbins, "Big Wheels: The Rotary Club at 75," New York Times, Sunday, Feb. 17, 1980, sec. 3, p. 3.

"Poverty in the U.S.," International Herald Tribune, Sept. 29, 2000.

Journals
D. Kenny and J.F. Marshall, "Contextual Marketing: The Real Business of the Internet," Harvard Business Review 78 (November-December 2000): 119-125.

T.J. Allen and S. Cohen, "Information Flow in R&D Labs," Administrative Science Quarterly 14 (December 1969): 12-19.

M.C. Jensen and W.H. Meckling, "The Nature of Man," Journal of Applied Finance 7, no. 2 (1994): 4, 15-19.

"GM Powertain Suppliers Will See Global Pricing," Purchasing 124, no. 2 (Feb. 12, 1998): 10-11.

Popular Magazines
S. Spencer, "Childhood's End," Harper's, May 1979, 16-19.

E. Neuborne, "E-Tailers, Deliver or Die," Business Week, Oct. 23, 2000, 16.

"To Have and To Hold," Economist, June 16, 2001, 9-11.

Internet Sources
Usage note: Internet sources are those that exist solely online. A print publication that has an Internet incarnation is not considered to be an "Internet source."

D. McCullagh, "ACLU Loses Digital Copyright Battle," April 9, 2003, news.com.com

"Toyota Expanding China Links," April 9, 2003, edition.cnn.com

A. Huffington, "Corporate America's 'Most Wanted'," April 2, 2003, www.salon.com

Working Papers
N. Repenning and J. Sterman, "Capability Traps and Self-Controlling Attribution Errors in the Dynamics of Process Improvement," working paper 4372-02, MIT Sloan School of Management, Cambridge, Massachusetts, June 2002, http://papers.ssrn.com/sol3/papers .cfm?abstract_id=-320380.

McKinsey & Co., Inc., "Succeeding at Cross-Border Alliances: Lessons From Winners," working paper, London, 1991.

D. Ready, "Developing Global Capability—Project Overview," working paper, International Consortium for Executive Development Research, Lexington, Massachusetts, June 1997.

White Papers
"The Road to Recovery," white paper, Sibson Consulting Group, New York, November 2001, p. 2.

Dissertations
J.P. Voges "Supply Chain Design in the Volatile Semiconductor Capital Equipment Industry"(Ph.D. diss., MIT Sloan School of Management and MIT Department of Mechanical Engineering, 2002), http://theses.mit.edu/

Forthcoming Books
M. Tushman, "Managing Innovation and Change" (New York: McGraw-Hill, in press).

Forthcoming Articles
M. Tushman, "An Information Processing Approach," Academy of Management Review, in press.

SMR Special Style: Multiple Citations in One Reference
G. Farris, "Managing Informal Dynamics in R&D," Harvard Business Review 64 (January-February 1986): 5-11; and F. Andrews and G. Peters, "Personnel Psychology" (New York: McGraw-Hill, 1986).

No Author Specified
"Federal Express Uses a Three-Level Recovery System," Service Edge (December 1990): 5.

"Poverty in the U.S.," International Herald Tribune, Sept. 29, 2000.

818

Papers and Presentations at Meetings
J. Donehey and G. Overholser, "Capital One" (presentation at the Ernst & Young Embracing Complexity Conference, Boston, Aug. 2-4, 1998).

J. Kluge, "Simply Superior Sourcing" (paper presented at the Fifth International Annual International Purchasing and Supply Education and Research Association Conference, Eindhoven, Netherlands, April 2, 1996).

Case Studies
R.M. Kanter, "FCB and Publicis (A): Forming the Alliance," Harvard Business School case no. 9-393-099 (Boston: Harvard Business School Publishing, 1993).

Organization, Association or Corporation as Author
International Monetary Fund, "Survey of African Economies," vol. 7, "Algeria, Mali, Morocco, and Tunisia" (Washington, D.C.: IMF, 1977).

Government Reports
Securities and Exchange Commission, "Annual Report for the Securities and Exchange Commission for the Fiscal Year" (Washington, D.C.: Government Printing Office, 1983), 42.

Personal Communications
D.B. Johnson, interview with authors, Nov. 11, 1997.

To inquire about a manuscript's status, send a e-mail to **smrsubmissions@mit.edu** or call 617-253-3959.

For further information, please contact David Smagalla at **smagalla@mit.edu** or call 617-253-3959.

Mountain Plains Journal of Business and Economics

ADDRESS FOR SUBMISSION:

Gerald E. Calvasina, Editor
Mountain Plains Journal of Business and
   Economics
Southern Utah University
Department of Business
351 W. Center Street
Cedar City, UT 84720
USA
Phone: 435-586-1976
E-Mail: calvasina@suu.edu
Web: http://www.mountainplains.org/

PUBLICATION GUIDELINES:

Manuscript Length: 21-25
Copies Required: One
Computer Submission: Yes
Format: MS Word
Fees to Review: 50.00 US$

Manuscript Style:
   See Manuscript Guidelines

CIRCULATION DATA:

Reader: Academics
Frequency of Issue: No Reply
Sponsor/Publisher: Mountain Plains
   Management Association

REVIEW INFORMATION:

Type of Review: Blind Review
No. of External Reviewers: 2
No. of In House Reviewers: 1
Acceptance Rate: 25-35%
Time to Review: 1 - 2 Months
Reviewers Comments: Yes
Invited Articles: 0-5%
Fees to Publish: 0.00 US$

MANUSCRIPT TOPICS:
Business Information Systems (MIS); Business Law, Public Responsibility & Ethics; Direct Marketing; Global Business; Labor Relations & Human Resource Mgt.; Marketing Research; Marketing Theory & Applications; Organizational Behavior & Theory; Organizational Development; Production/Operations; Public Administration; Sales/Selling; Services; Small Business Entrepreneurship; Strategic Management Policy

MANUSCRIPT GUIDELINES/COMMENTS:

Submission Guidelines
The *Mountain Plains Journal of Business and Economics* is entirely electronic. All articles will be submitted, reviewed, and published electronically via email and/or the Internet. Papers may be submitted for possible publication in any of the functional areas of business, including Accounting, Economics, Finance, Marketing, Management, MIS, Business Law, etc. Papers may be submitted for peer review in the following manner:

1. Prepare your paper in a Microsoft Word format that is compatible with Windows 98, Windows NT or higher. We will accept manuscripts for REFEREE purposes in ANY format. Upon acceptance for publication, the manuscript must be converted to the following format.

The typeface standard is 12 point Times New Roman, left justified, single-spaced. Let all headings throughout the manuscript be capitalized and centered. If you must use subheadings, they should be typed at the left margin with initial caps. Manuscripts should begin with a title (16 point font), followed by author's) and affiliations (12 point font). Use 12 point, Times New Roman type. Following the manuscript title, all manuscripts should begin with an abstract except cases. Double space between paragraphs, and indent the first sentence in each paragraph. Insert all tables in the manuscripts in portrait mode.

2. **Citations, References, and Footnotes**. Use APA style for all publications. The *American Psychologist's Association Style Manual* does not employ footnotes. Instead, a citation is handled in the body of the text (Calvasina & Roberts, 2004), by putting the last names of the authors, followed by the year of the publication within parenthesizes. References should be prepared in general accordance with the APA. Please use italics in place of underlines. Double space between references and do not indent in any way.

Multinational Business Review

ADDRESS FOR SUBMISSION:

Hongxi John Zhao, Editor
Multinational Business Review
Saint Louis University
Boeing Institute of International Bus.
John Cook School of Business
3674 Lindell Boulevard, Suite 332
St. Louis, MO 63108
USA
Phone: 314-977-3630
E-Mail: mbr@slu.edu
Web: mbr.slu.edu

PUBLICATION GUIDELINES:

Manuscript Length: 7,000 Words
Copies Required: Three
Computer Submission: Yes
Format: MS Word
Fees to Review: 50.00 US$
   30.00 US$ Journal Subscribers

Manuscript Style:
  , Journal of International Business
Studies

CIRCULATION DATA:

Reader: Business Persons, Academics
Frequency of Issue: 3 Times/Year
Sponsor/Publisher: Boeing Institute of
  International Business / John Cook
  School of Business / St. Louis University

REVIEW INFORMATION:

Type of Review: Blind Review
No. of External Reviewers: 2
No. of In House Reviewers: 1
Acceptance Rate: 30%
Time to Review: 8 weeks
Reviewers Comments: Yes
Invited Articles: 0-5%
Fees to Publish: 0.00 US$

MANUSCRIPT TOPICS:

Business Information Systems (MIS); Global Business; Marketing Research; Marketing Theory & Applications

MANUSCRIPT GUIDELINES/COMMENTS:

Multinational Business Review (MBR) solicits and welcomes articles of interest to academics as well as practitioners, with at least one "Practitioner Insights" article per issue. Collaborative papers between academicians and practitioners are encouraged, especially with corporate case studies with a global scope. All submission should be original, not previously published, not accepted for publication, and not under consideration by another journal. The only exception is papers presented at a conference as a work-in-progress and subsequently published in conference proceedings. Specific formatting guidelines and submission instructions for email and mail are provided on the website. Should an article be accepted for publication, the author will receive special instructions for final submittal. *MBR* will have the copyright to all published articles—authors will be asked to sign a Copyright Release Form. Approval of a final proof will be required prior to publication.

Naval Research Logistics

ADDRESS FOR SUBMISSION:

David Simchi-Levi, Editor-in-Chief
Naval Research Logistics
  ELECTRONIC SUBMISSION ONLY
Massachusetts Institute of Technology
School of Engineering
77 Masachusetts Avenue, Room I-171
Cambridge, MA 02139-4307
USA
Phone: 617-258-8409
E-Mail: dslevi@mit.edu
  kerrigan@mit.edu
Web: http://nav-wiley.manuscript
  central.com/

PUBLICATION GUIDELINES:

Manuscript Length: 30 Pages Average
Copies Required: Electronic
Computer Submission: Yes Online
Format: MS Word, PDF, Text
Fees to Review: 0.00 US$

Manuscript Style:
    See Manuscript Guidelines

CIRCULATION DATA:

Reader: Academics
Frequency of Issue: 8 Times/Year
Sponsor/Publisher: Logic Tools, IBM,
  General Motors, SAP AG, MIT Leaders
  for Manufacturing, ONR / John Wiley &
  Sons

REVIEW INFORMATION:

Type of Review: Editorial Review
No. of External Reviewers: 2
No. of In House Reviewers: 0
Acceptance Rate: 0-5%
Time to Review: 4 - 6 Months
Reviewers Comments: Yes
Invited Articles: 0-5%
Fees to Publish: 0.00 US$

MANUSCRIPT TOPICS:
Operations   Research/Statistics;   Production/Operations;   Technology/Innovation;
Transportation/Physical Distribution

MANUSCRIPT GUIDELINES/COMMENTS:

Aims and Scope
Naval Research Logistics is a premier peer-reviewed journal in operations research, applied statistics, and general quantitative modeling. Founded in 1954, *NRL* has a distinguished history of publication of both seminal methodological contributions and innovative applications. *NRL's* original focus on naval applications has been greatly extended for many years to a wide range of civilian and military problems.

The types of articles most sought after by *Naval Research Logistics* fall into the following classes: (i) modeling and analysis of problems motivated by current real-world applications, (ii) exploratory modeling and analysis of problems motivated by potential future real-world applications, (iii) major methodological advances, and (iv) expository pieces of exceptional clarity. Areas represented include (but are not limited to) probability, statistics, simulation, optimization, game theory, scheduling, reliability, inventory, decision analysis, and combat models.

Special issues devoted to a single topic are published occasionally. Proposals for special issues are welcomed by the Editorial Board.

Readership
Operations researchers, systems analysts and programmers, economists, statisticians

Instructions to Authors
Naval Research Logistics is now receiving submitted manuscripts online at:
http://mc.manuscriptcentral.com/nrl.

Submit all new manuscripts online. Launch your web browser and go to **http://mc.manu scriptcentral.com/nrl.** Check for an existing user account. If you are submitting for the first time, and you do not find an existing account, create a new account. Follow all instructions.

Manuscript file, tables, and figures must be submitted separately. You do not need to mail any paper copies of your manuscript at this time.

At the end of a successful submission, a confirmation screen with manuscript number will appear and you will receive an e-mail confirming that the manuscript has been received by the journal. If this does not happen, please check your submission and/or contact tech support at **support@scholarone.com.**

Authors of manuscripts accepted for publication in the *Journal* will be asked, on acceptance, to mail to the *Journal* Office a printout of the accepted version of the manuscript along with required copyright and permissions forms and a disk(s) containing the corresponding manuscript file, figures, and tables. Accepted manuscripts should be mailed to the Editor-in-Chief, Dr. David Simchi-Levi, Naval Research Logistics, Massachusetts Institute of Technology, School of Engineering, 77 Massachusetts Avenue, Room I-171, Cambridge, MA 02139-4307.

Submission of a manuscript to the Editor implies that the paper has not been published, that it is not being submitted for publication elsewhere, and that, if the work reported is officially sponsored, it has been released for publication. A publication agreement may be obtained from the editor or the publisher. A copy of the publication agreement appears in most issues of the journal. Only original papers will be accepted and copyright in published papers will be vested in the publisher. It is the author's responsibility to obtain written permission to reproduce material that has appeared in another publication. A copy of that agreement, signed by the author, is required before a manuscript can be accepted for publication. (In the case of a "work made for hire," the agreement must be signed by the employer.)

A short abstract (200 words maximum) is required. It should be complete and self-contained, giving the scope and emphasizing the main conclusions, results, or significance of the work described.

Equations and symbols should be typed wherever possible; all ambiguous symbols must be clearly defined in the margin (e.g., 1, l; k, κ; x, χ).

Figures should be professionally prepared and submitted in a form suitable for reproduction (camera-ready copy). Computer-generated graphs are acceptable only if they have been printed with a good quality laser printer. The maximum final size for a figure in this journal is 12 x 20-cm; lettering is reduced to a 1.5-mm height.

All color figures will be reproduced in full color in the online edition of the journal at no cost to authors. Authors are requested to pay the cost of reproducing color figures in print. Authors are encouraged to submit color illustrations that highlight the text and convey essential scientific information. For best reproduction, bright, clear colors should be used. Dark colors against a dark background do not reproduce well; please place your color images against a white background wherever possible. Please contact Carol Ann McNelis at 201-748-6009/cmcnelis@wiley.com for further information.

To ensure that your digital graphics are suitable for print purposes, please go to Rapid Inspector at http://rapidinspector.cadmus.com/wi/index.jsp. This free, stand-alone software application will help you to inspect and verify illustrations right on your computer.

Wiley's Journal Styles and EndNote
EndNote is a software product that we recommend to our journal authors to help simplify and streamline the research process. Using EndNote's bibliographic management tools, you can search bibliographic databases, build and organize your reference collection, and then instantly output your bibliography in any Wiley journal style.

Download Reference Style for this Journal. If you already use EndNote, you can download the reference style for this journal.

How to Order. To learn more about EndNote, or to purchase your own copy of EndNote.

Technical Support. If you need assistance using EndNote, contact endnote@isiresearch soft.com, or visit www.endnote.com/support.

Literature references should be indicated in text by an Arabic number in square brackets. All literature citations should be grouped together at the end of the manuscript in alphabetical order and numbered consecutively. For journal references, supply author(s), title, journal title, volume, page range, and year of publication; for unpublished material, give as much information as possible [e.g., for lectures of symposia list author(s), paper title, symposium title, sponsor, location, and date]. Sample references follow:

Journal Article
[1] E. S. Kramer, S. S. Magliveras, and D. M. Mesner, t-designs from the large Mathieu groups, Discrete Math 36 (1981), 171-189.

Book
[2] T. Beth, D. Jungnickel, and H. Lenz, Design theory, Cambridge University Press, Cambridge, England, 1986.

Edited Book
[3] C. C. Lindner, and C. A. Rodger, "Decomposition into cycles II," Cycle systems in contemporary design theory: A collection of surveys, J. H. Dinitz and D. R. Stinson (Editors), Wiley, New York, 1992, pp. 325-369.

Proceedings
[4] P. K. Brayton, D. Coppersmith, and A. J. Hoffman, Self-orthogonal Latin squares, Teorie Combinatorie, Proc. Rome Conf, 1976, pp. 509-517.

Authors will receive **proofs** that must be corrected and returned to the publisher within 48 hours of receipt. No new material may be inserted in the text at the proofreading stage. A reprint order form is sent with the proofs. Reprints must be ordered and prepaid when the proofs are returned.

Guidelines for Electronic Submission
Authors are strongly encouraged to deliver the final, accepted version of their manuscript on a disk.

- **Storage Medium.** 3½ inch disk in IBM MS-DOS or Macintosh format.
- **Software.** LaTeX is preferred.
- **All TeX files will be accepted.** However, if you prefer to use the macros created by the publisher, they are available via the Internet on the John Wiley & Sons, Inc. FTP server. The address is: ftp.wiley.com/public/journals/tex/navalr. Log in as anonymous and use your e-mail address as a password. For more information see the README file in the navalr subdirectory.
- **Illustrations.** Electronic illustrations are encouraged, but not required. Submit each article's illustrations in a separate directory on the same disk as the article. TIFF and EPS files or native application files are accepted. For grey scale and color figure submissions please contact us for more detailed instructions.
- **File names.** Submit each journal article as one single file. Each file should be named using your last name (not to exceed 8 letters). If your last name exceeds eight letters it should be truncated to fit.
- Label all disks with your name, the title of your article, the file name, and the program used.
- The disk must be accompanied by hard copy printout.

Operations Research

ADDRESS FOR SUBMISSION:

David Simchi-Levi, Editor
Operations Research
Massachusetts Institute of Technology
Department of Civil and Environmental
Engineering
Cambridge, MA 02139
USA
Phone: 617-253-6160
E-Mail: dslevi@mit.edu
Web: http://or.pubs.informs.org;
http://mc.manuscriptcentral.com/opre

PUBLICATION GUIDELINES:

Manuscript Length: Any
Copies Required: Four
Computer Submission: Yes Online
Format:
Fees to Review: 0.00 US$

Manuscript Style:
Chicago Manual of Style

CIRCULATION DATA:

Reader: Academics
Frequency of Issue: Bi-Monthly
Sponsor/Publisher: Institute for Operations
Research and Management Science
(INFORMS)

REVIEW INFORMATION:

Type of Review: Editorial Review
No. of External Reviewers: 3
No. of In House Reviewers: 1
Acceptance Rate: 21-30%
Time to Review: 4 - 6 Months
Reviewers Comments: Yes
Invited Articles: 0-5%
Fees to Publish: 0.00 US$

MANUSCRIPT TOPICS:

Business Information Systems (MIS); Business Law, Public Responsibility & Ethics; Communication; Non-Profit Organizations; Operations Research/Statistics; Production/Operations; Services; Strategic Management Policy; Transportation/Physical Distribution

MANUSCRIPT GUIDELINES/COMMENTS:

Topics Include. Computing and Decision Technology; Decision Analysis; Environment, Energy and Natural Resources; Financial Engineering; Manufacturing, Service and Supply Chain Operations; Marketing Science; Military OR; Optimization; OR Forum; OR Practice; Revenue Management; Simulation; Stochastic Models; Telecommunications and Networking; Transportation.

Subscription can be found at: **www.informs.org/Pubs/PubsIndividual.pdf**.

General Considerations
To submit a paper to *Operations Research*, the author should visit the online submission site at **http://mc.manuscriptcentral.com/opre**

Papers not in the fields covered by the Area Editors should besubmitted to the Editor.

Papers should **not** be sent to the Associate Editors.

Submission of a manuscript is a representation that the paper has neither been published nor submitted for publication elsewhere, and that, if the work is officially sponsored, it has been released for open publication.

Manuscripts will not be returned to an author unless specifically requested, or unless reviewers have provided annotations that will be of use to the author.

The text should be arranged as follows: title page, abstract, introduction, main sections, appendix, acknowledgment, and references. Appendices and an acknowledgment are optional. If a paper is accepted for publication, the Editor may request (or require) that supporting appendix material is placed oniine at the *Operations Research* web site. Authors should consider this either during the initial submission phase or during the final revisions of the paper and may wish to design their papers accordingly.

Personal Web Sites. Upon acceptance of a paper to *Operations Research,* the author must remove all copies of the paper from any web sites. The copyright belongs to INFORMS and placement of the paper on a web site is a violation of the copyright transfer agreement. Prior to publication in *Operations Research*, the authors must submit a signed copy of the Authors' Web Site Disclosure Form.

Observe the following points in preparing manuscripts. Papers not conforming closely to these instructions may be returned to their authors for appropriate revisions or may be delayed in the review process.

1. **Readability.** The abstract and the introduction of every paper must be free of unnecessary jargon and clearly readable by any INFORMS member. These sections should be written in an expository style that will be comprehensible to readers who are not technical experts in the subject matter.

2. **Title Page.** Each paper should have a title page that contains the author(s)' name(s) and address(es). The usual acknowledgments should be placed in a separate section at the back of the manuscript.

3. **Abstract.** Preface each article with a self-contained, one-paragraph abstract that summarizes the problem and the principal results and conclusions. It should not contain formulas, references or abbreviations, nor exceed 200 words.

4. **Introduction.** The introduction must clearly state the problem, the results to be found in the paper and their significance to the OR community. It should not contain equations or mathematical notation. Section numbering and headings begins here.

5. **Main Sections**. The main sections of the paper must be readable, the level of the mathematics and/or the terminology appropriate to the topic, and the material logically presented.

6. **Style**. The message of the paper will be enhanced if it is presented in active, forceful, and concise prose. Good writing is a craft at least as difficult as doing operations research. While the Editor and staff will correct minor lapses from good style in the manuscript, they cannot undertake wholesale revisions of poorly written papers. There is no set limit to the number of pages for a paper; however, conciseness and clarity of presentation are important publication criteria.

7. **Spacing and Format**. Double-space manuscripts throughout, including the abstract, subsidiary matter (list of captions, for example), and references. In general, keep figures and tables to a minimum. Each page of the manuscript should be numbered. Indent the first line of each paragraph.

8. **Footnotes**. *Operations Research* does not use footnotes; incorporate subsidiary material that would otherwise appear in footnotes in the main text, possibly in parentheses or brackets, or place it in a Notes section at the end of the text, before the Acknowledgment and References. Designate notes by using superscript numerals placed in serial order throughout the text.

9. **Acknowledgments**. Place acknowledgments of presentation, support, and assistance in a final section that precedes the References, not on the title page.

10. **References**. List only those references that are cited in the text. References in the text should be cited by the author's surname and the year of publication, for example, Flood (1962). If the reference has two or three authors, cite all of the authors' surnames and the year of publication—Flood, Smith and Jones (1982). If the reference has more than three authors, cite the first author's surname followed by et al. and the year of publication—Brown et al. (1985).

If there are more than one reference by the same author with the same year of publication, the first citation appearing in the text would read Flood (1962a), the second citation would read Flood (1962b), etc. Do not use parentheses or brackets for dates when the citation is already enclosed within parentheses.

At the end of the paper list references alphabetically by the last name of the first author. Do not number the reference list. Double-space this final section.

For journal references, give the author, year of publication, title, journal name, volume, and pages, for example:
FLOOD, M. M. 1962. New Operations Research Potentials. *Opns. Res.* 10, 423-436.

For book references, give the author, year of publication, title, publisher, city, state, and pages, for example:

MORSE, P. M., AND G. E. KIMBALL. 1951. Methods of Operations Research. John Wiley, New York, 44-65.

For references to working papers or dissertations cite the author, title, type of document, department, university, and location, for example:

ROSENWEIN, M. 1986. Design and Application of Solution Methodologies to Optimize Problems in Transportation Logistics. Ph.D. Dissertation. Department of Decision Sciences, University of Pennsylvania, Philadelphia.

11. **Mathematical Expressions.** Within the text, use the solidus whenever possible in preference to built-up fractions: e.g., $a/(1-b)$ exponentials in the form $\exp(\ )$; avoid subscripts or superscripts on subscripts or superscripts; and, in general, minimize unusual typographical requirements. For displayed equations, use built-up fractions. Avoid lengthy equations that will take several lines to typeset (possibly by defining terms of the equations in separate displays).

Make subscripts and superscripts large and clear, and shown in a clearly inferior or superior position. The letter l and the numeral 1, and the letter O and the numeral 0, which are identical on most keyboards, should be identified. Symbols and Greek letters should be identified clearly. On their first occurrence, label unusual or ambiguous symbols by marginal notes. The difference between upper and lower case letters should be clear.

Display only those mathematical expressions that must be numbered for later reference or that need to be emphasized. Number displayed equations consecutively throughout the paper; do not number equations by section numbers. Appendix equations can be labeled A1, A2, etc. The numbers should be placed in parentheses to the right of the equation.

12. **Tables.** Tables should be numbered with Arabic numerals, have a title, and be referred to sequentially in the text. Column headings should be brief and not use abbreviations. Do not use vertical rules. The use of footnotes is encouraged; designate these by lower case letters. The submission of original tables suitable for reproduction is not necessary; all tables will be typeset for consistency. Each table should be on a separate sheet and not interleaved in the text.

13. **Figures.** Figures should be professionally drawn or laser-printed and suitable for photographic reproduction. All figures must be in black and white. Color figures will be printed in black and white and do not scan properly. The author is responsible for the quality of the final form of the figure(s). Figures are scanned and corrections on page proofs are costly. Do not clutter the figure with information that makes it difficult to read. To avoid an undesirable moiré effect when scanned, figures should be shaded with a coarse pattern rather than a fine screen. Line weights should be consistent and at least .25 points after reduction. Lettering in the body of the figure should be proportional to the graphic and be typed.

Most figures will be reduced to approximately 3¼" in width. For optimal quality, please submit final figures close to that size. All details on the figures should be checked carefully because correction on proofs necessitates reshooting.

Each figure must be cited and will be placed in the order mentioned in the text. Each figure must have a caption and a number (Arabic). Do not place the caption on the original of the figure. Place captions on a separate sheet. Do not differentiate between illustrations and figures.

14. Subject Classification Scheme for the OR/MS Index. Subject Classification Keywords Determine the appropriate subject classifications (up to 3) and accompanying descriptive phrases for all work submitted. Choose from one to three subject categories for each manuscript. For every category chosen, write a short phrase that puts the paper in context. (The phrase can be a concise rendering of the title, or it may specify some aspect of the paper that is import ant but not apparent in the title.) The length of each phrase, including spaces and punctuation, should not exceed 60 characters. This information will be printed on the title page of every article, technical note, and letter that is published.

Subject categories and phrases must appear on the title page of the manuscript.

15. Reprints. *Operations Research* does not have paper charges, nor does it supply free reprints. Authors of accepted articles may order reprints at reasonable rates at the time they submit their corrected galley proofs. Reprints of individual articles are not available from INFORMS.

Managing Editor. Janet Kerrigan, Department of Civil and Environmental Engineering, Massachusetts Institute of Technology 30 Wadsworth Street, 1-176 Cambridge, MA 02139, **kerrigan@MIT.EDU** Phone (617) 258-8409, Fax (617) 324-2546.

Oxford Journal

ADDRESS FOR SUBMISSION:

Atul Gupta, Editor
Oxford Journal
PO Box 11172
Lynchburg, VA 24501
USA
Phone: 434-385-8667
E-Mail: editorijbe@yahoo.com
Web: www.facultyforum.com/oj

CIRCULATION DATA:

Reader: Academics
Frequency of Issue: Yearly
Sponsor/Publisher: Association for
    Business & Economics Research (ABER)

PUBLICATION GUIDELINES:

Manuscript Length: 16-20
Copies Required: Electronic
Computer Submission: Yes Email
Format: MS Word, PDF
Fees to Review: 0.00 US$

Manuscript Style:
    See Manuscript Guidelines

REVIEW INFORMATION:

Type of Review: Blind Review
No. of External Reviewers: 2
No. of In House Reviewers: 0
Acceptance Rate: 11-20%
Time to Review:
Reviewers Comments:
Invited Articles: 0-5%
Fees to Publish: 0.00 US$

MANUSCRIPT TOPICS:

Advertising & Promotion Management; Business Education; Business Law, Public Responsibility & Ethics; Communication; Direct Marketing; E-Commerce; Global Business; Health Care Administration; Labor Relations & Human Resource Mgt.; Marketing Research; Marketing Theory & Applications; Non-Profit Organizations; Office Administration/Management; Operations Research/Statistics; Organizational Behavior & Theory; Organizational Development; Production/Operations; Public Administration; Purchasing/Materials Management; Sales/Selling; Services; Small Business Entrepreneurship; Strategic Management Policy; Technology/Innovation; Tourism, Hospitality & Leisure; Transportation/Physical Distribution

MANUSCRIPT GUIDELINES/COMMENTS:

Oxford Journal is intended to be an outlet for theoretical and empirical research contributions for scholars and practitioners in the business field. In addition to manuscript submitted by leading scholars and practitioners to a double-blind referee process, the journal also publishes in its executive forum column invited papers by selected authors with a topic of special concern. IBJR invites manuscripts in the area of: Management Information Systems; Business Law; Public Responsibility and Ethics; Global Business; Marketing Theory and Applications; Accounting; Economics; Finance & Investment; General Management; General Business Research; Business & Economics Education; Production/Operations Management;

Organizational Behavior & Theory; Strategic Management Policy; Labor Relations & Human Resource Management; Technology & Innovation; Public Administration and Small Business Entrepreneurship.

Style Guidelines and Submission Requirements

Please review all guidelines and revise your manuscript as needed to comply with *OJ's* style guidelines and submission requirements. Ignoring these requirements may lead to significant delays, as they cause reviewers, editors, and staff to take on additional work to complete the processing of your manuscript. In some cases, the Editor may return the manuscript for editing before considering the manuscript as an official submission to *OJ*.

Publication Requirements

Authors submitting their manuscript to *OJ* for publication consideration must certify that:

a.   None of the contents of their manuscript has been copyrighted, published, or accepted for publication by another journal, or is under review by another journal. Authors whose manuscripts utilize data that are reported in any other manuscript, published or not, are required to inform the editor at the time of submission in a cover letter explaining the duplication.

b.   This manuscript uses appropriate citations for the reproduction of someone else's original words or expression of ideas.

c.   This manuscript has not been previously submitted to *OJ* for review.

d.   All working papers, prior drafts, and/or final version of submitted manuscripts that are posted on a website will be taken down during the review process.

Lastly, the editor may ask the authors to submit copies of related papers to the *OJ* office to facilitate an objective review of the manuscript.

Submission Format

All manuscripts must be submitted electronically through the E-mail to **Editorijbe@yahoo.com**

While *OJ* will consider exceptions, submitted manuscripts should be no more than 30 double-spaced pages excluding references, appendixes, tables, and figures. If a manuscript extends beyond the recommended page limit, the Editor may reject the manuscript based on lack of fit with the Journal's objectives.

All manuscripts should be double-spaced in 12-point Times New Roman font with consecutively numbered pages. Page numbers should be continued through the manuscript, including for pages of references, appendixes, tables, and figures. Allow margins of one inch on all four sides of every page.

Manuscript elements (other than the separate Abstract entry required) must be saved as unlocked files in Adobe Portable Document Format (PDF) and submitted via E-mail. PDF files have identical computer and print appearance allowing author formatting to be maintained during the review process. Note that you must use Adobe Acrobat or Adobe's online service to convert your file to a PDF file format.

Abstract
The abstract, which may be composed of up to 250 words, must clearly and succinctly convey the manuscript's subject matter, significance and contribution.

In the submission process, the Corresponding Author will be expected to type the abstract, or to cut and paste it from a Word document, into a form.

The Abstract should also be included in the Main Body of the Manuscript.

Title Page
To maintain a double-blind review, the title page must be prepared and submitted as a separate PDF document from the main body of the manuscript.

In addition to the title of the manuscript, the title page must include the authors' names, affiliations, ground and email addresses, and phone numbers. Acknowledgements should appear at the bottom of the title page.

Main Body of the Manuscript
The manuscript's main body should include title, abstract, and the text of the manuscript, followed by references, appendixes, tables, and figures. The first page of the main body should include the title in boldface capital-and-lower-case letters followed by an abstract of no more than 250 words.

Major or first-level headings should appear in boldface capital letters throughout the manuscript with four to six major headings for most manuscripts. Most manuscripts begin with an ABSTRACT major heading following by an INTRODUCTION heading. Second-level headings should be typed in boldface capital-and-lower-case letters. Third-level headings should be in boldface italic letters beginning with the first word capitalized and the remaining words in lower-case letters. All headings are to be left-justified.

Cover Letter (Optional)
During the on-line manuscript submission process in the E-mail, you have the option to submit a cover letter to the editor. All submission documents, including the cover letter, must be provided in PDF file format.

Review Areas
To facilitate the review process, authors must indicate suitable key words for their manuscripts to identify the primary Topic Areas their manuscripts address, and the Methodological Areas they utilize.

During the Manuscript Submission process, you must identify and rank order at least one and no more than five Topic Area(s) and at least one and no more than three Methodological Area(s). In preparation for your submission, it is recommended that all authors actively participate in the selection and ranking of their manuscript's key words.

Mathematical Notation

All equations should be set on separate lines, centered, and numbered consecutively in parentheses that appear flush with the right margin of the page.

Tables and Figures

Tables and Figures should clarify and supplement the text, and not duplicate what is already stated in words.

Tables should be used when data can be presented more economically in this form than in narrative form. Visual representations of the manuscript's concepts should be labeled as Figures.

Tables and Figures should be consecutively numbered in Arabic numerals from the beginning to the end of the article and should appear on separate pages from the text. Table and Figure notations appear with boldface type for the word Table or Figure and the Table or Figure number, followed by a colon. The Table or Figure title should be in regular type with the first word capitalized and the remaining words in lower-case letters.

The Table or Figure number and Table or Figure title should be left-justified on the page as in the following example:
Table 1: Measurement items
The position of the Table or Figure on the page should be as follows:

Insert Table/Figure Here

Footnotes or End Notes

OJ does not allow the use of footnotes or endnotes within the text of the manuscript. However, footnotes to Tables are allowed and should be used to explain the designations of the Table, such as columns or row headings. Each footnote should be designated by a superscript small letter beginning with the letter "a".

Reference Citations

All references in the body of the text should be in the format of Name (Date). The date should be represented by the year of the publication. Name refers to the last name. In the case of multiple citations, please place them in alphabetical order and utilize an ampersand between them. Multiple references to work by one author or a group of authors with the same year of publication should be differentiated with the addition of small letters (a, b, etc.) after the year.

Reference List Style

Authors are responsible for the accuracy of their reference lists. Be sure you have a complete reference for each citation, and a citation for each reference.

The reference styles should follow these *OJ* style guidelines:
References should be listed at the end of the manuscript alphabetically by the last name of the first author. If there is no indication of an individual author, use the editor, corporate author, or periodical name.

All book/article/chapter/dissertation/website titles should be provided with the first letter of the first word of the title in upper case and the other words in lower case.

All book names, dissertation titles and website articles should be provided in italics.

All periodical names should be provided in italics with the first letter of every word capitalized.

Multiple authors should be listed in alphabetical order and separated by a comma and an ampersand (&).

Book Entries
If single author:
Author's last name, first initial. middle initial. (year). Book title. City, State of publication: Publisher.
Example: Bollen, K. A. (1989). Structural equations with latent variables. New York, NY: Wiley.

If multiple authors, list authors alphabetically and separate by a comma and an ampersand (&):
First author's last name, first initial. middle initial., & Second author's last name, Second author's first initial. middle initial. (year). Book title. City, State of publication: Publisher.
Example: Brown, C. V., & Sambamurthy, V. (1999). Repositioning the IT organization to facilitate business transformation. Cincinnati, OH: Pinnaflex Press.

If a later edition:
Author's last name, first initial. middle initial. (year), Book title (edition number). City, State of publication: Publisher.
Example: Nunnally, J. C. (1978). Psychometric theory (2nd ed.). New York, NY: McGraw-Hill.

Chapters in Books
Chapter author's last name, first initial. middle initial. (year), Chapter title. In book editor's first initial. last name, (Ed.), Book title. City of publication: Publisher, pages x-y.
Example: Winter, S. (1987). Knowledge and competence as strategic assets. In D. J. Teece (Ed.), The competitive challenge: Strategies for industrial innovation and renewal. Cambridge, MA: Ballinger, 159-184

Periodical Entries
Author's last name, first initial. middle initial (year). Article title, Periodical Title, Arabic Volume Number x (Arabic Issue Number y), pages x-y.
Example: Barney, J. B. (1991). Firm resources and sustained competitive advantage. Journal of Management, 17(1), 99-120.

836

Unpublished Papers, Dissertations, and Presented Paper Entries
Author's last name, first initial. middle initial. (year), Title of paper / dissertation / presented paper entry. Definition of type (e.g., doctoral dissertation), affiliation (e.g., Arizona State University, City, State/Country.
Example: Zitzler, E. (1999). Evolutionary algorithms for multiobjective optimization: Methods and applications. Doctoral dissertation, Swiss Federal Institute of Technology (ETH), Zurich, Switzerland.

Proceedings, Published Reports, Monographs, and Specific Editions
Author's last name, first initial. Middle initial. (year). Proceeding/Report/Monograph title. Proceedings of the Conference Name, City, State: Publisher. pages x-y.
Example: Schaffer, J. D. (1985). Multiple objective optimization with vector evaluated genetic algorithms. Proceedings of the First International Conference on Genetic Algorithms. Hillsdale, NJ: Lawrence Erlbaum Associates. 93-100.

Websites and URLs
Author's last name, first initial. middle initial. (year). Title of reference, accessed month, day, year, [available at Insert URL here].
Example: Bitpipe (2004). Readership and usage of white papers by corporate and IT management, accessed July 14, 2004, [available at http://itresearch.forbes.com/detail/RES/1079371988_689.html&src=FEATURE_SPOTLIGHT].

PASOS: Journal of Tourism and Cultural Heritage

ADDRESS FOR SUBMISSION:

Agustin Santana, Editor
PASOS: Journal of Tourism and Cultural
   Heritage
ELECTRONIC SUBMISSION ONLY
   revista.pasos@canarias.org
Phone: (34) 922317740
E-Mail: asantana@ull.es
Web: www.pasosonline.org

CIRCULATION DATA:

Reader: Academics
Frequency of Issue: 3 Times/Year
Sponsor/Publisher: Universidad de La
   Laguna and Direccion General de
   Patrimonio (Gobierno de Canarias)

PUBLICATION GUIDELINES:

Manuscript Length: 16-20
Copies Required: Electronic
Computer Submission: Yes Email
Format: PDF
Fees to Review: 0.00 US$

Manuscript Style:
   See Manuscript Guidelines

REVIEW INFORMATION:

Type of Review: Blind Review
No. of External Reviewers: 2
No. of In House Reviewers: 1
Acceptance Rate: 50%
Time to Review: 1 - 2 Months
Reviewers Comments: Yes
Invited Articles: 11-20%
Fees to Publish: 0.00 US$

MANUSCRIPT TOPICS:

Marketing Research; Organizational Behavior & Theory; Organizational Development; Public Administration; Tourism, Hospitality & Leisure

MANUSCRIPT GUIDELINES/COMMENTS:

PASOS. Journal of Tourism and Cultural Heritage is an free internet publication dedicated to the academic and management-based analysis of the diverse processes inscribed within the tourist system, with a particular emphasis on the uses of culture, the environment and territory, people, communities and spaces, integral heritage. It encourages articles from inter and trans-disciplinary perspectives, from both scientific and management points of view. Its objective is to provide a forum for the discussion of methodologies and theories as well as the presentation of case studies and the results of empirical research. It hopes to contribute to ongoing debates surrounding attempts to comprehend the phenomenon of tourism and to develop diverse approaches to the prevention of the undesirable consequences of tourism as well as enhance the quality of life of the residents of tourist destinations.

Style

In order to simplify the process of edit-ing and publication contributors are requested to comply with the following editorial guidelines:

Submission of original manuscripts. papers should be sent to the following email address: **revista.pasos@canarias.org** inserting *For Publication* in the 'Subject' box.

Language. Articles will be published in the language in which they are submitted.

Margins. 3 centimetres on all sides.

Font. Times New Roman or Arial, in 10-point or similar. The same font should be used in the footnotes, but in 9-point. There should be no variation in fonts or text size throughout the text. Highlighted paragraphs or words should be indicated in italics.

Notes. These should always be placed at the end of the article and written in the same font as the main body (Times New Roman or Arial) in 9-point.

Title and author note(s). The title of the article should be written in lower case and highlighted in bold, at the top of the first page. This should be accompanied by the author(s) full name(s) and title(s), indicating clearly their institutional affiliation, specialism and email address. If it is desired, further biographic details may be inserted in a separate note, not exceeding 60 words.

Abstract. An abstract must be included (max. 110-120 words) in the same language as the main article. This should be accompanied by a translation in English, or, Spanish, if the language of the article is English.

Key words. A list of 5 – 7 key words should be provided, which relate to the principal themes in the article.

Text Articles should be typed, 1.5 spaces apart, exceeding no more than 9,000 words (max. 35 pages), including the title, biographic information, abstract, introduction, relevant appendices, con-clusion, acknowledgements (if relevant) and bibliography.

Tables, Diagrams and Figures. These can be included in the article where necessary. They should be referenced in the main text and/or situ-ated where convenient and accompanied by an explanatory sub-heading. Colour graphics can be used.

Abbreviations and Acronyms. These should be spelt out in full and clearly defined where they initially appear in the text.

References and Bibliography. The standard Harvard system should be used, indicating the author and date of publication of the relevant work. For example: (Smith, 2001) or (Nash, 1990; Smith 2001). Where it is necessary to include a more precise citation the page number should be included (Smith, 2001: 34). The bibliography should be in alphabetical order at the end of the article, and written in the following format:

Smith, Valene L. and Brent, Mary-Ann
2001 "Introduction to hosts and guests revisited: Tourism issues of the 21st century". In Smith, Valene L. & Brent, Mary-Ann (Eds.), Hosts and guests revisited: Tourism issues in the 21st century (pp. 1-14). New York: Cognizant Communications.

Smith, Valene L.
1998 "War and tourism. An American ethnogra-phy". Annals of Tourism Research, 25(1): 202-227

Urry, J.
1990 The tourist gaze: leisure and travel in contemporary societies. London: Sage

For other kinds of publications, the name of the author, date of publication, title and place of publication/conference title, should be stated.

Rights and Obligations of the Author. The authors are entirely responsible for the content of the article. The editors reserve the right to re-print articles which appear, in subsequent collections.

Pennsylvania Journal of Business and Economics

ADDRESS FOR SUBMISSION:

Leon Markowicz, Editor
Pennsylvania Journal of Business and
   Economics
Lebanon Valley College
Lynch 124A
Annville, PA 17003
USA
Phone: 717-867-6104
E-Mail: markowic@lvc.edu
Web:

PUBLICATION GUIDELINES:

Manuscript Length: 6-10
Copies Required: Three + Zip Disk
Computer Submission: Yes If Accepted
Format: MS Word
Fees to Review: 20.00 US$

Manuscript Style:
   American Psychological Association

CIRCULATION DATA:

Reader: Academics
Frequency of Issue: 2 Times/Year
Sponsor/Publisher: Association of
   Pennsylvania University Business and
   Economic Faculties (APUBEF)

REVIEW INFORMATION:

Type of Review: Blind Review
No. of External Reviewers: 2
No. of In House Reviewers: 1
Acceptance Rate: 35%
Time to Review: 2-4 Months
Reviewers Comments: Yes
Invited Articles: 0-5%
Fees to Publish: 0.00 US$

MANUSCRIPT TOPICS:

Advertising & Promotion Management; Business Education; Business Information Systems (MIS); Business Law, Public Responsibility & Ethics; Communication; Direct Marketing; E-Commerce; Global Business; Health Care Administration; Labor Relations & Human Resource Mgt.; Marketing Research; Marketing Theory & Applications; Non-Profit Organizations; Office Administration/Management; Operations Research/Statistics; Organizational Behavior & Theory; Organizational Development; Public Administration; Purchasing/Materials Management; Retailing; Sales/Selling; Services; Small Business Entrepreneurship; Strategic Management Policy; Technology/Innovation; Tourism, Hospitality & Leisure; Transportation/Physical Distribution

MANUSCRIPT GUIDELINES/COMMENTS:

The *APUBEF Journal* is a refereed journal aimed at publishing the papers of faculty from the business and economics disciplines within the State System of Higher Education Universities in Pennsylvania, or from business and economics faculty at comparable institutions from within Pennsylvania and from surrounding states. While theoretical works are encouraged, most published papers are empirical or pedagogical in nature.

Send all paper submissions to Leon Markowicz, Pennsylvania Journal of Business and Economics, Lebanon Valley College, Lynch 124A, Annville, PA 17003, 717-867-6104, **markowic@lvc.edu**

Manuscript Style
1. Papers **must** be submitted on a zip disk using MS Word. Three high-quality, hard copies of the paper **must** accompany the disk: one with author information, two without. Printer setup should be HP LaserJet 4.

2. Use 10-point Times New Roman font for the body of the paper and all headings including the heading for **references**. Use 1" margins at top and bottom and 1.25 left and right.

3. Single-space the **text**. Double-space between paragraphs, and indent the first line five spaces using the tab key. Use full-justification.

4. Spell-check before sending the paper, and correct all grammatical errors. Also, edit the paper to address the comments and suggestions of the reviewers and editor.

Specific Requirements
1. Start the manuscript with the **full title**, centered in capitals, bold print. Following a space, each author and university should be identified, one author per line. No titles (Dr., Mr., Mrs., etc.) are to be used; nor should rank be indicated. Please, no fancy type styles other than ones specified. NO headers, footers or page numbers should be incorporated.

2. After the last author's name and affiliation, double-space, center, and type the heading **abstract**, bold and all caps. All papers **must** have an abstract of no more than 150 words, which provides a brief synopsis of the paper.

3. The next heading is **introduction**, bold and all caps. Double-space before and after. All major headings MUST follow this format. Secondary headings MUST be in bold print, left justified, first letter capitalized then lower case, with a space above and below each heading.

4. **Mathematical expressions and notations** should be used judiciously and all symbols should be identified.

5. **Tables** should be arranged sequentially in the order in which the tables are first mentioned in the text and placed at the end of the manuscript. Type the word Table and its Arabic numeral flush-left at the top of the table, double-space, then type the table title flush-left above the table. The explanatory notes to a table such as probability tables, explanations of acronyms, etc., should appear below the table. Use the same 10-point Times NewRoman font as used in the text and the tab function to construct the tables. If a "camera-ready" table is to be used, send the original and not a reduced copy for incorporation in the journal.

6. **Figures** (such as graphs, drawings, photographs, and charts) must be consecutively numbered in Arabic numerals, with their captions in the order they appear in the text. All illustrations must be camera-ready; photographs must be of professional quality, and drawings

must be prepared in ink. Illustrations should be identified on the back in light pencil with the name of the author and the figure number.

7. Either **footnotes** or **endnotes** are permitted, but not encouraged. In most cases, the material they contain can be incorporated in the text. If footnotes are used, use the automatic footnote function (Control F7), and specify a Times New Roman 10-point font for their text. Endnotes should be in the same 10-point Times New Roman font as the text and placed after the references.

References

1. When citing references in the text, please use parenthesis, author's name, comma and date of publication, i.e., (Wilson, 1996). For up to three authors, cite each and use the "&" for "and", i.e., (Dawes, Dowling & Peterson, 1992). For more than three authors, use the surname of the first author followed by "et al." comma and the year, i.e., (Cravens et al., 1988). Multiple reference citations in parentheses should be arranged alphabetically and a semi-colon used to separate them, i.e., (Cravens et al., 1988; Dawes, Dowling & Peterson, 1992; Wilson, 1996). Text citations must correspond accurately to the references in the reference list.

2. References should be listed alphabetically at the end of the manuscript. References with the same authors in the same order are arranged according to the year of publication, the earliest first.

3. An American Psychological Association format is used for the references.

For a Journal Article
Buzzell, R.D., Gale, B.T., & Sultan, R.G.M. (1975). Market share—a key to profitability. *Harvard Business Review, 75*(1), 97-106.

For a Book
Czepiel, J.A. (1992). *Competitive Marketing Strategy*. Englewood Cliffs, NJ: Prentice-Hall.

For more information and examples please refer to the *Publication Manual of the American Psychological Association.*

Psychology & Marketing

ADDRESS FOR SUBMISSION:

Rajan Nataraajan, Executive Editor
Psychology & Marketing
Auburn University
College of Business
Dept of Marketing
235 Business Building
Auburn University, AL 36849
USA
Phone: 334-844-2465/2450
E-Mail: rajan@business.auburn.edu
Web: www.wiley.com

CIRCULATION DATA:

Reader: Academics, Business Persons
Frequency of Issue: Monthly
Sponsor/Publisher: Interscience/Wiley

PUBLICATION GUIDELINES:

Manuscript Length: 30-35
Copies Required: Five
Computer Submission: Yes·
Format: Contact Editor
Fees to Review: 0.00 US$

Manuscript Style:
  American Psychological Association

REVIEW INFORMATION:

Type of Review: Blind Review
No. of External Reviewers: 3
No. of In House Reviewers: 1
Acceptance Rate: 11-20%
Time to Review: 3 Months
Reviewers Comments: Yes
Invited Articles: 0-5%
Fees to Publish: 0.00 US$

MANUSCRIPT TOPICS:

Marketing Research; Marketing Theory & Applications

MANUSCRIPT GUIDELINES/COMMENTS:

Manuscripts should be submitted in *quintuplicate* to Rajan Nataraajan, Ph.D., Executive Editor, *Psychology & Marketing*, Department of Marketing and Transportation, College of Business, 235 Business Building, Auburn University, Auburn, AL 36849-5246. Articles should be no longer than 35 double-spaced pages, comments no longer than 5 double-spaced pages. Manuscripts must adhere to the instructions on reference citations, preparation of tables and figures, and manuscript format as described in the *Publication Manual of the American Psychological Association* (4th ed.). Readers' comments on published articles must be submitted no later than one month from the date of the issue containing the article being commented on in order to ensure timeliness. All articles as well as comments are subject to editorial review. Journal policy prohibits an author from simultaneously submitting a manuscript for consideration to another journal while that manuscript is under consideration for publication in *Psychology & Marketing*.

844

Figures should be professionally prepared and submitted in a form suitable for reproduction (camera-ready copy). Computer-generated graphs are acceptable only if they have been printed with a good quality laser printer.

References should be compiled on a separate sheet at the end of the article. Examples follow:

Journal
Lichenstein, D. R., Bloch, P. H., & Black, W. C. (1988) Correlates of price acceptability. *Journal of Book Consumer Research*, 15, 243-252.

Lilien, G. L., & Kotler, P. (1983). Marketing decision making. New York: Harper and Row.

Article in Edited Book
Brown, E. D., & Sechrest, L. (1980). Experiments in cross-cultural research. In H. C. Triandis & J. W. Berry (Eds.), Handbook of cross-cultural psychology (Vol. 2, pp. 297–318). Boston: Allyn and Bacon, Inc.

Conference Proceeding
Schaninger, C., Buss, C., & Grover, R. (1982). The effect of sex roles on family finance handling and decision influence. In Bruce Walker (Ed.), An assessment of marketing thought and practice, Educators' Conference Proceedings, Series 48 (pp. 43–47). Chicago: American Marketing Association.

Copyright. No article can be published unless accompanied by a signed publication agreement, which serves as a transfer of copyright from author to publisher. A publication agreement may be obtained from the editor or the publisher. A copy of the publication agreement appears in most issues of the journal. Only original papers will be accepted and copyright in published papers will be vested in the publisher. It is the author's responsibility to obtain written permission to reproduce material that has appeared in another publication.

Correspondence. All other correspondence should be addressed to the Publisher, Professional/Trade Group, John Wiley & Sons, Inc., 605 Third Ave., New York, NY 10158.

Disk Submission Instructions
Please return your final, revised manuscript on disk as well as hard copy. The hard copy must match the disk.

The journal strongly encourages authors to deliver the final, revised version of their accepted manuscripts (text, tables, and, if possible, illustrations) on disk. Given the near-universal use of computer word-processing for manuscript preparation, we anticipate that providing a disk will be convenient for you, and it carries the added advantages of maintaining the integrity of your keystrokes and expediting typesetting. Please return the disk submission slip below with your manuscript and labeled disk(s).

GUIDELINES FOR ELECTRONIC SUBMISSION
Text
Storage Medium. 3½" high-density disk in IBM MS-DOS, Windows, or Macintosh format.

Software and Format. Microsoft Word 6.0 is preferred, although manuscripts prepared with any other microcomputer word processor are acceptable. Refrain from complex formatting; the Publisher will style your manuscript according to the Journal design specifications. Do not use desktop publishing software such as Aldus PageMaker or Quark XPress. If you prepared your manuscript with one of these programs, export the text to a word processing format. Please make sure your word processing program's "fast save" feature is turned off. Please do not deliver files that contain hidden text. For example, do not use your word processor's automated features to create footnotes or reference lists.

File Names. Submit the text and tables of each manuscript as a single file. Name each file with your last name (up to eight letters). Text files should be given the three-letter extension that identifies the file format. Macintosh users should maintain the MS-DOS "eight dot three" file-naming convention.

Labels. Label all disks with your name, the file name, and the word processing program and version used.

Illustration files for full color images to be in a CMYK color space. If possible, ICC or ColorSync profiles of your output device should accompany all digital image submissions.

Storage Medium. Submit as separate files from text files, on separate disks or cartridges. If feasible, full color files should be submitted on separate disks from other image files. 3½" high-density disks, CD, Iomega Zip, and 5¼" 44- or 88-MB SyQuest cartridges can be submitted. At authors' request, cartridges and disks will be returned after publication.

Software and Format. All illustration files should be in TIFF or EPS (with preview) formats. Do not submit native application formats.

Resolution. Journal quality reproduction will require greyscale and color files at resolutions yielding approximately 300 ppi. Bitmapped line art should be submitted at resolutions yielding 600-1200 ppi. These resolutions refer to the output size of the file; if you anticipate that your images will be enlarged or reduced, resolutions should be adjusted accordingly.

File Names. Illustration files should be given the two- or three-letter extension that identifies the file format used (i.e., .tif, .eps).

Labels. Label all disks and cartridges with your name, the file names, formats, and compression schemes (if any) used. Hard copy output must accompany all files.

Qualitative Market Research - An International Journal

ADDRESS FOR SUBMISSION:

Len Tiu Wright, Editor
Qualitative Market Research - An
   International Journal
De Montfort University
Leicester Business School (Bede Island)
The Gateway
Leicester, LE1 9BH
UK
Phone: +44 (0) 178-250-6096
E-Mail: lwright@dmu.ac.uk
Web: www.emeraldinsight.com/qmr.htm

PUBLICATION GUIDELINES:

Manuscript Length: 21-25
Copies Required: Three + Two 3.5' Disks or
   CD
Computer Submission: Yes
Format: MS Word, Windows 98 or Later
Fees to Review: 0.00 US$

Manuscript Style:
   Uniform System of Citation (Harvard
   Blue Book)

CIRCULATION DATA:

Reader: Academics, Business Persons
Frequency of Issue: Quarterly
Sponsor/Publisher: Emerald Group
   Publishing Limited

REVIEW INFORMATION:

Type of Review: Blind Review
No. of External Reviewers: 2-3
No. of In House Reviewers: 0
Acceptance Rate: 40%
Time to Review: 1 - 3 Months
Reviewers Comments: Yes
Invited Articles: 0-5%
Fees to Publish: 0.00 US$

MANUSCRIPT TOPICS:
Direct Marketing; E-Commerce; Marketing Research; Marketing Theory & Applications; Technology/Innovation

MANUSCRIPT GUIDELINES/COMMENTS:

Topics Include. Qualitative Market Research; Qualitative Theory & Applications in Marketing; Qualitative Software/Technology/Innovation/Direct Marketing in the Market Research Industry; Other topics related to Qualitative Research

Copyright
Articles submitted to the journal should be original contributions and should not be under consideration for any other publication at the same time. Authors submitting articles for publication warrant that the work is not an infringement of any existing **copyright** and will indemnify the publisher against any breach of such warranty. For ease of dissemination and to ensure proper policing of use, papers and contributions become the legal copyright of the publisher unless otherwise agreed. Submissions should be sent to the Editor.

Editorial Objectives

Qualitative Market Research: An International Journal aims to further the frontiers of knowledge and understanding of qualitative market research and its applications, exploring many contemporary issues and new developments in marketing. Examples of areas covered include:

- Qualitative perspectives of relationships & complexities in buyer and supplier behaviour
- Commissioning and selling qualitative research
- Research design processes
- Questionnaire enquiry & interviewing, focus groups, projective and enabling techniques
- Qualitative sampling techniques foe qualitative research, data handling, & interpretation
- Applications of information technology
- Use of qualitative software
- Use of qualitative research to enhance quantitative work
- Stimulus material for use in qualitative research on advertising
- Interdisciplinary applications, e.g., sociology, economics, and cultural studies
- Related fields in psychoanalysis, phenomenology, discourse analysis, ethnography, semiotics, and grounded theory
- Analysis and case studies from public and private, profit and not-for-profit sectors
- International qualitative marketing research
- Contemporary developments in qualitative literature
- Ethical and legislative implications in data privacy and control

The journal aims to break new ground by raising awareness of the dichotomy of principles and practices in research in an analytical and practical way.

Editorial Scope

The content is targeted at an international readership and the areas and issues covered by the journal will be treated from cross-national and cross-cultural perspectives. The journal has the scope to cover both a breadth and depth of academic and practitioner research. Case studies and practical applications, which demonstrate the effectiveness of the methodology described, and comparative studies are also encouraged.

Reviewing Process

All papers are subjected to a double-blind reviewing process and all reviews are normally undertaken by members of the Journal's Editorial Board.

Manuscript Requirements

The MCB Journal Article Review Form (JAR) in getting authors' permission for publishing their papers with MCB are found on the MCB website at:

http://www.emeraldinsight.com/literaticlub/jarforms.htm

Three copies of the manuscript and a 3.5" disc should be submitted in double line spacing with wide margins. All authors should be shown and **author's details** must be printed on a separate sheet and the author should not be identified anywhere else in the article.

As a guide, articles should be around 6,000 - 8,000 words in length. A separate page needs to be supplied showing the **title** and brief **autobiographical note** about the author(s) including full name, affiliation, e-mail address, and full international contact details.

The first page of the manuscript should show the **title** of not more than eight words followed by a **structured abstract** of no more than 250 words. Up to six **key words** should be included which encapsulate the principal subjects covered by the article.

Writing the Structured Abstract
To produce a structured abstract for the journal and Emerald database, please complete the following fields about your paper. There are four fields which are obligatory (Purpose, Design, Findings and Value); the other two (Research limitations/implications and Practical implications) may be omitted if they are not applicable to your paper. Abstracts should contain no more than 250 words. Write concisely and clearly. The abstract should reflect only what appear in the original paper. For more information and guidance on structured abstracts visit:
        http://www.emeraldinsight.com/literaticlub/editors/editorialadmin/abstracts

Where there is a **methodology**, it should be clearly described under a separate heading. **Headings** must be short, clearly defined and not numbered. **Notes** or **Endnotes** should be used only if absolutely necessary and must be identified in the text by consecutive numbers, enclosed in square brackets and listed at the end of the article.

Figures, charts and **diagrams** should be kept to a minimum. They must be black and white with minimum shading and numbered consecutively using Arabic numerals with a brief title and labelled axes. In the text, the position of the figure should be shown by typing on a separate line the words "take in Figure 2". Good quality originals must be provided.

Tables should be kept to a minimum. They must be numbered consecutively with Roman numerals and a brief title. In the text, the position of the table should be shown by typing on a separate line the words "take in Table IV".

Photos and illustrations must be supplied as good quality black and white original half tones with captions. Their position should be shown in the text by typing on a separate line the words "take in Plate 2".

References to other publications should be complete and in Harvard style. They should contain full bibliographical details and journal titles should not be abbreviated. For multiple citations in the same year use a, b, c immediately following the year of publication. References should be shown within the text by giving the author's last name followed by a comma and year of publication all in round brackets, e.g. (Fox, 1994). At the end of the article should be a reference list in alphabetical order as follows:

For Books
Surname, initials and year of publication, title, publisher, place of publication, e.g., Wright, L.T. and Crimp, M. (2000), The Marketing Research Process, FT Prentice-Hall, UK.

For Articles
Surname, initials, year "title", journal, volume, number, pages, e.g., Henry, P. (2005), Social class, market situation and consumer metaphors of social (dis)empowerment, *Journal of Consumer Research*, Vol. 31 March, pp. 766-778.

Sinkovics, R., Penz, E. and Ghauri, P. (2005), "Analysing textual data in international marketing research". *Qualitative Market Research – An International Journal*, Vol. 8 No. 1, pp. 9-38

Final Submission of the Article
Once accepted for publication, two good printed final versions of the manuscript must be provided, accompanied by either two 3.5" disks or two CD-Rewritable disks (not CD-Recordable disks) of the same version labelled with: disk format; author name(s); title of article; journal title; file name.

Each article must be accompanied by a completed and signed Journal Article Record Form available from the Editor or on http://www.emeraldinsight.com/literaticlub/jarforms.htm.

The manuscript will be considered to be the definitive version of the article. The author must ensure that it is complete, grammatically correct and without spelling or typographical errors.

In preparing the disk, please use one of the following formats: Word, Word Perfect, Rich text format or TeX/LaTeX. Figures, which are provided electronically, must be in TIF, GIF or PIC file extensions. All figures and graphics must also be supplied as good quality originals.

Final Submission Requirements. Manuscripts must
- Be clean, good quality hard copy
- Include an abstract and keywords
- Have Harvard style references
- Include any figures, photos and graphics as good quality originals
- Be accompanied by a labelled disk
- Be accompanied by a completed Journal Article Record Form

Technical assistance is available from MCB's World Wide Web Literati Club on http://www.literaticlub.co.uk. The Notes for Contributors in preparing manuscripts are found on the MCB website at **http://www.emeraldinsight.com/rpsv/journals/qmr/notes.htm**

Circulation. Available via the MCB Emerald database in over 800 universities worldwide

Regional Business Review

ADDRESS FOR SUBMISSION:

Janet Marta, Editor
Regional Business Review
Northwest Missouri State University
800 University Drive
Maryville, MO 64468-6001
USA
Phone: 660-562-1859
E-Mail: jmarta@mail.nwmissouri.edu
Web:

CIRCULATION DATA:

Reader: Academics, Business Persons
Frequency of Issue: Yearly
Sponsor/Publisher: Melvin D. & Valorie G.
  Booth College of Business &
  Professional Studies

PUBLICATION GUIDELINES:

Manuscript Length: 16-20
Copies Required: Three
Computer Submission: Yes Disk, Email
Format: MS Word
Fees to Review: 0.00 US$

Manuscript Style:
  Chicago Manual of Style

REVIEW INFORMATION:

Type of Review: Blind Review
No. of External Reviewers: 1
No. of In House Reviewers: 1
Acceptance Rate:
Time to Review: 1 - 2 Months
Reviewers Comments: Yes
Invited Articles: 0-5%
Fees to Publish: 0.00 US$

MANUSCRIPT TOPICS:

Advertising & Promotion Management; Communication; Direct Marketing; E-Commerce; Global Business; Health Care Administration; Marketing Research; Marketing Theory & Applications; Marketing Theory & Applications; Sales/Selling; Services; Small Business Entrepreneurship; Tourism, Hospitality & Leisure; Transportation/Physical Distribution

MANUSCRIPT GUIDELINES/COMMENTS:

Authors should submit manuscripts electronically, as an attachment to an e-mail to the editor. Manuscripts must be double-spaced, with at least a one-inch margin on all sides; and about 15-25 pages in length. To assist in blind reviewing, the author's (authors') name(s) should appear on the title page only. In the case of multiple authors, please indicate in a cover letter the author with whom we should correspond.

Please avoid endnotes and footnotes and follow *Chicago* guidelines for references.

Research in Consumer Behavior

ADDRESS FOR SUBMISSION:

Russell W. Belk, Editor
Research in Consumer Behavior
University of Utah
David Eccles School of Business
1645 E. Campus Center Drive
Salt Lake City, UT 84112-9305
USA
Phone: 801-581-7401
E-Mail: mktrwb@business.utah.edu
Web: http://www.business.utah.edu/
~mktrwb/

CIRCULATION DATA:

Reader: Academics
Frequency of Issue: Yearly
Sponsor/Publisher: Elsevier Inc.

PUBLICATION GUIDELINES:

Manuscript Length: 30+
Copies Required: Four
Computer Submission: Yes Disk, Email
Format: MS Word, ASCII, Upon
   Acceptance
Fees to Review: 0.00 US$

Manuscript Style:
   Chicago Manual of Style, American
   Psychological Association, Journal of
   Consumer Reasearch

REVIEW INFORMATION:

Type of Review: Blind Review
No. of External Reviewers: 3
No. of In House Reviewers: 1
Acceptance Rate: 30%
Time to Review: 1 - 2 Months
Reviewers Comments: Yes
Invited Articles: 0-5%
Fees to Publish: 0.00 US$

MANUSCRIPT TOPICS:
Advertising & Promotion Management; Communication; Consumer Behavior; Direct
Marketing; Global Business; Marketing Research; Marketing Theory & Applications; Non-
Profit Organizations; Tourism, Hospitality & Leisure

MANUSCRIPT GUIDELINES/COMMENTS:

RCB seeks qualitative empirical research, quantitative empirical research, theoretical papers,
and methodological papers concerning any aspect of consumer acquisition, consumption, and
disposition. A wide variety of theoretical and methodological perspectives will be considered.
Manuscripts should be in the 25-50-page range and should be written following,
approximately, *Journal of Consumer Research* style guidelines. All manuscripts will be blind
reviewed. Authors will receive a copy of the volume in which their paper appears and 25
reprints of their chapter.

Author's Responsibilities
The author is responsible for correct spelling and punctuation, accurate quotations with page
numbers, complete and accurate references, relevant content, coherent organization, legible
appearance, and so forth. The author must proofread the manuscript after it is typed, making

all corrections and changes before submitting the manuscript. Before submitting the manuscript to the editor please use the checklist on last page of pamphlet to be sure all necessary material is included.

The author is also responsible for preparing the manuscript on a word processor. Just as word processing eliminates a good amount of retyping, submitting a disk provides an opportunity to eliminate duplicate keyboarding by the typesetter. One key to success is compatibility. Therefore, the following steps should be followed closely.

1. Use a word processing program that is able to create a PC-compatible MSWord file.
2. Submit online or via e-mail or on a disk or CD-ROM.
3. Structure manuscript to follow guidelines.
   - Keep entire manuscript on one (1) file
   - Use no headers or footers, but include page numbers.

Volume Editor's Responsibility
The volume editor is responsible for reviewing all printed manuscripts and disks before submission for publication.

General Instructions
Paper. Preparethe manuscript for either A3 or A4 paper. Include tables, photos (black and white only), and illustrations within the same Word file as the text material.pages. Use 12-point Times New Roman or Times Roman font.

Double Spacing. Double space between ALL lines of the manuscript, which includes the title, headings, footnotes, quotations, references, figure captions, and all parts of tables. Never use single-spacing or one-and-a-half spacing.

Margins. Leave uniform margins of 1½ inch at the top, bottom, right, and left of every page. The length of each typed line is 5½ inch. Do not justify lines; leave the right margin uneven. DO NOT hyphenate words at the end of a line; let a line run short or long rather than break a word. Type no more than 25 lines of text on a manuscript page.

Headings. Most manuscripts use from one to four headings. The four levels should appear as:

CENTERED ALL UPPERCASE HEADING

Centered Uppercase and Lowercase Heading

Flush Left, Underlined, Uppercase and Lowercase Side Heading

    Indented, underlined, lowercase paragraph heading ending with a period

Paragraphs and Indentation. Indent the first line of every paragraph and the first line of every footnote five spaces. Type the remaining lines of the manuscript to a uniform left-hand margin.

Quotations. Direct quotations must be accurate. Quotations of 40 words or less should be incorporated into the text and enclosed by double quotation marks ("). Display quotations of more than 40 words should appear as a double-spaced block with no quotation marks. DO NOT single-space. Indent 5 spaces from the left margin and 5 spaces from the right margin.

Permission to Quote. Any direct quotation, regardless of length must be accompanied by a reference citation that includes the author, year of publication, and page number(s). If you quote at length from a copyrighted work, you will also need written permission from the owner of the copyright. It is the author's responsibility to obtain permission. A copy of the letter of permission must accompany the manuscript.

Statistical and Mathematical Copy. Type all signs and symbols in mathematical , Times New Roman, or Times Roman font.

Parts of a Manuscript. Order of manuscript pages: Number all pages consecutively. Arrange the pages of the manuscript as follows:
- Title page (page 1)
- Abstract (page 2)
- Text (page 3)
- Appendixes (start each on a separate page)
- Author acknowledgement notes
- Notes (use sparingly and only if necessary to clarify text; start on a new page)
- References (start on a new page)
- Tables (start each on a separate page)
- Figures (start each on a separate page)

This arrangement is not the way the printed paper will appear; it is necessary for handling by the copy editor and the typesetter.

After the manuscript pages are arranged in the correct order, number them consecutively, beginning with the title page. Number ALL pages. Type the number in the upper right-hand corner using Arabic numerals. Identify each manuscript page by typing an abbreviated title above the page number.

Title Page. The title page includes 4 elements:
- The title in uppercase letters.
- The Author(s) in uppercase and lowercase letters.
- An abbreviated title to be used as a running head. The running head should be a maximum of 70 characters, which includes all letters, punctuation, and spaces between words.
- Complete mailing address and phone number of each author.

Abstract. Begin the abstract on a new page. Type the word "ABSTRACT" in all uppercase letters, centered at top of page. Type the abstract itself as a single paragraph, double-spaced, indent 5 spaces from the left margin and 5 spaces from the right margin.

Text. Begin the text on a new page. The sections of the text follow each other without a break.

Appendices. Double-space the appendices and begin each on a separate page. Type the word "APPENDIX" in all uppercase letters and identifying capital letters in the order in which they are mentioned in text, centered at the top of the page. If there is only one appendix, do not use an identifying letter.

Author Acknowledgement Notes. This note is neither numbered nor is it mentioned in text. Type the word "ACKNOWLEDGMENT" in all uppercase letters, centered at top of a new page. Type the acknowledgment itself as a double-spaced single paragraph.

Notes. Notes that are mentioned in text are numbered consecutively throughout the chapter. Double-space the notes and begin on a separate page. Center the word "NOTES" in all uppercase letters at the top of the page. Indent the first line of each note 5 spaces and type the notes in the order in which they are mentioned in text.

References. Each series has it's own individual style, whether it be APA, ASA, reference notes, or a style unique to their discipline. For the style that you must follow, consult the *Publication Manual of the American Psychological Association* (THIRD Edition), *The Chicago Manual of Style.*

References cited in text **must** appear in the reference list; conversely, each entry in the reference list must be cited in text. It is the author's responsibility to make certain that each source referenced appears in both places and that the text citation and reference list are identical.

Important. (1) Foreign language volumes, parts, numbers, editions, and so on must be translated into their English equivalents. (2) Elsevier does not use either op. cit. or loc. cit. A short-title form is required. Ibid. is acceptable.

Items to be included in a full reference are:
Book: Author's full name
        Complete title of the book
        Editor, compiler, or translator, if any
        Series, if any, and volume or number in series
        Edition, if not the original
        Number of volumes
        Facts of publication – city where published, publisher, date of publication
        Volume number, if any
        Page number(s) of the particular citation
Article in a Periodical:
        Author's full name
        Title of the article
        Name of the periodical
        Volume (and number) of the periodical
        Date of the volume or issue
        Page number(s) of the particular citation

Unpublished Material
  Title of document, if any, and date
  Folio number or other identifying material
  Name of collection
  Depositor, and city where it is located

Tables. Tables are numbered consecutively in the order in which they are first mentioned in text and are identified by the word "Table" and an Arabic numeral. Double-space each table, regardless of length, and begin each table on a separate page. Type the short title of the manuscript and the page number in the upper right-hand corner of every page of a table. Tables are complicated to set in type and more expensive to publish than text. Therefore, they should be reserved for important data directly related to the content of the paper. Refer to every table and its data in text. Do not write "the table above/below " or "the table on p. 32" because the position and page number of a table cannot be determined until the text is typeset. In text, indicate the approximate placement of each table by a clear break in the text, inserting:

TABLE 1 ABOUT HERE

set off, and double-spaced above and below. Do not abbreviate table headings. Limit the use of rules to horizontal rules only. Draw all rules in pencil.

Figures. Figures are also numbered consecutively in the order in which they are first mentioned in text. Use the word "Figure" and an Arabic numeral. Indicate the location of each figure by a clear break, inserting:

INSERT FIGURE 1 ABOUT HERE

set off double-spaced above and below.

Careful adherence to these instructions will ensure the high quality appearance of your paper.

Research Journal of Business Disciplines

ADDRESS FOR SUBMISSION:

John Gill, Editor
Research Journal of Business Disciplines
PO Box 1399
Clinton, MS 39060-1399
USA
Phone: 601-877-6450
E-Mail: msabd@jam.rr.com
Web: www.msabd.org

CIRCULATION DATA:

Reader: Academics
Frequency of Issue: Yearly
Sponsor/Publisher: MidSouth Association
of Business Disciplines

PUBLICATION GUIDELINES:

Manuscript Length: Less than 26 Pages
Copies Required: Three
Computer Submission: Yes Email
Format: Adobe, MS Word, WordPerfect
Fees to Review: 90.00 US$

Manuscript Style:
, Accounting Horizons

REVIEW INFORMATION:

Type of Review: Blind Review
No. of External Reviewers: 2
No. of In House Reviewers: 2
Acceptance Rate: 41-50%
Time to Review: 1 - 2 Months
Reviewers Comments: Yes
Invited Articles: 0-5%
Fees to Publish: 25.00 US$ / Co-Author

MANUSCRIPT TOPICS:

Advertising & Promotion Management; Business Education; Business Information Systems (MIS); Business Law, Public Responsibility & Ethics; Communication; Direct Marketing; E-Commerce; Global Business; Labor Relations & Human Resource Mgt.; Marketing Research; Marketing Theory & Applications; Non-Profit Organizations; Office Administration/Management; Operations Research/Statistics; Organizational Behavior & Theory; Organizational Development; Production/Operations; Purchasing/Materials Management; Sales/Selling; Services; Small Business Entrepreneurship; Strategic Management Policy; Technology/Innovation; Tourism, Hospitality & Leisure; Transportation/Physical Distribution

MANUSCRIPT GUIDELINES/COMMENTS:

The *Research Journal of Business Disciplines* is the official publication of the MidSouth Association of Business Disciplines.

To be eligible for submission to the *Journal*, manuscripts must have completed a documented process of public scrutiny by academic peers or practitioners. Papers presented at the Association's annual meeting meet this eligibility requirement. Under certain circumstances the Association may allow this requirement to be met by alternate methods. Such manuscripts must, in the editor's opinion, have receive sufficient, relevant feedback from academic peers and/or practitioners via some public forum to be eligible for submission to the *Journal*.

The Association's annual meeting is held at various locations in the southeastern or southwestern US during the first or second week of October. Information about the Association, the *Journal*, and the annual meeting can be obtained from our website www.msabd.org. Written requests for information on the Association, the *Journal*, and the annual meeting should be addressed to Vicky Gill, Executive Director, MSABD, P.O. Box 1399, Clinton, MS 39060-1399, USA. The email address is **msabd@jam.rr.com**.

Format Instructions
Papers submitted for initial review may be in practically any reasonable formatting schema. Accepted papers must be submitted in their final proof version to the *Research Journal of Business Disciplines* on 8.5 by 11.0 paper following the general style of *Issues in Accounting Education* and/or *Accounting Horizons*. MSABD will provide an MS Word template to format final submissions; contact the editor to obtain the template prior to making the final submission.

Submission Deadline
Papers presented at the annual meeting in October must be submitted to the *Journal* by January 15 of the year following presentation. Other submissions will be considered as they are received.

Retail Education Today

ADDRESS FOR SUBMISSION:

David J. Burns, Editor
Retail Education Today
Xavier University
Williams College of Business
Department of Marketing
315 Hailstones Hall
Cincinnati, OH 45207
USA
Phone: 513-745-3956
E-Mail: Burnsd@xavier.edu
Web: www.acraretail.org

PUBLICATION GUIDELINES:

Manuscript Length:
Copies Required: Two
Computer Submission: Yes
Format:
Fees to Review: 0.00 US$

Manuscript Style:
     See Manuscript Guidelines

CIRCULATION DATA:

Reader: Academics
Frequency of Issue: Quarterly
Sponsor/Publisher: American Collegiate
     Retailing Association

REVIEW INFORMATION:

Type of Review: Blind Review
No. of External Reviewers: 1
No. of In House Reviewers: 1
Acceptance Rate:
Time to Review: 2 - 3 Months
Reviewers Comments: Yes
Invited Articles: 0-5%
Fees to Publish: 0.00 US$

MANUSCRIPT TOPICS:
Business Education; Marketing Theory & Applications; Retailing; Sales/Selling

MANUSCRIPT GUIDELINES/COMMENTS:

Papers will be reviewed in any format. Authors of accepted papers will be sent the style guidelines and will be requested to make the appropriate changes.

Review of Business Research

ADDRESS FOR SUBMISSION:

Bhavesh M. Patel & Eric Girard, Editors
Review of Business Research
PO Box 2536
Ceres, CA 95307
USA
Phone: 440-582-5978
E-Mail: Review@iabe.org
Web: www.iabe.org

CIRCULATION DATA:

Reader: Academics, Business Persons
Frequency of Issue: 2 Times/Year
Sponsor/Publisher: International Academy
    of Business and Economics (IABE)

PUBLICATION GUIDELINES:

Manuscript Length: 11-15
Copies Required: One
Computer Submission: Yes Disk, Email
Format: MS Word
Fees to Review: 0.00 US$

Manuscript Style:
    Chicago Manual of Style

REVIEW INFORMATION:

Type of Review: Blind Review
No. of External Reviewers: 2
No. of In House Reviewers: 1
Acceptance Rate:
Time to Review: 2 - 3 Months
Reviewers Comments: Yes
Invited Articles: 11-20%
Fees to Publish: 0.00 US$

MANUSCRIPT TOPICS:

Accounting; Advertising & Promotion Management; Business Education; Business Information Systems (MIS); Business Law, Public Responsibility & Ethics; E-Business; E-Commerce; Economics; Finance; Global Business; Health Care Administration; Labor Relations & Human Resource Mgt.; Marketing Research; Marketing Theory & Applications; Operations Research/Statistics; Organizational Behavior & Theory; Organizational Development; Production/Operations; Public Administration; Purchasing/Materials Management; Services; Small Business Entrepreneurship; Strategic Management Policy; Technology/Innovation; Tourism, Hospitality & Leisure; Transportation/Physical Distribution

MANUSCRIPT GUIDELINES/COMMENTS:

Please use following manuscript Guidelines for submission of your papers for the review. Papers are reviewed on a continual basis throughout the year. Early Submissions are welcome! Please email your manuscript to **Review@iabe.org**.

ensure proper policing of use papers/articles/cases and contributions become the legal copyright of the IABE unless otherwise agreed in writing.

General Information. These are submission instructions for review purpose only. Once your submission is accepted you will receive submission guidelines with your paper acceptance letter. The author(s) will be emailed result of the review process in about 6-8 weeks from submission date. Papers are reviewed and accepted on a continual basis. Submit your papers early for full considerations!

Typing. Paper must be laser printed/printable on 8.5" x 11" white sheets in Arial 10-point font single-spaced lines justify style in MS Word. All four margins must be 1" each.

First Page. Paper title not exceeding two lines must be CAPITALIZED AND CENTERED IN BOLD LETTERS. Author name and university/organizational affiliation of each author must be printed on one line each. Do NOT include titles such as Dr., Professor, Ph.D., department address email address etc. Please print the word "ABSTRACT" in capitalized bold letters left justified and double-spaced from last author's name/affiliation. Abstract should be in italic. Please see the sample manuscript.

All other Headings. All other section headings starting with INTRODUCTION must be numbered in capitalized bold letters left justified and double-spaced from last line above them. See the subsection headings in the sample manuscript.

Tables Figures and Charts. All tables figures or charts must be inserted in the body of the manuscripts within the margins with headings/titles in centered CAPITALIZED BOLD letters.

References and Bibliography. All references listed in this section must be cited in the article and vice-versa. The reference citations in the text must be inserted in parentheses within sentences with author name followed by a comma and year of publication. Please follow the following formats:

Journal Articles
Khade Alan S. and Metlen Scott K. "An Application of Benchmarking in Dairy Industry" *International Journal of Benchmarking* Vol. III (4) 1996 17

Books
Harrison Norma and Samson D. Technology Management: Text and Cases McGraw-Hill Publishing New York 2002

Internet
Hesterbrink C. E-Business and ERP: Bringing two Paradigms together October 1999; PricewaterhouseCoopers *www.pwc.com.*

Author Profile(s). At the end of paper include author profile(s) not exceeding five lines each author including name highest degree/university/year current position/university and major achievements. For example:

Author Profile:
Dr. Tahi J. Gnepa earned his Ph.D. at the University of Wisconsin Madison in 1989. Currently he is a professor of international business at California State University Stanislaus and Managing Editor of Journal of International Business Strategy (JIBStrategy).

Manuscript. Absolutely no footnotes! Do not insert page numbers for the manuscript. Please do not forget to run spelling and grammar check for the completed paper. Save the manuscript on your diskette/CD or hard drive.

Electronic Submission. Send your submission as an MS Word file attachment to your Email to **Review@iabe.org**.

Schmalenbach Business Review

ADDRESS FOR SUBMISSION:

Wolfgang Ballwieser, Managing Editor
Schmalenbach Business Review
University of Munich
Munich School of Management
Ludwigstr. 28/RG
80539 Munich,
Germany
Phone: +49-89-2180-6309
E-Mail: sbr@bwl.uni-muenchen.de
Web: www.sbr-online.de

CIRCULATION DATA:

Reader: Academics, Business Managers
Frequency of Issue: Quarterly
Sponsor/Publisher:

PUBLICATION GUIDELINES:

Manuscript Length: 26-30
Copies Required: Two
Computer Submission: No
Format: N/A
Fees to Review: 0.00 US$

Manuscript Style:
    See Manuscript Guidelines

REVIEW INFORMATION:

Type of Review: Blind Review
No. of External Reviewers: 1-2
No. of In House Reviewers: 1
Acceptance Rate: 37%
Time to Review: 2 - 3 Months
Reviewers Comments: Yes
Invited Articles: 0-5%
Fees to Publish: 0.00 US$

MANUSCRIPT TOPICS:
Marketing Research; Marketing Theory & Applications; Organizational Behavior & Theory; Technology/Innovation

MANUSCRIPT GUIDELINES/COMMENTS:

Call for Papers
The *Schmalenbach Business Review - SBR* - is the international edition of the oldest and most prestigious German journal of business, named "Schmalenbachs Zeitschrift für betriebswirtschaftliche Forschung" (zfbf). *SBR's* goal is to publish original and innovative research. The journal covers topics especially in accounting, finance, taxation, marketing and organisation, but is open for further subjects. Thus, *SBR* attempts to bring together the most important management areas. This approach of not specializing in one specific subject, such as accounting or finance, stands in the tradition of German business research journals.

Schmalenbach Business Review (SBR) publishes original research of general interest in business administration. Authors are invited to submit theoretical as well as empirical papers which are innovative.

SBR is soliciting contributions from all fields of business administration. Traditionally, most papers are in the field of:

- Accounting
- Finance
- Marketing
- Organization

but this list is by no means exhaustive.

Every submission is refereed by two referees, at least one review is double-blind. Every effort is made to ensure a quick turnaround time; usually the reviewing time does not exceed 90 days. The journal's internationally composed board of editors and ad hoc referees guarantee the high quality standard of the journal. The Editor conducts a desk rejection when he believes the probability of acceptance is insufficient to cause the authors to wait for the outcome of the full review. For example, the manuscript might be a poor fit with the journal or the manuscript might fail to provide new findings over the extant literature. A maximum of one referee report will be provided.

Manuscripts should be sent in duplicate, together with an data file without the author's name. The data file can be separately sent as an attachment of an e-mail. The address is:

Wolfgang Ballwieser; Managing editor of *SBR*
Munich School of Management; University of Munich
Ludwigstr. 28/RG; D-80539 Munich; Germany
Email: **sbr@bwl.uni-muenchen.de**

Information to Authors

Submission of a paper to *SBR* implies that the paper is unpublished original work by the author(s) and is not under consideration for publication elsewhere. Authors declare this explicitly.

PAPER GUIDELINES

General

Submissions should not exceed 25 pages/6000 words. Please print in Times New Roman, 12 point, 1.5 spaced, left and right margin 3 cm. Accentuation in the text and the footnotes should be made by italics. Do not use bold print.

Structure

1 ((bold))
1.1 (italics)
1.1.1 ((italics))
and so on

Do not use specific abbreviations in the main text. Exceptions can be made at usually abbreviated nouns such as USA, EU, p., km, or technical terms such as Ltd., API.

Add an abstract of approximately 10-15 lines to every paper, keywords and the *JEL*-Classification.

First Page
The names of the authors should be marked with an asterisk (*). In the footnote the profession and corresponding address should be given.

The first page should contain only the names and information about the authors, the title of the paper and the abstract. The second page should start with the title without reference to the authors and then commence with the text.

Tables and Illustrations
Tables and illustrations should be separated from the text as originals to allow a good quality of reproduction. Electronic submission is allowed.

Every table or illustration should have a heading, printed in italics. References in the text should be printed in italics and are not abbreviated [see table 3]

References
References in the body text should be reduced to a minimum.

Citations are made according to the author-year-principle directly in the body text. Footnotes should only contain additional sources and comments, should be numbered consecutively and placed at the bottom of the relevant page. They should be kept to a minimum (for example, no more than one per three or four pages) and should be concise (for example, no more than three lines long).

For citations, please cite only the last name [e.g. (Rappaport (1975, 179))]. If there is more than one author separate the names using a slash [e.g. Jensen and Meckling (1976, 156) say...or (Jensen and Meckling (1976))]. If there is more than one reference in a footnote, separate the references with a semicolon [e.g. (Mattessich (1995, 149); Watts/Zimmerman (1986, 139)]. As short form for several authors the abbreviation "et al." might be used. To ensure uniqueness of references in case of the same authors and publications in the same year, use letters to distinguish them (e.g., Bromwich (2004a, 2004b)).

List of References
Do not use abbreviations for journals.

The literature should be cited with last name, given name (not abbreviated), year of publication (in brackets), title, and source with place of publication according to the following examples:

Book
  title of the publication, place of publication: publishing company [e.g. Watts, Ross L. and Jerold L. Zimmerman (1986), *Positive Accounting Theory*, New Jersey et al.: Prentice-Hall.]

Journal article

title of the article, name of journal volume, pages [e.g. Jensen, Michael C. and Wil-liam H. Meckling (1976), Theory of the firm: Managerial behavior, agency costs and ownership structure, *Journal of Financial Economics* 3, 305-60.]

Article in edited volume

title of the article, in name(s) of the editor(s), title of the book, place of publication: publishing company, pages [e.g. Grossman, Sanford J. and Oliver D. Hart (1982), Corporate financial structure and managerial incentives, in John J. McCall (ed.), *The Economics of Information and Uncertainty*, Chicago, Ill.: University of Chicago Press, 123-55.]

Unpublished work

Theissen, Erik (2001), *Price Discovery in Floor and Screen Trading Systems*, Working Paper, University of Bonn.

Service Industries Journal (The)

ADDRESS FOR SUBMISSION:

Ronald Goldsmith, Co-Editor
Service Industries Journal (The)
Florida State University
College of Business
Marketing Department
Tallahassee, FL 32306-1110
USA
Phone: 850-644-4401
E-Mail: rgoldsm@garnet.acns.fsu.edu
Web: www.frankcass.com

CIRCULATION DATA:

Reader: Academics
Frequency of Issue: 8 Times/Year
Sponsor/Publisher: Taylor & Francis, Ltd.

PUBLICATION GUIDELINES:

Manuscript Length: 16-20
Copies Required: Four
Computer Submission: Yes
Format: MS Word, Rich Text
Fees to Review: 0.00 US$

Manuscript Style:
, Publisher Guidelines

REVIEW INFORMATION:

Type of Review: Blind Review
No. of External Reviewers: 3
No. of In House Reviewers: 1
Acceptance Rate: 0-5%
Time to Review: 1-3 Months
Reviewers Comments: Yes
Invited Articles: 0%
Fees to Publish: 0.00 US$

MANUSCRIPT TOPICS:
Services; Services Management

MANUSCRIPT GUIDELINES/COMMENTS:

Editors
Gary Akehurst, University of Wales School of Management and Business, Cledwyn Building, Aberystwyth, Ceredigion, SY23 3DD, UK

Ronald Goldsmith, Florida State University, College of Business, Marketing Department, Tallahassee, Florida 32306-1110, USA

Barry Howcroft, Loughborough University Business School, Banking Centre, Loughborough, Leicestershire, LE11 3TU, UK

Nicholas Alexander, University of Wales School of Management and Business, Cledwyn Building, Aberystwyth, Ceredigion, SY23 3DD, UK

Manuscripts and editorial correspondence should be sent to Ronald Goldsmith in USA or one of the editors in the UK (see addresses above).

About the Journal
Service industries generate over two-thirds of GNP and employment in developed countries, and their importance is growing in developing countries. We must understand how they have developed, are developing and how we can improve the management of services. Services industries include retailing and distribution; financial services, including banking and insurance; hotels and tourism; leisure, recreation and entertainment; professional and business services, including accountancy, marketing and law.

The Service Industries Journal, an international journal of service management, exists to improve our knowledge of service industries, service businesses and the effective management of services. This multidisciplinary journal was the first of its kind and has established a first class international reputation for the quality of its articles.

Guide to Journal Contributors
Manuscript. Articles submitted for consideration should be sent to any of the editors at the above address by electronic file (preferably in Microsoft Word or Rich Text format) plus each manuscript should be submitted in hard copy, in triplicate (four copies would be more helpful).

Authors are asked to submit their articles presented according to the following instructions, as editors will not undertake retyping of manuscripts prior to publication.

Manuscripts must be typewritten on one side only, and **double-spaced** with ample margins throughout, including pages of notes and references. All pages should be numbered consecutively.

There is no standard length for articles, but 5,000-6,000 words (including notes and references) is a useful target. Authors should inform the editor of the exact length of the article at the time of submission.

The article title should not exceed ten words in length. The author's name should appear on the first page, in capitals and centred underneath the title. The author's affiliation with address should appear in a footline on the first page. Acknowledgements, if any, should appear at the end of the article before the endnotes.

The article should begin with an indented and underlined summary of less than 100 words, describing the main arguments and conclusions of the article.

As no author corrections, updating or additions are allowed at proof stage, authors must make a final check of their article for content, style, proper names, quotations and references. Check especially consistency of capitalisation, use of italics, hyphenation (minimal use of these is preferable), and spelling (e.g. of place names). Check for missing or duplicated numbers indicating notes.

Preparation of Electronic Files or Diskettes. Following peer review and acceptance for publication, authors are requested to submit the paper in electronic format or 3.5" computer diskettes (either IBM/PC or Macintosh-compatible) of their revised manuscripts along with a printed copy of the final manuscript. The following formats are preferred: Microsoft Word; WordPerfect; and rich text files (RTF). Please do not embed footnotes, references, or any other text; list them in the foreground at the end of the text proper. Identify the diskette by providing lead author's name, manuscript title, name of computer file, and word-processing program, type and version number used.

Please keep at least one copy of the diskette. Diskettes will be returned after use upon request.

There is a risk that spelling mistakes, capital letters, etc. in original copy will be faithfully translated into typeset copy, so please check copy carefully before sending it.

Use the number 1, not lowercase l, for numerals, and for zero use 0, not upper case O.

Printout. Copy presented on diskette must be accompanied by a printout. The printout and the diskette must agree with each other. If corrections are made on the word processor, a new printout must be made. The printout must be: double-spaced; in letter quality, **not draft** mode; without line-end hyphenation, and preferably unjustified, on plain paper, not greenlined computer paper.

Tables/Camera-Ready Artwork. Tables, figures and maps should be kept to a minimum (preferably no more than 4 per article) and should be grouped in an Appendix at the end of the article. They must be sufficiently black and clear and of good quality to be reproduced photographically. Tables should be produced on separate pages. Headings, sources and notes for tables and figures will be set by the typesetter. Tables, if created in a word processor, may appear in the main text file, but do not apply frames or tints.

The type area of a journal page is 144mm x 177mm. Please do not use more than 110 characters across (including spaces) for upright tables, or 175 characters across for landscaped ones. Avoid landscaped tables where possible, and consider reversing rows and columns to convert to an upright table. So that tables in different articles appear standard throughout the journal, please do not use more than three horizontal lines, as shown in the example, and avoid vertical lines (rules) as far as possible. Follow the style of column headings closely.

Graphic elements, including tables (with the exception of those created in word processors as described above), figures, charts and photographs should be attached as separate items and saved in black and white in uncompressed TIF or JPG format. Tints should be avoided: use open patterns instead.
- As camera-ready artwork cannot be corrected at proof stage, double check for accuracy and consistency before submission.
- Do not mark up amendments or changes on any tables submitted as artwork for reproduction. This applies particularly to changes from American spelling: e.g. 'labor' to 'labour'. If any amendments or changes are necessary, these should be made before submission of camera-ready artwork.
- Ensure spelling is consistent with the text of an article: e.g. 'fertiliser' in text, but 'fertilizer' in table; 'defence' in text, but 'defense' in table (or vice versa).

Technical Matter
- Equations, tables and diagrams should not be used unless essential to making the author's point and, where possible, should be placed in an appendix at the end of the article.
- Symbols or Greek letters must be absolutely clear for the typesetter.
- If mathematics must be included please note that the typesetter can: turn any English or Greek letter, in upper or lower case, roman, italic or bold, into a first or second order superior; put a bar over any character but not over a group of characters.

Journal Style
Authors will be responsible for ensuring that their manuscripts correspond with the Journal style. Particular attention is drawn to the following points.

Spelling. British spelling should be used throughout, and where there is an alternative -ise (rather than -ize) endings (i.e. organise rather than organize).

Subheadings. Main subheadings should be in capital letters, ranged left above the section, and sub-subheadings should have capital letters only for major words, and be underlined and ranged left above the section. Third-level subheadings should be underlined and run on as part of the paragraph (with a space above) and typed with a capital letter only for the first word.

Notes and References. Simple references without accompanying comments to be inserted in square brackets at the appropriate place in the text, stating author's surname, publication date of work, and (where appropriate) page numbers: [Livesey, 1979: 22-3]. If reference is made in the article to more than one work in the same year by the author, a lower case letter should be used to distinguish them: [Sparks, 1982a: 24-56].

References with Comments. To appear as notes, indicated consecutively throughout the article by raised numerals corresponding to the list of notes placed at the end of the article. Notes should be kept to a minimum. Bibliographical references within the notes should follow the system described above.

A reference list should appear after the list of notes. It should contain all the works referred to, listed alphabetically by the author's surname (or name of sponsoring organisation where there is no identifiable author). Please double check that all authors mentioned in text are in the reference list, with the same spelling of names, and that they are in correct alphabetical order. Style should follow: author's surname, forename and/or initials, date of publication, title of publication (italicised), place of publication and publisher. All of this information must be provided. Thus (note especially punctuation):

Dawson, J.A. and D. Kirby, (1979) *Small scale retailing in the United Kingdom,* 2nd edition, Farnborough: Saxon House.

Sparks, L., (1982a) Female and part-time employment within superstore retailing, *European Journal of Marketing,* 16(3), July, pp.278-94.

Sparks, L., (1982b) Employment in hypermarkets and superstores, in A.B. Smith (ed.), *Employment trends in England and Wales,* Oxford: Basil Blackwell.

Book reviews should be preceded by full publication information in the following form: *The Business of Tourism,* by J.C. Holloway. Plymouth: MacDonald & Evans, 1983. Pp.x + 246. E14.95 (paperback). ISBN 0-71210594-8.

The reviewer's name (in capital letters) and affiliation (underlined, ranged at the left) should appear at the end of the review.

While every care is taken, the Publishers cannot accept responsibility for loss of or damage to authors' manuscripts. Authors should keep at least one copy of their article.

Services Marketing Quarterly

ADDRESS FOR SUBMISSION:

Bob Stevens & David Loudon, Co-Editors
Services Marketing Quarterly
University of Louisiana at Monroe
College of Business Administration
Monroe, LA 71209-0140
USA
Phone: 318-342-1201
E-Mail: bstevens@ulm.edu
   dlloudon@samford.edu
Web: www.haworthpressinc.com

PUBLICATION GUIDELINES:

Manuscript Length:
Copies Required: Electronic
Computer Submission: Yes Email Preferred
Format: MS Word
Fees to Review: 0.00 US$

Manuscript Style:
   American Psychological Association

CIRCULATION DATA:

Reader: Academics, Business Persons
Frequency of Issue: Quarterly
Sponsor/Publisher: Haworth Press, Inc.

REVIEW INFORMATION:

Type of Review: Peer Review
No. of External Reviewers: 1
No. of In House Reviewers: 1
Acceptance Rate:
Time to Review: 1 - 2 Months
Reviewers Comments:
Invited Articles: 6-10%
Fees to Publish: 0.00 US$

MANUSCRIPT TOPICS:

Advertising & Promotion Management; Communication; Direct Marketing; E-Commerce; Global Business; Marketing Research; Marketing Theory & Applications; Non-Profit Organizations; Sales/Selling; Services; Services Marketing; Small Business Entrepreneurship; Tourism, Hospitality & Leisure; Transportation/Physical Distribution

MANUSCRIPT GUIDELINES/COMMENTS:

Co-Editor. David Loudon, Samford University, School of Business, Birmingham, AL 35229. Phone: 205-726-4314; Email: **dlloudon@samford.edu**

About the Journal
Services Marketing Quarterly is an applied journal for marketing all types of services. It is devoted to supplying "how-to" marketing tools for specific sectors of the expanding service sector of the economy.

Each issue of this unique quarterly periodical is a basic resource for all service managers. Specific tools, cases, and methodologies used by other professionals in various service industries are offered for examination.

The distinguished practitioners and academicians share their experiences in developing, implementing, and evaluating their marketing campaigns and programs, and explore the latest marketing issues and methodologies.

Services Marketing Quarterly demonstrates the applicability of marketing to specific services. It bridges a gap between theory and application by simply and clearly presenting marketing methodologies that can assist you in marketing your service.

Instructions for Authors

1. **Manuscripts** should be submitted as an e-mail attachment (preferable), or on a diskette, to the Editors. All editorial inquiries should be directed to the Editors.

2. **Original Articles Only**. Submission of a manuscript to this *Journal* represents a certification on the part of the author(s) that it is an original work, and that neither this manuscript nor a version of it has been published elsewhere nor is being considered for publication elsewhere.

3. **Copyright**. Copyright ownership of your manuscript must be transferred officially to The Hawthorn Press, Inc., before we can begin the peer-review process. The Editor's letter acknowledging receipt of the manuscript will be accompanied by a statement fully explaining this. All authors must sign the form and return the original to the Editor as soon as possible. Failure to return the copyright form in a timely fashion will result in delay in review and subsequent publication. A Manuscript Submission & Limited Copyright Transfer Form may be printed from http://www.haworthpress.com/pdfs/Jmanuscript.pdf .

4. **Manuscript Length**. Your manuscript may be approximately 5,000 words (15-25 double-spaced pages, including references, tables, and figures). Lengthier manuscripts or shorter viewpoint/opinion pieces will be considered at the discretion of the Editor. Sometimes, lengthier manuscripts may be considered if they can be divided up into sections for publication in successive journal issues.

5. **Manuscript Style**. References, citations, and general style of manuscripts for this journal should follow the APA style, as outlined in the latest edition of the *Publication Manual of the American Psychological Association*. References should be double-spaced and placed in alphabetical order. The use of footnotes within the text is discouraged. Words should be underlined only when it is intended that they be typeset in italics. If an author wishes to submit a paper that has been already prepared in another style, he or she may do so. However, if the paper is accepted (with or without reviewer's alterations), the author is fully responsible for retyping the manuscript in the correct style as indicated above. Neither the Editor nor the Publisher is responsible for re-preparing manuscript copy to adhere to the journal's style.

6. **Manuscript Preparation**

Margins. Leave at least a 1" margin on all four sides.
Cover Page. Include a cover page with the following:
- Article title
- Full authorship
- An ABSTRACT of about 100 words

- 5 or 6 KEY WORDS that identify article content
- An introductory footnote with authors' academic degrees, professional titles, affiliations, postal and email addresses, and any desired acknowledgment of research support or other credit
- A header or footer on each page with abbreviated title and pg number of total (e.g., pg 2 of 7)

7. **Spelling, Grammar, and Punctuation**. You are responsible for preparing manuscript copy which is clearly written in acceptable, scholarly English, and which contains no errors of spelling, grammar or punctuation. Neither the Editor nor the Publisher is responsible for correcting errors of spelling and grammar. The manuscript, after acceptance by the Editor, must be immediately ready for typesetting as it is finally submitted by the author(s).
Check your paper for the following common errors:
- Dangling modifiers
- Misplaced modifiers
- Unclear antecedents
- Incorrect or inconsistent abbreviations

Also, check the accuracy of all arithmetic calculations, statistics, numerical data, text citations, and references.

8. **Inconsistencies Must Be Avoided**. Be sure you are consistent in your use of abbreviations, terminology, and in citing references, from one part of your paper to another.

9. **Preparation of Tables, Figures, and Illustrations**. Any material that is not textual is considered artwork. This includes tables, figures, diagrams, charts, graphs, illustrations, appendices, screen captures, and photos. Computer-generated figures should be in black and white and/or shades of gray (preferably no color, for it does not reproduce well). Camera-ready art must contain no grammatical, typographical, or format errors and must reproduce sharply and clearly in the dimensions of the final printed page (4½ x 6½ inches). Photos and screen captures must be on a disk as a TIFF file, or other graphic File format such as JPEG or BMP. For rapid publication we must receive black-and-white glossy or matte positives (white background with black images and/or wording) in addition to files on disk. Tables should be created in the text document file using the software's *Table* feature.

Both a printed hard copy and a disk copy of the art must be provided. Each piece of art should be sent in its own file, on a disk and be clearly labeled. We reserve the right to (if necessary) request new art, alter art, or if all else has failed in achieving art that is presentable, delete art. If submitted art cannot be used, the Publisher reserves the right to redo the art and to charge the author a fee for this service.

10. **Alterations Required by Referees and Reviewers**. A paper may be accepted by the Editor contingent upon changes that are mandated by anonymous specialist referees and members of the Editorial Board. If the Editor returns your manuscript for revisions, you are responsible for retyping any sections of the paper to incorporate these revisions (if applicable, revisions should also be put on disk).

11. **Typesetting**. You will not receive galley proofs of your article. Editorial revisions, if any, must therefore be made while your article is still in manuscript. The final version of the manuscript will be the version you see published. Typesetting errors will be corrected by the production staff of The Haworth Press, Inc. Authors are expected to submit manuscripts, disks, and art that are free from error.

12. **Electronic Media**. Please submit your article (in Microsoft Word format) as an e-mail attachment or by sending a diskette containing the article. Authors are advised that no revisions of the manuscript can be made after acceptance by the Editor for publication.

13. **Reprints**. The senior author will receive two copies of the journal issue and 25 complimentary reprints of his or her article. The junior author will receive two copies of the journal issue. An order form for the purchase of additional reprints will also be sent to all authors at this time. (Approximately 4-6 weeks is necessary for the preparation of reprints.) Please do not query the *Journal*'s Editor about reprints. All such questions should be sent directly to The Haworth Press, Inc., Production Department, 37 West Broad Street, West Hazleton, PA 18202. To order additional reprints (minimum 50 copies), please contact The Haworth Document Delivery Center, 10 Alice Street, Binghamton, NY 13904-1580; Tel (800) 342-9678 or Fax (607) 722-6362.

Simulation & Gaming: An Interdisciplinary Journal of Theory, Practice & Research

ADDRESS FOR SUBMISSION:

David Crookall, Editor
Simulation & Gaming: An Interdisciplinary
     Journal of Theory, Practice & Research
University of Nice Sophia Antipolis
     ELECTRONIC SUBMISSION ONLY
France
Phone:
E-Mail: simulation-gaming@wanadoo.fr
     simulation.gaming@gmail.com
Web: www.unice.fr/sg/

PUBLICATION GUIDELINES:

Manuscript Length: 6-30
Copies Required: Electronić
Computer Submission: Yes Email Required
Format: MS Word
Fees to Review: 0.00 US$

Manuscript Style:
     American Psychological Association

CIRCULATION DATA:

Reader: Business Persons, Academics
Frequency of Issue: Quarterly
Sponsor/Publisher: ABSEL / Sage
     Publications

REVIEW INFORMATION:

Type of Review: Blind Review
No. of External Reviewers: 2-3
No. of In House Reviewers: 0-1
Acceptance Rate: 21-30%
Time to Review: 2 - 3 Months
Reviewers Comments: Yes
Invited Articles: 6-10%
Fees to Publish: 0.00 US$

MANUSCRIPT TOPICS:

Business Education; Business Information Systems (MIS); Business Law, Public Responsibility & Ethics; Communication; Global Business; Health Care Administration; Labor Relations & Human Resource Mgt.; Marketing Theory & Applications; Non-Profit Organizations; Operations Research/Statistics; Organizational Behavior & Theory; Organizational Development; Production/Operations; Public Administration; Services; Small Business Entrepreneurship; Strategic Management Policy; Technology/Innovation; Tourism, Hospitality & Leisure; Transportation/Physical Distribution

MANUSCRIPT GUIDELINES/COMMENTS:

Simulation & Gaming: An Interdisciplinary Journal of Theory, Practice and Research is the world's foremost scientific review devoted to academic and applied issues in the increasingly popular methodology of simulation/gaming as used in education, training, consultation and research round the world. Simulation/gaming is to be taken in its broadest meaning, to encompass such areas as simulation, computerized simulation, gaming, simulation/gaming, policy exercises, planning exercises, debriefing, analytic discussion, post-experience analysis, modeling, virtual reality, game theory, role-play, role-playing, play, active learning, experiential learning, learning from experience, toys, playthings, structured exercises, debriefing. This quarterly journal examines the methodologies and explores their application to real-world problems and situations.

The broad scope and multidisciplinary nature of *S&G* is demonstrated by the variety of its readers and contributors. They work in sociology, political science, economics, education, cognition, psychology, social-psychology, social psychology, management, business, marketing, government, entrepreneurship, environmental issues, health, medicine, research methodology, communication, environment, policy, planning, educational, technology, computing, geography, climate change, multi-culturalism, multi-cultural, intercultural, culture, organization studies, negotiation, history, peace studies, business, statistics, decision making, conflict management, cognition, communication, political science, language learning, media, learning theory, international studies, took, educational technology, information technology.

All standard manuscripts submitted to *S&G* for publication must be written within the spirit, scope and format of the journal. To make sure that your manuscript is correctly written, please consult both:
- several recent issues of the journal and
- the Guide for *S&G* Authors - **www.unice.fr/sg/**

Before submitting your manuscripts, you must obtain a *Ms ID*, see website.

The Guide is couched in rather dogmatic terms because it is vital that the instructions are followed carefully at the outset. Submissions will not be processed until they conform to this Guide.

This Guide is in several sections. These are clustered into four broad areas:
- **Overview**. The scope of *S&G*, the substance of papers, the types of paper published in *S&G*. It also contains special author guides for reviews and for ready-to-use games.
- **Process**. The things that you must do or the steps that you must take, such getting a ms ID, having your ms reviewed, and sending the author agreement.
- **Structure**. The things that you must include in your ms, to get your it into shape for review and publication, such as laying out your ms in certain ways or including certain elements (abstract, keywords, etc.). The check list will help you here.
- **Guest**. Notes to help you prepare a proposal to guest edit a symposium issue of *S&G*.

To **navigate** the pages of this Guide for *S&G* Authors, you may use the following:
- the header of these pages.
- the panel to the left.
- the *Table of Contents*.
- the links in each page.

Other information regarding *S&G* is in other parts of the web - **www.unice.fr/sg/**

Calls for Papers
Symposium issues currently open for submitting papers.
Below is a list of special, theme issues of *S&G* that are currently being prepared. If you wish to contribute to one of these, be in touch directly with the Guest Editor of the issue concerned.

Current symposium issues include:
- Internet & computing
- Natural resources
- Assessment
- Video games
- Facilitation
- Utilities
- History
- Previous

Symposium issues planned for the future
- ˙Collaborative learning.
- Ethical issues.

For a list of past symposium issues, see website.

What to send to Guest Editors.
When contacting a Guest Editor, make sure that you send a one- to two-page outline proposal containing the following elements:
- A working title.
- Your name, address, phone, fax, e-mail, etc.
- A set of objectives for the proposed paper.
- A working plan.
- (Possibly one or two offprints of previous papers that might help.)
- An assurance that you subscribe to, or at least that you are familiar with, *S&G*. It is impossible to write a paper without knowing the journal.

Proposing to guest edit a symposium issue.
You are encouraged to guest edit a symposium issue of *S&G*. In principle, most topics can form the basis of a symposium issue. Almost all the topics of papers published in *S&G* could be expanded into a special issue.

To start the ball rolling, please send an outline proposal containing the following elements to the editor:
- A working **title**.
- A one- to two-page **proposal**, with the following: delimitation of the theme, outlining rational & objectives, target audience(s), list of possible authors, list of sub-topics, possible members of your ad hoc editorial board.
- A short résumé or CV (one page maximum).

- Notes on any previous editorial experience. Previous editorial experience is not required. On the contrary, one can learn a great deal about editing from guest editing a special issue of a journal. *S&G* is happy to provide this opportunity to those who are motivated and willing to work hard.
- Possibly one or two offprints of previous papers that might help.
- An assurance that you subscribe to, or at least that you are familiar with, *S&G*. It is impossible to guest edit without knowing the journal.
- **Contact details**. Name, address, telephone and fax numbers and e-mail address(es). It is essential to have reliable e-mail facilities in order to guest edit a special issue.

Before submitting an outline, you should look at some recent copies of *Simulation & Gaming*. They can be consulted in a good library or purchased from Sage Publications.
- Sage Publications, 2455 Teller Road, Thousand Oaks, CA 91320, USA; telephone: +1 805-499-0721; fax: +1 805-499-0871; **www.sagepub.com/**.
- Sage Publications, 6 Bonhill Street, London EC2A 4PU, UK; telephone: +44 (0)171 374 0645; fax: +44 (0)171 374 8741; **www.sagepub.co.uk/**.

Southwest Business and Economics Journal

ADDRESS FOR SUBMISSION:

Syed Ahmed, Editor
Southwest Business and Economics Journal
Cameron University
School of Business
Business Research Center
2800 W. Gore Boulevard
Lawton, OK 73505
USA
Phone: 580-581-2430
E-Mail: syeda@cameron.edu
Web: http://www.Cameron.edu/academic/
business/brc/soce.html

PUBLICATION GUIDELINES:

Manuscript Length: 11-20
Copies Required: Three
Computer Submission: Yes
Format: MS Word
Fees to Review: 0.00 US$

Manuscript Style:
American Psychological Association

CIRCULATION DATA:

Reader: Academics, Buiness Persons
Frequency of Issue: Yearly
Sponsor/Publisher: Cameron University

REVIEW INFORMATION:

Type of Review: Blind Review
No. of External Reviewers: 1-2
No. of In House Reviewers: 0-1
Acceptance Rate: 30-35%
Time to Review: 2 - 3 Months
Reviewers Comments: Yes
Invited Articles: 0-5%
Fees to Publish: 60.00 US$

MANUSCRIPT TOPICS:

Business Information Systems (MIS); Economics; Finance; International Business; Management; Marketing Theory & Applications; Organizational Theory & Application

MANUSCRIPT GUIDELINES/COMMENTS:

Editorial Information

The *Southwest Business and Economics Journal* is published once a year by the Business Research Center, School of Business, Cameron University, Lawton. OK.

The *Southwest Business and Economics Journal* provides a bridge of communication between the business community and the academia. Articles related to all business areas and regional economic development are welcome. The journal publishes refereed articles from the academic community and an occasional invited article from business practitioners. The target audience includes both academics and the business and professional community. Priority will be given to subjects dealing with interpretations or new understandings, and solutions to problems faced by business and government leaders.

880

Author Guidelines

1. All submitted work must be original work that is not under submission to another journal or under consideration for publication in another form.

2. Authors must submit three double-spaced typewritten copies of their paper. Three copies of the paper should be submitted, in addition to the e-mail submission as an attached MS-WORD document.

3. The cover page shall contain the title of the paper, author's name, and affiliation. This page will be removed when the paper is sent to a referee. The first page of text should contain the title but not the name of the author.

4. A separate abstract of not more than 100 words should be included.

5. Each table and figure should be on a separate page at the end of the paper, with proper instructions about their placement in the paper.

6. Footnotes must be consecutively numbered and typed on a separate page and double-spaced.

7. Cite references in the text, placing the publication date in parentheses, e.g., "Banz (1981) was the first..." References should follow APA guidelines.

8. *Southwest Business and Economics Journal* will hold exclusive rights after acceptance.

9. Authors are advised to mention their office and residence telephone numbers and convenient times for contact.

10. The paper should be submitted to the Editor.

We accept computer submissions formatted in Word.

Southwestern Business Administration Journal

ADDRESS FOR SUBMISSION:

Felix Ayadi, Editor
Southwestern Business Administration
    Journal
Texas Southern University
School of Business
3100 Cleburne
Houston, TX 77004
USA
Phone: 713-313-7738
E-Mail: ayadi_fo@tsu.edu
  sbaj@tsu.edu
Web: http://www.tsu.edu/academics/
  business/SBAJ/index.asp

PUBLICATION GUIDELINES:

Manuscript Length: 21-25
Copies Required: Three
Computer Submission: Yes Preferred
Format: MS Word
Fees to Review: 0.00 US$

Manuscript Style:
  See Manuscript Guidelines

CIRCULATION DATA:

Reader: Academics, Business Persons
Frequency of Issue: 2 Times/Year
Sponsor/Publisher: Texas Southern
  University & Organizational Behavior
  Teaching Society

REVIEW INFORMATION:

Type of Review: Blind Review
No. of External Reviewers: 2
No. of In House Reviewers: 1
Acceptance Rate: 25%
Time to Review: 2 - 3 Months
Reviewers Comments: Yes
Invited Articles: 0-5%
Fees to Publish: 0.00 US$

MANUSCRIPT TOPICS:

Advertising & Promotion Management; Business Education; Business Law, Public Responsibility & Ethics; Communication; E-Commerce; Global Business; Health Care Administration; Labor Relations & Human Resource Mgt.; Marketing Theory & Applications; Organizational Behavior & Theory; Organizational Development; Public Administration; Small Business Entrepreneurship; Strategic Management Policy; Technology/Innovation

MANUSCRIPT GUIDELINES/COMMENTS:

The above topics are acceptable as long as they address the teaching and learning process.

About the Journal

The *Southwestern Business Administration Journal* (SBAJ) is a refereed publication. The aim of this journal is to provide a forum for current thoughts, techniques, theories, issues, trends, and innovations in teaching and learning within the business administration field. Its general focus is to enhance the teaching and learning process. The *SBAJ* is published in spring and fall of every year. All manuscripts submitted to the journal will be subject to a double-blind referee process.

Submission Format

Manuscripts should be in English

Manuscripts should be typed on a standard size paper (8.5" by 11 ") and must not exceed 25 pages, including references, appendixes, tables, and figures.

The manuscript must use Microsoft Word or rich text format and should be typed in a 12-point font. It must be double-spaced (excluding references, appendixes, tables, and figures). All margins are one inch.

The title page should include the title of the manuscript and appropriate contact information (authors' names, affiliations, complete address, contact numbers, and e-mail addresses).

The second page should repeat the title of the manuscript and a brief (not to exceed 100 words) abstract. Excluding title page, the manuscript should not contain the name of the author or any affiliation that would allow the reviewer to determine authorship

Main headings should be centered and typed in all capitals. Example: INTRODUCTION.

Secondary headings should be typed, flush with the left margin and in small letters, with major words beginning with capitals. Example: Learning Models.

Tables, figures, and graphs should be included where they are discussed. Do not include notations like "Insert Table 1 About Here".

Do not paginate within the manuscript. Pencil in page numbers on the bottom of the hard copy.

Do not use footnotes in your manuscript.

Citations should be made in the text by inclosing the cited author's name and the year of the work cited in parentheses. Example: Several studies (Johnson, 1999; Smith, 1998; Green, 1997) support this finding, OR, Results reported by Ball (1985) suggest ……..

Direct quotations must give a page number(s); these follow the date of publication and are separated from it by a colon. Example: Johnson indicated that writing is a difficult process (1995: 6).

Periodical reference example:
   Johnson, C. L. (1994). The art of writing. *Academy of Management Journal*, 32, 112-125.

Periodical reference example:
   Jacobs, B., & Gurley, M.A., (1990). When writing works. *Studies in Management*, 33, 75-87.

Book reference example:
Johnson, C. L. (1994). *The art of writing*. New York, Macmillan.

Working paper reference example:
Becker, K.L. & Kepler, H.R., (2004). How to finance a budget deficit. NBER Working Paper No. 398. Retrieved September 23, 2004 from the National Bureau of Economic Research database.

References to materials on the internet must be given in brackets in the text such as:
www.tsu.edu/businesspaper.html (with download date indicated)

Assumptions

Authors have submitted original work and made every effort to ensure accuracy of the manuscript.

Accepted ethical standards have been applied in the research and/or preparation of the manuscript submitted for publication.

Authors have obtained appropriate permissions so that the publication of the manuscript would not violate any copyright or any personal or proprietary rights of others.

Publication decisions are based on the recommendations of the journal's editorial board. Submissions are typically assigned to at least two reviewers for consideration. Weak or inappropriate submissions may be returned to authors without formal reviews.

Sport Marketing Quarterly

ADDRESS FOR SUBMISSION:

Jacquelyn Cuneen, Editor
Sport Marketing Quarterly
Bowling Green State University
The G. M. Eppler Complex
Bowling Green, OH 43403
USA
Phone: 419-372-7231
E-Mail: smq@bgnet.bgsu.edu
Web: http://www.fitinfotech.com/smq/
 smq.tpl

CIRCULATION DATA:

Reader: Academics, Business Persons,
 Industry Professionals
Frequency of Issue: Quarterly
Sponsor/Publisher: Fitness Information
 Technology

PUBLICATION GUIDELINES:

Manuscript Length: 11-25
Copies Required: Electronic
Computer Submission: Yes Email
Format: MS Word
Fees to Review: 0.00 US$

Manuscript Style:
 American Psychological Association

REVIEW INFORMATION:

Type of Review: Blind Review
No. of External Reviewers: 2
No. of In House Reviewers: 1
Acceptance Rate: 20%
Time to Review: 1 - 2 Months
Reviewers Comments: Yes
Invited Articles: 0-10%
Fees to Publish: 0.00 US$

MANUSCRIPT TOPICS:
Advertising & Promotion Management; All Related to Sports; Communication; E-Commerce; Marketing Research; Marketing Theory & Applications; Strategic Management Policy; Tourism, Hospitality & Leisure

MANUSCRIPT GUIDELINES/COMMENTS:

Topics Include. Sport Advertising & Promotion Management; Sport Communication; Sport E-Commerce; Sport Marketing Research; Sport Marketing Theory & Applications; Strategic Marketing Policy in Sport Organizations; Sport Tourism, Sport Hospitality & Leisure

Publisher. Fitness Information Technology, a division of the International Center for Performance Excellence, West Virginia University, 262 Coliseum – WVU, Box 6116, Morgantown, WV 26505 USA. Web: www.fitinfotech.com. For Subscription Information: 304-293-6888

Sport Marketing Quarterly represents a unique publishing concept for sport marketing industry professionals and academicians. These two groups of marketing professionals are represented in a landmark publication that facilitates the exchange of ideas in sport marketing. For the practicing sport professional, *SMQ* provides a vehicle for sharing **marketing successes.**

For academicians, *SMQ* provides a forum for sharing research. For both constituencies, *SMQ* provides an opportunity to work together in the business of marketing sport.

Publishing categories for *SMQ* include:
- Professional
- Media
- Amateur
- Advertising
- Promotion
- Special Events
- Facility, Arena, and/or Stadium Marketing
- International
- Research
- Miscellaneous As Appropriate

Sport Marketing Quarterly Manuscript Submission Guidelines

1. Manuscripts submitted to *SMQ* should not be submitted to another publication while under review for *SMQ*.

2. Manuscripts submitted to *SMQ* should be written in Microsoft Word or saved in rich text format and should be submitted electronically, via email attachment, to **smq@bgnet.bgsu.edu**.

3. Authors' names should not appear anywhere in the manuscript. A cover sheet listing the manuscript title and the order of authors as well as the primary author's name, mailing address, preferred phone and fax numbers and email address should accompany each manuscript. In addition, information regarding each author's rank, institution, and research interests should be listed. If appropriate, identify if the manuscript is derived from a master's thesis or doctoral dissertation.

4. A 150-word abstract should preface each manuscript. Manuscripts should be double-spaced with 1.5-inch margins, using an easily readable 12-point font. Authors should follow the style of the *Publication Manual of the American Psychological Association* in preparing all text, tables, and figures (e.g., italics used to report statistical information, indented second line in references listing).

5. Tables and figures should be submitted in electronic and paper form. The Editorial Board will consult the hard copies of the tables and figures to verify content, and the production department will use the hard copies to verify formatting. Indicate the software that was used to create the figures. Adobe Illustrator, CorelDraw, Pagemaker, and QuarkXPress are the preferred software for *SMQ* figures.

6. Manuscripts should not exceed 25 pages, including text, tables, figures, charts, footnotes, and references.

7. Manuscripts submitted to *SMQ* undergo double-blind review. Reviewers' comments will be returned via email attachment written in Microsoft Word or saved in rich text format. The Editor will examine all manuscripts and determine if the content is congruent with the focus of the journal. If the content of the manuscript is not congruent with *SMQ's* focus, the Editor will return the manuscript to the author(s) with an explanation. If the content of the manuscript is congruent with *SMQ's* focus, the Editor will determine if the manuscript should be "Previewed" or "Reviewed." The Editor will ask for a Preview when the manuscript has been examined and determined that there may be questions related to the concept, writing, methodology, results, discussion, or implementation. Previewers will provide the Editor with a general rationale for rejection OR disagree with the Editor's opinion, in which case a full review will be conducted. The Editor will ask for a Review when the manuscript has been read and determined to be of acceptable or high quality in concept, writing, methodology, results, discussion, or implementation. A Review will be conducted in the traditional manner.

8. The Editor will provide authors with a completed review as soon as possible.

9. Authors warrant that the manuscript is original except for excerpts and illustrations from copyrighted works as may be included with permission of the copyright owner, such permissions to be obtained by the authors at their own expense. The manuscripts submitted to the publisher must contain the appropriate credit line, if any, required by copyright holders of material adapted or reprinted for use.

10. Authors of manuscripts accepted for publication will be required to transfer copyright to Fitness Information Technology, publisher of *SMQ*.

All inquiries about reviews related to refereed research manuscripts should be directed to: Jacquelyn Cuneen, Editor **smq@bgnet.bgsu.edu**

Sport Marketing Quarterly **Case Study Submission Guidelines**
1. As the intent of the Case Study section is to provide case studies that can be used in the classroom, case study submissions to *SMQ* should summarize a challenge facing a sport organization and challenge the reader to develop a solution based on the facts provided in the case.

2. Case study submissions should follow all of the submission and style requirements listed above for manuscripts with the exception that the case study should not exceed 18 pages including tables, charts, etc.

3. In addition to the case study, submissions should also be accompanied by a separate file that includes teaching notes for the case. In the teaching notes, authors should outline the following: a brief summary of the case (150 words or less), the theoretical areas of sport marketing to which the case is applicable, information on how the challenge was addressed, and spaced. If accepted, the teaching notes will be posted on the FIT website as a service to instructors.

4. Case studies submitted to *SMQ* will undergo double-blind review. *SMQ* will attempt to provide feedback to case study authors within 6 weeks.

5. Accepted case studies will be sent to a practitioner (who is not employed by the organization described) who will provide a brief analysis of the case and discuss their recommendations for the case in question. The case and the response to the case will be published together.

6. Stipulations set forth in the manuscript submission guidelines with respect to originality and copyright transfer also apply to the Case Study section of *SMQ*.

All inquiries about reviews related to refereed Case Study manuscripts should be directed to: James. M. Gladden, Editor **jgladden@sportstudy.umass.edu**

Tourism

ADDRESS FOR SUBMISSION:

S. Corak, Editor-in-Chief
Tourism
Institute for Tourism Zagreb
Vrhovec 5
10000 Zagreb
Croatia
Phone: +385-1-39 09 666
E-Mail: sanda.corak@iztzg.hr
Web: www.iztzg.hr/tourism.htm

CIRCULATION DATA:

Reader: Academics, Business Persons
Frequency of Issue: Quarterly
Sponsor/Publisher: Ministry of Science,
　Education and Sports

PUBLICATION GUIDELINES:

Manuscript Length: 16-20
Copies Required: Three
Computer Submission: Yes
Format: Final Version
Fees to Review: 0.00 US$

Manuscript Style:
　See Manuscript Guidelines

REVIEW INFORMATION:

Type of Review: Blind Review
No. of External Reviewers: 2
No. of In House Reviewers: 1
Acceptance Rate: 40%
Time to Review: 1 - 2 Months
Reviewers Comments: Yes
Invited Articles: 0-5%
Fees to Publish: 0.00 US$

MANUSCRIPT TOPICS:

Business Information Systems (MIS); Direct Marketing; Marketing Research; Marketing Theory & Applications; Operations Research/Statistics; Services; Small Business Entrepreneurship; Strategic Management Policy; Transportation/Physical Distribution

MANUSCRIPT GUIDELINES/COMMENTS:

Topics Include. Tourism Planning and Management Issues, Market Research and Segmentation, Special Interest Tourism, Tourism Promotion and Marketing, Impacts of Tourism, Tourism Policy, Valuation of Public Goods, Education in Tourism, Tourism Forecasting, Research Methods in Tourism and Hospitality

Journal *Tourism* is an international academic and professional quarterly which welcomes articles on various aspects of travel and tourism. The journal emphasizes the broadness and interrelatedness of the tourist sector Manuscripts submitted to the journal can be processed expeditiously if they are prepared according to our guidelines. Manuscripts will be returned to the author with a set of instructions if they are not submitted according to our style guide.

Alterations Required by Reviewers. Articles are reviewed anonymously (two reviewers) and, if required, returned to authors for modification and/or completion. The author is responsible for retyping any sections of the paper to incorporate these revisions.

Length and Classes of Articles. The Journal publishes four main classes of articles: original scientific papers, preliminary communications, reviews and professional papers. All this are full-length articles and should be 4000-6000 words long. All these are full-length articles and should be 4000-6000 words long. Articles are reviewed anonymously (2 reviewers) and, if required, returned to authors for revision and/or completion. All papers should be accompanied by an abstract (200-250 words) and by up to six keywords. *Tourism* also publishes shorter items - research notes, agency reports and industry viewpoints (800 -2000 words), book and journal reviews (800-1000 words). Shorter items will be refereed by an Editorial Board member.

Manuscript Preparation. Manuscripts must be submitted in English, in triplicate (the original plus two photocopies) plus electronic version. One copy of the article should include the following information on the cover page: title of the article (90 letters maximum), name of author(s), academic attainment, present position and complete address (telephone/fax, e-mail). The other two copies should have only the article title.

Preparation of Tables, Figures, and Illustrations. Tables, figures, illustrations, and all other supplements should be enclosed on separate pages and the place where they are to be printed must be marked in the text.

Inconsistencies Must be Avoided. Authors should be consistent when using abbreviations, terminology, and in citing references in different parts of an article.

References. In the text, references are cited with parentheses using the author/ date style. Example: (Collins 2002). If there are three or more authors, quote all three names the first time you cite them in the body of the paper, then abbreviate this by quoting the first name and using et al. The list of all references should be placed at the end of the text in alphabetical order of authors. All cited references must be given in full, including the volume, issues and page numbers.

Periodicals
Lepp A. and Gibson H. (2003). Tourist roles, perceived risk and international tourism. Annals of Tourism Research, 30 (3), 606-624.

Books
Reisinger Y. and Turner L.W. (2003) Cross-cultural behaviour in tourism: concepts and analysis. Oxford: Butterworth Heinemann.

Article or Chapter in an Edited Book
MacLaurin D. J. (2002) Human resource issues for the convention industry. In: Weber K. and Chon K. S. (eds) Convention tourism: international research and industry perspectives. New York: The Haworth Hospitality Press. 79-99.

Reprints. The authors will receive one printed copy and the PDF version of their articles.

Submission of Final Manuscripts. Authors whose papers have been accepted for publication should provide and send by e-mail a revisited version of the manuscript. Tables, graphs, pictures, illustrations and other graphics should be in separate files and in the original programs in which they were created (e.g. for tables and graphs created in Excel, the authors should attach the original Excel files with an xls extension; photographs or maps should be in one of the following formats: jpg, tif, gif, bmp or cdr). The authors are fully responsible for the contents of the manuscript and the accuracy of all the enclosed data.

Tourism Analysis

ADDRESS FOR SUBMISSION:

Muzaffer Uysal & Geoffrey Crouch, Co-Eds
Tourism Analysis
Virginia Polytechnic Institute and State
  University
Dept of Hospitality & Tourism Mgmt.
362 Wallace
Blacksburg, VA 24061
USA
Phone: 540-231-8426
E-Mail: samil@vt.edu
  g.crouch@latrobe.edu.au
Web: http://www.cognizantcommunication.
  Com/filecabinet/Tourism_Analysis/
  ta.htm

PUBLICATION GUIDELINES:

Manuscript Length: 26-30
Copies Required: Three
Computer Submission: Yes .
Format: MS Word, Text File
Fees to Review: 0.00 US$

Manuscript Style:
  American Psychological Association,
  4th Edition

CIRCULATION DATA:

Reader: Academics, Practitioners
Frequency of Issue: Quarterly
Sponsor/Publisher: Cognizant
  Communication Corporation

REVIEW INFORMATION:

Type of Review: Blind Review
No. of External Reviewers: 2
No. of In House Reviewers: 1
Acceptance Rate: 45%
Time to Review: 1 - 2 Months
Reviewers Comments: Yes
Invited Articles: 0-5%
Fees to Publish: 0.00 US$

MANUSCRIPT TOPICS:
Business Information Systems (MIS); Direct Marketing; E-Commerce; Global Business; Marketing Research; Marketing Theory & Applications; Organizational Development; Services; Small Business Entrepreneurship; Tourism & Hospitality Research; Tourism, Hospitality & Leisure

MANUSCRIPT GUIDELINES/COMMENTS:

Aims and Scope
The aim of *Tourism Analysis* is to promote a forum for practitioners and academicians in the fields of Leisure, Recreation, Tourism, and Hospitality (LRTH). As an interdisciplinary journal, it is an appropriate outlet for articles, research notes, and computer software packages designed to be of interest, concern, and of applied value to its audience of professionals, scholars, and students of LRTH programs the world over. The scope of the articles will include behavioral models (quantitative-qualitative), decision-making techniques and procedures, estimation models, demand-supply analysis, monitoring systems, expert systems

892

and performance evaluation, assessment of site and destination attractiveness, new analytical tools, research methods and related areas such as validity and reliability, scale development, development of data collection instruments, methodological issues in cross-national and cross-cultural studies, and computer technology and use.

Information for Contributors

Send manuscripts to the Editors. Muzaffer Uysal, address above, or Geoffrey I. Crouch, Professor of Marketing, School of Business, Faculty of Law and Management, La Trobe University, Melbourne, Victoria 3086, Australia. Tel 61-3-9479-2450; Fax 61-3-9479-5971; **G.Crouch@latrobe.edu.au**

Manuscripts Submitted From Europe. Klaus Weiermair, Institute of Tourism and Service Economics, University of Innsbruck, Leopold-Franzens-Universitat, A-6020 Innsbruck, Austria. Tel 43-512-507-7081; Fax 43-512-507-2845; **Klaus.Weiewair@uibk. ac.at**

Manuscript Submission. Manuscripts must be submitted in triplicate. They should be typewritten on one side of the paper, double-spaced (including references), and should be checked carefully. All rights and permissions must be obtained by the contributor(s). These permissions should be sent upon acceptance of the manuscript for publication. Enclose a self-addressed envelope with the submitted manuscript. Electronic submission is also acceoted.

The title of the paper, all author names and corresponding affiliations, and name and complete mailing address for sending proofs should be included on a separate page, because manuscripts are sent out for blind review. Include telephone and fax numbers and e-mail address (if necessary) for the designated corresponding author.

Abstract. Provide an abstract of up to 300 words. It should contain an abbreviated representation of the content of the manuscript. Major results, conclusions, and/or recommendations should be given, followed by supporting details of method, scope, or purpose as appropriate. Supply 3 to 5 keywords suitable for indexing.

References should be placed at the end of the manuscript on a separate page, arranged in alphabetical order. Follow APA guidelines set forth in their *Publication Manual* (4th edition) for text and reference list citations, per these examples.

Text Citations
(Gunn, 1990) or (Fesenmaier et al., 1994; Mazanec, 1992, 1993; Uysal & Gitelson, 1994) or (Crompton, 1979, p. 411) (for quoted material).

Journal Citation
Crouch, I.G. (1994). The study of international tourism demand: A review of findings. Journal of Travel Research, 33(1), 12-23.

Book Citation
Witt, E.S., & Witt, C.A. (1992). Modeling & forecasting in tourism. London: Academic Press.

Chapter/Pages in Edited Book

Frechtling, C.D. (1994). Assessing the impacts of travel and tourism: Measuring economic benefits. In J.R. Brent Ritchie & C.R. Goeldner (Eds.), Travel, tourism, and hospitality research (2nd ed., pp. 367-391). New York: John Wiley & Sons.

Please note that citations such as "personal communication" should be cited parenthetically in the text only. Do not include in the reference list.

Figures. All figures should be prepared in a program that allows saving in .tif or .eps format. Do no incorporate figures within the text of the manuscript. Black and white line art (i.e., bar graphs, etc.) should be prepared without color unless the figure is to be printed in color. **Note-**There is a charge for printing figures in color.

Labeling and figure detail should be large enough to be legible after reduction to fit page parameters. Each figure must be cited in the text and legends for all illustrations should be included on a separate page. Do not incorporate figure legends as part of the figure and figure file. Place figure legend text at the end of the manuscript file. Include figure (graphic) files as separate files on the final disk.

Tables. Table material should not duplicate the text. Include each table on a separate page at the end of the manuscript or as separate files. Include a title for each table. Do not incorporate tables within the text of the manuscript.

Final Accepted Manuscripts. A final hard copy of the revised manuscript, including all table and figures, along with a disk containing all files (text, graphic, tables) should be mailed to the above address. Make sure that the hard copy and disk file match exactly and contain the final version of the manuscript. Label each figure in pencil on the back of the figure with author's name and figure number.

Page Proofs and Reprints. Page proofs will be sent to the designated corresponding contributor. A form for ordering reprints and copies of the journal issue in which the article appears will accompany the page proofs. Minor corrections only are allowed at proof stage.

Copyright. Publications are copyrighted for the protection of the authors and the publisher. A Transfer of Copyright Agreement will be sent to the author whose manuscript is accepted for publication. This form must be completed and returned to the Editor before the article can be published.

Although every effort is made by the publisher and editorial board to see that no inaccurate or misleading data, opinion, or statement appears in this journal, they wish to make it clear that the data and opinions appearing in the articles and advertisements herein are the sole responsibility of the contributor or advertiser concerned. Accordingly, the publisher, the editorial board, editors, and their respective employees, officers, and agents accept no responsibility or liability whatsoever for the consequences of any such inaccurate or misleading data, opinion, or statement.

Tourism and Hospitality Research

ADDRESS FOR SUBMISSION:

Mariam Hasan, Publisher
Tourism and Hospitality Research
Palgrave Macmillan
Houndmills
Basingstoke, RG21 6XS
UK
Phone:
E-Mail: submissions@palgrave.com
Web: http://www.palgrave-journals.com/
   thr/index.html

CIRCULATION DATA:

Reader: Academics, Business Persons
Frequency of Issue: Quarterly
Sponsor/Publisher: Palgrave Macmillan

PUBLICATION GUIDELINES:

Manuscript Length: See Guidelines
Copies Required:
Computer Submission: Yes Disk
Format: MS Word, WordPerfect
Fees to Review: 0.00 US$

Manuscript Style:
   Uniform System of Citation (Harvard
   Blue Book)

REVIEW INFORMATION:

Type of Review: Blind Review
No. of External Reviewers: 0-3
No. of In House Reviewers: 1
Acceptance Rate: 21-30%
Time to Review: 1 - 2 Months
Reviewers Comments: Yes
Invited Articles: 6-10%
Fees to Publish: 0.00 US$

MANUSCRIPT TOPICS:
Advertising & Promotion Management; Communication; Global Business; Labor Relations & Human Resource Mgt.; Office Administration/Management; Operations Research/Statistics; Organizational Behavior & Theory; Organizational Development; Production/Operations; Public Administration; Purchasing/Materials Management; Services; Small Business Entrepreneurship; Tourism, Hospitality & Leisure

MANUSCRIPT GUIDELINES/COMMENTS:

Tourism and Hospitality Research is firmly established as a leading and authoritative journal for tourism and hospitality researchers and professionals.

Instructions for Authors
1. Authors are requested to submit a hard copy of their manuscript as well as an electronic copy by email. Submissions should be addressed to:
   Mariam Hasan, Publisher
   Palgrave Macmillan
   Houndmills
   Basingstoke RG21 6XS, UK
   E-mail: **submissions@palgrave.com**

Please clearly state for which journal you are contributing.

2. Authors submitting papers for publication should specify which section of the *Journal* they wish their paper to be considered for: 'Academic Papers' or 'Practice Papers'. Papers submitted for publication in the 'Academic papers' section will be subject to strict double-blind refereeing and will be reviewed by at least two referees', those submitted as a practice paper will be refereed normally by one member of the Editorial Board.

3. Academic papers should normally be between 4000 to 6000 words; practice papers between 2000 and 4000 words in length. Papers outside these guidelines will be considered but authors should note that the review process will consider the length in relation to the content and the clarity of the writing. They should be typewritten double-spaced on A4 or US letter-sized paper and printed on one side of the paper only. Manuscripts should normally be submitted in English.

4. Submission on disk should be clearly labelled with the file name, the date, the author's name and the software package used. The preferred medium is a 3.5 inch disk for PC in Word or WordPerfect. Artwork on disk is preferred on 3.5 inch PC or Macintosh format disk in a dedicated drawing package, such as Adobe Illustrator/ Corel Draw/ Macromedia Freehand, rather than presentation, spreadsheet or database packages. Provide hard copy print out of each figure, clearly identified.

5. Authors will be given the opportunity to purchase offprints of their paper once typesetting has been finalised. The Publishers will send first-named authors up to three free copies of the issue containing their paper.

6. The first page of the manuscript should include a brief descriptive title and the author's name, affiliation, address, telephone and fax numbers and email address. A short description of the author (about 80 words) and, if appropriate, the organisation of which he or she is a member is requested. In the case of co-authors, their full details should also be included. All correspondence will be sent to the first named author, unless otherwise indicated.

7. The second page should contain the title of the paper, a summary or abstract, outlining the aims and subject matter of not more than 100 words in length, and up to six key words. The summary should provide a review of the paper and not simply repeat the conclusions.

8. The paper should begin on the third page and should not relist the title or authors. The paper should be sub-divided into sections. For simplicity, section headings should be in upper case and bold, while subsection headings should be in upper and lower case and bold.

9. Papers should be supported by actual or hypothetical examples wherever possible and appropriate. Authors should not seek to use the *Journal* as a vehicle for marketing any specific product or service and should avoid the use of language or slang that is not in keeping with the academic and professional style of the *Journal*.

10. Titles of organisations etc. should be written out first in full and thereafter in initials. Authors are asked to ensure the references to named people and/or organisations are accurate and without libellous implications.

11. Figures and other line illustrations should be submitted in good quality originals on a separate sheet and numbered consecutively and independently of any tables in the article. Each figure should be numbered and titled. In the text, the position of figures should be indicated by typing on a separate line the words "Figure 1 about here". A copy of the data should also be included where appropriate.

12. Each table should be submitted on a separate sheet, titled and numbered consecutively and independently of any figures in the article. All columns should have explanatory headings. Tables should not repeat data that are available elsewhere in the paper. In the text, the position of tables should be indicated by typing on a separate line the words "Table 1 about here".

13. Photographs and illustrations supporting papers may be submitted where appropriate. Photographs should be good quality positives, printed from the original negatives and in black and white only.

14. Papers should be supported by references. These should be set out according to the standard Harvard style as follows. In the text, references should be cited by the author's name and year of publication in brackets (Jones, 1994), or '. . . as noted by Jones (1994)'. Where there are two or more references to one author for the same year, the following form should be used: (Jones, 1993a) or (Jones, 1993b). Where references include three or more authors the form (Jones et al., 1994) should be used. A full list of references in alphabetical order should be given at the end of the paper citing the author(s) (with surname first), year, title, journal name and volume; and author(s), year, title, publisher and city for books. All references should be written as follows: Lundberg, C.C. (1997) 'Widening the conduct of hospitality inquiry: toward appreciating research alternatives', *Journal of Hospitality and Tourism Research*, 21, 1, 1-13. Ravenscroft, N.R. (1992) 'Recreation Planning and Development', Basingstoke: Macmillan Press Ltd.

15. No contribution will be accepted which has been published elsewhere, unless it is expressly invited or agreed by the Editors and the Publisher.

16. **Copyright**. Authors are responsible for obtaining permission from copyright holders for reproducing through any medium of communication those illustrations, tables, figures or lengthy quotations previously published elsewhere. Add your acknowledgements to the typescript, preferably in the form of an "Acknowledgements" section at the end of the paper. Credit the source and copyright of photographs or figures in the accompanying captions.

The journal's policy is to own copyright in all contributions. Before publication, authors assign copyright to the Publishers, but retain their rights to republish this material in other works written or edited by themselves, subject to full acknowledgement of the original source of publication.

The journal mandates the Copyright Clearance Center in the USA and the Copyright Licensing Agency in the UK to offer centralised licensing arrangements for photocopying in their respective territories.

17. All contributions sent to the Publisher, whether they are invited or not, must bear the author's full name and address, even if this is not for publication. Contributions, whether published pseudonymously or not, are accepted on the strict understanding that the author is responsible for the accuracy of all opinion, technical comment, factual report, data figures, illustrations and photographs. Publication does not necessarily imply that these are the opinions of the Editors, Editorial Board or the Publisher, not does the Editor of the Board accept any liability for the accuracy of such comment, report and other technical and factual information. All reasonable efforts are made to ensure accurate reproduction of text, photographs and illustrations. The Publisher does not accept responsibility for mistakes, be they editorial or typographical, nor for consequences resulting from them.

Tourism Economics

ADDRESS FOR SUBMISSION:

Stephen Wanhill, Editor
Tourism Economics
Bournemouth University
School of Service Industries
Talbot Campus
Fern Barrow
Poole, BH12 5BB
UK
Phone: +44 1202 595017
E-Mail: swanhill@bournemouth.ac.uk
Web: www.ippublishing.com

CIRCULATION DATA:

Reader: Academics
Frequency of Issue: Quarterly
Sponsor/Publisher: IP Publishing Ltd

PUBLICATION GUIDELINES:

Manuscript Length: 21-25
Copies Required: Three
Computer Submission: No
Format: N/A
Fees to Review: 0.00 US$

Manuscript Style:
    Uniform System of Citation (Harvard
    Blue Book)

REVIEW INFORMATION:

Type of Review: Blind Review
No. of External Reviewers: 2
No. of In House Reviewers: 1
Acceptance Rate: 45%
Time to Review: 2 - 3 Months
Reviewers Comments: Yes
Invited Articles: 0-5%
Fees to Publish: 0.00 US$

MANUSCRIPT TOPICS:
Non-Profit Organizations; Tourism, Hospitality & Leisure

MANUSCRIPT GUIDELINES/COMMENTS:

Editorial Coverage
Tourism Economics, published quarterly, covers the business aspects of tourism in the wider context. It takes account of constraints on development, such as social and community interests and the sustainable use of tourism and recreation resources, and inputs into the production process. The definition of tourism used includes tourist trips taken for all purposes, embracing both stay and day visitors.

Articles address the components of the tourism product (accommodation; restaurants; merchandizing; attractions; transport; entertainment; tourist activities); and the economic organization of tourism at micro and macro levels (market structure; role of public/private sectors; community interests; strategic planning; marketing; finance; economic development).

Core subject areas:

- forecasting
- public policy (strategies, fiscal and other intervention policies)
- economic development
- market structures and competition
- sources of capital provision
- labour economics (quality and productivity issues)
- business aspects of marketing
- private and public sector interaction
- economic appraisal at sector and project level
- mathematical modelling
- developments in the components of the product
- structure of the tourism industry (including such issues as ownership, corporate size, international operations, etc)
- regional economic effects of tourism developments
- analysis of international data on tourism, such as WTO statistics

Each issue of the journal also includes a section entitled 'Databank', which provides summary and analysis of the latest tourism data. This varies from statistics on the global picture to those related to a particular world region (as defined by the WTO). Databank provides an invaluable tool for the tourism researcher.

Notes for Authors
Please send papers to Professor Stephen Wanhil, School of Service Industries, Bournemouth University, Talbot Campus, Fern Barrow, Poole BH12 5BB, UK (see above.)

Papers will normally be about 5,000 words long. However, this is by no means inflexible and substantially shorter or longer papers will be considered where appropriate. Research notes and shorter report-style pieces will also be considered.

Presentation. Submissions should be double-spaced, printed on one side of the paper, and sent in triplicate. An electronic version is **not** required for the initial submission, but authors of accepted papers will need to supply a disk with their final draft.

The **title page** should contain full names and addresses of the authors, their professional status or affiliation and the address to which correspondence should be sent. As this page will not be forwarded to referees, the title of the article (without authors) should be repeated on the first page of the text.

An **abstract** should be provided, comprising 80-100 words. Between three and six **key words** should appear below the abstract, highlighting the main topics of the paper. The **text** should be organized under appropriate cross-headings (not numbered paragraphs) and where possible these should be not more than 800 words apart.

References should follow the Harvard system. That is, they should be shown within the text as the author's surname (or authors' surnames) followed by a comma and the year of publication all in round brackets: for example, (Smith, 1998). At the end of the article a bibliographical list should be supplied, organized alphabetically by author (surnames followed by initials—all authors should be named). Bibliographic information should be given in the order indicated by the following examples:

Articles

Knapman, B., and Stoeckl, N. (1995), 'Recreation user fees: an Australian empirical investigation', *Tourism Economics*, Vol 1, No 1, pp 5–15.

Books

Manning, R.E. (1999), *Studies in Outdoor Recreation: Search and Research for Satisfaction*, Oregon State University Press, Corvallis, OR.

Notes should be numbered consecutively in the text and typed in plain text at the end of the paper (not as footnotes on text pages).

Tables and **illustrations** should be presented separately at the end of the text.

Refereeing. The anonymity of both authors and referees will be maintained throughout the refereeing process. There will be a minimum of two referees for each paper.

Copyright. Unless otherwise indicated, articles are received on the understanding that they are original contributions, and have not been published or submitted for publication elsewhere. Wherever possible, authors are asked to assign copyright to IP Publishing Ltd. Relevant authors' rights are protected.

Tourism in Marine Environments

ADDRESS FOR SUBMISSION:

Michael Luck, Editor-in-Chief
Tourism in Marine Environments
Auckland University of Technology
School of Hospitality and Tourism
Faculty of Applied Humanities
Private Bag 92006
Auckland,
New Zealand
Phone: +64 9 921 9999 ext. 5833
E-Mail: micha.lueck@aut.ac.nz
Web: http://www.cognizantcommunication.
com/filecabinet/Tme/tme.html

PUBLICATION GUIDELINES:

Manuscript Length: 5,000-7,000 Words
Copies Required: Four
Computer Submission: Yes Email Preferred
Format: MS Word
Fees to Review: 0.00 US$

Manuscript Style:
American Psychological Association

CIRCULATION DATA:

Reader: Academics, NGOs, Governmental
Organizations
Frequency of Issue: 2 Times/Year
Sponsor/Publisher: Cognizant
Communication Corporation

REVIEW INFORMATION:

Type of Review: Blind Review
No. of External Reviewers: 2
No. of In House Reviewers: 2
Acceptance Rate:
Time to Review: Varies
Reviewers Comments: Yes Blind Copy
Invited Articles: 0-5%
Fees to Publish: 0.00 US$

MANUSCRIPT TOPICS:
Global Business; Marine Environments; Tourism, Hospitality & Leisure

MANUSCRIPT GUIDELINES/COMMENTS:

Aims and Scope
Tourism in Marine Environments is an interdisciplinary journal dealing with variety of management issues in marine settings. It is a scientific journal that draws upon the expertise of academics and practitioners from various disciplines related to the marine environment, including tourism, marine science, geography, social sciences, psychology, environmental studies, economics, marketing, and many more.

The marine environment has long been one of the most attractive settings for tourism. Marine tourism, as defined by Orams (*Marine tourism: Development, impacts and management.* Routledge; 1999, p. 9) includes 'those recreational activities that involve travel away from one's place of residence and which have as their host or focus the marine environment (where the marine environment is defined as those waters which are saline and tide-affected)'. Thus, it includes a wide spectrum of activities, such as scuba diving and snorkeling, wind surfing, fishing, observing marine mammals and birds, the cruise ship and ferry industry, all beach activities, sea kayaking, visits to fishing villages and lighthouses, maritime museums, sailing and motor yachting, maritime events, Arctic and Antarctic tourism, and many more.

Tourism in Marine Environments aims to contribute to the process of theory building, and to be the leading source for research reports and analysis related to all forms of marine tourism. It is governed by an international editorial board consisting of experts in marine tourism, marine science, and related fields. This board conducts most of the manuscript reviews and therefore plays a large role in setting the standards for research and publication in the field. The Editor-In-Chief receives and processes all manuscripts, from time to time modifies the editorial board, and works to ensure a continuous improvement in quality.

Information for Contributors

To expedite the review process, all manuscripts submitted to *Tourism in Marine Environments* (*TME*) must be prepared according to the following format.

Send manuscripts to the Editor-in-Chief.

Manuscript Submission. Authors are encouraged to submit manuscripts by e-mail (attachment in Word format). Hardcopy manuscripts must be submitted in quadruplicate. They should be typewritten on one side of the paper, double spaced (including references), and should be checked carefully. All rights and permissions must be obtained by the contributor(s). These permissions should be sent upon acceptance of the manuscript for publication.

Writing Style. The paper must be written in the third person and all submissions must be in English. Readers need to grasp information quickly; thus, authors should use straightforward declarative sentences, making every effort to help readers understand the concepts presented. All articles should be comprehensible to all readers, regardless of their areas of specializations and academic backgrounds. Papers may include tables, drawings, charts, or photographs.

Paper Length. Articles should be limited to 5,000-7,000 words. Each figure and table counts for approximately 300 words. Book Reviews, Commentaries, and Research Notes should be between 600 and 1,200 words in length.

Cover Page. This should bear a short informative title (title/subtitle 50 letters maximum). To facilitate blind review, no names or affiliations appear on the cover page.

Title Page. The article title is repeated on the title page, followed by all authors' names and affiliations. The corresponding author should be designated, with complete mailing address, as well as telephone and fax numbers, and e-mail address.

Abstracts and Keywords. The article abstract (between 110 and 120 words, including keywords) should state concisely what was done and why, what was found, and what was concluded, and end with a list of up to five keywords pertinent to the central theme.

Text. The paper itself will be composed of three parts: introduction, the study, and conclusion. Headed with an appropriate title, the study (or the main body of the paper) is in turn divided into subtitled sections. The whole submission should be arranged in the following order: cover sheet, title page, abstract and key words, introduction, the study, conclusion, acknowledgment, biographical note, reference list, figure captions, tables. Do not use text footnotes. Extra explanatory material can be included as an Appendix.

Biographical Note. A 65-word biosketch of the author(s) should be included. Manuscripts accepted for publication have to include a biographical sketch (current position, prior significant professional experience, technical interests, education, important activities, and professional affiliations) of all authors.

Abbreviations and Terminologies. These should be fully spelled out and defined when first used in the text.

References. In the text, references are cited using the author/date style following the APA *Publication Manual* (4th ed.). Examples: (Fennell, 1999) or (Duffus & Dearden, 1990; Hall, 2001, 2002). The reference list, placed at the end of the text, must be typed double-spaced in alphabetical order of authors. A referenced article should contain all authors' names, year of publication, title of the article, name of the publication, volume, and inclusive page numbers. A referenced book should list author name(s), year of publication, title of the book, place of publication, and publisher per the following examples:

Journal Article
Orams, M. (1996). An interpretation model for managing marine wildlife-tourist interaction. *Journal of Sustainable Tourism, 4*(4), 81-95.

Book
Gill, P., & Burke, C. (1999). *Whale watching in Australian & New Zealand waters*. Sydney: New Holland Publishers.

Book Chapter
Cater, E., & Goodall, B. (1992). Must tourism destroy its resource base? In A.M. Mannion & S.R. Bowlby (Eds.), *Environmental issues in the 1990s* (pp. 309-323). Chichester: John Wiley & Sons.

Please note that citations such as "personal communication" should not be included in the reference list, but may be added parenthetically in the text.

Figures. All figures should be prepared in a program that allows saving in .tif or .eps format. (Do not incorporate figures within the text of the manuscript.) Black and white line art (i.e., bar graphs, etc.) should be prepared without color unless the figure is to be printed in color. (Note - There is a charge for printing figures in color). Labeling and figure detail should be large enough to be legible after reduction to fit page parameters. Each figure must be cited in the text and legends for all illustrations should be included on a separate page. (Do not incorporate figure legends as part of the figure and figure file.) Place figure legend text at the end of the manuscript file. Include figure (graphic) files as separate files on the final disk.

Tables. Table material should not duplicate the text. Include each table on a separate page at the end of the manuscript or as separate files. Include a title for each table. (Do not incorporate tables within the text of the manuscript.)

Final Accepted Manuscripts. A final hard copy of the revised manuscript, including all tables and figures, along with a disk containing all files (text, graphics, tables) should be mailed to the above address. (Make sure that the hard copy and disk file match exactly and contain the final version of the manuscript.) Label each figure in pencil on the back of the figure with author's name and figure number.

Commentary, Research Notes, and Book Reviews. *TME* also solicits submission to these Departments. The above general format applies; for any queries prospective contributors are asked to contact the respective Editor. In order to avoid unnecessary delays, please send submissions directly to the appropriate Editor.

Evaluation. *TME* is a refereed journal. All manuscripts are evaluated by at least two independent referees. The paper evaluation is double blind and anonymous: neither referees nor the authors are aware of each other's identities.

Copyright and Originality. All authors must sign the "Transfer of Copyright" agreement before the article can be published. This transfer agreement enables Cognizant Communication Corp. (CCC) to protect the copyrighted material for the authors, but does not relinquish the author's proprietary rights. The copyright transfer covers the exclusive rights to reproduce and distribute the article, including reprints, photographic reproductions, microfilm, or any other reproductions of similar nature and translations, as well as the right to adapt the article for use in conjunction with computer systems and programs, and reproduction of publication in machine-readable form and incorporation in retrieval systems. Authors are responsible for obtaining from the copyright holder permission to reproduce any material for which copyright exists.

Page Proofs/Offprints. Page proofs will be sent to the designated corresponding author before publication. Minor corrections only are allowed at this stage. An offprint order form will accompany the page proof.

Although every effort is made by the publisher and editorial board to see that no inaccurate or misleading data, opinion, or statement appears in this journal, they wish to make it clear that the data and opinions appearing in the articles and advertisements herein are the sole responsibility of the contributor or advertiser concerned. Accordingly, the publisher, the editorial board, editors, and their respective employees, officers, and agents accept no responsibility or liability whatsoever for the consequences of any such inaccurate or misleading data, opinion, or statement.

Tourism Management

ADDRESS FOR SUBMISSION:

Chris Ryan, Editor
Tourism Management
University of Waikato
Department of Tourism and Hospitality
 Management
Private Bag 3105
Hamilton,
New Zealand
Phone: +64 7 838 4259
E-Mail: caryan@waikato.ac.nz
 stcpan@mngt.waikato.ac.nz
Web: www.ees.elsevier.com/jtma

PUBLICATION GUIDELINES:

Manuscript Length: 26-30
Copies Required: Electronic
Computer Submission: Yes·Online
Format:
Fees to Review: 0.00 US$

Manuscript Style:
 American Psychological Association

CIRCULATION DATA:

Reader: Business Persons, Academics;
 Researchers in Commerce & Gov't
Frequency of Issue: 6 Times/Year
Sponsor/Publisher: Elsevier Inc.

REVIEW INFORMATION:

Type of Review: Blind Review
No. of External Reviewers: 3
No. of In House Reviewers: 0
Acceptance Rate: 10%
Time to Review: 3-4 Months
Reviewers Comments: Yes
Invited Articles: 1%
Fees to Publish: 0.00 US$

MANUSCRIPT TOPICS:
Advertising & Promotion Management; Marketing Research; Organizational Behavior & Theory; Services; Small Business Entrepreneurship; Tourism, Hospitality & Leisure

MANUSCRIPT GUIDELINES/COMMENTS:

Description
Tourism Management is the leading international journal for all those concerned with the planning and management of travel and tourism. Tourism comprises a multitude of activities which together form one of the world's fastest growing international sectors. The journal takes an interdisciplinary approach and includes planning and policy aspects of international, national and regional tourism as well as specific management studies.

The journal's contents reflect its integrative approach - including primary research articles, discussion of current issues, case studies, reports, book reviews and listings of recent publications, and forthcoming meetings. Articles are relevant to both academics and practitioners, and are the results of anonymous reviews by at least two referees chosen by the editor for their specialist knowledge.

Audience
Academics and researchers, government departments and NTOs, consultants and planners in the tourism, hotel and airline industries.

Guide for Authors
Tourism Management is an international journal which publishes original research in tourism, analysis of current trends, and information on the planning and management of all aspects of travel and tourism. The journal emphasizes the broadness and interrelatedness of the tourism industry. Articles, which should take a multisectoral approach, may cover geography, economics, transportation, hotels and catering, sociology, marketing or development studies.

Tourism Management aims to publish articles that are directly relevant to its readers and of interest to both academics and practitioners, with a minimum of technical jargon. Subjects covered should be treated in such a way as to appeal to as wide a range as possible, and those reporting research should attempt to draw management implications from their results. The use of examples is encouraged.

Submission of Papers
From 1st October 2005, all manuscripts should be submitted electronically through the Elsevier Editorial System (EES) which can be accessed at **http://ees.elsevier.com/jtma**. The system will automatically convert your source files to a single Adobe Acrobat PDF version of the article, which will be used during the peer-review process. Please note that even though manuscript source files are converted to PDF at submission for the review process, these source files will be needed for further processing after acceptance. If you are not able to submit your paper to JTMA electronically please contact the Editor Chris Ryan at **caryan@waikato.ac.nz** for further instructions.

Submission of an article implies that the work described has not been published previously (except in the form of an abstract or as part of a published lecture or academic thesis), that it is not under consideration for publication elsewhere, that its publication is approved by all authors and tacitly or explicitly by the responsible authorities where the work was carried out, and that, if accepted, it will not be published elsewhere in the same form, in English or in any other language, without the written consent of the Publisher. The Editors reserve the right to edit or otherwise alter all contributions, but authors will receive proofs for approval before publication.

Upon acceptance of an article, authors will be asked to transfer copyright (for more information on copyright see http://authors.elsevier.com). This transfer will ensure the widest possible dissemination of information. A letter will be sent to the corresponding author confirming receipt of the manuscript. A form facilitating transfer of copyright will be provided. If excerpts from other copyrighted works are included, the author(s) must obtain written permission from the copyright owners and credit the source(s) in the article. Elsevier has preprinted forms for use by authors in these cases: contact ES Global Rights Department, P.O. Box 800, Oxford, OX5 1DX, UK; phone: (+44) 1865 843830, fax: (+44) 1865 853333, e-mail: permissions@elsevier.com

Preparation of Text

Please write your text in good English (American or British usage is accepted, but not a mixture of these). Italics are not to be used for expressions of Latin origin, for example, in vivo, et al., per se. Use decimal points (not commas); use a space for thousands (10 000 and above).

Double spacing and wide (3 cm) margins should be used. (Avoid full justification, i.e., do not use a constant right-hand margin.) Ensure that each new paragraph is clearly indicated.

Provide the following data on the title page (in the order given).

Title. Concise and informative. Titles are often used in information-retrieval systems. Avoid abbreviations and formulae where possible.

Author names and affiliations. Where the family name may be ambiguous (e.g., a double name), please indicate this clearly. Present the authors' affiliation addresses (where the actual work was done) below the names. Indicate all affiliations with a lower-case superscript letter immediately after the author's name and in front of the appropriate address. Provide the full postal address of each affiliation, including the country name, and, if available, the e-mail address of each author.

Corresponding author. Clearly indicate who is willing to handle correspondence at all stages of refereeing and publication, also post-publication. Ensure that telephone and fax numbers (with country and area code) are provided in addition to the e-mail address and the complete postal address.

Present/permanent address. If an author has moved since the work described in the article was done, or was visiting at the time, a 'Present address' (or 'Permanent address') may be indicated as a footnote to that author's name. The address at which the author actually did the work must be retained as the main, affiliation address. Superscript Arabic numerals are used for such footnotes.

Abstract. A concise and factual abstract is required (maximum length 150 words). The abstract should state briefly the purpose of the research, the principal results and major conclusions. An abstract is often presented separate from the article, so it must be able to stand alone. References should therefore be avoided, but if essential, they must be cited in full, without reference to the reference list.

Keywords. Immediately after the abstract, provide a maximum of 8 keywords, avoiding general and plural terms and multiple concepts (avoid, for example, 'and', 'of'). Be sparing with abbreviations: only abbreviations firmly established in the field may be eligible.

Arrangement of the Article

Subdivision of the article. Divide your article into clearly defined and numbered sections. Subsections should be numbered 1.1 (then 1.1.1, 1.1.2, ?), 1.2, etc. (the abstract is not included in section numbering). Use this numbering also for internal cross-referencing: do not just refer to 'the text.' Any subsection, ideally, should not be more than 600 words. Authors are urged to write as concisely as possible, but not at the expense of clarity. Figure legends, figures, schemes. Present these, in this order, at the end of the article. They are described in more detail below. High-resolution graphics files must always be provided separate from the main text file (see Preparation of illustrations). Tables. Number tables consecutively in accordance with their appearance in the text. Place footnotes to tables below the table body and indicate them with superscript lowercase letters. Avoid vertical rules. Be sparing in the use of tables and ensure that the data presented in tables do not duplicate results described elsewhere in the article.

References

Responsibility for the accuracy of bibliographic citations lies entirely with the authors. Citations in the text: Please ensure that every reference cited in the text is also present in the reference list (and vice versa). Any references cited in the abstract must be given in full. Unpublished results and personal communications should not be in the reference list, but may be mentioned in the text. Citation of a reference as 'in press' implies that the item has been accepted for publication.

Citing and listing of web references. As a minimum, the full URL should be given. Any further information, if known (author names, dates, reference to a source publication, etc.), should also be given. Web references can be listed separately (e.g., after the reference list) under a different heading if desired, or can be included in the reference list.

Text. Citations in the text should follow the referencing style used by the American Psychological Association. You are referred to the *Publication Manual of the American Psychological Association*, Fifth Edition, ISBN 1-55798-790-4, copies of which may be ordered from http://www.apa.org/books/4200061.html or APA Order Dept., P.O.B. 2710, Hyattsville, MD 20784, USA or APA, 3 Henrietta Street, London, WC3E 8LU, UK. Details concerning this referencing style can also be found at http://humanities.byu.edu/linguistics/Henrichsen/APA/APA01.html.

List. References should be arranged first alphabetically and then further sorted chronologically if necessary. More than one reference from the same author(s) in the same year must be identified by the letters "a", "b", "c", etc., placed after the year of publication.

Examples

Reference to a journal publication
Van der Geer, J., Hanraads, J. A. J., & Lupton R. A. (2000). The art of writing a scientific article. *Journal of Scientific Communications*, 163, 51-59.

Reference to a book
Strunk, W., Jr., & White, E. B. (1979). *The elements of style*. (3rd ed.). New York: Macmillan, (Chapter 4).

Reference to a chapter in an edited book
Mettam, G. R., & Adams, L. B. (1994). How to prepare an electronic version of your article. In B. S. Jones, & R. Z. Smith (Eds.), *Introduction to the electronic age* (pp. 281-304). New York: E-Publishing Inc.

Preparation of Artwork

Number figures consecutively with Arabic numerals. Please visit our Web site at http://authors.elsevier.com/artwork, for detailed instructions on preparing electronic artwork.

When uploading your files, please do not use PDFs as source files for illustrations as these are large and slow down the journal site, which inconveniences users. Please use standard drawing programs for line figures (e.g., Adobe etc.). Please save all illustrations, including scanned photographs, micrographs and plates, in a simple file format such as Jpeg. The site will build all of your source files into a PDF. Please also remember to approve the PDF promptly.

Color figures in the printed issue can be accepted only if the authors defray the full cost. However, if together with your accepted article, you submit usable color figures, then Elsevier will ensure, at no additional charge, that these figures will appear in color on the Web (e.g., ScienceDirect and other sites) regardless of whether these illustrations are reproduced in color in the printed version.

For color reproduction in print, you will receive information regarding the costs from Elsevier after receipt of your accepted article. Please note: Because of technical complications that can arise in converting color figures to "gray scale" (for the printed version should you not opt for color in print), please submit in addition usable black-and-white files corresponding to all the color illustrations.

Captions. Ensure that each illustration has a caption. A caption should comprise a brief title (not on the figure itself) and a description of the illustration. Keep text in the illustrations themselves to a minimum but explain all symbols and abbreviations used.

Tables

Tables should be numbered consecutively with Arabic numerals in order of appearance in the text. Type each table double-spaced on a separate page with a short descriptive title typed directly above and with essential footnotes below.

Language Editing

Information on author-paid and pre-accept language editing services available to authors can be found at http://authors.elsevier.com/LanguageEditing.html.

Proofs

When your manuscript is received by the Publisher it is considered to be in its final form. Proofs are not to be regarded as 'drafts'. One set of page proofs in PDF format will be sent by e-mail to the corresponding author, to be checked for typesetting/editing. No changes in, or additions to, the accepted (and subsequently edited) manuscript will be allowed at this stage. Proofreading is solely your responsibility. A form with queries from the copyeditor may accompany your proofs. Please answer all queries and make any corrections or additions required. Elsevier will do everything possible to get your article corrected and published as quickly and accurately as possible. In order to do this we need your help. When you receive the (PDF) proof of your article for correction, it is important to ensure that all of your corrections are sent back to us in one communication. Subsequent corrections will not be possible, so please ensure your first sending is complete. Note that this does not mean you have any less time to make your corrections, just that only one set of corrections will be accepted.

Online Publication
Your article will appear on Elsevier's online journal database ScienceDirect as an "Article in Press" within approximately 4-6 weeks of acceptance. Articles in Press for this journal can be viewed at **http://www.sciencedirect.com/science/journal/0265931X**. An Article in Press may be cited prior to its publication by means of its unique digital object identifier (DOI) number, which does not change throughout the publication process.

Enquiries
Authors can keep a track on the progress of their accepted article, and set up e-mail alerts informing them of changes to their manuscript's status, by using the "Track a Paper" feature of Elsevier's Author Gateway http://authors.elsevier.com. For privacy, information on each article is password-protected. The author should key in the "Our Reference" code (which is in the letter of acknowledgement sent by the publisher on receipt of the accepted article) and the name of the corresponding author. In case of problems or questions, authors may contact the Author Service Department, E-mail: authorsupport@elsevier.com.

Tourism Review International

ADDRESS FOR SUBMISSION:

Laura Jane Lawton, Editor-in-Chief
Tourism Review International
University of South Carolina
Sch. Of Hotel, Restaurant & Tourism Mgmt
College-Hospitality, Retail & Sport Mgmt
701 Assembly Street, Carolina Coliseum
Columbia, SC 29208
USA
Phone: 803-777-7111
E-Mail: llawton@gwm.sc.edu
Web:
    http://www.cognizantcommunication.com

PUBLICATION GUIDELINES:

Manuscript Length: 21-25
Copies Required: Electronic
Computer Submission: Yes Email
Format: MS Word
Fees to Review: 0.00 US$

Manuscript Style:
    American Psychological Association

CIRCULATION DATA:

Reader: Academics, Industry Related
Frequency of Issue: Quarterly
Sponsor/Publisher: Cognizant
    Communication Corporation

REVIEW INFORMATION:

Type of Review: Blind Review
No. of External Reviewers: 3
No. of In House Reviewers: 0
Acceptance Rate: 11-20%
Time to Review: 2 - 3 Months
Reviewers Comments: Yes
Invited Articles: 0-5%
Fees to Publish: 0.00 US$

MANUSCRIPT TOPICS:

Advertising & Promotion Management; E-Commerce; Marketing Research; Small Business Entrepreneurship; Tourism, Hospitality & Leisure

MANUSCRIPT GUIDELINES/COMMENTS:

Aims and Scope

Tourism Review International is a peer-reviewed journal that advances excellence in all fields of tourism research, promotes high-level tourism knowledge, and nourishes cultural awareness in all sectors of the tourism industry by integrating industry and academic perspectives. Its international and interdisciplinary nature ensures that the needs of those interested in tourism are served by documenting industry practices, discussing tourism management and planning issues, providing a forum for primary research and critical examinations of previous research, and by chronicling changing tourism patterns and trends at the local, regional and global scale.

INFORMATION FOR CONTRIBUTORS

Submission

Article and Research Note manuscripts. Sent to Dr. Laura Jane Lawton, Editor-in-Chief, Tourism Review International, School of Hotel, Restaurant, & Tourism Management, College of Hospitality, Retail, & Sport Management, University of South Carolina, 701 Assembly Street, Carolina Coliseum, Columbia, SC 29208 USA. Tel: (803) 777-7111; Fax: (803) 777-1727; E-mail: **llawton@gwm.sc.edu**

Book Review manuscripts. Please submit to the appropriate Editor as listed on the inside cover page of this journal issue.

To expedite the review process, manuscripts (including all Figures and Tables) should be submitted by E-mail as an attached Word file. Alternatively, hard copies may be submitted in triplicate, accompanied by a copy on disk (e.g., Word 2002). All manuscripts must be typewritten on one side of the paper, double spaced (including references), and should be checked carefully prior to submission. All rights and permissions must be obtained by the contributor(s).

Format Requirements (in sequence)

Cover Page. This contains the title of the manuscript (50 words maximum), all author names and their corresponding affiliations as well as complete mailing address, telephone and fax number, and E-mail. The designated corresponding author must be identified by an asterisk (*).

Title Page. The second page consists of the manuscript title, abstract (maximum of 200 words that reflects an abbreviated representation of the content of the manuscript including purpose, method, main results, conclusions, and/or recommendations), and up to six key words for indexing purposes. To facilitate the double-blind review process (see 'Evaluation' below); no material that identifies the author(s) should be placed on this page.

Text. The text should consist of an Introduction, main body (including literature review, method, results, analysis, and discussion, as appropriate) and Conclusions. Text citations should adhere to the following examples: (Digance, 2003) or (Buckley, 2001, 2002; Sirakaya et al., 2001; Teo & Li, 2003) or (Butler, 1980, p.7) (for quoted material). Abbreviations should be fully spelled out in parentheses the first time that they are used in the text.

Acknowledgements. These will immediately follow the Conclusions.

Endnotes. A small number of Endnotes (e.g. no more than five) may follow the Acknowledgements. Do not use Footnotes – all important information should be incorporated in the text.

Quotations. Should be extracted and indented if they consist of forty words or more.

References should be placed at the end of the manuscript on a separate page, arranged in alphabetical order. Follow *APA* guidelines set forth in their *Publication Manual* (5th edition) for text and reference list citations, as per the following examples:

Journal article
Strange, C., & Kempa, M. (2003). Shades of dark tourism: Alcatraz and Robben Island. *Annals of Tourism Research*, 30(2), 386-405.

Book
Weaver, D. B., & Lawton, L. J. (2002). *Tourism management* (2nd ed.). Milton, QLD: John Wiley & Sons, Australia, Ltd.

Chapter in edited book
Var, T., & Ap, J. (1998). Tourism and world peace. In W. F. Theobald (Ed.), *Global tourism* (2nd ed., pp. 44-57). Oxford, UK: Butterworth Heinemann.

Please note that citations such as "personal communication" should be cited parenthetically in the text only. Do not include in the reference list.

Figures. All figures should be kept to a minimum and be prepared in a program that allows saving in .tif (preferred) or .eps format. Do not incorporate figures within the text of the manuscript. Black and white line art (i.e., bar graphs, etc.) should be prepared without color unless the figure is to be printed in color. (Note there is a charge for printing figures in color). Labeling and figure detail must be large enough to be legible after reduction to fit page parameters. Each figure must be cited in the text and legends for all illustrations should be included on a separate page. Do not incorporate figure legends as part of the figure and figure file. Place figure legend text at the end of the manuscript file following the reference section. Include figure (graphic) files as separate files on the final accepted manuscript disk. Photographs should be presented in a .tif file (no color unless they are to be printed in color). The desired position of each Figure in the text must be indicated by typing on a separate line the words "Figure 1 about here".

Tables follow the Figures and should be constructed to be intelligible without reference to the text. Include a title caption and headings for columns. Avoid very wide or very long tables that would not fit on one printed page. The same information should not be duplicated in other tables and figures. Place tables on separate pages at the end of the manuscript. Do not imbed tables within the text of the manuscript. The position of each Table in the text must be indicated by typing on a separate line the words "Table 1 about here".

Word length. Articles should be between 5,000 and 10,000 words, including all of the above sections. Book Reviews and Research Notes should be between 500 and 1,500 words.

Evaluation
Tourism Review International is a refereed journal. All manuscripts are subject to a double-blind process of peer review involving at least two independent referees.

Final Accepted Manuscript
The final version of the manuscript, including all figures and tables must be submitted electronically as an attached Word file to the Editor-in-Chief.

Biographical note
Manuscripts accepted for publication must include a biographical sketch (no more than 100 words) of each author, indicating their current position and affiliation, highest education attained (including institution and year), prior significant professional experience, and main research interests.

Copyright and Originality. All authors must sign a Transfer of Copyright agreement and return it to the Editor before their article can be published. This transfer agreement enables Cognizant Communication Corporation to protect the copyrighted material for the authors, but does not relinquish the author's proprietary rights. The copyright transfer covers the exclusive rights to reproduce and distribute the article, including reprints, photographic reproductions, microfilm, or any other reproductions of similar nature and translations, as well as the right to adapt the article for use in conjunction with computer systems and programs, and reproduction of publication in machine-readable form and incorporation in retrieval systems. Authors are responsible for obtaining from the copyright holder permission to reproduce any material for which copyright exists.

Page proofs and reprints. Page proofs will be sent to the designated corresponding author prior to publication. Minor changes only are allowed at this stage. A form for ordering reprints and additional copies of the journal issue in which the article appears will accompany the page proofs. A copy of the journal will be mailed to the Corresponding Author of each article, research note or book review after publication.

Although every effort is made by the publisher and editorial board to see that no inaccurate or misleading data, opinion, or statement appears in this Journal, they wish to make it clear that the data and opinions appearing in the articles and advertisements herein are the sole responsibility of the contributor or advertiser concerned. Accordingly, the publisher, the editorial board, editors, and their respective employees, officers, and agents accept no responsibility or liability whatsoever for the consequences of any such inaccurate or misleading data, opinion, or statement.

Tourism Today

ADDRESS FOR SUBMISSION:

Craig Webster, Editor-in-Chief
Tourism Today
College of Tourism & Hotel Management
Larnaka Ave, Aglangia
PO Box 20281
2150 Nicosia,
Cyprus
Phone: +357 22 462846
E-Mail: craig@cothm.ac.cy
Web: www.cothm.ac.cy

CIRCULATION DATA:

Reader: Academics
Frequency of Issue: Yearly
Sponsor/Publisher: College of Tourism and
   Hotel Management

PUBLICATION GUIDELINES:

Manuscript Length: 16-20
Copies Required: Three
Computer Submission: Yes Email
Format: MS Word
Fees to Review: 0.00 US$

Manuscript Style:
   See Manuscript Guidelines

REVIEW INFORMATION:

Type of Review: Blind Review
No. of External Reviewers: 2
No. of In House Reviewers: 0
Acceptance Rate: 80%
Time to Review: 2 - 3 Months
Reviewers Comments: Yes
Invited Articles: 6-10%
Fees to Publish: 0.00 US$

MANUSCRIPT TOPICS:
Tourism, Hospitality & Leisure

MANUSCRIPT GUIDELINES/COMMENTS:

Manuscript Submission Procedure
Manuscripts should be written as understandably and concisely as possible with clarity and meaningfulness. Submission of a manuscript to *Tourism Today* represents a certification on the part of the author(s) that it is an original work and has not been published elsewhere; manuscripts that are eventually published may not be reproduced for one year following publication in *Tourism Today*. Submit your paper, book reports and conference reports via e-mail to the Editor: **Craig@cothm.ac.cy**. Feedback regarding the submission will be returned to the author(s) within one or two months of the receipt of the manuscript. Submission of a manuscript will be held to imply that it contains original unpublished work not being considered for publication elsewhere at the same time. Each author will receive three complimentary copies of the issue. Contributors can correct first proofs, if time permits it.

Manuscript Length

Full papers should be between 2.500 and 4.000 words. Research notes or case studies should be up to 1,500 words. Commentaries should be up to 1,200 words. Book and conference reviews should be 1,000 words long.

Manuscript Style and Preparation

- All submissions (full papers, research notes, case studies, commentaries, and book or conference reviews) must have a title of no more than 14 words.
- Manuscripts should be double-line spaced, and have at least a one-inch margin on all four sides. Pages should be numbered consecutively.
- The use of footnotes within the text is discouraged – use endnotes instead. Endnotes should be kept to a minimum, be used to provide additional comments and discussion and should be numbered consecutively in the text and typed on a separate sheet of paper at the end of the article.
- Quotations must be taken accurately from the original source. Alterations to the quotations must be noted. Quotation marks (" ") are to be used to denote direct quotes. Inverted commas (' ') should denote a quote within a quotation.
- Include the name(s) of any sponsor(s) of the research contained in the manuscript.
- Tables, figures and illustrations are to be included in the text and to be numbered consecutively (in Arabic numbers) with the titles.
- Tables, figures and illustrations should be kept to a minimum.
- The text should be organized under appropriate section headings, which, ideally, should not be more than 500 words apart. Section headings should be marked as follows: primary headings should be typed in bold capitals and underlined; secondary headings should be typed with italic capital letters. Authors are urged to write as concisely as possible, but not at the expense of clarity.
- Author(s) are responsible for preparing manuscripts which are clearly written in acceptable, scholarly English, and which contain no errors of spelling, grammar, or punctuation. Neither the Editor nor the Publisher is responsible for correcting errors of spelling or grammar.
- Images should be supplied as files that can be opened and edited in Adobe Photoshop (bitmapped images) or Illustrator (vector images). Transparencies (up to 4 x 5") and photo prints (up to A3 size) are also acceptable.

Manuscript Presentation

For submission, manuscripts of full papers, research notes and case studies should be arranged in the following order of presentation:

- **First page**: title, subtitle (if required), author's name and surname, affiliation, full postal address, telephone and fax numbers, and e-mail address. Respective names, affiliations and addresses of co-authors should be clearly indicated. Also, include an abstract of not more than 150 words, acknowledgements (if any), and up to 6 keywords that identify article content.
- **Second page**: title, an abstract of not more than 150 words and up to 6 keywords that identify article content. Do not include the author(s) details and affiliation(s) in this page.
- **Subsequent pages**: main body of text (including tables, figures and illustrations); list of references; appendixes; and footnotes (numbered consecutively).

Reference Style
In the text, references should be cited with parentheses using the "author, date" style - for example (Ford, 2001; Jackson 1998, 2002). Page numbers for specific points or direct quotations must be given. The Reference list, placed at the end of the manuscript, must be typed in alphabetical order of authors. The specific format is:

- *For journals*: Tribe, J. (2002) The philosophic practitioner. *Annals of Tourism Research*, 29(2), 338-357.
- *For books and monographs*: Teare, R. and Ingram, H. (1993) *Strategic Management: A Resource-Based Approach for the Hospitality and Tourism Industries*. London, Cassell.
- *For chapters in edited books*: Sigala, M. and Christou, E. (2002) Use of Internet for enhancing tourism and hospitality education: lessons from Europe. In K.W. Wober, A.J. Frew and M. Hitz (Eds.) *Information and Communication Technologies in Tourism*, Wien: Springer-Verlag.
- *For reports*: Edelstein, L. G. & Benini, C. (1994) *Meetings and Conventions*. Meetings market report (August), 60-82.

Tourism, Culture & Communication

ADDRESS FOR SUBMISSION:

Brian King & Lindsay Turner, Co-Editors
Tourism, Culture & Communication
Victoria University
School of Hospitality, Tourism
  and Marketing
PO Box 14428 MC
Melbourne, Victoria, 8001
Australia
Phone: 613 9919 4430
E-Mail: brian.king@vu.edu.au
Web: www.cognizantcommunication.com

CIRCULATION DATA:

Reader: Academics
Frequency of Issue: 3 Times/Year
Sponsor/Publisher: Cognizant
  Communication Corporation

PUBLICATION GUIDELINES:

Manuscript Length: 5,000-8,000 Words
Copies Required: Three
Computer Submission: Yes Disk, Email
Format: MS Word
Fees to Review: 0.00 US$

Manuscript Style:
  American Psychological Association

REVIEW INFORMATION:

Type of Review: Blind Review
No. of External Reviewers: 2
No. of In House Reviewers: 1
Acceptance Rate: 21-30%
Time to Review: 2 - 3 Months
Reviewers Comments: Yes
Invited Articles: 6-10%
Fees to Publish: 0.00 US$

MANUSCRIPT TOPICS:

Advertising & Promotion Management; Communication; Direct Marketing; Marketing Research; Marketing Theory & Applications; Tourism, Hospitality & Leisure

MANUSCRIPT GUIDELINES/COMMENTS:

Aims and Scope

Tourism, Culture & Communication is international in its scope and will place no restrictions upon the range of cultural identities covered, other than the need to relate to tourism and hospitality. The journal seeks to provide interdisciplinary perspectives in areas of interest that may branch away from traditionally recognized national and indigenous cultures, for example, cultural attitudes toward the management of tourists with disabilities, gender aspects of tourism, sport tourism, or age-specific tourism.

The focus will be on high-quality research, and a double-blind referring process will be applied. *Tourism, Culture & Communication* will consist of main articles, major thematic reviews, position papers on theory and practice, and substantive case studies. A Reports section will provide coverage of specific initiatives and projects, of work in progress, and of major conferences and seminars.

Information for Contributors
Send manuscripts to: Brian King, address above; E-mail: **Brian.King@vu.edu.au**

Manuscript Submission. Manuscripts must be submitted in triplicate, including all figures and tables. They should be typewritten on one side of the paper, double spaced (including references), and should be checked carefully. All rights and permissions must be obtained by the contributor(s). These permissions should be sent upon acceptance of the manuscript for publication. Enclose a self-addressed envelope with the submitted manuscript.

Title. The title of the paper, all author names and corresponding affiliations, and name and complete mailing address for mailing proofs should be included on a separate page, because manuscripts are sent out for blind review. Include telephone and fax numbers and e-mail address (if applicable) for the designated corresponding author.

Abstract. Provide an abstract of up to 300 words. It should contain an abbreviated representation of the content of the manuscript. Major results, conclusions, and/or recommendations should be given, followed by supporting details of method, scope, or purpose as appropriate. Supply 3 to 5 keywords suitable for indexing.

References should be placed at the end of the manuscript on a separate page, arranged in alphabetical order. Follow APA guidelines set forth in their *Publication Manual* (4th edition) for text and reference list citations, per the examples.

Text citations
(Gunn, 1990) or (Fesenmaier et al., 1994; Mazanec, 1992, 1993; Uysal & Gitelson, 1994) or (Crompton, 1979, p. 411) (for quoted material).

Journal citation
Crouch, I. G. (1994). The study of international tourism demand: A review of findings. Journal of Travel Research, 33(1), 12-23.

Book citation
Witt, E. S., & Witt, C. A. (1992). Modeling and forecasting in tourism. London: Academic Press.

Chapter/pages in edited book
Frechtling, C. D. (1994). Assessing the impacts of travel and tourism: Measuring economic benefits. In J. R. Brent Ritchie & C. R. Goeldner (Eds.), Travel, tourism, and hospitality research (2nd ed., pp. 367-391). New York: John Wiley & Sons.

Please note that citations such as "personal communication" should be cited parenthetically in the text only. Do not include in the reference list. NOTE: Check carefully that all references listed are cited in the text, and that all text citations are included in the reference list.

Figures. All figures should be prepared in a program that allows saving in .tif or .eps format. (Do no incorporate figures within the text of the manuscript.) Black and white line art (i.e., bar graphs, etc.) should be prepared without color unless the figure is to be printed in color (note there is a charge for printing figures in color). Labeling and figure detail should be large enough to be legible after reduction to fit page parameters. Each figure must be cited in the text and legends for all illustrations should be included on a separate page. (Do not incorporate figure legends as part of the figure and figure file.) Place figure legend text at the end of the manuscript file. Include figure (graphic) files as separate files on the final disk.

Tables. Table material should not duplicate the text. Include each table on a separate page at the end of the manuscript or as separate files. Include a title for each table. (Do not incorporate tables within the text of the manuscript.)

Final Accepted Manuscripts. A final hard copy of the revised manuscript, including all table and figures, along with a disk containing all files (text, graphic, tables) should be mailed to the above address. (Make sure that the hard copy and disk file match exactly and contain the final version of the manuscript.) Label each figure in pencil on the back of the figure with author's name and figure number.

Computer Disks. Please observe the following criteria: 1) Specify what software was used, including which release (e.g., Word 97). 2) Specify what computer was used. 3) Include both program file and ASCII (plain text) file on the disk. 4) The file should be single spaced and should use the wrap-around end-of-line feature (i.e., no return at the end of the line). All textual elements should begin flush left, with no paragraph indents. Place two returns after every element, such as title, headings, paragraphs, etc. 5) Keep a backup file for reference and safety.

Page Proofs and Reprints. Page proofs will be sent to the designated corresponding contributor. A form for ordering offprints and copies of the journal issue in which the article appears will accompany the page proofs. Minor corrections only are allowed at proof stage.

Copyright. Publications are copyrighted for the protection of the authors and the publisher. A Transfer of Copyright Agreement will be sent to the author whose manuscript is accepted for publication. This form must be completed and returned to the Editor before the article can be published.

Although every effort is made by the publisher and editorial board to see that no inaccurate or misleading data, opinion, or statement appears in this journal, they wish to make it clear that the data and opinions appearing in the articles and advertisements herein are the sole responsibility of the contributor or advertiser concerned. Accordingly, the publisher, the editorial board, editors, and their respective employees, officers, and agents accept no responsibility or liability whatsoever for the consequences of any such inaccurate or misleading data, opinion, or statement.

Tourist Studies

ADDRESS FOR SUBMISSION:

Mike Crang & Adrian Franklin, Editors
Tourist Studies
University of Durham
Department of Geography
South Road
Durham, DH1 3LE
UK
Phone: +44 191 334 1899
E-Mail: m.a.crang@durham.ac.uk
Web: http://www.sagepub.co.uk/journal.
    aspx?pid=105798

PUBLICATION GUIDELINES:

Manuscript Length: 26-30
Copies Required: Five
Computer Submission: Yes Email
Format: MS Word
Fees to Review: 0.00 US$

Manuscript Style:
    See Manuscript Guidelines

CIRCULATION DATA:

Reader: Academics
Frequency of Issue: 3 Times/Year
Sponsor/Publisher: Sage Publications

REVIEW INFORMATION:

Type of Review: Blind Review
No. of External Reviewers: 3
No. of In House Reviewers: 1
Acceptance Rate: 21-30%
Time to Review: 4 - 6 Months
Reviewers Comments: Yes
Invited Articles: 6-10%
Fees to Publish: 0.00 US$

MANUSCRIPT TOPICS:
Office Administration/Management; Tourism, Hospitality & Leisure

MANUSCRIPT GUIDELINES/COMMENTS:

Description
Tourist Studies is a multi-disciplinary journal providing a platform for the development of critical perspectives on the nature of tourism as a social phenomenon. Theoretical and multi-disciplinary. *Tourist Studies* provides a critical social science approach to the study of the tourist and the structures which influence tourist behaviour and the production and reproduction of tourism. The journal examines the relationship between tourism and related fields of social inquiry. Tourism and tourist styles consumption are not only emblematic of many features of contemporary social change, such as mobility, restlessness, the search for authenticity and escape, but they are increasingly central to economic restructuring, globalization, the sociology of consumption and the aestheticization of everyday life. *Tourist Studies* analyzes these features of tourism from a multi-disciplinary perspective and seeks to evaluate, compare and integrate approaches to tourism from sociology, socio-psychology, leisure studies, cultural studies, geography and anthropology.

Global Perspective

Tourist Studies takes a global perspective of tourism, widening and challenging the established views of tourism presented in current periodical literature.

Tourist Studies includes: Theoretical analysis with a firm grounding in contemporary problems and issues in tourism studies, qualitative analyses of tourism and the tourist experience, reviews linking theory and policy, interviews with scholars at the forefront of their fields, review essays on particular fields or issues in the study of tourism, review of key texts, publications and visual media relating to tourism studies, and notes on conferences and other events of topical interest to the field of tourism studies

Manuscript Submission Guidelines

Submission of mss. Five identical copies of the manuscript, each fully numbered, labelled and typed in double spacing throughout, on one side only on white A4 or US standard size paper, plus a disk version of the article, should be sent to either:

Adrian Franklin, The School of Sociology and Social Work, University of Tasmania GPO Box 252-17, Hobart, Tasmania, Australia 7001. Email: **Adrian.Franklin@utas.edu.au**
or
Mike Crang, University of Durham, Department of Geography, Science Laboratories, South Road, Durham, DH1 3LE, UK. Email: **M.A.Crang@durham.ac.uk**

Covering letter. Please attach to every submission a letter confirming that all authors have agreed to the submission and that the article is not currently being considered for publication by any other journal.

Format of mss. Each manuscript should contain:

- Title page with full title and subtitle (if any). For the purposes of blind refereeing, full name of each author with current affiliation and full address/phone/fax/email details plus short biographical note should be supplied on a separate sheet. Owing to the broad range of subject matter, authors are asked to specify two or more subfields or areas of inquiry to which their paper pertains and are encouraged to include the names of one or more potential referees.
- abstract of 100-150 words
- up to 10 key words
- main text and word count -- suggested target is about 8000 words. Text to be clearly organized, with a clear hierarchy of headings and subheadings and quotations exceeding 40 words displayed, indented, in the text. Texts of a length greatly exceeding this will be considered as interest warrants and space permits.
- end notes, if necessary, should be signalled by superscript numbers in the main text and listed at the end of the text before the references
- references in both the text and end notes should follow Harvard style. References are cited in the text thus: (author, date: page)
- an alphabetical references section should follow the text (and end notes if any), using the Harvard system.

Tables. Tables should be typed (double line-spaced) on separate sheets and their position indicated by a marginal note in the text. All tables should have short descriptive captions with footnotes and their source(s) typed below the tables.

Illustrations. All line diagrams and photographs are termed 'Figures' and should be referred to as such in the manuscript. They should be numbered consecutively. Line diagrams should be presented in a form suitable for immediate reproduction (i.e. not requiring redrawing), each on a separate A4 sheet. They should be reproducible to a final printed text area of 115 mm x 185 mm. Illustrations on disk should be supplied as TIFF or EPS files at high resolution. Photographs should preferably be submitted as clear, glossy, unmounted black and white prints with a good range of contrast. Slides are also acceptable. All figures should have short descriptive captions typed on a separate sheet.

Authors are responsible for obtaining permissions from copyright holders for reproducing any illustrations, tables, figures or lengthy quotations previously published elsewhere. Permission letters must be supplied to Sage Publications.

Style. Use a clear readable style, avoiding jargon. If technical terms or acronyms must be included, define them when first used. Use non-racist, non-sexist language and plurals rather than he/she.

Spellings. UK or US spellings may be used with '-ize' spellings as given in the *Oxford English Dictionary* (e.g. organize, recognize).

Punctuation. se single quotation marks with double quotes inside single quotes. Present dates in the form 1 May 1998. Do not use points in abbreviations, contractions or acronyms (e.g. AD, USA, Dr, PhD)

Disks. On acceptance of your manuscript for publication, you will be asked to supply another diskette (IBM-compatible or Mac) of the final version.

Copyright. Before publication authors are requested to assign copyright to Sage Publications, subject to retaining their right to reuse the material in other publications written or edited by themselves and due to be published preferably at least one year after initial publication in the Journal.

Proofs and Offprints. Authors will receive proofs of their articles and be asked to send corrections to: Mike Crang, Department of Geography, Science Laboratories, South Road, Durham, DH1 3LE, UK within 2 weeks. They will receive a complimentary copy of the journal and 25 offprints of their article. Reviewers receive 5 offprints.

Reviews. *Tourist Studies* includes a section in which books and other significant contributions to the field are reviewed. This includes both essay length and shorter contributions.

Books for review and manuscripts of reviews should be sent to: Mike Crang, Department of Geography, Science Laboratories, South Road, Durham, DH1 3LE, UK

Transportation

ADDRESS FOR SUBMISSION:

David T. Hartgen, Editor
Transportation
University of North Carolina
Department of Geography & Earth Science
Charlotte, NC 28223
USA
Phone: 704-687-4308
E-Mail: dthartge@email.uncc.edu
Web: www.springeronline.com/journal/
11116

PUBLICATION GUIDELINES:

Manuscript Length: 25 Pages Maximum
Copies Required: Three
Computer Submission: Yes Disk, Email
Format: MS Word
Fees to Review: 0.00 US$

Manuscript Style:
See Manuscript Guidelines

CIRCULATION DATA:

Reader: Academics, Government,
Consulting
Frequency of Issue: Bi-Monthly
Sponsor/Publisher: Springer

REVIEW INFORMATION:

Type of Review: Editorial Review
No. of External Reviewers: 3
No. of In House Reviewers: 0-1
Acceptance Rate: 21-30%
Time to Review: 2 - 3 Months
Reviewers Comments: Yes
Invited Articles: 0-5%
Fees to Publish: 0.00 US$

MANUSCRIPT TOPICS:
Marketing Research; Operations Research/Statistics; Planning; Policy; Research; Transportation/Physical Distribution

MANUSCRIPT GUIDELINES/COMMENTS:

Editor-in-Chief
Martin G. Richards, Editor-in-Chief, The Old School House, Coldharbour, Dorking, Surrey RH5 6HF, UK. **martinrichards1@aol.com**

Editors
Kay Axhausen, ETH – Hönggerberg, CH - 8093 Zurich, Switzerland. **axhausen@ivt.baug. ethz.ch.**

David T. Hartgen, The University of North Carolina at Charlotte, Department of Geography and Earth Sciences, Charlotte, NC 28223, USA. **dthartge@mail.uncc.edu**

Ryuichi Kitamura, Department of Transportation Engineering, Faculty of Engineering, Kyoto University, Sakyo-ku, Kyoto 606-8501, Japan. **rkitamura@term.kuciv.kyoto-u.ac.jp**

Statement of Purpose

Although the transportation needs of cities and nations around the world may differ in key details, they have much in common. By sharing research findings and practical experiences, every city and every nation can benefit.

Transportation seeks to assist in that vital exchange of information, through the publication of carefully selected papers, which help to advance the international fund of knowledge.

Transportation focuses on issues of direct relevance to those concerned with the formulation of policy, the preparation and evaluation of plans, and the day-to-day operational management of transport systems. It is concerned not only with the policies and systems themselves, but also with their impacts on, and relationship with, other aspects of the social, economic and physical environment.

Transportation aims at being relevant to all parts of the world, industrialised, newly industrialised or developing. The journal has no modal bias, and is totally apolitical. Our mission is simply to help improve the transportation of people and goods through a better understand and appreciation of the key opportunities and constraints.

Papers published in *Transportation* are subjected to peer review in accordance with standard international practice for scholarly journals. They are only accepted for publication once the authors have adequately responded to advice given by the referees. Publication of a paper in *Transportation* therefore accords with the normal requirements of academic appointment and promotion panels.

Submission of Manuscripts

Papers for publication to *Transportation* should be submitted directly to a member of the Editorial Board. Any paper submitted should be accompanied by a statement that the paper has not been published or submitted for publication elsewhere in the current or any essentially similar form.

Although authors may submit papers to any Editor, the Editors prefer that authors from:

- North America submit their papers to David T Hartgen
- Asia and Australasia submit their papers to Ryuichi Kitamura
- Continental Europe to Kay Axhausen
- The UK, Africa and South America submit their papers to Martin Richards.

Contact Details

Authors must provide the full postal address, telephone and fax numbers and e-mail address for the corresponding author. All contact between the authors and both the Editors and the Publisher will be with the corresponding author, who is totally responsible for ensuring all his/her co-authors are kept fully informed.

Presentation and Preparation of the Manuscript

Manuscripts should be written in standard English and submitted in triplicate together with an electronic copy in Word format, either on a 3.5in disk or by e-mail to the appropriate Editor. The author should retain the original.

No page charges are applicable, but prospective authors should contain their papers to a total length of no more than 25 pages, including all figures, table etc, prepared in accordance with the guidance given below.

Particular attention should be given to consistency in the use of technical terms and abbreviations. Authors whose mother tongue is not English should have their manuscripts checked for the quality of the English before submission to the Journal. For those manuscripts that may require it, language editing is available through the Journal at charge to the author.

Manuscripts should be typed in Arial 11 point with standard double-spacing throughout on one side of DIN A4 (21 x 29 cm) or US letter paper (8.5 x 11 inch), with 2.5 cm wide (1 inch) margins. All papers (including the tables, figures, legends and references) should be numbered consecutively. The manuscript should be arranged in the order set out below:

Title page (page 1)
- The title should be brief but informative.
- A subtitle may be used to supplement and thereby shorten an excessively long main title.
- The name(s), affiliations and full address(es) must be provided for all authors, using "&" before the name of last author and indicating the corresponding author (see above).

Key words/Abstract/Abbreviations (page 2)
- Key words (a maximum of 6, in alphabetical order, suitable for indexing).
- Abstract (brief and informative, not to exceed 250 words).
- Abbreviations (arranged alphabetically; only those which are not familiar and/or commonly used).

Main text
- The relative importance of headings and subheadings should be clear.
- The approximate location of figures and tables should be indicated in the text.
- New paragraphs should be clearly indented.
- The use of footnotes should be avoided. However, if essential, they should be typed on the appropriate page, but clearly separated from the text with a line of space above them.

After the main text
- Acknowledgements (also grants, support etc., if any) should follow the text and precede the references.
- Notes (if any) should be numbered consecutively in the text with superscript numerals and listed in numerical order, after the Acknowledgements.

References
- The literature references should be arranged alphabetically, typed double-spaced, and in the text referred to as: author and year of publication, e.g., (Willson 2001; Redmond & Mokhtarian 2001; Lam et al. 2002).
- Citations of personal communications and unpublished data should be avoided, unless absolutely necessary. Such citations should, in text, appear only as: WD Smith, pers. comm., CS Andrew, unpubl., and not in the reference list.

References should follow the style shown below:
Periodicals
May, AD, Shepherd & SP, Timms, PM (2000) Optimum transport strategies for European cities. *Transportation* 27: 285-315.

Books (edited by someone other than the author of article)
Kitamura, R, Yamamoto,. & Fujii, S (1998), Impacts of the Hanshin-Awaji earthquake on traffic and travel. In: Cairns, S, Hass-Klau C & Goodwin PB (eds) *Traffic Impact of Highway Capacity Reductions: Assessment of the Evidence*. London: Landor.

Books (identical author and editor)
Louviere, JJ, Hensher, DA & Swait, JF (2000) *Stated Choice Methods and Analysis*. Cambridge: Cambridge University Press.

Tables
- Each table should be typed on a separate page and numbered with Arabic numerals 'as Table x', followed by the title.
- Horizontal rules should be indicated and vertical rules avoided. Table-footnotes should be marked with superscript letters.
- Each table must be mentioned in the text and its location indicated in the margin.
- Tables may be edited by the publisher to permit more compact typesetting.

Figures
- Each figure should be mentioned in the text numbered with Arabic numerals as 'Fig. x'.
- Line drawings should be in a form suitable for reproduction without modification. Extremely small type should be avoided as figures are often reduced in size.
- Photographs should be supplied as black-and-white, high contrast glossy prints. Colour plates may be inserted at the author's own expense.
- Where multi-part figures are used, each part should be clearly identified in the legend, preferably with (lower case) letters.
- Figures to be placed landscape should be avoided if possible.
- Identify each illustration, on the back, by lightly writing author's name and figure number, also indicate the top of each figure.
- Figure legends should be typed on the appropriate page after References.

Notes on Contributors
Authors should include a brief summary of their professional background; this will be published in the same issue of the Journal as their paper. The summary should no longer than 50 words, counting an abbreviation as a word.

Abbreviations and Units
Only SI units and abbreviations should be used. Abbreviations should be explained when they first appear in the text. If a non-standard abbreviation is to be used extensively, it should be defined in full on page 2 as mentioned above. Whenever in doubt use SI (Système International d'Unités).

Monetary values should be expressed in the local currency and US$s.

Proofs and Offprints

The author will be sent an offprint order form and 2 proofs for proofreading. One set of corrected proofs together with the manuscript should be returned to the Publisher within 3 days of receipt of the material. 50 offprints will be supplied free of charge.

Transportation Journal

ADDRESS FOR SUBMISSION:

John C. Spychalski, Editor
Transportation Journal
The Pennsylvania State University
College of Business Administration
413 Business Building
University Park, PA 16802
USA
Phone: 814-865-2872
E-Mail: jcs2@psu.edu
Web: www.astl.org

CIRCULATION DATA:

Reader: Academics, Business Persons,
  Government
Frequency of Issue: Quarterly
Sponsor/Publisher: American Society of
  Transportation and Logistics (ASTL)

PUBLICATION GUIDELINES:

Manuscript Length: 16-20
Copies Required: Four + Disk
Computer Submission: No
Format: N/A
Fees to Review: 0.00 US$

Manuscript Style:
  Chicago Manual of Style, Current
  Edition

REVIEW INFORMATION:

Type of Review: Blind Review
No. of External Reviewers: 3
No. of In House Reviewers: 0
Acceptance Rate: 15%
Time to Review: 2 - 3 Months
Reviewers Comments: Yes
Invited Articles: 0%
Fees to Publish: 0.00 US$

MANUSCRIPT TOPICS:

Business Information Systems (MIS); Purchasing/Materials Management; Strategic Management Policy; Technology/Innovation; Transportation/Physical Distribution

MANUSCRIPT GUIDELINES/COMMENTS:

Topics Include. Transportation/Logistics/Supply Chain Mgmt-Related; Transportation Policy & Planning; Transportation/Logistics Supply Chain Research & Education Methods.

The *Journal* is published quarterly by the AST&L, to disseminate research findings and original writings on transportation, logistics, and related fields. Manuscripts are sought from educators, professionals working in the field, and government officials. The editorial review board strives to balance the *Journal*, to keep it practical for business people who need usable information in a forthright format, yet scholarly enough to stimulate educators.

In addition, there is a book review section which provides information on recently published professional reading material in the field. Each Winter Issue contains an index of all articles published in the preceding year.

The *Transportation Journal* articles cover such areas as Logistics/Physical Distribution/ Supply Chain Management; Management Information Systems & Computer Applications in Transport and Logistics; Motor, Rail, Water, Air, & Pipeline Transport; Intermodal Transport; International Transport; Transport Security; Regulation/Law, Transport Management Policies, Practices, and Performance; Transport Costing, Pricing, and Finance; and Transport Policy.

Manuscript Guidelines

1. Articles should broaden and deepen the body of theoretical and/or empirical knowledge in logistics, supply chain management and transportation.

2. Submission

Send manuscripts—4 printed copies, 1 digital copy—to: Dr. John C. Spychalski, 413 Business Building, University Park, PA 16802. An explanatory letter of transmittal should accompany the manuscript. The title page should indicate each author's academic rank or professional title and employer affiliation, including location. The first page of the text should contain the title of the article but not the author's name. Papers submitted to the *Journal* must be neither previously published nor submitted elsewhere for review simultaneously.

3. Format

Manuscripts should be typewritten and double spaced on one side only of medium-weight opaque bond paper. Margins should be at least one inch on all sides and pages should be numbered consecutively.

4. Endnotes

Endnotes are used to elaborate on information presented in the article text. If endnotes are used, they must be numbered consecutively in the text throughout the article and must be indicated by superscript numerals following the punctuation. All endnote entries must be double-spaced at the end of the article and must appear before references (see #5 below).

5. References

References citing source materials must be listed at the end of the article and must include, in order, the following information: author (last name first for lead author, first name first for other authors), year of publication (in parenthesis), title, name of journal, volume number, issue number, and inclusive page numbers. Entries for book references must include, in order, author (last name first for lead author, first name first for other authors), year of publication (in parenthesis), title, city of publication, and publisher.

Reference citations in the text of the article must be enclosed in parenthesis, as follows: (Author, year if more than one publication by the same author is listed at the end of the article, and specific page numbers cited).

Web-based citations must be in the form specified in the University of Chicago's *A Manual of Style,* current edition.

6. Numbers and Tabular Material

Arabic numerals should be used for quantities for 11 or greater and for percentages. The word "percent" should be used in text material (e.g., 15 percent). Figures should be numbered consecutively in Arabic numerals. Figures should be originals and professionally drawn (i.e., camera-ready) for direct reproduction by the *Journal's* printer.

7. Other Sources of Style Information

See the University of Chicago's *A Manual of Style,* current edition.

Transportation Research Part E: Logistics and Transportation Review

ADDRESS FOR SUBMISSION:

W. K. Talley, Editor-in-Chief
Transportation Research Part E: Logistics
   and Transportation Review
Old Dominion University
College of Business & Public Admin.
Department of Economics
Norfolk, VA 23529-0221
USA
Phone: 757-683-3534
E-Mail: wktalley@odu.edu
Web: www.elsevier.com

PUBLICATION GUIDELINES:

Manuscript Length: No Restriction
Copies Required: Three or 1 Electronic
Computer Submission: Yes
Format: PC Compatible
Fees to Review: 0.00 US$

Manuscript Style:
   Uniform System of Citation (Harvard
   Blue Book)

CIRCULATION DATA:

Reader: Academics, Business Persons
Frequency of Issue: 6 Times/Year
Sponsor/Publisher: Elsevier Inc.

REVIEW INFORMATION:

Type of Review: Blind Review
No. of External Reviewers: 2
No. of In House Reviewers: No Reply
Acceptance Rate: 30%
Time to Review: 3-4 Months
Reviewers Comments: Yes
Invited Articles: 6-10%
Fees to Publish: 0.00 US$

MANUSCRIPT TOPICS:

Operations   Research/Statistics;   Production/Operations;   Technology/Innovation;
Transportation/Physical Distribution

MANUSCRIPT GUIDELINES/COMMENTS:

Description

Transportation Research Part E: The Logistics and Transportation Review publishes informative articles drawn from across the spectrum of logistics and transportation research. Subjects include, but are not limited to:

- Transport economics including cost and production functions, capacity, demand, pricing, externalities, modal studies
- Transport infrastructure and investment appraisal
- Evaluation of public policies
- Empirical studies of management practices and performance
- Logistics and operations models, especially with application
- Logistics and supply-chain management topics

Guide for Authors

Manuscripts should be submitted in quadruplicate to the Editor-in-Chief. They should be accompanied by a covering letter mentioning the title of the paper and the name of the corresponding author, together with mailing address, telephone and fax numbers and if available e-mail address.

Electronic Manuscripts

Authors are encouraged to submit a computer disk (5.25" or 3.5" HD/DD disk) containing the *final* version of the paper along with the *final* manuscript to the editorial office. Please observe the following criteria: (1) Send only hard copy when first submitting your paper. (2) When your paper has been refereed, revised if necessary and accepted, send a disk containing the final version with the final hard copy. Make sure that the disk and the hard copy match exactly. (3) Specify what software was used, including which release (e.g. WordPerfect 6.0) (4) Specify what computer was used (either IBM-compatible PC or Apple Macintosh). (5) Text, tables and illustrations (if available on disk) should be supplied as separate files. (6) The files should follow the general instructions on style/arrangement and, in particular, the reference style of this journal as given below. (7) The file should be single-spaced and should use the wrap-around end-of-line feature (i.e. no returns at the end of each line). All textual elements should begin flush left, no paragraph indents. Place two returns after every element such as title, headings, paragraphs, figure and table call-outs. (8) Keep a back-up disk for reference and safety.

Style of Manuscript

All sections of the manuscript (abstract, text, references) should be double-spaced, using a single typeface and style. Use underlining only for definitions and subsections; do not underline for emphasis. Footnotes should be limited in number and size, and should not contain mathematical expressions.

The abstract should describe in straightforward language the contents of the paper, but not its motivation. It should explain briefly the procedures and the results, and must not contain abbreviations and acronyms.

Figures are photo-reproduced and authors will be required to furnish camera-ready artwork or glossy prints. Each figure should be placed on a separate sheet of paper, and should be typed on a separate page at the end of the manuscript.

Tables and their captions should be typed on separate sheets, numbered consecutively and indicated in the text at their approximate position.

Equations should be clearly displayed, with any unusual symbols (including Greek letters) identified in the margin.

Equation numbers should be placed in the right margin and numbered continuously, not by section.

The Harvard system of references is used. In the body of the text, a paper is referred to by the author's surname, with the year of publication in parentheses, and at the end of the paper complete references are given alphabetically by author's surnames; journal titles should not be abbreviated, e.g.

Kanafani, A. and Abbas, M.S. (1987) Local air service and economic impact of small airports. *Journal of Transportation Engineering* 113, 42-55.

Button, K.J. (1982) *Transport Economics.* Heinemann, London.

Nash, C.A. (1988) Integration of public transport: an economic assessment. In *Bus Deregulation and Privatisation: An International Perspective,* eds J.S. Dodgson and N. Topham, pp. 17-46 Wiley, New York.

Jones, M. (1995) Cost considerations in research funding. Report of the SERC Working Group, London.

Proofs
Before publication an authors' proof will be sent to the corresponding author at the address shown on the Editor-in-Chief's covering letter. It is important that authors read the proof very carefully and answer all queries on the page proofs and return the proof to the publisher within a short time (usually 48 hours). Except for typographical errors, changes should be kept to a minimum and rewriting the text is not permitted. Authors may be charged for changes other than the correction of typographical errors. Authors are urged to check their proof carefully, since late corrections cannot be accepted. Reprints Along with page proofs, the corresponding author will receive a form for ordering reprints and full copies of the issue in which the paper appears. Twenty-five free reprints are provided; orders for additional reprints must be received before printing in order to qualify for lower prepublication rates. All co-author reprint requirements should be included on the reprint order form.

Copyright

Transportation Science

ADDRESS FOR SUBMISSION:

Hani Mahmassani, Editor-in-Chief
Transportation Science
  ELECTRONIC SUBMISSION ONLY
University of Maryland
Maryland Transportation Initiative
College Park, MD 20742-3021
USA
Phone: 301-405-0752
E-Mail: masmah@umd.edu
Web: http://transci.pubs.informs.org/

CIRCULATION DATA:

Reader: Academics
Frequency of Issue: Quarterly
Sponsor/Publisher: INFORMS / Cadmus

PUBLICATION GUIDELINES:

Manuscript Length: 15-30
Copies Required: Online Submission Only
Computer Submission: Yes Online
Format: See Guidelines
Fees to Review: 0.00 US$

Manuscript Style:
  See Manuscript Guidelines

REVIEW INFORMATION:

Type of Review: Peer Review
No. of External Reviewers: 3
No. of In House Reviewers: 2
Acceptance Rate: 11-20%
Time to Review: 4 - 6 Months
Reviewers Comments: Yes
Invited Articles: 0-5%
Fees to Publish: 0.00 US$

MANUSCRIPT TOPICS:
Logistics; Operations Management & Research; Transportation/Physical Distribution

MANUSCRIPT GUIDELINES/COMMENTS:

Editorial Policy
Transportation Science publishes original contributions and surveys on phenomena associated with all modes of transportation, present and prospective, including mainly such aspects as planning, design, economic, operational, and social. Excluded are physical design aspects of such items as vehicles, highway pavements, railroads, roadbeds, or other components. Contributions in related areas such as location may be of interest as long as their relevance to demonstration is clearly demonstrated (e.g., papers on the location of bus depots, or airline hubs, etc.). Studies that advance the analytical, experimental, and observational tools for the study of transportation problems are also welcome, as are critical review articles dealing with the status and direction of the above subjects. Of particular interest is scientific work on transportation processes that contribute to the understanding of the characteristics and behavior of transportation systems. Book reviews within the scope of the journal are also published.

All papers submitted for publication are refereed and accepted solely on the basis of quality and importance. The contribution of each paper should be clearly stated in the introduction. Decisions regarding the publication of the paper are based on the value of the contribution to the field of transportation science. Criteria such as relationship with existing literature, length, and style are taken into account. A clear indication on the suitability of a manuscript is usually provided after the first round of refereeing. As a rule, manuscripts can undergo only one major revision.

Instructions to Authors
Manuscripts for publication should be submitted online through the manuscript central website, at: **http://mc.manuscriptcentral.com/transci**. Submission of a manuscript is a representation that the paper has been neither published nor submitted for publication elsewhere, and that, if the work is officially sponsored, it has been released for open publication.

Manuscripts must be double-spaced throughout with the original in typewritten or equally legible form. They should contain no footnotes. Figures are required in a form suitable for photographic reproduction. Any one of a number of forms will be acceptable, e.g., laser printer drawing, original black ink drawings, or high-quality glossy prints. Lettering should be uniform in size and style and sufficiently large to be legible after reduction. Figures should be designated by Arabic numbers and referred to in the text by number. Figure legends should be collectively provided on a separate sheet rather than placed on the figures themselves. Tables may be typed on sheets separated from the text. Each table should have a caption that makes the table entries clearly independent of the text; complicated column headings should be avoided. All tables should be numbered and referred to in the text by number.

In mathematical expressions, authors are requested in general to minimize unusual or expensive typographical requirements; for example: authors are requested to use the solidus wherever possible in preference to built-up fractions, to write complicated exponentials in the form exp() and to avoid subscripts and superscripts on subscripts or superscripts. Subscripts and superscripts should be shown large and clear, Greek letters and unusual symbols should be labeled on first occurrence, as should subscript "zero", to distinguish it from the letter "oh". Whether each letter is capital or lower case should be unambiguous. Equation numbers must be at the right.

Each paper must be accompanied by an abstract of about 100 to 200 words. The abstract should be adequate as an index and should summarize the principal results and conclusions. The first section of the article should not be numbered. References to related previous work should be reasonably complete, and grouped at the end of the paper. References in the text should be cited by the author's surname and the year of publication, e.g., (Jansson, 1980), (Marguier and Ceder, 1984). The following format should be used for references.

Article in a Journal
W.B. Powell and I.A. Koskosidis, "Shipment Routing Algorithms with Tree Constraints", *Transportation Science* 26, 230-245 (1992).

Chapter in a Book
H.N. Pasaraftis, "Dynamic Vehicle Routing Problems," in *Vehicle Routing: Methods and Studies*, B.L. Golden and A.A. Assad (eds), 223i-248, North-Holland, Amsterdam, 1988.

Working Paper
B. Gavish and S.C. Graves, "Scheduling and Routing in Transportation and Distribution Systems: Formulations and New Relaxations", Working Paper 8202, Graduate School of Management, University of Rochester, Rochester, NY, 1981.

Book
I. Prigogine and R. Herman, *Kinetic Theory of Vehicular Traffic*, Elsevier, New York (1971).

Dissertation
P. Jaillet, Probabilistic Traveling Salesman Problems, Ph.D. thesis, Massachusetts Institute of Technology, Cambridge, MA (1985)

Presentation at a Conference
K. Ashok and M. Ben-Akiva, "Estimation and Prediction of Time-Dependent Origin-Destination Flows with a Stochastic Mapping to Path Flows and Link Flows," presented at Optimization Days, Montreal, May 1996.

Authors are responsible for revising their proofs, and should limit alterations to the strict minimum. The editorial management of INFORMS reserves the right to accept only those changes that affect the accuracy of the text.

Western Journal of Communication

ADDRESS FOR SUBMISSION:

A. Cheree Carlson, Editor
Western Journal of Communication
Arizona State University
HDSHC
Tempe, AZ 85287-1205
USA
Phone: 480-965-5147
E-Mail: western.journal@asu.edu
Web:

CIRCULATION DATA:

Reader: Academics
Frequency of Issue: Quarterly
Sponsor/Publisher: Professional Association

PUBLICATION GUIDELINES:

Manuscript Length: 20-30
Copies Required: Four
Computer Submission: No
Format: N/A
Fees to Review: 0.00 US$

Manuscript Style:
    American Psychological Association, or
    MLA Style Manual

REVIEW INFORMATION:

Type of Review: Blind Review
No. of External Reviewers: 2
No. of In House Reviewers: 2
Acceptance Rate: 20%
Time to Review: 3 Months
Reviewers Comments: Yes
Invited Articles: 0-5%
Fees to Publish: 0.00 US$

MANUSCRIPT TOPICS:
Communication; Organizational Behavior & Theory

MANUSCRIPT GUIDELINES/COMMENTS:

Topics Include. International/Intercultural Communication; Interpersonal/Human Communication; Persuasion & Nonverbal Communication; Rhetorical & Applied Communication

The *Western Journal of Communication* publishes original scholarship that advances our understanding of human communication. Research from diverse theoretical and methodological perspectives is encouraged. That diversity is reflected in *WJC's* history of publishing scholarship in rhetorical and communication theory, interpersonal communication, media studies, philosophy of communication, cultural and critical theory, health communication, freedom of speech, gender and communication, performance studies, and applied communication. Research accessible to both scholarly audiences and the learned public is encouraged.

Research involving the use of human subjects must be approved by an institutional review board to be published in *WJC*.

Authors should submit four copies of each manuscript, double-spaced and using 12 characters per inch. Attach a separate title page that indicates:

1. Manuscript title
2. The full name and title of each author
3. Each contributor's address, telephone number, e-mail address, and fax number, and
4. The history of the manuscript, where appropriate.

Manuscripts must conform to either the *MLA Style Manual*, 6th Edition or the *Publication Manual of the American Psychological Association*, 5th Edition.

WJC follows a policy of blind, peer review. Each manuscript is typically read by three reviewers with expertise in the study's subject matter, methodology, and theoretical perspective. Manuscripts must not be under consideration by any other publication. Manuscripts will not be returned to authors. Send submissions to the Editor.

World Transport Policy & Practice

ADDRESS FOR SUBMISSION:

John Whitelegg, Editor-in-Chief
World Transport Policy & Practice
53 Derwent Road
Lancaster, LA1 3ES
UK
Phone: +44 1524 63175
E-Mail: john.whitelegg@phonecoop.coop
Web: www.eco-logica.co.uk/wtpp

CIRCULATION DATA:

Reader: Academics, Practitioners
Frequency of Issue: Quarterly
Sponsor/Publisher: Eco-Logica Ltd

PUBLICATION GUIDELINES:

Manuscript Length: 11-15
Copies Required: Two
Computer Submission: Yes
Format: Any
Fees to Review: 0.00 US$

Manuscript Style:
   See Manuscript Guidelines

REVIEW INFORMATION:

Type of Review: Blind Review
No. of External Reviewers: 1
No. of In House Reviewers: 1
Acceptance Rate: 21-30%
Time to Review: 1 - 2 Months
Reviewers Comments: Yes
Invited Articles: 21-30%
Fees to Publish: 0.00 US$

MANUSCRIPT TOPICS:
Global Business; Strategic Management Policy; Technology/Innovation; Transportation/Physical Distribution

MANUSCRIPT GUIDELINES/COMMENTS:

Topics Include. Design of Cities & Rural Areas; Development of Ideas of Sustainability; Global Business; International Links; Links Improving Health, Economy, & Environment; Passenger & Freight Transportation; Transport Corridors

Description
The journal provides a high-quality medium for the development and international dissemination of original and creative ideas in world transport. International experts in transport, the environment, economics and ecology contribute probing papers dealing in an informed and even-handed manner with key issues in transport, case studies and reports of trials, and assess the difficulties of balancing social, economic and ecological considerations as we strive to develop a better transport system in all respects. "Increasing the comfort zone for hesitant administrators and politicians, pioneering new concepts for activists, community groups, entrepreneurs and business, and through our joint efforts, energy and personal choices, placing them and ourselves firmly on the path to a more sustainable and more just society."

Articles

Contributions are welcome. Whether you are a novice author or an experienced one, the Editor would like to invite you to consider sharing your thoughts and experiences with others like yourself. We can promise a considered and constructive review of your article and, for contributions deemed suitable, publication in the journal.

Please read through the **Contributor Guidelines** section of Web site for further background and details, and if you find that to your liking feel free to contact John Whitelegg, the Editor, who will be pleased to offer comments on drafts, work in progress, or ideas which you believe could be made into an article.

Also, if you have ideas or proposals for articles or topics, we will be pleased to hear from you.

Book and Report Reviews

We welcome reviews of current books of interest to our readers, and of official reports and documents that might benefit from open discussion by qualified international professionals. Contact us first with a short note outlining your intended contribution, so that we can agree on format and length in advance, thus sparing you time and trouble in getting your good materials into print.

Special and Joint Editions

The concept of working closely with other groups and events to develop focused special editions is one that has been important in the past when the journal was a paper product, but in its new electronic life is one to which we are giving far more emphasis.

Guidelines for Contributors

Contributions to *World Transport Policy & Practice* are welcome. Whether you are a novice author or an experienced one, the Editor would like to invite you to consider sharing your thoughts and experiences with others like yourself. We can promise a considered and constructive review of your article and, for contributions deemed suitable, publication in *World Transport Policy & Practice*. Please read through the following guidelines and feel free to contact the Editor, who will be pleased to offer comments on drafts, work in progress, or ideas which you believe could be made into an article.

Editorial Objectives

The journal aims to provide validated information about the latest developments in transport policy to enable local authorities, governments, consultancies, NGOs and supra national organisations to speed up their policy development and implement new ideas from around the world. It aims to:

- Cover all passenger and freight transport
- Deal with global as well as local issues
- Include the development of the ideas of sustainability, the design of cities and rural areas, transport corridors and international links to improve health, the economy and the environment.

Article Composition

Articles should normally be between 2,000 and 4,000 words. Shorter articles can be published as "Comment" pieces. Responses to papers which have appeared in the journal, either as letters to the Editor or as response articles, will be welcomed. Submitting articles by e-mail attachment or on paper with a disk

By Email. Articles for publication may be submitted by e-mail attachment to **john. whitelegg@phonecoop.coop**. It is useful if authors indicate what software is required to read any attachments and if they include the letter combination 'zq' in the title. Please DO NOT name articles 'whitelegg', 'wtpp' or variations of these. Authors are advised that they may need to provide a version on paper and/or on 3.5" disk prepared on a Macintosh or PC system.

On Paper. Articles should be typescript and double-spaced with wide margins. Please send two copies. Manuscripts will not normally be returned, so you should ensure you retain a copy. Please supply the article on paper of no less than 80 gsm weight with high-quality print. This will enable electronic scanning if needed. Please supply the same version of the article on a 3.5" disk prepared on a Macintosh or PC system in ASCII format. Mark the disk clearly with your name, the article title and the software you have used. Where there is ambiguity, the disk version will normally be considered definitive.

Presentation

Headings and subheadings should be used at approximately 500-750 word intervals. Please ensure that headings and subheadings are clearly identified.

Charts, Diagrams and Figures. These should be called "Figures" and numbered consecutively (e.g. Figure 1, Figure 2, etc.). Please make sure they are clear and can be reproduced easily. In addition, please provide the raw data so that we can redraw them, if necessary. Indicate where in the text they should appear "(Figure 1 about here)". Each figure should have a brief title (e.g. "Figure 1. Schematic of the Programme").

Tables should be numbered consecutively, independently of figures. Indicate in the text where they should appear. Give them a brief title. Please ensure that they are clear and legible. Authors should not use many tabs or spaces between columns of data—normally, one tab is sufficient.

Maps are especially welcome. They should be numbered consecutively, independently of figures and tables and their location in the text should be indicated. Please ensure that they are clear, uncluttered and legible. They should have a title.

Measurements. SI units should be used throughout.

Abstracts and Keywords

- Write an abstract of 75 words or so which summarises the main points of the article. It should be sufficient for a reader to decide whether they want to read the whole article.
- Please also note up to six keywords or descriptors which describe the content of the article. These would include geographical area, if specific, industry, functions, managerial activity and process.

References

- Authors should keep references to a minimum, ideally no more that ten to fifteen.
- References should be confined to essential items only and those that are necessary to establish key steps in an argument or key areas of support for a particular proposition.
- Reference citations within the text should be by the author's last name, followed by a comma and year of publication enclosed in parentheses.
- A reference list should follow the article, with references listed in alphabetical order in the following form:
- Books: Surname, Initials, (Year of Publication), Title, Publisher, Place of Publication.
- Articles: Surname, Initials, (Year of Publication), "Title", Journal, Volume, Number, Pages.

Originality. The author should indicate if a paper has been presented elsewhere. If the author does not do so, the Editor will assume that the paper is an original contribution. Papers appearing in *World Transport Policy & Practice* should not be published elsewhere without the written consent of the Publisher of the journal.

Copyright. Authors submitting articles for publication must warrant that the work is not an infringement of any existing copyright. Papers and contributions published become the legal copyright of the publisher, unless otherwise agreed.

Written Communication

ADDRESS FOR SUBMISSION:

Christina Haas, Editor
Written Communication
Kent State University
Department of English
PO Box 5190
Kent, OH 44242
USA
Phone: 330-672-4512
E-Mail: chaas@kent.edu
  oazeri@kent.edu
Web: www.sagepub.com

CIRCULATION DATA:

Reader: Academics
Frequency of Issue: Quarterly
Sponsor/Publisher: Sage Publications

PUBLICATION GUIDELINES:

Manuscript Length: Less than 9,000 Wds
Copies Required: Four
Computer Submission: Yes If Accepted
Format: Latest Version MS Word
Fees to Review: 0.00 US$

Manuscript Style:
    American Psychological Association

REVIEW INFORMATION:

Type of Review: Blind Review
No. of External Reviewers: 2
No. of In House Reviewers: 1
Acceptance Rate: 6-10%
Time to Review: 2-4 Months
Reviewers Comments: Yes
Invited Articles: 0-5%
Fees to Publish: 0.00 US$

MANUSCRIPT TOPICS:
Anthropology; Communication; History; Journalism; Linguistics; Mass Communication; Psychology; Rhetoric; Sociology; Technical Communication; Writing

MANUSCRIPT GUIDELINES/COMMENTS:

Aims and Scope
Written Communication is an international multidisciplinary journal that publishes theory and research in writing from fields including anthropology, English, education, history, journalism, linguistics, psychology, and rhetoric. Among topics of interest are the nature of writing ability; the assessment of writing; the impact of technology on writing (and the impact of writing on technology); the social and political consequences of writing and writing instruction; nonacademic writing; literacy (including workplace and emergent literacy and the effects of classroom processes on literacy development); the social construction of knowledge; the nature of writing in disciplinary and professional domains; cognition and composing; the structure of written text and written communication; relationships among gender, race, class and writing; and connections among writing, reading, speaking, and listening. Also of interest are review essays and reviews of research on topics important to writing researchers. No worthy topic related to writing is beyond the scope of the journal.

Theoretical and applied contributions of articles in *Written Communication* are made explicit and will be relevant to teachers and researchers from a range of scholarly disciplines. Published articles will collectively represent a wide range of methodologies, but the methodology of each study must be handled expertly.

Manuscript Submission Guidelines

Editorial Policy Statement. *Written Communication* is an international multidisciplinary journal that publishes theory and research in writing from fields including anthropology, English, history, journalism, linguistics, psychology, and rhetoric. Among topics of interest are the nature of writing ability; the assessment of writing; the impact of technology on writing (and the impact of writing on technology); the social and political consequences of writing and writing instruction; nonacademic writing; literacy (including workplace and emergent literacy and the effects of classroom processes on literacy development); the social construction of knowledge; the nature of writing in disciplinary and professional domains; cognition and composing; the structure of written text and written communication; relationships among gender, race, class and writing; and connections among writing, reading, speaking, and listening. Also of interest are review essays and reviews of research on topics important to writing researchers. No worthy topic related to writing is beyond the scope of the journal. Published articles will collectively represent a wide range of methodologies, but the methodology of each study must be handled expertly.

Guidelines for Submission. Prospective authors are strongly urged to acquaint themselves with previously published issues of the journal, particularly the Editor's Comments in Volume 11, Number 1 (January 1994). Submitting an essay indicates that the work reported has not been previously published, that the essay--in present or revised form--is not being considered for publication in other journals or in edited volumes, and that the author(s) will not allow the essay to be so considered before notification in writing of an editorial decision by Written Communication. Submission should generally not exceed 9,000 words and must follow the American Psychological Association's (5th edition) guidelines for publication. All authors should (a) include with each copy an abstract of 100-150 words; (b) select five to seven keywords (which do not appear in the title) to facilitate electronic search; (c) provide a cover page which includes the title of the submission, author names(s), institutional affiliations(s), mailing address(es), and three to four-sentence biographical statements for each author. Author name(s) should not appear anywhere else in the manuscript. Note that the entire manuscript should be single-sided and double-spaced, including the abstract, block quotations, tables, figures, notes and references. *Written Communication* does not normally return submitted manuscripts to authors. Domestic submissions: Send four copies to Editor, Written Communication, in care of Kent State University, Department of English, P.O. Box 5190, Kent, OH 44242. An electronic version is needed only if and when the manuscript is accepted for publication. Faxed manuscripts will not be accepted. International submissions only: Mail one copy of the manuscript to the above address by airmail. Send an electronic version as an attachment by email. Written Communication: Tel: (330) 672-4512. Fax: (330) 672-3152. E-mail: **chaas@kent.edu** or **oazeri@kent.edu**

Journal Name	Type Review	No. Ext. Rev.	Accept. Rate	Page
Advertising & Promotion Management				
Academy of Business Journal	Blind	2	6-10%	1
Academy of Marketing Science Review	Blind	3	6-10%	4
Academy of Marketing Studies Journal	Blind	3	21-30%	11
Agribusiness: An International Journal	Blind	2	11-20%	17
American International College Journal of Business	Editorial	0	90%	25
American Journal of Business and Economics	Blind	2	21-30%	26
Annals of Tourism Research: A Social Sciences Journal	Blind	3+	11-20%	32
Annual Advances in Business Cases	Blind	3	30%	36
Asia Pacific Journal of Marketing and Logistics	Blind		11-20%	49
Asia Pacific Journal of Tourism Research	Blind	2	31-40%	51
Australasian Leisure Management	Editorial	1	21-30%	53
Business Case Journal	Blind	3	11-20%	60
California Business Review		2		63
California Journal of Business Research	Blind	2	25%	66
CASE Journal (The)	Blind	2	21-30%	72
Case Research Journal	Blind	3	11-20%	74
Cornell Hotel and Restaurant Administration Quarterly	Blind	3	11-20%	86
Decision Sciences	Blind	3	11-20%	91
ESIC Market	Blind	2	21-30%	105
Global Business and Economics Review	Blind	3	0-5%	122
Harvard Business Review	Editorial	0	0-5%	132
Health Marketing Quarterly	Blind	3	21-30%	135
Industrial Marketing Management	Blind	3	20-25%	143
International Journal of Advertising	Blind	3+	21-30%	154
International Journal of Bank Marketing	Blind	2	21-30%	157
International Journal of Business & Economics	Blind		11-20%	163
International Journal of Business and Public Administration	Blind	2	10-20%	165
International Journal of Business Disciplines	Blind	2	40-50%	169
International Journal of Business Strategy	Blind	2	11-20%	171
International Journal of Business Studies	Blind	2	11-20%	174
International Journal of E-Business	Blind	2	21-30%	191
International Journal of Electronic Marketing and Retailing	Blind	3	11-20%	216
International Journal of Hospitality and Tourism Administration	Blind	2	60%	231
International Journal of Hospitality Management	Blind	2-3	21-30%	234
International Journal of Management Theory & Practices	Blind	3	6-10%	283
International Journal of Market Research	Blind	2	6-10%	288
International Journal of Mobile Communications	Blind	1	25%	293
International Journal of Research in Marketing	Blind	3	11-20%	328

E-Commerce

Journal Name	Type Review	No. Ext. Rev.	Accept. Rate	Page
Journal of the International Society of Business Disciplines	Blind	2	21-30%	745
Journal of Travel & Tourism Marketing	Blind	3	21-30%	761
Journal of Vacation Marketing	Blind	2	50%	768
Journal of Website Promotion	Blind	2	21-30%	772
Management Science	Editorial	3	11-20%	780
Marketing Education Review	Blind	3	30%	784
Marketing Letters	Editorial	2	21-30%	794
Marketing Management Journal	Blind	3	21-30%	801
Marketing Review (The)		0		803
Midwestern Business and Economic Review	Blind	2	35-40%	810
Oxford Journal	Blind	2	11-20%	831
Pennsylvania Journal of Business and Economics	Blind	2	35%	840
Qualitative Market Research - An International Journal	Blind	2-3	40%	846
Regional Business Review	Blind	1		850
Research Journal of Business Disciplines	Blind	2	41-50%	856
Review of Business Research	Blind	2		859
Services Marketing Quarterly	Peer	1		871
Southwestern Business Administration Journal	Blind	2	25%	881
Sport Marketing Quarterly	Blind	2	20%	884
Tourism Analysis	Blind	2	45%	891
Tourism Review International	Blind	3	11-20%	911

Global Business

Journal Name	Type Review	No. Ext. Rev.	Accept. Rate	Page
Academy of Business Journal	Blind	2	6-10%	1
Academy of Marketing Science Review	Blind	3	6-10%	4
Advances in International Marketing	Blind	3	11-20%	13
Agribusiness: An International Journal	Blind	2	11-20%	17
American International College Journal of Business	Editorial	0	90%	25
American Journal of Business and Economics	Blind	2	21-30%	26
Anatolia: An International Journal of Tourism Hospitality and Research	Blind	3	21-30%	29
Annals of Tourism Research: A Social Sciences Journal	Blind	3+	11-20%	32
Annual Advances in Business Cases	Blind	3	30%	36
Asia Pacific Business Review	Blind	20+	21-30%	46
Asia Pacific Journal of Marketing and Logistics	Blind		11-20%	49
Asia Pacific Journal of Tourism Research	Blind	2	31-40%	51
Business Case Journal	Blind	3	11-20%	60
California Journal of Business Research	Blind	2	25%	66
California Management Review	Blind	3	4-8%	69
CASE Journal (The)	Blind	2	21-30%	72
Case Research Journal	Blind	3	11-20%	74
Consortium Journal of Hospitality and Tourism	Blind	3	25-30%	83

Journal Name	Type Review	No. Ext. Rev.	Accept. Rate	Page
Oxford Journal	Blind	2	11-20%	831
Pennsylvania Journal of Business and Economics	Blind	2	35%	840
Regional Business Review	Blind	1		850
Research in Consumer Behavior	Blind	3	30%	851
Research Journal of Business Disciplines	Blind	2	41-50%	856
Review of Business Research	Blind	2		859
Services Marketing Quarterly	Peer	1		871
Simulation & Gaming: An Interdisciplinary Journal of Theory, Practice & Research	Blind	2-3	21-30%	875
Southwestern Business Administration Journal	Blind	2	25%	881
Tourism Analysis	Blind	2	45%	891
Tourism and Hospitality Research	Blind	0-3	21-30%	894
Tourism in Marine Environments	Blind	2		901
World Transport Policy & Practice	Blind	1	21-30%	940

Health Care Administration

Journal Name	Type Review	No. Ext. Rev.	Accept. Rate	Page
American International College Journal of Business	Editorial	0	90%	25
American Journal of Business and Economics	Blind	2	21-30%	26
CASE Journal (The)	Blind	2	21-30%	72
Case Research Journal	Blind	3	11-20%	74
Global Business and Economics Review	Blind	3	0-5%	122
Health Marketing Quarterly	Blind	3	21-30%	135
International Journal of Business & Economics	Blind		11-20%	163
International Journal of Business and Public Administration	Blind	2	10-20%	165
International Journal of Business Disciplines	Blind	2	40-50%	169
International Journal of Business Strategy	Blind	2	11-20%	171
International Journal of Business Studies	Blind	2	11-20%	174
International Journal of E-Business	Blind	2	21-30%	191
International Journal of Electronic Business	Blind	2-3	11-20%	198
International Journal of Food Safety Management	Blind	3	11-20%	223
International Journal of Information and Computer Security	Blind	2-3	11-20%	239
International Journal of Information Policy and Law	Blind	2-3	11-20%	246
International Journal of Internet and Enterprise Management	Blind	2-3	11-20%	260
International Journal of Internet Marketing and Advertising	Blind	2-3	11-20%	267
International Journal of Management Theory & Practices	Blind	3	6-10%	283
International Journal of Mobile Communications	Blind	1	25%	293
International Journal of Sport Management	Blind	3	21-30%	338
Journal of American Academy of Business, Cambridge (The)	Blind	2	36-38%	398
Journal of Applied Business and Economics	Blind	2	11-20%	401

Journal Name	Type Review	No. Ext. Rev.	Accept. Rate	Page
International Journal of Information Policy and Law	Blind	2-3	11-20%	246
International Journal of Integrated Supply Management	Blind	2		253
International Journal of Internet and Enterprise Management	Blind	2-3	11-20%	260
International Journal of Internet Marketing and Advertising	Blind	2-3	11-20%	267
International Journal of Management Theory & Practices	Blind	3	6-10%	283
International Journal of Mobile Communications	Blind	1	25%	293
International Journal of Product Development	Blind	3	11-20%	316
International Journal of Sport Management and Marketing	Blind	3	11-20%	340
International Journal of Tourism Research	Blind	2	60%	355
Journal of Academy of Business and Economics	Blind	2	15-25%	386
Journal of Applied Business and Economics	Blind	2	11-20%	401
Journal of Business and Behavioral Sciences	Blind	3	11-20%	417
Journal of Business and Economic Perspectives	Blind	2	21-30%	418
Journal of Business and Economics	Blind	2	21-30%	421
Journal of Business Disciplines	Blind	3	12-20%	424
Journal of Business Research	Blind	2	6-10%	429
Journal of Business, Industry and Economics	Blind	2	20%	432
Journal of International Business and Economics	Blind	2	21-30%	551
Journal of Marketing	Blind	3	11%	587
Journal of Quality Assurance in Hospitality & Tourism	Blind	2	60%	669
Journal of Retailing and Consumer Services	Blind	3	11-20%	690
Journal of Sport Management	Blind	3	18-22%	710
Journal of World Business	Blind	2	11-20%	777
Midwestern Business and Economic Review	Blind	2	35-40%	810
MIT Sloan Management Review	Blind	2	7%	812
Mountain Plains Journal of Business and Economics	Blind	2	25-35%	819
Oxford Journal	Blind	2	11-20%	831
Pennsylvania Journal of Business and Economics	Blind	2	35%	840
Research Journal of Business Disciplines	Blind	2	41-50%	856
Review of Business Research	Blind	2		859
Simulation & Gaming: An Interdisciplinary Journal of Theory, Practice & Research	Blind	2-3	21-30%	875
Southwestern Business Administration Journal	Blind	2	25%	881
Tourism and Hospitality Research	Blind	0-3	21-30%	894

Marketing Research

Academy of Business Journal	Blind	2	6-10%	1
Academy of Marketing Science Review	Blind	3	6-10%	4

9733972

Journal Name	Type Review	No. Ext. Rev.	Accept. Rate	Page
Journal of Hospitality & Leisure Marketing	Blind	2	50%	538
Journal of International Business and Economics	Blind	2	21-30%	551
Journal of International Business Strategy	Blind	2	11-20%	556
Journal of International Consumer Marketing	Blind	2	11-20%	559
Journal of International Food & Agribusiness Marketing	Blind	2	21-30%	564
Journal of Marketing	Blind	3	11%	587
Journal of Marketing Channels	Blind	2	12-16%	591
Journal of Marketing Education	Blind	3	11-20%	599
Journal of Marketing for Higher Education	Blind	2	21-30%	602
Journal of Marketing Management	Blind	2	11-20%	606
Journal of Marketing Research	Blind	2	11-20%	610
Journal of Marketing Theory and Practice	Blind	3	15%	617
Journal of Medical Marketing	Blind	2	21-30%	622
Journal of Nonprofit & Public Sector Marketing	Blind	3	20-25%	625
Journal of Pharmaceutical Marketing & Management	Blind	2	25%	634
Journal of Political Marketing		3	21-30%	638
Journal of Product and Brand Management	Blind	2	25%	643
Journal of Promotion Management	Blind	2	21-30%	648
Journal of Public Affairs	Blind	2	40%	653
Journal of Public Policy & Marketing	Blind	3+	11-20%	657
Journal of Quality Assurance in Hospitality & Tourism	Blind	2	60%	669
Journal of Relationship Marketing	Blind	3	11-20%	676
Journal of Research in Marketing and Entrepreneurship	Blind	40	11-20%	678
Journal of Retailing	Blind	2-3	10-15%	685
Journal of Retailing and Consumer Services	Blind	3	11-20%	690
Journal of Service Research	Blind	3	20%	698
Journal of Services Marketing	Blind	3	21-30%	702
Journal of Services Research	Blind	2	21-30%	706
Journal of Strategic International Business	Blind	2	11-20%	715
Journal of Targeting, Measurement, and Analysis for Marketing	Blind	3	50%	726
Journal of the Academy of Business Research	Blind	2	80%	737
Journal of the Academy of Marketing Science	Blind	2-4	10-15%	738
Journal of the Association of Marketing Educators	Blind	0	6-10%	741
Journal of the International Academy for Case Studies	Blind	2	25%	743
Journal of the International Society of Business Disciplines	Blind	2	21-30%	745
Journal of Travel & Tourism Marketing	Blind	3	21-30%	761
Journal of Vacation Marketing	Blind	2	50%	768
Management Science	Editorial	3	11-20%	780
Marketing Education Review	Blind	3	30%	784

Non-Profit Organizations

Journal Name	Type Review	No. Ext. Rev.	Accept. Rate	Page
International Journal of Product Development	Blind	3	11-20%	316
International Journal of Sport Management and Marketing	Blind	3	11-20%	340
Journal of Academy of Business and Economics	Blind	2	15-25%	386
Journal of Applied Business and Economics	Blind	2	11-20%	401
Journal of Business and Economic Perspectives	Blind	2	21-30%	418
Journal of Business and Economics	Blind	2	21-30%	421
Journal of Business Disciplines	Blind	3	12-20%	424
Journal of Business, Industry and Economics	Blind	2	20%	432
Journal of International Business and Economics	Blind	2	21-30%	551
Journal of Marketing	Blind	3	11%	587
Journal of Political Marketing		3	21-30%	638
Journal of the Academy of Business Education	Blind	3	11-20%	734
Journal of the International Society of Business Disciplines	Blind	2	21-30%	745
Midwestern Business and Economic Review	Blind	2	35-40%	810
Oxford Journal	Blind	2	11-20%	831
Pennsylvania Journal of Business and Economics	Blind	2	35%	840
Research Journal of Business Disciplines	Blind	2	41-50%	856
Tourism and Hospitality Research	Blind	0-3	21-30%	894
Tourist Studies	Blind	3	21-30%	921

Operations Research/Statistics

Journal Name	Type Review	No. Ext. Rev.	Accept. Rate	Page
American International College Journal of Business	Editorial	0	90%	25
American Journal of Business and Economics	Blind	2	21-30%	26
Annual Advances in Business Cases	Blind	3	30%	36
Asia Pacific Journal of Tourism Research	Blind	2	31-40%	51
California Management Review	Blind	3	4-8%	69
CASE Journal (The)	Blind	2	21-30%	72
Case Research Journal	Blind	3	11-20%	74
Cornell Hotel and Restaurant Administration Quarterly	Blind	3	11-20%	86
Decision Sciences	Blind	3	11-20%	91
Global Business and Economics Review	Blind	3	0-5%	122
International Journal of Business	Blind	1-2	15-20%	161
International Journal of Business & Economics	Blind		11-20%	163
International Journal of Business and Public Administration	Blind	2	10-20%	165
International Journal of Business Disciplines	Blind	2	40-50%	169
International Journal of Business Strategy	Blind	2	11-20%	171
International Journal of Business Studies	Blind	2	11-20%	174
International Journal of E-Business	Blind	2	21-30%	191
International Journal of Integrated Supply Management	Blind	2		253
International Journal of Logistics Management	Blind	3+	21-30%	274

Journal Name	Type Review	No. Ext. Rev.	Accept. Rate	Page
Transportation Research Part E: Logistics and Transportation Review	Blind	2	30%	932

Organizational Behavior & Theory

Journal Name	Type Review	No. Ext. Rev.	Accept. Rate	Page
Agribusiness: An International Journal	Blind	2	11-20%	17
Air Force Journal of Logistics	Blind	3	40%	23
American International College Journal of Business	Editorial	0	90%	25
American Journal of Business and Economics	Blind	2	21-30%	26
Anatolia: An International Journal of Tourism Hospitality and Research	Blind	3	21-30%	29
Annals of Tourism Research: A Social Sciences Journal	Blind	3+	11-20%	32
Asia Pacific Business Review	Blind	20+	21-30%	46
Asia Pacific Journal of Tourism Research	Blind	2	31-40%	51
California Management Review	Blind	3	4-8%	69
CASE Journal (The)	Blind	2	21-30%	72
Case Research Journal	Blind	3	11-20%	74
Cornell Hotel and Restaurant Administration Quarterly	Blind	3	11-20%	86
Decision Sciences	Blind	3	11-20%	91
Family Business Review	Blind	2	8-13%	118
FIU Hospitality & Tourism Review (The)	Blind	2	21-30%	121
Global Business and Economics Review	Blind	3	0-5%	122
International Journal of Business	Blind	1-2	15-20%	161
International Journal of Business & Economics	Blind		11-20%	163
International Journal of Business and Public Administration	Blind	2	10-20%	165
International Journal of Business Disciplines	Blind	2	40-50%	169
International Journal of Business Strategy	Blind	2	11-20%	171
International Journal of Business Studies	Blind	2	11-20%	174
International Journal of E-Business	Blind	2	21-30%	191
International Journal of Electronic Marketing and Retailing	Blind	3	11-20%	216
International Journal of Hospitality and Tourism Administration	Blind	2	60%	231
International Journal of Hospitality Management	Blind	2-3	21-30%	234
International Journal of Integrated Supply Management	Blind	2		253
International Journal of Management Theory & Practices	Blind	3	6-10%	283
International Journal of Mobile Communications	Blind	1	25%	293
International Journal of Product Development	Blind	3	11-20%	316
International Journal of Technology Marketing	Blind	3	11-20%	347
International Journal of Tourism Research	Blind	2	60%	355
International Research in the Business Disciplines	Blind	2	11-20%	368

Journal Name	Type Review	No. Ext. Rev.	Accept. Rate	Page
International Journal of Physical Distribution & Logistics Management	Blind	3	21-30%	312
International Journal of Product Development	Blind	3	11-20%	316
International Journal of Sport Management and Marketing	Blind	3	11-20%	340
International Journal of Technology Marketing	Blind	3	11-20%	347
International Journal on Media Management (The)	Blind	2-3	39%	361
International Research in the Business Disciplines	Blind	2	11-20%	368
International Review of Retail, Distribution and Consumer Research	Blind	2	33%	371
Journal of Academy of Business and Economics	Blind	2	15-25%	386
Journal of Applied Business and Economics	Blind	2	11-20%	401
Journal of Business and Behavioral Sciences	Blind	3	11-20%	417
Journal of Business and Economic Perspectives	Blind	2	21-30%	418
Journal of Business and Economics	Blind	2	21-30%	421
Journal of Business Disciplines	Blind	3	12-20%	424
Journal of Business Research	Blind	2	6-10%	429
Journal of Business, Industry and Economics	Blind	2	20%	432
Journal of Business, Industry and Economics	Blind	2	20%	432
Journal of Communication Management	Blind	3	50%	440
Journal of Database Marketing and Customer Strategy Management	Blind	3	50%	479
Journal of Direct, Data and Digital Marketing Practice	Blind	2	60%	485
Journal of Food Products Marketing	Blind		31-50%	517
Journal of International Business and Economics	Blind	2	21-30%	551
Journal of Marketing	Blind	3	11%	587
Journal of Quality Assurance in Hospitality & Tourism	Blind	2	60%	669
Journal of Service Research	Blind	3	20%	698
Journal of Sport Management	Blind	3	18-22%	710
Journal of Sustainable Tourism	Blind	3	60%	721
Journal of Targeting, Measurement, and Analysis for Marketing	Blind	3	50%	726
Journal of the International Society of Business Disciplines	Blind	2	21-30%	745
Marketing Intelligence & Planning	Blind	2	40%	790
Marketing Review (The)		0		803
Midwestern Business and Economic Review	Blind	2	35-40%	810
Mountain Plains Journal of Business and Economics	Blind	2	25-35%	819
Oxford Journal	Blind	2	11-20%	831
PASOS: Journal of Tourism and Cultural Heritage	Blind	2	50%	837
Pennsylvania Journal of Business and Economics	Blind	2	35%	840
Research Journal of Business Disciplines	Blind	2	41-50%	856
Review of Business Research	Blind	2		859

Journal Name	Type Review	No. Ext. Rev.	Accept. Rate	Page
Journal of Business, Industry and Economics	Blind	2	20%	432
Journal of International Business and Economics	Blind	2	21-30%	551
Journal of International Marketing	Blind	2	20%	570
Journal of Marketing	Blind	3	11%	587
Journal of Political Marketing		3	21-30%	638
Journal of Public Affairs	Blind	2	40%	653
Journal of Public Policy & Marketing	Blind	3+	11-20%	657
Journal of Public Procurement	Blind	3	20-30%	665
Journal of Public Transportation	Editorial	2	60%	667
Journal of Retailing and Consumer Services	Blind	3	11-20%	690
Journal of Service Research	Blind	3	20%	698
Journal of Sport Management	Blind	3	18-22%	710
Journal of the Academy of Business Research	Blind	2	80%	737
Journal of the International Society of Business Disciplines	Blind	2	21-30%	745
Midwestern Business and Economic Review	Blind	2	35-40%	810
Mountain Plains Journal of Business and Economics	Blind	2	25-35%	819
Oxford Journal	Blind	2	11-20%	831
PASOS: Journal of Tourism and Cultural Heritage	Blind	2	50%	837
Pennsylvania Journal of Business and Economics	Blind	2	35%	840
Review of Business Research	Blind	2		859
Simulation & Gaming: An Interdisciplinary Journal of Theory, Practice & Research	Blind	2-3	21-30%	875
Southwestern Business Administration Journal	Blind	2	25%	881
Tourism and Hospitality Research	Blind	0-3	21-30%	894

Purchasing/Materials Management

Journal Name	Type Review	No. Ext. Rev.	Accept. Rate	Page
Academy of Marketing Science Review	Blind	3	6-10%	4
American International College Journal of Business	Editorial	0	90%	25
American Journal of Business and Economics	Blind	2	21-30%	26
CASE Journal (The)	Blind	2	21-30%	72
Consortium Journal of Hospitality and Tourism	Blind	3	25-30%	83
Cornell Hotel and Restaurant Administration Quarterly	Blind	3	11-20%	86
Decision Sciences	Blind	3	11-20%	91
Global Business and Economics Review	Blind	3	0-5%	122
Industrial Marketing Management	Blind	3	20-25%	143
International Journal of Business & Economics	Blind		11-20%	163
International Journal of Business and Public Administration	Blind	2	10-20%	165
International Journal of Business Disciplines	Blind	2	40-50%	169
International Journal of Business Strategy	Blind	2	11-20%	171
International Journal of Business Studies	Blind	2	11-20%	174
International Journal of E-Business	Blind	2	21-30%	191
International Journal of Electronic Business	Blind	2-3	11-20%	198

Journal Name	Type Review	No. Ext. Rev.	Accept. Rate	Page
Journal of Marketing	Blind	3	11%	587
Journal of Marketing Channels	Blind	2	12-16%	591
Journal of Marketing Management	Blind	2	11-20%	606
Journal of Public Procurement	Blind	3	20-30%	665
Journal of Retailing	Blind	2-3	10-15%	685
Journal of Retailing and Consumer Services	Blind	3	11-20%	690
Journal of Strategic International Business	Blind	2	11-20%	715
Journal of Transportation Management	Blind	2	30%	755
Marketing Review (The)		0		803
Midwestern Business and Economic Review	Blind	2	35-40%	810
Oxford Journal	Blind	2	11-20%	831
Pennsylvania Journal of Business and Economics	Blind	2	35%	840
Research Journal of Business Disciplines	Blind	2	41-50%	856
Review of Business Research	Blind	2		859
Tourism and Hospitality Research	Blind	0-3	21-30%	894
Transportation Journal	Blind	3	15%	929

Retailing

Journal Name	Type Review	No. Ext. Rev.	Accept. Rate	Page
British Food Journal	Blind	2	50%	55
Journal of Business, Industry and Economics	Blind	2	20%	432
Journal of Food Products Marketing	Blind		31-50%	517
Journal of Marketing	Blind	3	11%	587
Pennsylvania Journal of Business and Economics	Blind	2	35%	840

Sales/Selling

Journal Name	Type Review	No. Ext. Rev.	Accept. Rate	Page
Academy of Business Journal	Blind	2	6-10%	1
Academy of Marketing Science Review	Blind	3	6-10%	4
Academy of Marketing Studies Journal	Blind	3	21-30%	11
Agribusiness: An International Journal	Blind	2	11-20%	17
American International College Journal of Business	Editorial	0	90%	25
American Journal of Business and Economics	Blind	2	21-30%	26
Annual Advances in Business Cases	Blind	3	30%	36
Asia Pacific Journal of Marketing and Logistics	Blind		11-20%	49
Asia Pacific Journal of Tourism Research	Blind	2	31-40%	51
Australasian Leisure Management	Editorial	1	21-30%	53
Business Case Journal	Blind	3	11-20%	60
California Business Review		2		63
CASE Journal (The)	Blind	2	21-30%	72
Case Research Journal	Blind	3	11-20%	74
Cornell Hotel and Restaurant Administration Quarterly	Blind	3	11-20%	86
ESIC Market	Blind	2	21-30%	105
Global Business and Economics Review	Blind	3	0-5%	122
Harvard Business Review	Editorial	0	0-5%	132
Industrial Marketing Management	Blind	3	20-25%	143
International Journal of Business & Economics	Blind		11-20%	163

Journal Name	Type Review	No. Ext. Rev.	Accept. Rate	Page
Journal of International Food & Agribusiness Marketing	Blind	2	21-30%	564
Journal of International Marketing	Blind	2	20%	570
Journal of Marketing	Blind	3	11%	587
Journal of Marketing Communications	Blind	2	40%	595
Journal of Marketing Education	Blind	3	11-20%	599
Journal of Marketing Management	Blind	2	11-20%	606
Journal of Marketing Theory and Practice	Blind	3	15%	617
Journal of Medical Marketing	Blind	2	21-30%	622
Journal of Personal Selling & Sales Management	Blind	3	11-20%	629
Journal of Product and Brand Management	Blind	2	25%	643
Journal of Promotion Management	Blind	2	21-30%	648
Journal of Quality Assurance in Hospitality & Tourism	Blind	2	60%	669
Journal of Relationship Marketing	Blind	3	11-20%	676
Journal of Retailing	Blind	2-3	10-15%	685
Journal of Retailing and Consumer Services	Blind	3	11-20%	690
Journal of Selling and Major Account Management	Blind	3	21-30%	695
Journal of Services Marketing	Blind	3	21-30%	702
Journal of Strategic International Business	Blind	2	11-20%	715
Journal of the Academy of Business Education	Blind	3	11-20%	734
Journal of the Academy of Business Research	Blind	2	80%	737
Journal of the Academy of Marketing Science	Blind	2-4	10-15%	738
Journal of the Association of Marketing Educators	Blind	0	6-10%	741
Journal of the International Academy for Case Studies	Blind	2	25%	743
Journal of the International Society of Business Disciplines	Blind	2	21-30%	745
Journal of Travel & Tourism Marketing	Blind	3	21-30%	761
Journal of Vacation Marketing	Blind	2	50%	768
Journal of Website Promotion	Blind	2	21-30%	772
Marketing Education Review	Blind	3	30%	784
Marketing Intelligence & Planning	Blind	2	40%	790
Marketing Letters	Editorial	2	21-30%	794
Marketing Management	Blind	2+	21-30%	797
Marketing Management Journal	Blind	3	21-30%	801
Marketing Review (The)		0		803
Midwestern Business and Economic Review	Blind	2	35-40%	810
Mountain Plains Journal of Business and Economics	Blind	2	25-35%	819
Oxford Journal	Blind	2	11-20%	831
Pennsylvania Journal of Business and Economics	Blind	2	35%	840
Regional Business Review	Blind	1		850
Research Journal of Business Disciplines	Blind	2	41-50%	856
Retail Education Today	Blind	1		858
Services Marketing Quarterly	Peer	1		871

Journal Name	Type Review	No. Ext. Rev.	Accept. Rate	Page
International Journal of Information Policy and Law	Blind	2-3	11-20%	246
International Journal of Integrated Supply Management	Blind	2		253
International Journal of Internet and Enterprise Management	Blind	2-3	11-20%	260
International Journal of Internet Marketing and Advertising	Blind	2-3	11-20%	267
International Journal of Management Theory & Practices	Blind	3	6-10%	283
International Journal of Mobile Communications	Blind	1	25%	293
International Journal of Operational Research	Blind	3	11-20%	304
International Journal of Sport Management and Marketing	Blind	3	11-20%	340
International Journal of Technology Marketing	Blind	3	11-20%	347
International Research in the Business Disciplines	Blind	2	11-20%	368
Journal of Academy of Business and Economics	Blind	2	15-25%	386
Journal of Applied Business and Economics	Blind	2	11-20%	401
Journal of Applied Case Research	Blind	2	21-30%	404
Journal of Business and Behavioral Sciences	Blind	3	11-20%	417
Journal of Business and Economic Perspectives	Blind	2	21-30%	418
Journal of Business and Economics	Blind	2	21-30%	421
Journal of Business Disciplines	Blind	3	12-20%	424
Journal of Business Research	Blind	2	6-10%	429
Journal of Business, Industry and Economics	Blind	2	20%	432
Journal of Digital Business	Blind	3	New J	482
Journal of Food Products Marketing	Blind		31-50%	517
Journal of International Business and Economics	Blind	2	21-30%	551
Journal of International Business Strategy	Blind	2	11-20%	556
Journal of Marketing	Blind	3	11%	587
Journal of Marketing Management	Blind	2	11-20%	606
Journal of Quality Assurance in Hospitality & Tourism	Blind	2	60%	669
Journal of Research in Marketing and Entrepreneurship	Blind	40	11-20%	678
Journal of Retailing	Blind	2-3	10-15%	685
Journal of Retailing and Consumer Services	Blind	3	11-20%	690
Journal of Services Marketing	Blind	3	21-30%	702
Journal of Services Research	Blind	2	21-30%	706
Journal of the Academy of Business Research	Blind	2	80%	737
Journal of the International Academy for Case Studies	Blind	2	25%	743
Journal of the International Society of Business Disciplines	Blind	2	21-30%	745
Journal of Travel & Tourism Marketing	Blind	3	21-30%	761
Marketing Review (The)		0		803

Journal Name	Type Review	No. Ext. Rev.	Accept. Rate	Page
American International College Journal of Business	Editorial	0	90%	25
Anatolia: An International Journal of Tourism Hospitality and Research	Blind	3	21-30%	29
Annals of Tourism Research: A Social Sciences Journal	Blind	3+	11-20%	32
Australasian Leisure Management	Editorial	1	21-30%	53
Business Case Journal	Blind	3	11-20%	60
California Business Review		2		63
California Journal of Business Research	Blind	2	25%	66
CASE Journal (The)	Blind	2	21-30%	72
Cornell Hotel and Restaurant Administration Quarterly	Blind	3	11-20%	86
Current Issues In Tourism	Blind	3	21-30%	88
Event Management	Blind	2	50%	115
FIU Hospitality & Tourism Review (The)	Blind	2	21-30%	121
Global Business and Economics Review	Blind	3	0-5%	122
Information Technology & Tourism	Blind	2	40%	146
Information Technology in Hospitality	Blind	2	60%	150
International Journal of Business & Economics	Blind		11-20%	163
International Journal of Business and Public Administration	Blind	2	10-20%	165
International Journal of Business Disciplines	Blind	2	40-50%	169
International Journal of Business Strategy	Blind	2	11-20%	171
International Journal of Business Studies	Blind	2	11-20%	174
International Journal of Consumer Studies	Blind	2	21-30%	183
International Journal of E-Business	Blind	2	21-30%	191
International Journal of Electronic Business	Blind	2-3	11-20%	198
International Journal of Hospitality Management	Blind	2-3	21-30%	234
International Journal of Information and Computer Security	Blind	2-3	11-20%	239
International Journal of Information Policy and Law	Blind	2-3	11-20%	246
International Journal of Internet and Enterprise Management	Blind	2-3	11-20%	260
International Journal of Internet Marketing and Advertising	Blind	2-3	11-20%	267
International Journal of Management Theory & Practices	Blind	3	6-10%	283
International Journal of Mobile Communications	Blind	1	25%	293
International Journal of Sport Management and Marketing	Blind	3	11-20%	340
International Journal of Tourism Research	Blind	2	60%	355
Journal of Applied Business and Economics	Blind	2	11-20%	401
Journal of Business and Behavioral Sciences	Blind	3	11-20%	417
Journal of Business and Economic Perspectives	Blind	2	21-30%	418
Journal of Business Disciplines	Blind	3	12-20%	424

Notes

Notes

Notes

Notes

Notes